THE WAY TO LIBERATION

Indological Studies in Japan

The Japanese Association for South Asian Studies

Established in 1988

- **Office Bearers as of 1 July 2000**

  President

  Noboru Karashima, Taisho University

  General Secretary

  Yoshihiro Matsunami, Taisho University

  Members of the Board of Executive Directors

  Gen'ichi Yamazaki, Kokugakuin University
  Haruka Yanagisawa, University of Tokyo
  Hiroshi Yamashita, Tohoku University
  Masaichi Tanaka, Kyoto University
  Michio Yano, Kyoto Sangyo University
  Nariaki Nakazato, University of Tokyo
  Takako Hirose, Daito University
  Teiji Sakata, Takushoku University
  Tsukasa Mizushima, University of Tokyo
  Yasumasa Sekine, Japan Women's University

- **Head Office** (until September 2000)

  c/o Department of Indian Culture, Taisho University
  3-20-1 Nishi-Sugamo, Tashima-ku, Tokyo, Japan 170-8470
  Tel. +81-3-3918-7311 (ex. 541)
  Fax. +81-3-5394-3037
  E-mail. jasas@mail.tais.ac.jp

- **Publications in English**

  1 *JJASAS* (*Journal of the Japanese Association for South Asian Studies*), (annual publication in Japanese and English, the current issue: No. 10)
  2 Newsletter (annual publicatin, the current issue: No. 7)
  3 Japanese Studies on South Asia Series
  - No. 1 H. Kotani ed., *Caste System, Untouchability and the Depressed,* Manohar, New Delhi, 1997.
  - No. 2 N. Karashima ed., *Kingsip in Indian History*, Manohar, New Delhi, 1999.
  - No. 3 S. Mayeda ed., *The Way to Liberation*, Manohar, New Delhi, 2000.

Japanese Studies on South Asia No. 3

THE WAY TO LIBERATION

Indological Studies in Japan

in two volumes

VOLUME I

Edited by

SENGAKU MAYEDA

in collaboration with

Y. Matsunami, M. Tokunaga and H. Marui

MANOHAR

2000

First published 2000

ISBN 81-7304-367-1 (Set)
ISBN 81-7304-374-4

Published by
Ajay Kumar Jain for
Manohar Publishers & Distributors
4753/23 Ansari Road, Daryaganj
New Delhi 110 002

Printed at
Print Perfect
A-23, Mayapuri, Phase II
Delhi 110 064

Contents

Preface

For the past 100 years, papers, books and periodicals in the field of Indological studies in Japan have increased enormously year by year in number, diversity of subject, and methodology. However, these achievements by Japanese scholars have overwhelmingly been published in Japanese and, therefore, they have hardly been accessible to most Indian, European, and American scholars. This tendency remains true even today.

It was for the purpose of rectifying the present situation even in some small measure that I edited and published in September 1989 a special volume entitled *Japanese Studies in Indian Philosophy* in *Acta Asiatica: Bulletin of the Institute of Eastern Culture*, Toho Gakkai, Tokyo. At that time, then four young scholars contributed articles to that volume along with a select bibliography, 'Studies on Indian Philosophy in Japan 1963-1987'.

The present work entitled, *The Way to Liberation: Indological Studies in Japan*, in two volumes, was planned with the same aim. It consists of articles written by comparatively younger Japanese scholars who are at present actively engaged in the various fields of Indological studies and, in addition, select bibliographies of Indological publications in Japan of the past ten years from 1987 to 1997.

The first volume contains twenty articles divided into two groups, I: Epics and Purāṇas and II: Hindu Philosophical Traditions. The first group comprises two articles; one is Muneo Tokunaga's which treats the metre of the *Mahābhārata*, and the other is by Hiromichi Hikita's which takes up for discussion the destiny of the dead and their funeral ceremonies performed by their relatives with the *Garuḍapurāṇa* as its main source.

The second group contains eighteen articles classified into ten sub-groups and arranged in accordance with their topics, i.e. Introduction, Sāṃkhya, Yoga, Nyāya and Navya-Nyāya, Vaiṣeśika, Mīmāṃsā, Vedānta, Vyākaraṇa, Kashmir Śaivism, and Tamil religious thought. In the Introduction, Sengaku Mayeda puts forth the argument for the existence of two currents of thought, *Sat* and *Asat*, that lie at the basis of Indian philosophy.

There are two articles on Sāṃkhya. Shujun Motegi discusses the problem of the knower that cognizes the outer world and attains the knowledge for the final emancipation based on the arguments found in the *Yuktidīpikā* while Koki Aruga investigates the concept of bondage (*bandha*) in the Sāṃkhya tradition. In regards to Yoga, Ko Endo clarifies the concept of *prasaṃkhyāna* in the *Yogabhāṣya* and criticizes J. Bader's opinion that the deliberating practice of *parisaṃkhyāna* which Śaṃkara proposed in his *Upadeśasāhasrī* was formulated from *prasaṃkhyāna* detailed in the *Yogasūtra* and *Yogabhāṣya*.

There are two articles on Nyāya and Navya-Nyāya. Hiroshi Marui surveys earlier studies and observations on Jayanta's works and then conducts a careful investigation on the question of authenticity of the *Nyāyakalikā*, a digest of the Nyāya system, while Toshihiro Wada examines the concept of liberation in Navya-Nyāya, focusing on Śaśadhara and his *Nyāyasiddhāntadīpa* and briefly referring to Gaṅgeśa and his *Tattvacintāmaṇi*. Next, two articles are devoted to Vaiṣesika. Keiichi Miyamoto investigates the terms *sāmānya* and *viśeṣa* to clarify the true intention of the Sūtrakāra as to whether or not the particular universal (*sāmānyaviśeṣa*) is an independent category. Yasutaka Muroya examines the process of theoretical transformation by Praśastapāda by observing the aspects of the genesis and impermanence of sound (*śabda*).

There are two articles on Mīmāṃsā. Kiyotaka Yoshimizu examines the nature of *apūrva* described by Śabara and then clarifies Kumārila's own views on the role of *apūrva* within the structure of a sacrifice by elucidating how he estimated the various views on the nature of *apūrva* in his time. The other writer Kei Kataoka also takes up *apūrva* for discussion and attempts to reconstruct the Mīmāṃsā *apūrva*-theory through the term *dharma-abhivyakti-vāda,* the theory of *dharma*-manifestation.

As for the field of Vedānta, there are four articles, of which the first by Shoun Hino is an attempt to establish historical perspective on the Vedānta philosophy. In the second article Hiroyuki Sato analyzes the theory of definition given in Sarvajñātman's *Saṃkṣepaśārīraka*. Shokei Matsumoto in the third article asserts that Rāmānuja's two different views on the means to liberation are derived from the fact that he was a religious leader of the Śrīvaiṣṇava school as well as a philosopher of the Vedānta school. Hiroaki Ikebe in the fourth article examines the position of the commentary by Madhva and discusses *karmayoga* and *jñānayoga* in his system, their characters, their mutual relationships, and their function in the ladder to emancipation.

There are two articles on Vyākaraṇa. Akihiko Akamatsu makes an attempt at examining the two concepts, *abhyudaya* and *niḥśreyasa,* in Bhartṛhari's *Vākyapadīya*. Junzo Tanizawa investigates the theory of meaning with respect to the proper name (*yadṛcchāśabda*) and the name (*saṃjñā*) advanced by Indian grammarians from the point of view of contemporary controversy surrounding proper names.

The next topic is Kashmir Śaivism. In his essay Hirohisa Toda investigates the doctrine of liberation in the Trika system, so-called Kashmir Śaivism, contrasting it with that of the dualistic Śaivism, namely the Śaivasiddhānta. The last paper is in the field of Tamil religious thought. Takanobu Takahashi takes up C.G. Beschi (1680-1747) who erroneously translated 'soft shoulders' as 'soft skin' in a couplet from the *Tirukkuraḷ,* despite his reputation as an extremely effective missionary among Tamil people and among non-Indians one of the best versed in Tamil language and literature. Taking into consideration the social and cultural changes in Tamil history, Takahashi clarifies the factors that led a man of the stature of Beschi to misunderstand such a popular expression.

The second volume of this book is now in preparation. It is planned to consist of articles in the fields of Veda and Upaniṣad, Jainism, Buddhism (Early and Mahāyāna), modern and contemporary philosophers. As mentioned above, the second volume will include select bibliographies of Indological publications in Japan from 1987 to 1997.

I am deeply grateful to the Musashino Women's College and Rev. Kojun Terada for their generous financial aids which have enabled me to publish this book. Many thanks are also due to my colleagues, Professor Yoshihiro Matsunami, Taisho University, Professor Muneo Tokunaga, Kyoto University, and Professor Hiroshi Marui, University of Tokyo, without whose hearty cooperation this book could not have been completed on schedule. I also wish to extend my sincere gratitude to the contributors who set aside precious time in order to cooperate in the preparation of this book. I cannot conclude this preface without expressing my deep gratitude to my colleague, Professor Kenneth K. Tanaka, Musashino Women's University, who has kindly taken the great trouble to make useful suggestions on and correct the English language of many contributors and to Ms. Katsue Ikeda, Research Assistant, Mejiro University, who has worked extremely hard to prepare the camera-ready manuscripts for printing.

11 April 2000 SENGAKU MAYEDA

Contributors

SENGAKU MAYEDA: Professor, Musashino Women's University. *Śaṅkara's Upadeśasāhasrī, Critically Ed. with Introduction and Indices,* Tokyo, 1973. *A Thousand Teachings: The Upadeśa-sāhasrī of Śaṅkara*, New York, 1992.*The Philosophy of Vedānta with Special Reference to Śaṅkara* (in Japanese), Kyoto, 1980.

MUNEO TOKUNAGA: Professor, Kyoto University. *The Bṛhad-devatā: Text Reconstructed from the Manuscripts of the Shorter Recension with Introduction, Explanatory Notes, and Indices*, Kyoto, 1997. 'Statistic Survey of the Śloka in the *Mahābhārata*' in *Memoirs of the Faculty of Letters, Kyoto University*, Kyoto, 1993.

HIROMICHI HIKITA: Professor, Aichi Gakuin University. *A Study of the Hindu Tantrism* (in Japanese), Tokyo, 1997. '*Sātvata Saṃhitā*: An Annotated Translation, Chapter 25 (1)' in *Transaction of Humanity*, Aichi Gakuin University,10, 1996.

SHUJUN MOTEGI: Professor, Shinshu University. *Yukutidīpikā, The Most Significant Commentary on the Sāṃkhyakārikā*(coed. with Prof. A. Wezler), Stutgart, 1998. 'The Teachings of Pañcaśikha in the Mokṣadharma' in *Asiatische Studien*, LIII. 3, 1999.

KOKI ARUGA: Research Fellow, the Japan Society for the Promotion of Science. 'On Vācaspatimiśra's Explanation of the Cause of *saṃyoga*' (in Japanese) in *Journal of Indian and Buddhist Studies*, 41-2, Tokyo, 1993. 'Siddhasena's Description of Sāṃkhya: On *Sāṃkhyaprabodhadvātriṃśikā* 12,15' (in Japanese) in *Bukkyo Bunka Kenkyu Ronshu*, 2, Tokyo, 1998.

KO ENDO: Associate Professor, Aichi Bunkyo University. 'The Works and Flourishing Period of Nārāyaṇa Tīrtha, the Author of the *Yogasiddhāntacandrikā*' in *Nagoya Studies in Indian Culture and Buddhism: Sambhāsā* 14, 1993.

HIROSHI MARUI: Professor, University of Tokyo. 'What Prompts People to Follow Injunctions?: An Elucidation of the Correlative Structure of Interpretations of *vidhi* and Theories of Action' in *Acta Asiatica* 57, 1987. 'Does Jayanta Refer to His Own Work as "*śastrāntara*" in the *Nyāyamañjarī*?' in *Journal of Indian and Buddhist Studies,* 47-2, 1999.

TOSHIHIRO WADA: Professor, Nagoya University. *Invariable Concomitance in Navya-Nyāya*, Delhi, 1990. 'The Structure of the World in Indian Realism and Its Schematization' in S. Bhate and M.M. Deshpande, eds., *Vācaspatyam: Pt. V. Bhagavat Felicitation Volume*, Pune, 1994.

KEIICHI MIYAMOTO: Professor, Kokugakuin University. *The Metaphysics and Epistemology of the Early Vaiśeṣikas*, Pune, 1996. *A Cow Really Exists—A Translation and Explanation of the Daśapadārthī* (in Japanese), Tokyo, 1999.

YASUTAKA MUROYA: Research Fellow, the Japan Society for the Promotion of Science. '*Pariṇāma* and *Abhivyakti* in the Sāṃkhya Argument for Satkāryavāda' (in Japanese) in *Studies in the History of Indian Thought*, 8, 1996.

KIYOTAKA YOSHIMIZU: Associate Professor, Hokkaido University. 'On the Logical Difference between *arthāpatti* and *anumāna*' (in Japanese) in *Hokkaido Journal of Indological and Buddhist Studies,* 14, 1999. '*Arthāpatti* and *anumāna* in the *Mimāṃsāsūtra*' (in Japanese) in *Journal of Indian and Buddhist Studies*, 48-2, 2000.

KEI KATAOKA: Research Fellow, the Japan Society for the Promotion of Science. 'The Mīmāṃsā Concept of *saṃskāra* in the Process of Cognizing a Word-Meaning' in *Journal of the Japanese Association for South Asian Studies*, 11, 1999.

SHOUN HINO: Professor, Gifu Pharmaceutical University. *Advaita Tradition Series* (12 vols), 1-10, Delhi, 1982-99. *Wisdom in Indian Tradition*, ed., Delhi, 1999. 'Tantrism in Kashmir Śaivism,' (in Japanese) in M. Tachikawa, ed., *Tantrism in India*, Tokyo, 1999.

HIROYUKI SATO: Research Fellow, the Eastern Institute, Inc. 'The Formation of Epistemology in the Advaita Vedānta with Special Reference to the *Vedāntaparibhāṣā*' (in Japanese) in *Studies in the History of Indian Thought*, 7, Kyoto, 1995. 'Comparative Study on Definition' (in Japanese) in *Studies in Comparative Philosophy*, 22, Tokyo, 1995.

SHOKEI MATSUMOTO: Professor, Daito Bunka University. *A Study of Rāmānuja* (in Japanese), Tokyo, 1991.

HIROAKI IKEBE: Graduate Student, Hokkaido University. 'Madhva's Salvation Theory' (in Japanese) in *Hokkaido Journal of Indological and Buddhist Studies*, 14, 1999. '*Karma* and Madhva,' (in Japanese) in *Journal of Indian and Buddhist Studies*, 48-2, 2000.

AKIHIKO AKAMATSU: Professor, Kyushu University. 'The Two Kinds of *Anumāna* in Bhartṛhari's *Vākyapadīya*' in *Journal of Indian Philosophy*, 27, 1999.

JUNZO TANIZAWA:Associate Professor, Shinshu University. *Vākyapadīya 3-14: Vṛttisamuddeśa, tr. into Japanese with Explanatory Notes* (1) (in Japanese), Tokyo, 1991. 'Perception in Indian Philosophy: Is *Nirvikalpakaṃ Pratyakṣam* Possible?' in *Journal of Japanese Association for South Asian Studies*, 7, 1995.

HIROHISA TODA: Research Fellow, the Eastern Institute, Inc. 'An Instance of Syncretism of the Spanda- and Pratyabhijñā-systems,' in *Studies of Buddhist Culture*, 1, Tokyo, 1997. 'Differences of View on 36 *tattvas* between the Dualist and the Monist in Śaivism,'(in Japanese) in *Memoirs of the Institute of Oriental Culture*, 137, Tokyo, 1999.

TAKANOBU TAKAHASHI: Professor, University of Tokyo. *Tamil Love Poetry and Poetics*, Leiden/New York/Koln, 1995. *Tirukkural: A Gnomic Work in Ancient Tamil* (Japanese translation), Tokyo, 1999.

I

EPIC AND PURĀṆA

1

Shift of Caesura in the *Triṣṭubh* of the *Mahābhārata*

MUNEO TOKUNAGA

In my article "Shift of Caesura in the Triṣṭubh of the Rāmāyaṇa"[1] I pointed out, on the basis of the accurate statistic data produced by computer, that the caesura of Triṣṭubh shifts its place from the fifth to the fourth syllable in the younger Books of the Rāmāyaṇa. The purpose of this paper is to see if there is a similar tendency in the Triṣṭubh meter of the Mahābhārata. Before entering into this topic, let us make a quick survey of some general features of this meter in the Mahābhārata.[2]

MAJOR PATTERNS OF *TRIṢṬUUBH*

In the Poona Critical Edition of the Mahābhārata, Śloka lines occupy 93.6 percent (141,513 lines)[3] and Triṣṭubh/Jagatī,[4] both regular and irregular,[5] 5.9 percent (8,975.5 lines or 17,951 pādas) of all the metrical lines (151,166 lines, i.e., 30,332 pādas).[6] Further, of all the Triṣṭubh/Jagatī pādas, 15,554 pādas are composed in Triṣṭubh (87%) and 2,397 pādas, including the even pādas of Aparavaktra (pg), in Jagatī (13%). Without the irregular patterns, Triṣṭubh counts 14,792 and Jagatī 2,369 pādas, again including the even pādas of Aparavaktra.

As to the first four syllables of the regular Triṣṭubh (14,792 pādas), 5,820 pādas begin with – – ∪ – (39.3%) and 4,872 with ∪ – ∪ – (32.9%). They are followed by the sequence – – – – (2,452:16.6%) and ∪ – – – (1,334:9.0%) in quantity. The other sequences are much smaller in number with less than 145 instances.

Table 1 shows all the variations and the statistics found in the beginning eight syllables of the regular Triṣṭubh. (I have used the following symbols for the various sequences of four syllables: a – – – –, b ∪ – – –, c – ∪ – –, d ∪ ∪ – –, e – – ∪ –, f ∪ – ∪ –, g – ∪ ∪ –, h ∪ ∪ ∪–, i – – – ∪, j ∪ – – ∪, k – ∪– ∪, l ∪ ∪ – ∪, m – – ∪ ∪, n ∪ – ∪ ∪, p ∪ ∪ ∪ ∪.)

Table 1

xa	xa	xb	xc	xd	xe	xf	xg	xh	total
ax		ab 1	ac 1398	ad 656		af 1	ag 379	ah 17	2452
bx	ba 1		bc 664	bd 410			bg 245	bh 14	1334
cx			cc 64	cd 48			cg 32	ch 1	145
dx			dc 20	dd 10			dg 10		40
ex		eb 1	ec 599	ed 354	ee 15		eg 4797	eh 54	5820
fx			fc 583	fd 342	fe 11		fg 3911	fh 25	4872
gx							gg 2		2
hx				hd 1					1
ix			ic 22	id 48			ij 4		74
jx			jc 7	jd 32			jg 4		43
kx				kd 1					1
lx			lc 1						1
mx			mc 2	md 2				mh 1	5
nx			nc 1	nd 1					2
total	1	2	3361	1905	26	1	9384	112	14972

There is a peculiarity in the variation and quantity of the eight syllables of Jagatī in the epic. The sequence ∪ – ∪ – occupies the overwhelming majority in this meter (1,946:82%). Except for 217 pādas with the opening – – ∪ –, the other patterns do not count more than 97, as we see in the next table (pg corresponds to the even pāda of Aparavaktra).

Table 2

	xc	xd	xg	xh	xl	total
ax	ac 7	ad 10	ag 27		al 1	45
bx	bc 3	bd 9	bg 84	bh 1		97
cx			cg 3			3
dx	dc 1					1
ex	ec 8	ed 5	eg 196	eh 8		217
fx	fc 18	fd 2	fg 1913	fh 13		1946
ix			ig 1			1
kx		kd 1				1
px			pg 58			58
total	37	27	2282	22	1	2369

Now, as to the regular Triṣṭubh of more than one thousand instances, we find four major patterns according to the break and the position of caesura: A (caesura after the 5th) x – ∪ – –, ∪ ∪ (4,440 pādas, 4440/14,792=30%), B (caesura after the 4th) x – x –, – ∪ ∪ (3,690: 25%), C (caesura after the 4th) x – x –, – ∪ – (3,174: 21%), D (caesura after the 4th) x – x –, ∪ ∪ – (1,755: 12%). These patterns are divided into the following subtypes.

Table 3

A^1	(eg)	– – ∪ – –, ∪ ∪ + cadence	(2414 pādas: 16.3%)
A^2	(fg)	∪ – ∪ – –, ∪ ∪ + cadence	(2026 pādas: 13.7%)
sum			(4440 pādas: 30%)
B^1	(eg)	– – ∪ –, – ∪ ∪ + cadence	(1703 pādas: 11.5%)
B^2	(fg)	∪ – ∪ –, – ∪ ∪ + cadence	(1424 pādas: 9.6%)
B^3	(ag)	– – – –, – ∪ ∪ + cadence	(346 pādas: 2.3%)
B^4	(bg)	∪ – – –, – ∪ ∪ + cadence	(217 pādas: 1.5%)
sum			(3690: 25%)
C^1	(ac)	– – – –, – ∪ – + cadence	(1379 pādas: 9.3%) [=Śālinī]
C^2	(bc)	∪ – – –, – ∪ – + cadence	(653 pādas: 4.4%)
C^3	(ec)	– – ∪ –, – ∪ – + cadence	(581 pādas: 3.9%)
C^4	(fc)	∪ – ∪ –, – ∪ – + cadence	(561 pādas: 3.8%)
sum			(3174: 21%)
D^1	(ad)	– – – –, ∪ ∪ – + cadence	(651 pādas: 4.4%)
D^3	(bd)	∪ – – –, ∪ ∪ – + cadence	(410 pādas: 2.8%)
D^4	(ed)	– – ∪ –, ∪ ∪ – + cadence	(354 pādas: 2.4%)
D^4	(fd)	∪ – ∪ –, ∪ ∪ – + cadence	(340 pādas: 2.3%)
sum			(1755: 12%)

The statistics tell us that 51% of the regular Triṣṭubh pādas have eg-fg pattern, the so-called classical or Upajāti type, with a caesura after the fifth or the fourth syllable (7,567 out of 14,792 instances).[7] Besides, a majority of the pattern with the break – ∪ – is stereotyped as Śālinī in the Mahābhārata (1,379/3,174=43%).

By the prominence of the classical type among the epic Triṣṭubh we are naturally tempted to compare the Books by the ratio of this type. My statistics have shown that the Books line up in the following order on this standard[8]:

10(98%) — 4(97%) — 9(86%) — 6(79%) — 11(79%) — 8(74%) — 3(72%) — 7(68%) — 12(61%) — 15(61%) — 1(52%) — 2(42%) — 14(39%) — 13(38%) — 5(37%) — 16-18(30%)[9]

Interestingly, 'Battle-Books' mostly spoken by Saṃjaya (Books 6-9), no doubt belonging to the older stratum, appear in the former part, while the Books 1 and 12-18, evidently later additions, in the latter part of the line. This fact probably indicates that the classical type, in general, decreases in number in the younger parts of the Mahābhārata. Since eg-fg is the only predominant pattern of Triṣṭubh, decrease of this pattern indicates increase of variety in Triṣṭubh, as well. What puzzles us with this order is the location of Books 10, 4, 2, for the result does not agree with our general understanding of the textual development of the Mahābhārata.[10] No one doubts that the Second Book is part of the oldest core of the Mahābhārata. Also, Book 10, here the Aiṣīka Parvan in which Vaiśaṃpāyana resumes his speech, cannot be placed in the oldest stratum of the epic. However, these situations are partly understandable, when we consider that Books of the Mahābhārata often contain various layers of different ages. It may, therefore, be necessary for us to reconsider the situations of these Books upon the result of a further analysis of Triṣṭubh in the minor parvaṇs of the Mahābhārata.[11]

SHIFT OF CAESURA IN THE *TRIṢṬUUBH* OF THE *MAHĀBHĀRATA*

Table 4 shows the statistics of all the Triṣṭubh/Jagatī verses in the minor parvans of the Mahābhārata, including hypermetric and catalectic (submetric) verses as well as those of irregular cadence. It also includes even pādas of Aparavaktra as a variant of the Jagatī meter (pg).[12] Parvans are, in this table, not arranged according to the order in the Mahābhārata but to the ratio of the classical type to all the Trimeter pādas found in themselves. Further, statistics are divided into eight groups according to the size of double figures (90-100, 80-89, 70-79, 60-69, 50-59, 40-49, 30-39, 0-29). The columns, from left to right, contain the name of minor parvan preceded by the Book number (left end),[13] total number of Triṣṭubh/Jagatī pādas in the parvan(C), total number of eg-fg (and its percentage in C), the number of eg-fg with caesura after the fifth syllable (A) (and its percentage in C), the number of eg-fg with caesura after the fourth syllable (B) (and its percentage in C), and the result of B divided by A (right end).

Table 4

parvan		tri-jag_all(C)	eg-fg (/C)	eg-fg_c5(A) (/C)	eg-fg_c4(B) (/C)	B/A
(group 90-100)						
3:	drau_satya	48	48 (100%)	30 (63%)	15 (31%)	0.50
7:	abhimanyu	67	67 (100%)	36 (54%)	25 (37%)	0.69
3:	yakṣayuddha	122	122 (100%)	59 (48%)	50 (41%)	0.85
10:	aiṣīka	60	59 (98%)	38 (63%)	15 (25%)	0.39
3:	ājagara	186	183 (98%)	86 (46%)	74 (40%)	0.86
4:	gograh	294	287 (98%)	142 (48%)	79 (27%)	0.56
15:	pāṇḍava	56	55 (98%)	25 (45%)	25 (45%)	1.00
4:	vairāṭa(all jag)	233	227 (97%)	148 (64%)	53 (23%)	0.36
4:	Kīcaka	36	35 (97%)	21 (58%)	11 (31%)	0.52
8:	ṛaṇabhūmi	232	226 (97%)	142 (61%)	64 (28%)	0.45
7:	ṣaṃśaptaka	36	34 (94%)	23 (64%)	8 (22%)	0.35
3:	ṅhoṣa	124	114 (92%)	67 (54%)	34 (27%)	0.51
9:	śalyavadha	188	169 (90%)	114 (61%)	45 (24%)	0.39
7:	ñayadratha	203	182 (90%)	99 (49%)	86 (42%)	0.87
Total		1885	1808 (96%)	1030 (55%)	584 (31%)	0.57
(group 80-89)						
6:	Bhīṣmavadha	723	629 (87%)	312 (43%)	231 (32%)	0.74
9:	ḥradapraveśa	150	130 (87%)	85 (57%)	32 (21%)	0.38
8:	ṣoḍaśayuddha	215	183 (85%)	104 (48%)	58 (27%)	0.56
3:	drau_hara	504	419 (83%)	208 (41%)	160 (32%)	0.77
9:	ṅadāyuddha	52	42 (81%)	19 (37%)	17 (33%)	0.89
9:	ṭīrthayātrā	80	64 (80%)	28 (35%)	25 (32%)	0.89
Total		1724	1467 (85%)	756 (44%)	523 (30%)	0.69
(group 70-79)						
3:	Kairāta	300	237 (79%)	128 (43%)	84 (28%)	0.66
11:	ṣtrī	24	19 (79%)	13 (54%)	5 (21%)	0.38
5:	ūdyoga	220	166 (75%)	97 (44%)	46 (23%)	0.47
5:	Karṇopanivāda	68	51 (75%)	22 (32%)	24 (35%)	1.09
1:	drau_sva	616	454 (74%)	251 (41%)	134 (22%)	0.53
8:	ṣaptadaśa	1983	1421 (72%)	752 (38%)	510 (26%)	0.68
12:	ṃokṣadharma	1211	867 (72%)	425 (35%)	326 (27%)	0.77
1:	Vaivāhika	72	52 (72%)	26 (36%)	18 (25%)	0.69
5:	ūlūkayāna	48	34 (71%)	20 (42%)	12 (25%)	0.60
3:	ṭīrthayātrā	976	687 (70%)	325 (33%)	269 (28%)	0.83
Total		5518	3988 (72%)	2059 (37%)	1428 (26%)	0.69

(group 60-69)					
7: ḍroṇābhiṣeka	172	118 (69%)	55 (32%)	51 (30%)	0.93
12: āpaddharma	172	114 (66%)	62 (36%)	35 (20%)	0.56
14: ānugītā	140	93 (66%)	43 (31%)	39 (28%)	0.91
1: āstīka	229	144 (63%)	73 (32%)	52 (23%)	0.71
6: Bhagavadgītā	327	203 (62%)	92 (28%)	71 (22%)	0.77
6: ñambūkhaṇḍa	28	17 (61%)	5 (18%)	12 (43%)	2.40
3: ṃārkaṇḍeya	338	203 (60%)	109 (32%)	72 (21%)	0.66
Total	1406	892 (63%)	439 (31%)	332 (24%)	0.76
(group 50-59)					
7: ṅhaṭotkaca	340	201 (59%)	106 (31%)	68 (20%)	0.64
5: Bhagavadyāna	52	28 (54%)	13 (25%)	10 (19%)	0.77
1: Pauṣya	69	35 (51%)	24 (35%)	9 (13%)	0.38
3: īndraloka	32	16 (50%)	8 (25%)	7 (22%)	0.88
Total	493	280 (57%)	151 (31%)	94 (19%)	0.62
(without 1: pauṣya)	424	245 (58%)	127 (30%)	85 (20%)	0.67
(group 40-49)					
2: ānudyūta	52	24 (46%)	9 (17%)	12 (23%)	1.33
5: Prajāgara	492	210 (43%)	92 (19%)	91 (18%)	0.99
12: ṛājadharma	727	302 (42%)	161 (22%)	103 (14%)	0.64
2: ḍyūta	543	221 (41%)	100 (18%)	94 (17%)	0.94
1: ṣaṃbhava	538	216 (40%)	135 (25%)	60 (11%)	0.44
Total	2352	973 (41%)	497 (21%)	360 (15%)	0.72
(without 1: saṃbhava)	1814	757 (42%)	362 (20%)	300 (17%)	0.83
(group 30-39)					
5: Yānasaṃdhi	615	241 (39%)	118 (19%)	92 (15%)	0.78
13: ānuśāsana	1230	473 (38%)	202 (16%)	185 (15%)	0.92
8: ṣaṃjayavacana	66	23 (35%)	11 (17%)	10 (15%)	0.91
5: ṣanatsujāta	201	66 (33%)	42 (21%)	19 (9 %)	0.45
16-18	156	47 (30%)	17 (11%)	24 (15%)	1.41
Total	2268	850 (37%)	390 (17%)	330 (15%)	0.85
(group 0-29)					
5: āmbā	102	26 (25%)	12 (12%)	10 (10%)	0.83
5: ṣaṃjayayāna	1139	277 (24%)	119 (10%)	127 (11%)	1.07
3: āraṇyaka	160	27 (17%)	15 (9 %)	11 (7 %)	0.73
7: ṇārāyaṇa	76	13 (17%)	5 (7 %)	6 (8 %)	1.20
14: ṣaṃvarta	276	35 (13%)	17 (6 %)	13 (5 %)	0.76
15: dhṛta_vana	40	4 (10%)	1 (3 %)	2 (5 %)	2.00

1:	ānukramaṇī	240	22 (9 %)	7 (3 %)	14 (6 %)	2.00
3:	Kuṇḍala	56	4 (7 %)	4 (7 %)	0 (0 %)	0.00
Total		2089	408 (20%)	180 (9 %)	183 (9 %)	1.02

A higher parvan in the row contains a larger number of classical type and shows, in corollary, a smaller variation of Triṣṭubh/Jagatī verse, while a lower one a smaller number of classical type and a larger variation of the verse. From the name column we infer that Books 3, 5, and to some extent 7, of which minor parvans reveal a wider distribution in the groups, consist of various layers, as far as the classical type of Triṣṭubh is concerned. On the other hand, the parvans of Book 4 concentrate in the uppermost rows. In other words, variation of Triṣṭubh/Jagatī is almost leveled out with the classical type in this Book, as has been pointed out by various scholars. We have good reason to believe that the Virāṭa Parvan was compiled at a certain time under a powerful supervision of a particular person or an editorial board.

Naturally A and B decrease in number in proportion to the quantity of eg-fg type. What is important, decrease occurs in A in a higher rate than in B. A, which is in average nearly twice as large as B in quantity in the first group, becomes in average equal to B in the last group.[14] Also, it must be noted that the decrease draws a less uneven line in A. It is evident from these facts that caesura shifts its position from the fifth to the fourth syllable in proportion to the amount of eg-fg type in the Mahābhārata. Since the groups 30-39 and 0-29 contain Books 16-18 and the Anukramaṇī Parvan of Book 1, we may be allowed to recognize a shift of caesura in the youngest Books of the Mahābhārata, just as we have seen in the youngest Books of the Rāmāyaṇa. Only the groups 50-59 (0.62) and 40-49 (0.72) disturb the increase rate in B/A. But the latter group produces a normal figure 0.83 if we exclude the Saṃbhava Parvan of Book 1 from it. Similarly, the figure 0.67 appears less abnormal for the former group without the Pauṣya Parvan, again of the first Book.

Needless to say, we cannot simply apply the shift of caesure to our chronological consideration of the whole Mahābhārata. But I deem this phenomenon an essential factor in understanding the development of Triṣṭubh and consequently of the text of the Mahābhārata.

We are not puzzled with Books 16-18 and the Anukramaṇī Parvan of Book 1, both occurring in the lowest groups of the table. However, the younger nature of Book 4, of which all the three parvans belong to the group 90-100, is undeniable for the majority of epic scholars. Also,

Book 2, of which the Dyūta Parvan is included in the group 40-49, a rather lower group, has been commonly considered a part of the oldest core of the Mahābhārata. In view of these contradictory facts, we are led to the assumption that standardization of epic Triṣṭubh advanced gradually towards the classical type (with the caesura after the fifth syllable), culminating in the Virāṭa parvan, and that the verse thereafter fell down into promiscuity in pattern in the latest stage of the textual development.

NOTES

1 *Journal of Indian and Buddhist Studies* (Indogaku Bukkyōgaku Kenkyū), Vol. XLII, No. 1, December 1993, pp. 1-7.

2 The statistics are based on my digital file *mbhtrig_met*. I have made this database available to the public in my anonymous ftp site of the Graduate School of Letters, Kyoto University (ftp://tiger.bun.kyoto-u.ac.jp/pub/mtokunag/) so that one can work on this database in one's own way with a program such as *grep* or *perl*. Previously, besides E.W. Hopkins and F. Edgerton, M.C. Smith made a detailed, painstaking analysis of the Triṣṭubh verses in the Mahābhārata. See her *The Warrior Code of India's Sacred Song*, Harvard Dissertations in Folklore and Oral Tradition (New York: Garland, 1922), which book unfortunately is not available to me. For this paper I consulted an account of the results of her metrical analysis offered by J. Brockington in his *The Sanskrit Epics* (Brill, 1998), pp. 120-127.

3 For the details on the epic Śloka, see my article "Statistic Survey of the Śloka in the Mahābhārata," *Memoirs of the Faculty of Letters, Kyoto University*, No. 34, Faculty of Letters, Kyoto University, 1995, pp. 1-37.

4 The epic Jagatī shows its own peculiarity in some circumstances. But I agree with Hopkins in the thought that Jagatī is basically the same as the Triṣṭubh except for an additional final syllable after the short eleventh syllable.

5 I use the word 'regular' in a wider sense. In this paper 'regular' pāda means any pāda of eleven (Triṣṭubh) or twelve (Jagatī) syllables with the cadence – ∪ – x (Triṣṭubh) or – ∪ – ∪ x (Jagatī), and 'irregular' pāda any pāda of 10-13 syllables (Triṣṭubh) or 11-13 syllables (Jagatī) with the respective cadence. Classical stereotyped meters are not considered here except for Vātormī, Śālinī and the even pāda of Aparavaktra.

6 The number and the percentage of Triṣṭubh/Jagatī lines for all the metrical lines show the following variation in the Books of the Mahābhārata — Book 1: 898 lines (6.3%), Book 2: 303.5 lines (6.2%), Book 3: 1,435 lines (6.2%), Book 4: 295.5 lines (7.9%), Book 5: 1,470.5 lines (11.8%), Book 6: 539 lines (4.8%), Book 7: 461 lines (2.8%), Book 8: 1,248 lines (15.5%), Book 9: 235 lines (3.4%), Book 10: 30 lines (1.9%), Book 11: 12 lines (0.8%), Book 12: 1,055 lines (4.0%), Book 13:

615 lines (4.6%), Book 14: 242 lines (4.3%), Book 15: 58 lines (2.7%), Books 16-18: 78 lines (6.7%). I distinguish strictly the word 'pāda (or 'foot'),' 'line' (2 pādas), 'verse' (2 lines) in this paper.

7 According to Oldenberg, the tendency to these features appears in the Triṣṭubh of the Brāhmaṇas and Upaniṣads. Cf. *ZDMG* 37, p. 21.

8 I scanned all the Triṣṭubh and Jagatī pādas, both regular and irregular, for the sake of clearer result.

9 Here are the exact data — 1: 938/1798(52%), 2: 254/607(42), 3: 2077/2870(72), 4: 573/591(97), 5: 1102/2941(37), 6: 849/1078(79), 7: 624/922(68), 8: 1853/2496(74), 9: 405/470(86), 10: 59/60(98), 11: 19/24(79), 12: 1283/2110(61), 13: 473/1230(38), 14: 190/484(39), 15: 71/116(61), 16-18: 47/156(30).

10 Instances of Book 11 seem too small in number for us to draw some conclusion.

11 Even a minor parvan is not always of a homogeneous nature, as Smith has shown in her work from the metrical point of view. Cf. *The Sanskrit Epics, loc. cit.*

12 I have omitted the following sporadic verses, mostly tag verses, because they do not have much statistic value: i.59.54, 125.32, 127.24, 195.4, 223.9, 11, 14, 16, ii.4.21, 5.114-115, iii.12.67-68, 295.17, 297.11, 298.27-28, iv.63.9, 12, 15-16, 27-28, 66.21, v.169.14, vii.155.28-30, 157.8-10, 159.41, xiv.13.9-10, 15.32-34, 51.50-56, 56.22-23, 63.15-17, xv.12.14, 25.17-18, 26.21-22.

13 Abbreviations are used for the names of minor parvans: drau_satya (draupadīsatyabhāmāsaṃvāda, iii.222-224), abhimanyu (abhimanyuvadha, vii.32-51), yakṣayuddha (iii.155-172), aiṣīka (x.10-18), ājagara (iii.173-178), gograh (gograhaṇa, iv.24-62), pāṇḍava (pāṇḍavavarṇana, xv.32), vairāṭa (iv.1-12), kīcaka (kīcakavadha, iv.13-23), raṇabhūmi (raṇabhūmivarṇana, viii.68), saṃśaptaka (saṃśaptakavadha, vii.16-31), ghoṣa (ghoṣayātrā, iii.225-243), śalyavadha (ix.1-16), jayadratha (jayadrathavadha, vii.61-121), bhīṣmavadha (vi.41-117), hradapraveśa (ix.17-28), ṣoḍaśayuddha divasaḥ (viii.7-21), drau_hara (draupadīharaṇa, iii.248-283), gadāyuddha (ix.54-64), tīrthayātrā (ix.29-53, iii.80-153), kairāta (iii.13-42), strī (xi.1-27), udyoga (v.1-21), karṇaopanivāda (v.138-148), drau_sva (draupadīsvayaṃvara, i.174-189), saptadaśa (saptadaśa-yuddha divasaḥ, viii.22-67), mokṣadharma xii.168-353), vaivāhika (i.190-191), ulūkayāna (v.157-160), droṇābhiṣeka, (vii.1-15), āpaddharma (xii.129-167), anugītā (xiv.16-50), āstīka (i.13-53), bhagavadgītā (vi.14-40), jambūkhaṇḍa (jambūkhaṇḍavinirmāṇa, vi.1-11), mārkaṇḍeya (mārkaṇḍeyasamāsyā, iii.179-221), ghaṭotkaca (vii.122-154), bhagavadyāna (v.70-137), pauṣya (i.3), indraloka (indralokābhigamana, iii.43-79), anudyūta (ii.66-72), prajāgara (v.33-41), rājadharma (xii.1-128), dyūta (ii.43-65), saṃbhava (i.62-123), yānasaṃdhi (v.46-69), anuśāsana (xiii.1-152), saṃjayavacana (viii.4), sanatsujāta (v.42-45), ambā (ambopākhyāna, v.170-197), saṃjayayāna (v.22-32), āraṇyaka (iii.1-11), nārāyaṇa (nārāyaṇāstramokṣa, vii.166-173), saṃvarta (saṃvartamaruttīya, xiv.3-10), dhṛta_vana dhṛtarāṣṭrasya vanagamanasaṃkalpa, xv.21), anukramaṇī (i.1), kuṇḍala (kuṇḍalāharaṇa, iii.284-294).

14 It may be noted that B gets twice as large as A in number in the Anukramaṇī Parvan. The dhrta_vana (Book 15), of which B/A shows the same rate, may be too small in quantity for our consideration.

2

Funeral Ceremonies and the Destiny of the Dead*

HIROMICHI HIKITA

INTRODUCTION

In Indian religion, especially in Hinduism, the destiny of the deceased in the future life was a major concern. The notion of hell had not clearly appeared in the Vedic scriptures, but became feared once the Upaniṣadic scriptures introduced the idea of transmigration (*saṃsāra*).[1] The fear of falling into hell not only forced people to do good but also compelled the living relatives to perform funeral ceremonies for the deceased. These benefited not only the dead but also the living relatives in the legal aspect, as the chief mourner became the legal inheritor of the properties of the deceased.[2]

In this paper, the destiny of the deceased and the funeral ceremony performed by the relatives will be described. The sources used are mainly the *Garuḍapurāṇa*, the scripture compiled in the early first millennium.[3] At the same time, this ceremony will be compared with that as seen in the *Pitṛmedhasūtras*,[4] the ancient scripture of the Vedic period.

Studies of death rituals commenced in the West with the reports of field surveys by Dubois,[5] Bose,[6] Albeerūnī,[7] etc. and then proceeded to philological studies at the same time as Vedic textual studies were being carried.[8] It is clear that hymns of the *Ṛg-veda* X.14-18 and *A*tharva-veda XVI describe funeral ceremonies. Scholars differ whether the hymns of the *Ṛg-veda* X.18.10-13 signify the burial of dead bodies or of the urns of bones after cremation. Roth,[9] Müller[10] and Monier Williams[11] advocated the former, while Caland,[12] Oldenberg[13] and Hillebrandt[14] advocated the latter based on the contents of the *Pitṛmedhasūtras*. Keith on his part asserted that the passages of the *Ṛg-veda* in question signify both burial and cremation equally.[15] The publication of the *Śrautakośa*[16] contributed enormously to the development of this study. Further, Kane made a comprehensive study of death rituals utilizing the Sūtra and the Smṛti literatures.[17] Abegg translated the *Garuḍapurāṇa*[18] in Germany with full notes indicating parallel passages in the other Purāṇas.[19]

THE DESTINY OF THE BODY

This Purāṇa gives us only a few descriptions of the deceased going to heaven because of merits accumulated in previous lives. In contrast there are many passages that describe the terrifying fate of those who must submit to the judgement of Yama, the god of death and suffer many kinds of terrible torments in the hell governed by this god. This kind of fearful destiny is due to a negative karma committed in previous lives. The kind of special bodies people adopt after death will now be explained in conjunction with their destinies.

First, the *ātman*,[20] on going out from the corpse along with the vital air (*prāṇa*), simultaneously takes on the special body carrying *ātman* to another body (*ātivāhika-deha).*[21] It is said that the deceased take on these special bodies within ten days after death, during which the cremation and collection of the bones are performed by their living relatives. The body then becomes divided into one for torments (*yātanā-deha*) and the celestial body (*divya-deha*)[22] according to the evil or good actions in life. The former, in the *Manusmṛti*, is 'another solid body composed of five elements (such as earth, etc.) produced in order that those who committed evil acts in their previous lives may suffer tortures after death.' (12.17)

This kind of body, similar to the corporeal body of this world, is composed of five organs of perception, five organs of action, vital air, intellect (*buddhi*) and mind (*manas*). It is too minute to discern with the naked eye. So it is also called 'the existence which goes everywhere at will' (*vāyu-bhūta*).[23] Simultaneously when a wicked person dies, his soul enveloped in this kind of body, is pulled out from his physical self[24] and dragged away by Yama's servants. It then beholds the way to Yama's residence, Yama himself and the terrible scenes of the various torments in hell.

On the other hand, the features of the celestial body in the *Manusmṛti*, rejoice in all the blessings in heaven.[25] 'If one does mostly good deeds and bad deeds slightly, one will acquire happiness in heaven, enveloped in the body composed of such elements.' (12.20)

Then the *ātman* takes on another body called *piṇḍa-deha* which is produced from ten balls of rice (*piṇḍa*)[26] offered each day for ten days by the living relatives. So this body is completed on the tenth day. The ball is of one cubit size (*hasta-mātra*). The first ball of rice makes up the head of the body and the last ball gives 'hunger' to it.[27] This body will be cast off when the rite of *sapiṇḍīkaraṇa* is performed after a year. And simultaneously another one named 'the body of enjoyment' (*bhoga-deha*) will appear. So we may assume that the *piṇḍa-deha* is utilized during the year as the soul of the deceased proceeds to Yama's abode while suffering various tortures. The *Garuḍapurāṇa* describes how the individual soul (*jīva*) abandons the *piṇḍa-deha* and acquires the *bhoga-deha* as follows.

> Dependent on the body produced from his deeds (= *bhoga-deha*), (the individual soul) abandons his former body (= *piṇḍa-deha*). His *puruṣa,* the size of a thumb, creeps along on the leaf of a *śamī*-tree. (8.40)
> Like a leech on the grass, the individual soul (*jīva*), dominated by his karma, helplessly proceeds step by step, walking and stopping. (41)

Since the body which this individual soul takes is clearly the *bhoga-deha*, it may be divided into either the celestial body of a virtuous man who enjoys blessings in the heaven[28] and the body of one who suffers tortures in the hell.[29] The relation between the time lapsed after death and the kind of bodies is important. From the last moment of life to the tenth day after death, the individual soul assumes the *ātivāhika-deha* which is divided into the *divya-deha* and the *yātanā-deha*, and from the tenth day to the first year, he assumes the *piṇḍa-deha*. From the first year onward, he assumes the *bhoga-deha* that is again divided into the *divya-deha* and the *yātanā-deha*.

The individual soul wrapped in the *piṇḍa-deha*, sets out for Yama's residence on the tenth day after death. The virtuous man can make his way to the eastern, western or northern gate of the residence, but the unvirtuous must go to the southern gate.[30] Though *GP* does not say anything about the way for the virtuous man, Sacred Books of the Hindus says that this way is very similar to heaven.[31] It is approximately eighty-six thousand *yojanas*[32] from this world to the city of Yama, the King of Morals (*dharma-rāja)*, the chief judge of the deceased. He proceeds there at the speed of two hundred forty-seven *yojana*s a day. The transgressor barely arrives, having been tortured by Yama's servants (*yama-kiṅkara*)[33] and drowned in the Vaitaraṇī river full of blood and pus,[34] after passing through such cities as Yāmya and Sauripura. Once in the city of Yama, the soul receives Yama's sentence.[35] Śravaṇa[36] observes all the acts of the people in this world and reports them to Citragupta[37] who records them thoroughly, distinguishing good acts from bad acts. Depending on such materials, Yama decides what kind of destiny is most appropriate to the individual soul. What is most interesting is that Yama's attitude toward the good is quite different from that toward the evil.[38] The good and faithful soul can see the appearance of the King of Morals, while the evil soul must face the awful appearance of Yama. Yama grants favours to those who know, practice and are connected with ethics (*dharma*). He instills horror in those who committed evil but gives happiness to those who were righteous.[39] After passing such sentences upon them, Yama indicates to the good the comfortable way to the world of Brahman,[40] while he indicates to the evil the terrible way to hell. Such dual dimensions can be seen in Yama's city.[41] The city and the palace become beautiful to the good but terrible places of punishment to the evil. The individual soul of those who did evil has to go to hell located near the tree named *śālmalī*,[42] be dragged by Yama's servants, namely, Pracanda, Candaka, etc.[43]

FUNERAL CEREMONIES PERFORMED BY RELATIVES

It is the deeds, good or bad, of the previous life that decide the destiny of the individual soul. However, not only the law of causality but also the performance of the funeral ceremony by the relatives determines the future. According to Hartland, this ceremony is performed so that the living might be released from the pollution of death and the soul of the dead given a complete enough rest to stop wandering about in the world of the living.[44] His definition of this ceremony seems to give weight to the living at the expense of the dead. He seems to have overlooked the effect of this ceremony through which the tortures falling on the individual soul can be reduced. This Purāṇa describes how the soul of the dead wanders about in this world as a ghost (*preta*) and causes family troubles, various diseases and calamities if the funeral ceremony is not performed for him.[45] The Purāṇa also describes how this ceremony grants benefit to the dead. Here I would like to describe the ceremony from the perspective of the dead and compare it with that in the Vedic texts.

First, the special rite is performed for the dying man in order to compensate for the crimes committed by him. He knows that his vital air is going out before long through various diseases falling upon him.[46] The relatives beginning with his son lay down the dying man near the *tulasī* tree,[47] besmear the place with cow-dung,[48] draw a *maṇḍala* for him,[49] scatter sesame around him,[50] spread *darbha*-grass there[51] and place a *śālagrāma* stone.[52] They carefully avoid placing him in the air.[53] They put gold and five jewels into his mouth, seeking eternal life for him.[54] The son is expected to offer all properties acquired by the dying man to the Brahmins. He is forbidden to desire these as his inheritance. This offering is considered sixteen times as valuable as the *aśvamedha*-sacrifice. If these are not offered, the son would be committing a crime as grave as killing Brahmins.[55] The offering mainly consists of sesame, iron, gold, cotton, salt,[56] seven kinds of grains,[57] land and cows.[58] This offering is given after expressing the intention (*saṃkalpa*)[59] of transferring merit obtained to the dying man. Whispering the eight- or ten-syllabled mantra of Viṣṇu[60] in the ears of the dying man is also considered useful in order to remove previous transgressions. On the other hand, the dying man recites the mantras mentioned above, meditates on Viṣṇu, fasts all day,[61] and performs the rite of abandonment on this occasion (*ātura-saṃnyāsa*)[62] by himself. Whether the dying man performs by himself or his relatives perform for him is mentioned in several Purāṇas but is scarcely mentioned in the Vedic corpus. Only the rite of whispering in the ears is mentioned in the Vedic literatures, but it is not the name of Viṣṇu but the Vedas that is to be whispered.[63] So we can assume that the development of Viṣṇuism is strongly connected with the increase in the sense of guilt.

The kinsmen purify the corpse and bring it to a crematory. The son with his shaved head, shaves off all of the hair of the dead, purifies him with water, decorates him with sandal paste, a garland of flowers, etc. and covers him with cloth.[64] He brings the dead body to the crematory. After binding the hands and feet to a litter (*śāvikā*),[65] the son carries the corpse out with his shoulders. Carrying it out at night is forbidden.[66] He offers balls of rice one by one at crossroads and at each appropriate place on the way to the crematory. Who carries the corpse is the most important matter. When the deceased belongs to the upper three castes, the carrier is expected to belong to the same caste as him. If a person of Śūdra caste touches the corpse, it is polluted and not suited for the rite of cremation.[67] A Śūdra can carry only the bodies of those who have no relatives.[68]

The son purifies the crematory and piles up firewood for the deceased. He selects the ground for burning the corpse[69] and purifies it according to the prescribed rules. Then he piles up firewood and places the corpse on it. Its process is described in detail as follows. First of all, he cleanses the ground, besmears it with cow-dung, draws a circle (*maṇḍala*), makes a mound (*vedi*),[70] sprinkles it with water and kindles the sacrificial fire.[71] Then with flowers and rice-grains in his hands, the son recites the mantra to Agni[72] and makes a fire-offering with mantras.[73] On the ground where the fire-wood has not been piled up, he piles up the wood of sandal, *tulasī* and *palāśa*.[74] Then he places the corpse with its head pointing north and offers balls of rice. Last he pours ghee onto the face of fire and of the deceased, reciting "*yamāya cāntakāya*."[75] What is to be noted here is the placing of the corpse to the north. Other Sūtra literature agrees with the placing of the corpse in the direction of the fire of Āhavanīya, namely in the south-east.[76] Monier Williams says the direction is the north,[77] but Caland and Kane indicate the south.[78] I can not solve the question as to why such a discrepancy occurred. On the other hand, the Sūtra literature mentions that one sacrifices a cow named Anuṣṭaraṇī,[79] takes out its internal organs and places each organ on the corresponding organ of the deceased. This rite is deemed to lessen the heat of fire for the deceased. Moreover these works prescribe that one places on the deceased sacrificial utensils like the *juhū, upabhṛt*, etc.[80] which he utilized in his lifetime. Such description cannot be found in this Purāṇa.

The son kindles the fire in the eastern corner of the pile of fire-wood[81] reciting the mantra, after placing the corpse on it. Generally, except on the day of *pañcaka*,[82] one performs the cremation soon after death. Ordinarily it is the chief mourner, here the son, that kindles the fire. The sacrificial fire which has been burning since his birth is used for cremation if the deceased is a householder who had maintained the sacred fire (*sāgnika*), but the domestic fire is used if he is not such a householder (*niragnika*).[83] When the corpse is half burned, he offers sesame and ghee, reciting the mantras and wailing.[84] At the time when they clearly see the fire blazing up and the corpse being wrapped with flames, the relatives beginning with the son dive into the water with their clothing (*avagāhana*),[85] and pour water mixed with sesame onto the stone, reciting the family and personal names of the dead. This ritual is called libation (*udaka-kriyā*). It begins with expressing his due intention (*saṃkalpa*) as well as offering for the dying. It is performed at the first watch (*yāma*) of the day, avoiding three junction times (*saṃdhyā*).[86] The order of the relatives who turn back from the crematory in a funeral procession is totally in reverse order from when they went there. Women take the lead in this procession.[87] They chew bitter fruits (*nimba*), recite the name of Viṣṇu and talk of the virtues of the deceased.[88]

The bones are collected (*asthi-saṃcayana*) on the fourth day after cremation.[89] Unfortunately *GP* does not make any reference to this ritual, but SBH gives a detailed description of the manner of collecting the bones, temporarily burying an urn in the earth, scattering the bones in the Ganges, etc.[90] The Sūtra literature generally refers to the custom of washing the bones with water and milk, putting them in an urn and burying that in the earth. Many of these texts also discuss the placing of grave marks at the burial site.[91]

Various rituals are performed ten days after death. This period is considered impure (*āśauca*).[92] The length of the period of impurity varies according to how close the living relatives are to the deceased, the caste to which the deceased belongs, the age of the deceased, etc.[93] During this impure period, the living relatives abstain from offerings, fire-oblations, study of the Vedas, blessings, etc. They are unable to lead a normal life during this period.[94] Normally this period lasts ten days,[95] and during which one ball of rice is offered each day.[96] These balls of rice make up the special body of the deceased (*piṇḍa-deha*) for reaching Yama's residence as mentioned above. Of the balls of rice offered each day, two-fourths become nutriment of the five elements (*bhūta*) of this special body, one-fourth becomes food for this body, and the last one-fourth becomes an offering to Yama.

Worship of the deceased individual (*ekoddiṣṭa*) is then performed. The purpose of this kind of worship, which belongs to ancestor worship (*śrāddha*),[97] is to worship the spirit of the deceased which has yet to attain the level of the ancestor (*pitṛ*). This is considered a modified form of *pārvaṇa-śrāddha*, namely, the ceremony of offering oblations to all ancestors at a *parvan*.[98] This rite is performed on the eleventh day after death to sustain the individual soul of the deceased in his one-year travel to the residence of Yama. *GP* does not mention the prescribed order of such rites as the invitation of the Brahmins, the recitation of the mantras and the entertainment of the Brahmins[99] but only makes mention of the arrangements of the offerings and the special rite of setting a bull free at the funeral (*vṛṣotsarga*). The offering consists of a jar full of sesame, a cow, the clothes worn by the deceased, his ornaments, vehicles, a bronze jar full of seven kinds of grains, a bed, thirteen kinds of items (*pada*), etc.[100] Among them, the bed[101] and seven of the thirteen kinds of items are highly valued. These seven are a parasol, sandals, a water-jar, clothes, a ring, a seat, and containers. If the son offers the first three items, the deceased easily passes through the burning spot or the forest of trees with knife-leaves. If he offers the last four items, the deceased can escape the awful tortures by the servants of Yama and can proceed to Yama's residence while eating to his heart's content.[102] Next, the main component of the rite of *vṛṣotsarga* consists of setting free a bull with four calves. This rite is considered to have had nothing to do originally with the funeral ceremonies.[103] The procedure is described as follows. First the auspicious Brahmins who are well versed in this rite are invited. The chief mourner cleanses himself on pure ground, repeating the mantras, offering oblations in the fire, and making offerings.[104] Then he worships the stars and performs *mātṛ-śrāddha*.[105] He offers a spoonful of oblation on the fire[106] and worships Viṣṇu on the stone named *śālagrāma*.[107] Embellishing a bull with clothing, ornaments, etc. he sets four female calves in front of it.[108] He brands a wheel (*cakra*) on the left belly and a trident (*triśūla*) on the right belly of the bull.[109] He circumambulates the bull and sets it free, reciting the mantras[110] and offering oblations in the fire. Feeding the Brahmins, he does the *ātma-śrāddha*.[111] It is not clear how this rite came to be incorporated into the funeral ceremony. Nevertheless it is clear that setting the bull free as well as offering the Vaitaraṇī cow was definitely considered efficacious for the deceased in this Purāṇa.

Last, the son performs the rite of *sapiṇḍīkaraṇ*a. This and the *ekoddiṣṭa* belong to the *śrāddha*. The former is performed in order to admit the newly deceased soul into the group of ancestors (*pitṛ*), while the latter is performed to celebrate this individual soul alone. As mentioned above, the deceased reaches the residence of Yama after having taken a journey for a year. Upon his arrival, he is able to enter the world of ancestors owing to this rite.[112] After the rite is over, the newly deceased soul sheds his own name and becomes a member of the group of ancestors. This rite is performed in the following manner.[113] First the son, as the main mourner, takes a bath and performs this rite on ground smeared with cow-dung. Then he worships all the deities with foot-washing water (*pādya*), water for reverence (*arghya*), water for mouth rinsing (*ācamana*), etc. He offers a scattered portion of rice (*vikira*)[114] to the bad ancestors (*kupitṛ*). Then he offers three balls of rice to three ancestors who appear as Vasu, Rudra and Arka.[115] He offers the fourth ball to the deceased. Dividing the fourth ball into three with a golden stick, he mixes these three portions with the first three balls respectively.[116] Lastly he makes offerings of sandal, *tulasī*, scents, lighting, food, and perfume.

THE FEATURES OF THIS RITE AS SEEN IN *GP* COMPARED WITH THE SŪTRA LITERATURE

The comparison of the funeral ceremony in the *GP* and the Sūtra literature shows that the former does not describe this ceremony as elaborately as the latter. Instead, the former incorporates the ancestor worship (*śrāddha*) into the funeral ceremony in the form of the *ekoddiṣṭa* and the *sapiṇḍīkaraṇa* rites. It may thus be safe to say that *GP* supports the funeral ceremony described mainly in the *Pitṛmedha-sūtras* and the ancestor worship described mainly in the *Gṛhyasūtras*, while sketching the essence of both works. On the other hand, *GP* encourages offerings by promoting the various benefits of this act. This text, like other Purāṇas does not pay much attention to the correct performance of the ceremony but encourages various kinds of offerings. This constitutes the main characteristic of the Purāṇas at least in the domain of the funeral ceremony. A Brahmin who performs this ceremony belongs to any school (*śākhā*) of any Veda. He is well versed in the systematic process of this ceremony as prescribed by his school. To his sponsors, he promotes the merits of performing such a ceremony. It was important for the Brahmins to obtain their livelihood through this ceremony. This seems to be the main motive for compiling the latter part (*uttara-khaṇḍa*) of this Purāṇa.

NOTES

* I would like to express my deepest gratitude to Dr. Einoo, Professor of Tokyo University, who kindly showed me his vast amount of cards of Sanskrit ritual terms he picked up from many texts.

1 A.B. Keith, *The Religion and Philosophy of the Veda and Upanishads*, Harvard Oriental Series, vol. 32, Motilal Banarsidass, Delhi, authorized reprint (1925) 1970, pp. 406-16.

2 J. Jolly, *Recht und Sitte*, Verlag von Karl J. Trübner, Strassburg, 1896, p. 84.

3 Ludo Rocher, *The Purāṇas. A History of Indian Literature*, vol. 2, fasc. 3, Otto Harassowitz, Wiesbaden, 1986, p. 177.

4 Cf. *The Pitṛmedhasūtra of Baudhāyana, Hiraṇyakeśin, Gautama*, edited by W. Caland, Kraus Reprint Ltd., Leipzig, reprint, 1896.

5 J.A. Dubois, *Hindu Manners, Customs and Ceremonies*, translated by H.K. Beauchamp, Oxford University Press, Delhi, 3rd edition (1906) 1978, pp. 482-500.

6 S.C. Bose, *The Hindoos as They Are*, Calcutta, 2nd edition, 1883, pp. 252ff.

7 Albeerūnī, *India*, translated by E. Schau, Neudruck, London, 1910, vol. 2, pp. 167-71.

8 Concerning the history of the study of this ceremony, see 'Death and Disposal of the Dead (Hindu),' by A. Hillebrandt, *Encyclopaedia of Religion and Ethics*, edited by J. Hastings, vol. 4, Edinburgh, (1911) 1971. On the relation between the destiny of the dead and the funeral, see D.R. Shastri, *Origin and Development of the Rituals of Ancestor Worship in India*, Calcutta, 1963. An archaeological survey of burial practice in India is P. Singh, *Burial Practice in Ancient India*, Varanasi, 1970.

9 R. Roth, Die 'Todtenbestattung in indischen Alterthum,' *ZDMG*, vol. 8, 1854, pp. 467-75.

10 M. Müller, 'Die Todtenbestattung bei den Brahmanen und Opfergebräuche im Veda,' *ZDMG*, vol. 9, 1855, pp. i-lxxxi.

11 Monier Williams, *Religious Life in Ancient India. Vedism, Brahmanism and Hinduism*, Delhi, reprint, 1990, p. 279.

12 W. Caland, *Die altindischen Todten- und Bestattungsgebräuche*, Amsterdam, 1896, pp. 162-7.

13 H. Oldenberg, *Die Religion des Veda*, Darmstadt, reprint, (1923) 1970, pp. 571-90.

14 A. Hillebrandt, *Ritual-Litteratur: vedische Opfer und Zauber*, Strassburg, 1897, pp. 87-92.

15 A.B. Keith, *Religion and Philosophy*, pp. 417-24.

16 This portion of the ceremony is found in the *Śrautakośa*, Poona, vol. 1 (Sanskrit section), 1958, pp. 764-823 and vol. 2 (English section), 1963, pp. 1033-132. Concerning the *Pitṛmedhasūtra*, see J. Gonda, *The Ritual Sūtras. A History of Indian Literature*, vol. 1, fasc. 2, Otto Harrassowitz, Wiesbaden, 1977, pp. 616-21.

17 P.V. Kane, *History of Dharmaśāstra*, Bhandarkar Oriental Research Institute, Poona, vol. 4, 1953, pp. 179-266.

18 Here in this article, I have used the *uttara-khaṇḍa of Garuḍa-purāṇa*, edited by Jibananda Vidyasagara, Calcutta, 1890 (= *GP*). Cf. the *preta-kalpa of Garuḍa-purāṇa* (Nag Publishers) and *The Garuḍa Purāṇa (Sāroddhāra) with English translation,* by E. Wood and S.V. Subrahmanyam (Sacred Books of the Hindus, vol. 9) Allahabad, 1911 (= SBH).

19 Emill Abegg, *Der Pretakalpa des Garuḍa-Purāṇa*, Berlin, 1956. This is the German translation of SBH.

20 The vital air of a virtuous man comes out through the upper openings such as the mouth, the eyes, the nostrils, the ears and the aperture in the crown of the head (*brahmarandhra*), while that of an unvirtuous man comes out through the lower openings such as the urethra, the anus, etc. The soul of the most atrocious man comes out along with the air known as *apāna*. See *GP* 1.16; 21.25. *Bṛhadāraṇyaka-upaniṣad* (4.4.2) describes how the *ātman* with the vital air comes out from the physical body.

Concerning the concept of identifying the apertures with the gates of castles, see *Kāṭhaka-upaniṣad* 2.2.1 and *Bhagavadgītā* 5.13.

21 We may see the term *ativāha* in *GP*18.10; 20.11, 12, 25; 24.11. P.V. Kane says that the *ātman* is wrapped with the body called *ativāhika*, composed of five elements. See P.V. Kane, *Dharmaśāstra*, p. 265. See also *Brahmasūtra* (*Brahmasūtraśaṃkarabhāṣyam*, edited J.L. Shastri, Motilal Banarsidass, Delhi, 1980) 4.3.4.4.

22 The virtuous man not only rejoices in heaven, but divine attendants come here in a divine chariot to meet him. See SBH 9.46-8.

23 *GP* 3.16; 9.1; 24.14. This special body called *ātivāhika-deha* is considered as similar to 'a subtle body' (*sūkṣma-deha* or *liṅga-deha*) of the Sāṃkhya Philosophy. But the body of the latter has the egotism (*ahaṅkāra*), while the body of the former has not it. See E. Frauvallner, *History of Indian Philosophy,* Delhi, 1973, pp. 286-8.

24 *GP* 5.22-23. We may see the description of the *aṅguṣṭha-mātra-puruṣa* being pulled out from its residence, the heart in the *Kāṭhaka-upaniṣad* 2.1.12, 13; 2.2.3; 2.3.17 and *Mahābhārata* (Poona edition, = *MBh*) 3.281.16.

25 The celestial body is not composed of the physical elements born from the father and mother, but of the brilliance (*tejas*) born from the deeds (*karman*) of one's previous life. See *MBh* 3.247.13. In another passage, *MBh* (18.3.39-40), Yudhiṣṭhira performs ablution in the Ganges, when he throws away his physical body and acquires the divine one.

26 *GP* 8.38-39. P.V. Kane (*Dharmaśāstra*, p. 265, fn. 594) calls the body composed of balls of rice *bhoga-deha,* which does not mean the body of enjoying fruits of one's previous deeds but of enjoying balls of rice offered by one's relatives. *Agnipurāṇa* (Nag Publishers, = *AgniP*, 368.10) calls it *preta-deha*; Albeerūnī (*India*, vol. 1, p. 63) calls it *ātivāhika-deha*; Monier Williams (*Religious Life*, p. 293) calls it *ūrdhva-deha*. Concerning the meaning of that ball of rice in the Vedic rituals, see 'piṇḍa' in Louis Renou, *Vocabulaire rituel védique*, Paris, 1954.

27 The process of composition of this *piṇḍa-deha* is related with the ball of rice offered by the relatives. The relevant parts of this body in brackets are enumerated as follows: the 1st ball (head), the 2nd ball (neck and shoulders), the 3rd ball (heart), the 4th ball (back), the 5th ball (knees), the 6th ball (waist), the 7th (genitals), the 8th (thighs), the 9th (knees and feet) and the 10th ball (hunger). Cf. Jolly, *Recht,* p. 156; *Piṇḍa-upaniṣad* 4.9; *Brahma-purāṇa* (in the śrāddha-kalpa of the *Caturvargacintāmaṇi* III-1, Bibliotheca Indica, = *Caturvarga*, p. 1459) and *Āditya-purāṇa* (in the śrāddha-kalpa of the *Caturvarga* III-1, p. 1596).

28 *GP* 16.33.

29 Concerning the descriptions of various hells in the Purāṇas, see W. Kirfel, *Die Kosmographie der Inder*, Hildesheim, reprint (1920) 1990, pp. 143-73 and P.V. Kane, *Dharmaśāstra*, pp. 161-5.

30 *GP* (23.16) mentions that the city of Yama as the king of justice is located in the direction between the south and the south-west.

31 SBH 14.51-8. On the description of the ways for the good, see *Padma-purāṇa* (*Ānandāśrama Sanskrit Series*, No. 131, = *PadmaP*) 2.15.19-25;

6.226.11-35; *Mārkaṇḍeyapurāṇa* (Nag Publishers, = *MārkP*) 10. 93-7.

32 *Bhāgavatapurāṇa* (Nag Publishers, = *BhāgP*, 3.20.24) says it is eighty-nine thousand *yojanas* away from this world.

33 On more descriptions of the terrible ways, see *MBh* 18.2.16-25; *PadmaP* 4.97.10; 6.227.1-48; *MārkP* 10.65; *BhāgP* 3.3.22.

34 *GP* 5.80.

35 On the descriptions of this river, see Monier Williams, *Religious Life*, p. 290, fn. 1; E. W. Hopkins, *Epic Mythology*, Delhi, reprint (1915) 1974, pp. 5 and 110; P.V. Kane, *Dharmaśāstra*, p. 164. Kirfel (*Kosmographie*, pp. 147-72) says that this river is found only in connection with hell and is divided into four kinds: the actual river, the river in hell, the river on the way to Yama's residence and the river flowing in front of the residence of the king of justice (*dharma-rāja*). *MBh* (3.81.70-71) describes this river as a sacred place (*tīrtha*) and *MBh* (3.114.4cd-6ab) mentions that Dharma, after performing a sacrifice at this river, went to heaven.

36 The relation between Śravaṇa in this Purāṇa and *spaś*, the servant of Varuṇa in the *Ṛg-veda*, is indicated in E. Abegg, *Pretakalpa*, p. 60, fn. 3.

37 See *AgniP* 369.9; *PadmaP* 3.2.27; 6.68.14; 6.240.75-6. E.W. Hopkins (*Epic Mythology*, p. 113) says that Citragupta as a recorder is found in the works later than Epic-literatures. Concerning his features and his name as one of Yama's names, see *Āśvalāyanagṛhyapariśiṣṭasūtra* (*Āśvalāyana-gṛhyasūtram*. Ānandāśrama Sanskrit Series, No. 105, 1936, pp. 141-83, = *ĀśvGPŚ*) 2.4; 2.6; *PadmaP* 3.30.38a; 4.16.18ff; 5.97.94b; 7.3.45d; 7.6.25; 7.9.82cd-83ab; 7.12.18; 7.20.47c, 48d, 49b; 7.23.45, 77a, 103a, 113d; *Bhaviṣya*P 4.89.12d; 4.164.25; *Skandapurāṇa* (Nag Publishers, Delhi, 2nd reprint, 1984, = *SkandaP*) 7.1.139; *Viṣṇudharmottarapurāṇa* (Nag Publishers, Delhi, 1985, = *ViṣṇudhP*) 3.51.5cd; *Śivapuāṇa* (Nag Publishers, Delhi, 1986, = *ŚivaP*) 3.8.50-51; 4.8.17; 5.7.3c.

38 *PadmaP* (6.209.56ab) gives the simile description. *saumyaḥ sa dharmiṇāṃ devaḥ sākṣād ugras tu pāpinām* / On the terrible appearance of Yama, see *PadmaP* 2.15.26-9.

39 *GP* 9.7; 23.22.

40 *PadmaP* (6.226.40-3) says that on seeing the good, the king of justice stands and welcomes them with his folded palms, gives them the *arghya*-water and recommends them to go to the paradise in a celestial chariot. *PadmaP* (6.226.44-9) also says that the good after being welcomed warmly by Yama, go to the world of Brahman, Viṣṇu or Indra according to the merits accumulated in their previous lives.

41 *GP* 23.15-39.

42 SBH (3.34-36) says that this tree of five-*yojana* wide and a *yojana* high, is similar to the blazing fire. Many sinful ones are hung on this tree, exhausted by hunger and thirst, and beaten by the messengers of Yama.

43 Concerning the location of the hell, see *Viṣṇu-purāṇa* (Nag Publishers = *ViṣṇuP*) 2.6.1; Kirfel, *Kosmographie*, p. 147.

44 See *Encyclopaedia of Religion and Ethics*, pp. 419-24.

45 *GP* chapters 10-12. E. Abegg tried to translate these chapters into German (*Pretakalpa*, pp. 229ff).

46 On the omen of death, see *MBh* 12.305.9-15.

47 *GP* 19.22-23. The *tulasī* is identified with the wife of Viṣṇu. Worshipping this tree, one can atone for one's crimes. See Vettam Mani, *Purāṇic Encyclopedia*, Motilal Banarsidass, Delhi, 1979, pp. 797-8; J.A. Dubois, *Hindu Manners*, pp. 649-51.

48 *GP* (19.10) says that goblins like *yātudhāna, piśāca, rākṣasa*, etc. cannot enter a place smeared with cow-dung or attack the dying within it.

49 SBH (9.3) says that one draws a *maṇḍala* with cow-dung. *GP* (19.12-13) and SBH (9.17) say that Brahmā, Viṣṇu, Rudra, etc. stand upon this *maṇḍala*.

50 *GP* 5.7; 19.6-8. *GP* (19.15) says that sesame is produced from the sweat of Viṣṇu. Cf. *Caturvarga* pp. 643-6.

51 See *GP* 5.7; 19.6-8, 25; Monier Williams, op. cit., p. 296; P.V. Kane, op. cit., p. 182. *GP* (19.19) says that at the tip of this grass stays Śiva, in its middle stays Viṣṇu and at the root stays Brahmā. Only by touching the grass, is a person able to go to heaven. On the relation between this grass and Viṣṇu's hair, see J.A. Dubois, op. cit., p. 651. *GP* (19.24) says that *darbha*-grass, sesame and *tulasī* are generally said to purify any crime (*pavitra*).

52 *GP* 5.7. This stone is held in the family of the Brahmin. See J.A. Dubois, *Hindu Manners*, pp. 648-9; Monier Williams, *Religious Life*, p. 296.

53 *GP* 10.41; 12.11-12. One who dies in a bed will be a ghost (*preta*).

54 *GP* 5.7-8; 19.6. *GP* (31.4) says that gold is the first son of Agni. *Śatapathabrāhmaṇa* (= *ŚB*, 12.5.2.6; 13.4.4.11) says that gold symbolizes immortality and that seven pieces of gold are put in the seven holes through which the vital air comes out (a mouth, two eyes, two ears and two nostrils).

55 *GP* 20.17-18.

56 The taste of salt comes from the body of Viṣṇu and satisfies the ancestors. By giving salt, every caste can open the celestial door.

57 These are rice-grains (*vrīhi*), barley (*yava*), wheat (*godhūna*), *mudga* peas, *māṣa* peas, millet (*priyaṅgu*) and *canaka* peas.

58 This cow is named Vaitaraṇī. On the way giving this cow, see *GP* 35.25-35; *SkandaP* 5.3.159.73-90.

59 Cf. P.V. Kane, op. cit., p. 183; W. Caland, op. cit., p. 8.

60 *GP* 20.34. The eight-syllabled mantra is *oṃ namo vāsudevāya*. The twelve-syllabled mantra is *oṃ namo bhagavate vāsudevāya.*

61 Fasting (*anaśana*) is described in *GP* 26.5-21.

62 Cf. P.V. Kane, op. cit., vol. 2, p. 963.

63 See *Gautamapitṛmedhasūtra* (ed. W. Caland = *GPS*) 1.1.1-9; *Bhāradvāja-pitṛmedhasūtra* (*Śrautakośa* = *BRPS*) 1.14; *Kauśikasūtra of Atharvaveda* (ed. M. Bloomfield, Motilal Banarsidass, Delhi, reprint, (1889) 1972) 80.3-4.

64 The rite of decorating the corpse is not found in *GP* but it is described elaborately in SBH (chapt. 10). Cf. W. Caland, op. cit., pp. 12-14; P.V. Kane, op. cit., vol. 4, p. 217. *Āśvalāyanagṛhyasūtra* (= *ĀśvGS*, Nārāyaṇa's commentary ad 4.1.15-17) describes the very ancient custom of taking his excrement away and filling him with ghee mixed with coagulated milk (*pṛṣad-ājya*). Cf. *Baudhāyanapitṛmedhasūtra* (ed. W.

Caland = *BDPS*, 1.2); *BRPS* 1.115-121; *APS* 31.1.12-22.

65 *GP* 25.41. J.A. Dubois (op. cit., p. 484) says that one binds a coconut to each corner of the litter and cuts it when seeing the crematory.

66 *GP* 25.42. The *Manusmṛti* (The Kashi Sanskrit Series, No.114 = *MS*, 5.92) says that one carries the corpse of a Śūdra out from the southern gate, of a Vaiśya from the western gate, of a Kṣatriya from the northern gate and of the Brahmin from the eastern gate.

67 Cf. *MS* 5.104; *Viṣṇusmṛti* (The Adyar Library Series, No. 93, = *VS*) 19.1-4; *Gautamadharmasūtra* (Ānandāśrama Sanskrit Series, No. 61 = *GDS*) 2.5.28; *Yājñavalkyasmṛti* (Nirnaya Sagar Press, = *YS*) 3.26.

68 See Kullūka Bhaṭṭa's commentary ad 10.15 in *MN*.

69 *GP* does not give any regulation, but the Sūtra literature mentions that one should select ground sloping down to the south as the crematory.

70 One heaps up sand to make this mound and places the fire on it.

71 *GP* 5.42.

72 *tvaṃ bhūta-kṛj jagad-yone tvaṃ loka-paripālakaḥ // saṃhāra-kārakas tasmād enaṃ svargaṃ mṛtaṃ naya /* (*GP* 5.43cd-44ab)

73 *GP* 5.45. *lomabhyaḥ svāhā. tvace svāhā...... pāyave svāhā. Vajasaneyi-saṃhitā* (= *VājS*) 39.10. *Taittirīyasaṃhitā* 7.3.16.2.

74 *GP* 5.13-14. Cf. W. Caland, op. cit., pp. 35-6.

75 *GP* 5.46-7.

76 For example, *AśvGS* (4.2.15) mentions that one spreads *kuśa*-grass (*barhis*), puts the skin of the black antelope with its hair upwards and places the corpse directing his head towards the direction of the fire of *Āhavanīya*.

77 Monier Williams, op. cit., p. 299.

78 W. Caland, op. cit., pp. 39-40; P.V. Kane, op.cit.,vol. 4, p. 213.

79 *Anuṣṭaraṇī* is otherwise called *rājagavī*. It is a cow to be sacrificed in the *pitṛmedha*. Some of the body and skin are placed in the relevant parts of the deceased. It is also released like a cow at the time of *madhuparka*. See *Āgniveśyagṛhyasūtra* (ed. L.A. Ravi Varma. Trivandrum Sanskrit Series, No. 144, University of Travancore, Trivandrum, 1940, = *ĀgnGS*) 3.5.3. Concerning the *rājagavī*, see *ĀgnGS* 3.5.6; 3.5.8. *ĀśvGS* (4.3.22-23) mentions that if two kidneys of a cow are not available, one may put two pieces of *piṇḍī* on the both hands of the deceased, and *Vaikhānasa-smārtasūtra* (ed. W. Caland, The Asiatic Society of Bengal, Calcutta, 5.3-5) mentions that in this case one may put gold and a ball of clay for Rudra on his body.

80 All the Sūtra works mention installation of these sacrificial utensils. On the visual form of those utensils, see M. Müller, 'Die Todtenbestattung', pp. vi-vii.

81 *GP* 5.47. On this occasion, the following mantra is recited; *asmāt tvam adhi jāto 'si tvad ayaṃ jāyatāṃ punaḥ / asau svargāya lokāya svāhā //* (*VājS* 35.22a-c; *ŚB* 12.5.2.15a-c; *Kātyāyanaśrautasūtra* 25.7.38a-c; *Taittirīya Āraṇyaka* 6.2.1a-b). Monier Williams (op. cit., p. 299) says that one recites the mantra of *Ṛg-veda* X.17.3 and that one kindles the fire in the east desiring the deceased to attain heaven.

82 This consists of five constellations (*nakṣatra*) beginning with *dhaniṣṭhā*

and ending in *revatī*. When one dies on this occasion, not only the dead can not attain the happy goal but also his relatives must suffer from various disasters. Therefore, during this inauspicious constellation (*ṛkṣa*), all the castes beginning with the Brahmins should abstain from cremation, libation, etc.

83 Cf. W. Caland, op. cit., p. 189.

84 *GP* 5.52. J.A. Dubois (op. cit., p. 486) mentions that one weeps oneself out before kindling the fire.

85 Cf. W. Caland, op. cit., pp. 76-77.

86 *GP* 24.17.

87 *GP* 24.26. *YS* (3.12) and W. Caland (op. cit., p. 79) mention that they go back home with the children or youngest men taking the lead.

88 On their attitude before entering their houses and their acts once inside, see *GP* 24.27-30ab; *YS* 3.13-14.

89 *GP* 24.15-16. See *VS* 19.10; *ViṣṇuP* 3.13-14. P.V. Kane (op. cit., vol. 4, p. 242) says that in modern times, one collects bones just after cremation. See also *ĀśvGS* 4.5.1-8; *ĀgnGS* 3.4.5; *ĀśvGPZ* 3.7; *ViṣṇudhP* 2.76.11-17.

90 SBH chapter 10. It mentions that one buries the urn in the earth, then takes it out, washes the bones with ghee and water, puts them in a casket and lets it float down a river. It is uncertain when the custom of scattering bones in a river began, but at least the Sūtra literature does not mention this custom. *GPS* (1.5.32-33) mentions that after regarding the ditch (*lekhā*) as the Sarasvatī river, one dips the urn in a ditch and buries it at the root of a tree.

91 Making the grave of the deceased (*loṣṭa-citi*) is noticed in *BDPS* 1.13-17; *BRPS* 1.10-12; 2.2-5. There we may find that one buries the urn in the earth, then takes it out, buries it again in another place and makes the grave on this place. See also *ĀgnGS* 3.8.1-3.

92 Cf. J.A. Dubois, op. cit., pp. 178-80; J. Jolly, op. cit., p. 155; W. Caland, op. cit., pp. 81-4; P.V. Kane, op. cit., vol. 4, pp. 277-92. There are two kinds of impurity, namely the impurity caused by birth (*janāśauca, sūtaka*) and that caused by death (*maraṇāśauca*). The latter commences at the moment of cremation if the deceased man is a householder who maintains the sacrificial fire and it commences at the moment of death if he does not maintain such a fire. See also *ŚivaP* 2.5.28.28-29; *ViṣṇudhP* 2.75; 3.232; *AgniP* 157-58; *ĀgnGS* 3.7.4; 3.10.2-4; *GDS* 14.

93 Cf. *MS* 5.59, 64, 71; *YS* 3.18. On the period of impurity caused by the death of a baby, a young boy, etc., see SBH chapter 13.

94 See *GP* 29.3; *MS* 4.110; *GDS* 2.5.43; *ViṣṇuP* 3.13.18; *ĀśvGS* 4.4.17-27.

95 SBH says that the impurity continues during ten days for the Brahmins and for the *sapiṇḍa*-relatives in the fourth degree. But *MS* (5.60) says the *sapiṇḍa*-relatives include the seventh degree.

96 The crematory and other sacred places are recommended for this offering of balls of rice, and middle watch (*madhyama-yāma*) is also recommended. *GP* (5.60-4) mentions elaborately the rite of offering ten balls. One puts each ball in a hole each day for ten days along with a handful of water (*jalāñjali*), rice (*odana*), barley-flour (*saktu*), roots of vegetables, fruits, etc. *GP* (25.33-37) also mentions that offering of these ten balls

belongs to three kinds of ancestor worship (*ṣoḍaśa-śrāddhāni*). The first consists of offering of the sixteen balls including these ten. Remaining six balls are offered at the place of death, on the way to the crematory, on the pile of firewood, in the hand of the dead, to the habitants of the crematory and on the bones.

97 P.V. Kane (op. cit., vol. 4, p. 334, fn. 751) defines the *śrāddha* as follows; *deśe kāle ca pātre ca śraddhayā vidhinā ca yat / pitṝn uddiśya viprebhyo dattaṃ śrāddham udāhṛtam //*. P. V. Kane (op. cit., p. 381) enumerates twelve kinds of *śrāddha: nitya-, naimittika-, kāmya-, vṛddhi-, sapiṇḍana-, pārvaṇa-, goṣṭhi-, śuddhi-, karmāṅga-, daivika-, yātrā-, puṣṭhi-śrāddha*. On the *śrāddha* as seen in the Purāṇas, see J.D.L. de Vries, *Der Śrāddhakalpa im Harivaṃśa und in fünf anderen Purāṇen*, Bonn, 1928. On this ceremony based on the Sūtra-literature, see W. Caland, *Altindischer Ahnencult*, Leiden, 1893; J. Gonda, *Vedic Ritual. The Non-solemn Rites*, Leiden-Köln, 1986.

98 P.V.Kane (op. cit., vol. 4, pp. 431-515) mentions this *pārvaṇa-śrāddha*. *YS* (1.251-2) mentions the difference between this *pārvaṇa-śrāddha* and *ekoddiṣṭa*. See also *SkandaP* 2.4.9.73a (in the *dīpāvalī* rite).

99 SBH chapter 12.

100 *GP* 4.30-31.

101 By offering the bed, the deceased can proceed to the city of Yama or of Indra, escaping tortures by servants of Yama. Even if he committed faults in his previous life, he would be able to attain heaven and enjoy being attended by celestial damsels (*apsaras*). See *GP* 24.63-6. When offering this bed embellished with various ornaments, he recites the following mantra to a Brahmin: *yathā kṛṣṇa tvadīyā hi aśūnyā kṣīra-sāgare // śayyā bhūyān mamāpīyaṃ tathā janmani janmani /* (*GP* 24.58cd-59ab). If the dead is a woman, he recites, *pretasya pratimā hy eṣā sarvopakaraṇair yutā / sarva-ratna-samāyuktā tava vipra niveditā // ātmā śambhuḥ śivā gaurī śakraḥ sura-gaṇaiḥ saha / tasmāc chayyā pradātavyā eṣa ātmā prasīdatu //* (*GP* 24.74-5).

102 *GP* 8.17-23.

103 I can enumerate three reasons why the rite of *vṛṣotsarga* had nothing to do with the rite of *ekoddiṣṭa*. The first reason is that *Pāraskaragṛhyasūtra* (= *PGS*, 3.9), *Śāṅkhāyanagṛhyasūtra* (= *ŚGS*, 3.2) and *VS* (chapt. 86) do not mention the relation between this rite and the rite of *ekoddiṣṭa*. The second reason is that *GP* does not fix the date of the rite, saying it to be performed on the eleventh day in one passage and to on auspicious occasions like *Kārttika*, etc. in another passage. The third reason is that *GP* mentions that the rite of *ātmaśrāddha* is for the living on this occasion. *SkandaP* (7.1.223.54cd) and *ĀśvGPŚ* (3.18) mention this rite in the context of the obsequies.

104 *GP* 4.18-19. The wood, the sacred places, a small cot, etc. are recommended as the best place for this rite. See *Caturvarga*, p. 1616.

105 On this *graha-yajña*, see P.V. Kane op. cit., vol. 5, pp. 753-6. On the rite of *mātṛśrāddha*, see pp. 1621-22.

106 On this *pūrṇāhuti*, see *VS* 86.9; p. 1622; *PGS* 3.9.4-5; H. Krick, *Das Ritual der Feuergründung. (Agnyādheya)*, Wien, 1982, pp. 415-19.

107 *GP* 4.21.

108 *GP* 4.22. SBH (12.21) describes the features of the bull that is fit to be set free. The black bull (*nīla*) at the age of three, without any missing limbs, is particularly recommended. On this black bull, see *Caturvarga*, p. 1620.

109 *GP* 4.32.

110 The mantra is as follows: *dharmas tvaṃ vṛṣa-rūpeṇa brahmaṇā nirmitaḥ purā / vṛṣotsarga-prabhāveṇa mām uddhara bhavārṇavāt //* (*GP* 4.24). *VS* (86.15-16) mentions the following mantra: *vṛṣo hi bhagavān dharmaś catuṣpādaḥ prakīrtitaḥ / vṛṇomi tam ahaṃ bhaktyā sa me rakṣatu sarvataḥ //* (15) *etaṃ yuvānaṃ patiṃ vo dadāmy anena krīḍantīś carata priyeṇa / mā hāsmahi prajayā mā tanūbhir mā radhāma dviṣate soma rājan //* (*VS* 86.16). Cf. *Ṛgveda* 10.128.5c-d; *Atharvaveda* 5.3.7c-d; *Taittirīyasaṃhitā* 4.7.14.2c-d.

111 This is also called *jīvacchrāddha*. See P.V. Kane, op. cit., vol. 4, pp. 542-4; *Caturvarga*, pp. 1704-17. See P.V. Kane, op. cit., vol. 1, p. 903. *Liṅgapurāṇa* 2.45.

112 *GP* (16.14) enumerates the first year, half a year, three and half months and the twelfth day after death as the best period for this rite. It is said that the day on which a year has passed after death is the best, but the twelfth day seems to have been common in those days. See *GP* 16.13.

113 Since *GP* does not mention the systematic process of this rite, I followed the description of SBH (13. 35-39). On the rite of *sapiṇḍīkaraṇa*, see Ś*GS* 5.9; *YS* 1.253-4; *ViṣṇuP* 3.13-27; *VS* 21.12-23; *PadmaP* 5.10.22-33; *MārkP* 27.12-8; *AgniP* 117.35-37; *ViṣṇudhP* 2.77; *ĀśvGPZ* 3.11. On the sacrifice of the ball as seen in the Vedic literatures, see O. Donner, *Piṇḍapitṛyajña, das Manenopfer mit Klössen bei den Indern. Abhandlung aus den vedischen Ritual*, Berlin, 1870.

114 This is offered to hostile beings in a sacrifice. See *MS* 3.245; *ViṣṇuS* 81.23; *The Pariśiṣṭa of the Atharvaveda* 44.4.3; P.V. Kane, op. cit., Vol. 4, pp. 446 and 470.

115 *vasūn vadanti tu pitṝn rudrāṃś caiva pitāmahān / prapitāmahāṃs tathādityāñ chrutir eṣā sanātanī //* (*MS* 3.284)

116 *YS* (1.253-254) mentions that one prepares four jars full of scent, water and sesame, and pours one of the four for the newly deceased into the other three jars, reciting *ye samānāḥ* (*VājS* 19.45a, 46b).

II

HINDU PHILOSOPHICAL TRADITIONS

3

What Lies at the Basis of Indian Philosophy*

SENGAKU MAYEDA

INTRODUCTION

In 1983 I had an opportunity to meet His Holiness Abhinava Vidyātīrtha (1917-1989) at Shringeri monastery, the headquarters of the Shankara School. On that occasion I casually noted that in Japan there were only a few scholars who were engaged in research on Indian philosophy although there were many researchers of Buddhism. Then His Holiness said as follows:

> Buddhism and our Non-dualism are exceedingly similar. The only point of difference lies in the fact that we, Advaitins, recognize the existence of a substantial entity but Buddhism does not do so.

From this remark I was fortunate enough to obtain a glimpse of His Holiness' views on Buddhism.

Although I was in agreement with his statement, I found it difficult to accept it in the light of Shankara's strong criticism of Buddhism in his commentary on the *Brahmasūtra* and his other books. We could scarcely expect a statement of that nature from an individual like His Holiness Vidyātīrtha. He, after all, is the successor of Shankara, a great exponent of Advaita Vedānta in the 8th century.

SHANKARA'S VIEW OF BUDDHISM

At this point it would be pertinent to explain Shankara's views on Buddhism and for this it would be most appropriate to turn to the source material, i.e. his commentary on the *Brahmasūtra*.[1]

Here in his commentary on the *Brahmasūtra*, just prior to his criticism of Buddhism, he undertakes a criticism of the Vaiśeṣika school and characterizes it as 'seminihilism' (*ardhavaināṣika*). In this connection he defines Buddhism as a whole as 'the doctrine which asserts the nihilism of everything,' (*sarvavaināṣikarāddhānta*) . Then, as I have pointed out elsewhere, he makes an attempt at 'critical classification of the Buddhist doctrines' on the criterion of what is asserted as real or, in other words, from his ontological point of view, and criticizes the following three types of Buddhist propounders: (1) 'the Buddhist who asserts the real existence of everything' (*Sarvāstitvavādin*), (2) 'the Buddhist who asserts the real existence of *Vijñāna*, i.e. Consciousness' (*Vijñānāstitvavādin*) and (3) 'the Buddhist who asserts the emptiness of everything' (*Sarvaśūnyatvavādin*). Not to mention 'the Buddhist who asserts the emptiness of everything', 'the Buddhist who asserts the real existence of consciousness ' as well as 'the Buddhist who asserts the real existence of everything ' commonly advocate 'the doctrine of entities having but momentary existence' (*kṣanabhaṅga*).[2] Therefore, in Shankara's understanding, Buddhism as a whole is a doctrine which asserts total nihilism. For Shankara, even that Buddhist doctrine which asserts that consciousness alone is real is nihilistic and without a shred of rationality (*upapatti*). Shankara adds that it is not possible to lead an ordinary life on the basis of such a nihilistic view.

And finally he concludes his criticism against the Buddha and Buddhism with the following words:

> No further special discussion is in fact required. From whatever new points of view the Buddha system is tested with reference to its probability, it gives way on all sides, like the walls of a well dug in sandy soil. It has, in fact, no foundation whatever to rest upon, and hence the attempts to use it as a guide in the practical concerns of life are mere folly.
> Moreover, by propounding the three mutually contradictory systems, teaching respectively the reality of the external world, the reality of consciousness only, and total nihilism, Buddha has himself made it clear either that he was a man given to making incoherent assertions, or else that hatred of all beings induced him to propound absurd doctrines by whose acceptance they would become thoroughly confused.....Buddha's doctrine has to be entirely disregarded by all those who have a regard for their own happiness.[3]

SHANKARA'S OPPONENTS' VIEW OF ADVAITA

It is, however, well-known that Shankara was criticized by his opponents as 'a Buddhist in disguise' (*pracchannabauddha*) and his philosophy as 'the doctrine affirming the world to be an illusion' (*mā-*

yāvāda)[4] which is but crypto-Buddhism.

Among the Vedāntins, Bhāskara (750-900) was probably one of the earliest critics of Shankara. He called the Māyāvādin 'one who depends on the doctrine of the Buddhist' (*Bauddhamatāvalambin*), and said that this position has been negated by the author of the *Brahmasūtra*.[5] Afterwards, Yāmuna (918-1038), Rāmānuja (1017-1037), Madhva (1197-1037), Vallabha (1473-1531) and other Vedāntins severely criticized the Advaita Vedānta, pointing out that it is in essence nothing but a Buddhist doctrine[6].

This is true of modern Indian scholars. For example, in his *A History of Indian Philosophy*, S. Dasgupta remarks,

> Shankara and his followers borrowed much of their dialectic form of criticism from the Buddhists. His Brahman was very much like the sunya of Nāgārjuna. ......I am led to think that Shankara's philosophy is largely a compound of Vijñānavāda and Śūnyavāda Buddhism with the Upanishad notion of the permanence of self superadded.[7]

Even S. Radhakrishnan who asserts that 'there is no doubt that Shankara develops his whole system from the Upaniṣads and the *Vedānta Sūtra* without reference to Buddhism,'[8] says as follows:

> We need not say that the Advaita Vedanta philosophy has been very much influenced by the Mādhyamika doctrine..... the Nirguṇa Brahman of Shankara and Nāgārjuna's śūnya have much in common.[9]

SHANKARA AND VIJÑĀNAVĀDINS

Then, what possibly could have been Shankara's own reaction to the charges that his doctrine resembled that of Buddhism?

First of all, we must admit that, judging from his writings, there is no room to doubt the fact that his knowledge of Buddhism was of a high standard and accurate. Moreover, it is very probable that those critics of Shankara appeared not only after his death but also during his lifetime. In fact, Shankara himself explicitly admits in his *Māṇḍūkyo-paniṣatkārikābhāṣya* that Buddhism is said to be in close similarity to the Advaita of his paramaguru Gauḍapāda.

However, Shankara was by no means easily amenable to accepting such a similarity between Non-dualism and Vijñānavāda. On the contrary he stressed in his *Māṇḍūkyopaniṣatkārikābhāṣya*[10] the

Advaitins' originality and difference from Buddhism on the following two points: first, the Advaita philosophy expounds the non-dual, Ultimate Reality which, unlike the Vijñānavādins' consisting of three components,[11] i.e. knowledge, object of knowledge, and knower, does not possess any similar components, and secondly the Advaita philosophy is based on the absolute authority of the Upaniṣads.

In this connection the Ālayavijñāna of the Vijñānavādins may come into question. It is the substratum of transmigratory existence assumed by them and corresponds to the unchangeable substratum, that is, the Ātman of the fourth stage whose existence is strongly asserted by the Shankara school. Shankara's critique against this Ālayavijñāna is found in his *Brahmasūtrabhāṣya*. In it, Shankara denies the possibility of Ālayavijñāna's being the substratum of residual impressions for the Vijñānavādins accept its momentariness while recognizing it as the substratum. In Shankara's view our daily activities like memory and recognition would presuppose the existence of a continuous entity (*anvayin*)that persists in all the three times, past, present and future, or else, an unchangeable, permanent (*kūṭasthanitya*), quiescent Ātman. Therefore, this Ātman is essentially different from the Ālayavijñāna.

Even if Shankara's Ātman and the Vijñānavādins' Ālayavijñāna differ in essence, they show mutual similarity in the function that they exercise within each system, and as both of the two systems equally assert the non-reality of the phenomenal world, they belong to similar monistic standpoint.

In this context it is quite interesting to note the following fact: Buddhist philosophers, Śāntarakṣita (725-788) and Kamalaśīla (740-796), probably Shankara's contemporaries in the 8th century, recognize the fact that even Non-dualism is as valid as Vijñānavāda, although they also point out that there is 'a slight mistake' (*alpāparādha*) in the Advaita assertion of the eternal nature of the Ātman.

TWO TRADITIONS IN THE HISTORY OF INDIAN PHILOSOPHY

In his work entitled *The Central Philosophy of Buddhism*,[12] T.V.R. Murti once asserted:

> There are two main currents of Indian philosophy—one having its source in the atma-doctrine of the Upanishads and the other in the anatma-doctrine of Buddha.

I think that nobody can deny his assertion. Then, how is it that the

Vedānta school, a representative of the orthodox (*āstika*) Brahmanical traditions, come to assume close similarity to Buddhism, a representative of the non-orthodox (*nāstika*) traditions?

One major reason for this is the fact that during their long history, the two traditions have exerted influence upon each other. They have gradually approached one another and eventually almost fused with one another. This is a fact that one might reasonably assume. Actually the process whereby these two traditions approached each other can be explained to a certain degree. In my opinion, the process in which these two philosophical traditions approached one another was more or less as follows.

One of the fundamental standpoints of early Buddhism is said to have been the suspension of judgement with respect to metaphysical problems (*avyākata*). Judging from this basic standpoint of Buddhism, I would think that it is first of all contrary to Buddhism even to consider the question as to whether the Ātman exists or does not exist. According to some able scholars of early Buddhism, the concept of non-Self as revealed in the *Suttanipāta*, i.e. a text which is reputed to belong to the earliest group of Pāli Buddhist scriptures, by no means denies the existence of the Ātman. Rather it stresses 'the rejection of attachment, particulary attachment to ego', 'the rejection of an undue adherence to something' and 'the refusal to be enslaved by anything.' I personally believe that the theory of non-Ātman as revealed in early Buddhism, is not to be construed as denying the existence of the Ātman as revealed in the Upaniṣads. As observed in the well-known metaphor of the poisoned arrow of Mālunkyaputta, the major concern of early Buddhism was the final release from pain and sorrow (*duhkha*) and attainment of *nirvāṇa.* With regard, however, to the question of the subject who experiences that pain and sorrow or the subject of transmigration, all judgement was suspended. Accordingly, it seems to me that the doctrine of non-Ātman as revealed in early Buddhism, is not in conflict with that of Ātman.

However, in the period of the Abhidharma the theory of anātman i.e. non-Self could not immune from changes in its connotation, and eventually came to mean 'the non-existence of Ātman'. In order, however, to prove the non-existence of many substantial entities called *dharma*s, i.e. existential elements were emphasized. When Mahāyāna Buddhism arose, these existential elements were severely criticized by Nāgārjuna, and accordingly the concept of *śūnyatā*, i.e. emptiness was propounded as the basis of Mahāyāna Buddhism.

However, just as Gautama Buddha was silent or suspended his judgement concerning the subject of pain and sorrow, Nāgārjuna was also silent or suspended his judgement concerning the subject observing that everything is *śūnyatā*. As a result of this, I believe that the Consciousness-only theory of the Yogācāra school and the theory of Buddha-nature were propounded in order to make clear, from the standpoint of *śūnyatā*, what Nāgārjuna left unsaid. In other words Buddhism finally came to take up such problems as the subject of pain and sorrow and that of cognition, concerning which any judgement was suspended in early Buddhism. These are actually nothing but the problems of Ātman and Brahman in the Vedānta Philosophy.

It was in the period of the Gupta dynasty that the Yogācāra school came to cope with those problems; in this period Buddhism was on the decline and Hinduism which received the support of the Gupta dynasty was on the upswing. Against such a background there arose the 'vedāntinization' of Buddhism, in other words, 'sanskritization' of Buddhism. To explain briefly, Buddhism was transformed from the pluralism of the Abhidharma into the monism of Ālayavijñāna by Nāgārjuna's theory of emptiness.

As is well-known, in the *Laṅkāvatārasūtra*, which was probably composed around the year A.D. 400, *tathāgatagarbha* or the matrix-embryo of the Tathāgata was not only at times identified with Ālayavijñāna,[13] but the definition of this *tathāgatagarbha* was also very similar to the Vedānta definition of Brahman. Besides, Brahman, Viṣṇu, and Īśvara were also used as synonyms of *tathāgata* and the highest Brahman came to be regarded as the ultimate state.[14] In the same *Sūtra*, Mahāprajña Bodhisattva raises the question to the Buddha as to whether the doctrine of the *tathāgatagarbha* is not the same as the heretical Ātman doctrine (*tīrthakarātmavāda*)[15].

On the other hand, the Vedānta school was formed with the *Brahmasūtra* as its foundation in the fifth century, comparatively later than other philosophical schools including the Buddhist; the Vedānta school established a system of Brahmanic monism based upon the Upaniṣads, responding in particular to the then rather influential dualistic Sāṃkhya school.

However, this realistic monism of the *Brahmasūtra* was of a character of difference-and-non-difference (*bhedābheda*), i.e. a dualistic monism, as it were. In denying such a standpoint and in the process of developing an absolute monism (*advaita*), that is, the Upaniṣadic thought of the identity of Brahman and Ātman, the realistic monism of the *Brahmasūtra* was gradually transformed and moved closer to the Buddhism which had a more advanced theoretical system than the Vedānta. While doing so, this Vedānta philosophy came to be 'Buddhisticized' considerably.

The gradual process of 'Buddhisticization' of the Vedānta school is reflected in the four chapters of the *Māṇḍūkyakārikā* of Gauḍapāda (640-690). This 'Buddhisticization' of the Vedānta school reached its highest point in the fourth chapter of this work composed before Shankara[16] who wrote a commentary on it.

What Shankara, born in South India in the eighth century, found before him were: first, the Mīmāṃsā school which was flourishing with excellent theoreticians like Kumārila (650-700), Prabhākara (ca.700), Maṇḍanamiśra (680-720) and others; second, a tide of popular Hinduism which grew by leaps and bounds among the masses; and third, a weakening, esoteric-oriented Buddhism which was the target of strong criticism by Kumārila and others; fourth, a thoroughly 'Buddhisticized' Vedānta school.

Just as Dayananda Sarasvati (1828-1883) severely criticized the downfall of Hinduism in the nineteenth century with the cry 'Return to the Vedas,' in the same way Shankara in his days, beholding the prosperity of the Mīmāṃsā school and the deplorable situation of his own Vedānta school, must have proclaimed 'Return to the Vedas.' This must be one of the reasons why there is no one who has left us so many commentaries of the Upaniṣads as Shankara.

With the purpose of reviving the Vedānta school from the standpoint of orthodox Brahmanism, Shankara, while using his profound knowledge of Buddhism, transmuted Buddhist doctrines in the *Māṇḍūkyakārikā* into Advaitism and achieved the re-'vedānticization' of the 'Buddhisticized' Vedāntic tradition.[17]

In this way, Buddhist doctrines, which had been absorbed into the pre-Shankara Vedānta philosophy and constituted an integral part of the *Māṇḍūkyakārikā*, were preserved without being removed and were vedānticized by Shankara. As a result, the realistic monism of the *Brahmasūtra* was transformed and developed into an illusionistic non-dualism, which, as he himself recognized, closely resembled the Buddhist doctrine.[18] For Shankara, Buddhism was an important target to overcome. For this reason he attacked it very severely in his works. Shankara was an epoch-making reformer in the history of Vedānta who turned the extremely Buddhisticized tradition of Vedānta towards the Vedāntic Vedānta or Upaniṣadic Vedānta.[19]

Shankara was aware of the fact that non-dualism was said to be similar to Buddhism, but he personally refused to accept this view. His reason for insisting that the highest truth is revealed only in Upaniṣads, is probably a conviction arising from his desire to purify Vedāntic philosophy of its Buddhistic influences and bring to light the original Vedāntic philosophy, which had developed as an interpretative science of the Upaniṣads.

By the process explained above the two traditions seem to have approached and resembled each other in spite of Shankara's denial.

WHAT LIES AT THE BASIS OF INDIAN PHILOSOPHY

In such a way the two traditions finally attained a high degree of similarity. However, the essential difference between the two systems, in view of Shankara and Śāntarakṣita, lies in the concept of Ātman and Ālayavijñāna, and we may further add that their difference lies in their source of knowledge as well.

Now, Ātman is everlasting while Ālayavijñāna is momentary. But both of them are in their essence pure consciousness. Therefore, their difference may appear trifling. In my opinion, however, their difference is essential and deep-rooted.

After examining the two main currents of thought carefully and even recognizing the similarity between the Absolute of Vedānta and that of the Mādhyamika or Vijñānavāda, T.V.R. Murti concluded that 'there could not be acceptance of any doctrinal content by either side from the other, as each had a totally different background of tradition and conception of reality.' I would like to discuss what lies in the background of the two main different currents of Indian philosophy.

If I were to express my conclusion in advance, I would say that the conflict between the concepts of Ātman and Ālayavijñāna takes its source from that of Sat (Being) and Asat (non-Being) which can be traced back to the creation myths of the *Ṛgveda.* Since I believe that this centuries-old conflict between Sat and Asat lies at the basis of Indian philosophy, I would like to set aside a little time to deal with this significant question.

THE CONFLICT BETWEEN SAT AND ASAT

In his inspiring paper entitled 'Early Philosophical Speculation in the Rig Veda,' W. Norman Brown (1892-1975) explained as follows:

> Vedic man did....consider that there were in the cosmos two kinds of being more powerful than humans whom he could influence. These were the gods (*deva*) and the demons (*rakṣas*). The gods were kind of bureaucracy administering and enforcing the Rta. They and human beings were held to occupy the surface of the earth, the vault of heaven, and the midair.... between those two. This part of the cosmos was known as the Sat 'Existent.' It had light, warmth, and moisture, and in it the ṛta prevailed. The demons occupied the Asat 'Non-Existent,' a fearsome region situated below the Sat, from which it could be reached by descending through a great chasm. The Asat was without light, warmth, and moisture, and in it the ṛta did not prevail. Rather, the Asat was without the ṛta (anṛta).
> ...The demons were relentless enemies of the ṛta and of all beings living in the ṛta, that is, gods and humans. The gods should be allied against the demons. To effect such an alliance was the basic purpose of the Vedic sacrifice.[20]

Furthermore, Vedic man tried to understand the operation of the universe and for this purpose it was essential to penetrate to the origin of the universe, particulary the origin of the Sat and Asat. In the *Ṛgveda* there are a number of theories in answer to this inquiry. According to Brown the myth of the hero god Indra and demon presumably demonstrates the earliest example of these theories.[21]

This Indra-Vṛtra myth begins with the precreation state of chaos. In this state all the elements of the Sat were in existence but were unorganized and were concealed in the Asat, where they were held in restraint under a huge cover or obstruction by the demon Vṛtra.

On the other hand the gods, who could not cope with this situation, probably arranged for the birth of Indra. As soon as Indra was born, he drank *soma* and finally slew Vṛtra. Then the cosmic Waters came out. The Sat was then differentiated from the Asat, and the Sat contained the Waters and the Sun. Thus being provided with warmth, light and moisture, the *Ṛta* was made to prevail in the Sat, and the demons continued to breed and endanger the beings living in the Sat.

It did not take long for Vedic man to be dissatisfied with the myth which was too naive to remain convincing. Vedic man continued to search for the origin of the Sat and the Asat. Finally Vedic man's efforts resulted in the *Nasadīya* hymn (10.129) of the *Ṛgveda* which starts by taking us back before the differentiation of the Sat and Asat, even before their very existence.[22] Neither Indra nor Vṛtra appear in this hymn but 'That One' (*tad ekam*) alone breathed, though uninspired by breath, by its own potentiality in a primeval state where there was neither Sat nor Asat. It brought about the separation of Sat from Asat. The *Nasadīya* hymn reads as follows:

> The sages by pious insight into their heart (that is, by introspection) found the relation (*bandhu*) of the Sat with the Asat.[23]

According to another hymn of the *Ṛgveda* 'the Sat was born from the Asat in the primitive ages of the gods.'[24] In the *Atharvaveda*[25] the Skambha, the support of the universe, is regarded as containing both Sat and Asat. Brahman is praised as 'the womb of both Sat and Asat' and it is said in other hymns of the *Atharvaveda*[26] that the Sat is established in the Asat while the living being rest securely in the Sat and that the gods who were born from the Asat were indeed great.

Further, in the *Brāhmaṇas* Asat is also regarded as a kind of fundamental principle, and there are many creation myths wherein Asat was the beginning of the universe. In the Upaniṣads this idea was transmitted, and we come across such passages as 'In the beginning this (universe) was Asat. Therefrom, verily Sat was produced.'[27] and 'In the beginning this (universe) was Asat. It became Sat.'[28] Judging from the above observation, the idea that Asat is the origin of Sat seems to have prevailed since the *Ṛgveda.*

It was, however, the famous Upaniṣadic philosopher Uddālaka Āruṇi who denied this idea completely. In imparting the philosophy of Sat to his son Śvetaketu, Āruṇi insisted that it was Sat alone that existed in the beginning and strongly rejected the view that Sat was produced from Asat.[29] I belive that this philosophy of Sat stressed by Āruṇi came to be regarded as the legitimate theory of the orthodox Brahmans while that of Asat probably vanished from the orthodox philosophical world.

In my opinion, however, although it disappeared from the orthodox philosophical world, the tradition of Asat was not totally destroyed but did continue to develop under such different forms as the non-orthodox systems (*Nāstika*) of philosophy like Materialism, Jainism and Buddhism. Furthermore, even orthodox systems (*Āstika*) of philosophy such as the Nyāya and Vaiśeṣika which assert the combination theory (Ārambhavāda) based upon the causation theory in which the effect is not existent in the cause fall within this stream of Asat. Even the *Ālayavijñāna* of the Yogācāra school seems to belong to this philosophical tradition of Asat.

In the beginning of the universe the Sat and the Asat as fundamental principles of the universe are undifferentiated from each other as seen in the case of 'That One' in the hymns of *Ṛgveda*. As in the *Atharvaveda*, the Sat and the Asat are 'twins', or rather they could be better described as 'Siamese twins' which have Brahman as their common womb. Indeed, they are like the two sides of a single sheet of paper. The orthodox Brahman philosophers look at the obverse side of a paper while the Buddhists look at the reverse side of the same paper. Both Shankara and Vasubandhu observed the same sheet of paper, but they did so from opposite directions.

CONCLUSION

Now, I would like to bring my paper to a conclusion. At the basis of Indian philosophy there were two main currents of thought: one accepted the Sat and the other accepted the Asat as the fundamental cause of the universe and human beings; both were orthodox Brahmanical traditions of thought. In Upaniṣads, however, Uddālaka Āruṇi denied the philosophy of Asat and advocated that of Sat. It seems to me that this was the turning point wherein the orthodox Brahmanical line adopted the standpoint of Sat. Against this, Buddhism and the other unorthodox schools took the standpoint of Asat.

Here I do hope that you will remember Murti's assertion that there are two main currents of Indian philosophy, each of which had a totally different background of tradition and conception of reality. However, he did not make clear what he meant by 'totally different background and conception of reality.' If we were to accept the traditions of Sat and Asat, it is easily understandable why Vedānta and Buddhism, by extension Hindu philosophy and Buddhist philosophy, still differ in some fundamental ways despite their apparent close similarities. In my view, it is the two currents of Sat and Asat that lie at the basis of Indian philosophy.

The concepts of Sat and Asat are entirely contradictory to each other from a logical point of view. However, if we were to retrace our steps to their original root, we would arrive at that unique and undifferentiated 'That One'. It should not be forgotten that Vedic man searched neither for being nor non-being but for their origin, 'That One'. The two traditions of Indian philosophy equally aim at the Absolute, the ultimate state of liberation (*mokṣa* or *nirvāṇa*), which transcends the world of normal human logic, the world of subject and object, the world of nescience (*avidyā*), the world of frivolous talk (*prapañca*), and the world of being and non-being.

NOTES

* The International Institute for Asian Studies, Leiden, the Netherlands, has kindly given me permission to reprint this paper which was originally published in the *India and Beyond: Aspects of Literature, Meaning, Ritual and Thought, Essays in Honour of Frits Staal,* ed. by Dr. Dick van der Meij, Leiden and Amsterdam, 1997, pp. 348-60. The substance of this paper is based upon my lecture in Japanese 'Indo-shiso no Kontei ni arumono' delivered at the University of Tokyo on 25 January, 1991 which was published in the *Shunjū,* No. 328, 1991, pp. 5-13 and an abridged text of this paper was read at the East-West Philosophers' Conference held at Massey University, Palmerston North, New Zealand from 12 August to 15, 1994. I would like to express my thanks to Professors Eli Franco and Anindita N. Balslev who kindly read through my original manuscript and gave me valuable suggestions. Thanks are also due to Mr. Richard A. Paulson and Professor Kenneth K. Tanaka who kindly took trouble to revise and correct my English.

1 Shankara *ad Brahmasūtra* II,2,18,22.

2 Ibid., II,2,31.

3 Ibid., II,2,32.

4 In fact it is wrong that Shankara's Advaita philosophy is called '*māyā-vāda.*' Cf. *A Thousand Teachings: The Upadeśasāhasrī of Shankara, tr. with Introduction and Notes* by S. Mayeda, Tokyo, 1979, pp. 78-79.

5 Bhāskara *ad Brahmasūtra* II,2,29.

6 For a detailed introduction, cf. H. Nakamura, *Shoki no Vedānta Tetsugaku* (*Early Vedānta Philosophy*), Tokyo, 1950, pp. 159-161; Yoshiaki Kodate, 'Vedānta Tetsugaku to Bukkyo-Kosho no Ichidanmen' ('An Aspect of the Vedānta-Buddhism Relations'), *Nihonbukkyogaku Nenpo* 23, 1957, pp. 257-75.

7 Vol. 1, Cambridge, 1951, pp. 493-94.

8 *Indian Philosophy*, vol. 2, New York, 1958, p. 472.

9 Ibid., vol. 1, p.668.

10 *Māṇḍūkyopaniṣatkārikā*, IV,99, p. 182 (śrīśaṅkaragranthāvaliḥ, sampuṭaḥ 4. Śrīvāṇīvilāsamudrāyantrālayaḥ, n.d.). There is a problem concerning the authenticity of this commentary. Cf. S. Mayeda, 'On the author of the Māṇḍūkyopaniṣad- and the Gauḍapādiya-Bhāṣya,' *The Adyar Library Bulletin*, vols. 31-2, 1967-8, pp. 73-94; T. Vetter, 'Zur Bedeutung des Illusionismus bei Śaṅkara,' *Festschrift für Erich Frauwallner, WZKSO* 12/13, 1968, pp. 407-; P. Hacker, 'Notes on the Māṇḍūkyopaniṣad and Śaṅkara's Āgamaśāstravivarana,' *P. Hacker Kleine Schriften*, Wiesbaden, 1978, pp. 252-254, note 2. Previously, K. Kumada, taking the hint from this *Kārikā*, IV, 99, wrote an article entitled 'The Fundamental Difference between Buddhistic and Vedāntic Philosophies, ' *Journal of Indian and Buddhist Studies*, vol. IX, no.1, 1961, pp. 410-403. There are different controversies concerning the interpretation of IV, 99 of the *Kārikā,* but I deal only with Shankara's commentary in this article.

11 The expression *jñānajñeyajñātṛbhedarahitam* likely presupposes *grāhya-*

grāhakasaṃvittibhedavān seen in Dharmakīrti's *Pramāṇavārttika* II,354. Incidentally, this famous verse is quoted in Shankara's *Upadeśasāhasrī* II,18,142. Cf. my article 'Śaṅkara to Bukkyo,' ('Shankara and Buddhism'), *Bukkyo Kenkyu* 3, 1973, pp. 104-189.

12 London, 1974, pp. 10-35.

13 *Laṅkāvatārasūtra,* pp. 221, line 12; 222, lines 6, 9; 223, lines 2, 6, 11; 235, lines 7,16.

14 Ibid., p. 153, line 9.

15 Ibid., p. 77, line 13-p. 79, line 9. Cf. H. Nakamura, *Early Vedānta Philosophy,* op. cit., pp. 199-204.

16 Cf. my article 'Śaṅkara to Bukkyo,' op.cit., p. 104.

17 Cf. my article 'On the Author of the Māṇḍūkyopaniṣad- and the Gauḍapādīya-Bhāṣya,' op.cit., pp. 88-93.

18 Cf. my article 'Śaṅkara to Bukkyo,' op. cit., p.103.

19 This may be one of the reasons that Shankara was more rigid and stricter with regard to the problem of caste than the author of the *Brahmasūtra* as well as his followers.

20 *India and Indology: Selected Articles by W. Norman Brown,* ed. by Rosana Rocher, Delhi, 1978, pp. 79-80.

21 Ibid., p. 80.

22 *India and Indology,* op. cit., p. 82.

23 *Ṛgveda* 10,129,4.

24 Ibid., 10,72,2; 3.

25 *Atharvaveda,* 10,7,10.

26 Ibid., 4,1,1; 5,6,1.

27 *Taittirīya Upaniṣad* II,7.

28 *Chāndogya Upaniṣad* III,19,1.

29 Ibid., VI,2,1-2.

4

The Knower in the Sāṃkhya

SHUJUN MOTEGI

PREFACE

One of the characteristic features of ancient Indian thought is that the final aim is to attain emancipation and escape this human life full of pain. The Sāṃkhya school of thought, which probably flourished in the fourth or fifth century AD, developed its philosophy by focusing on emancipation as the final goal. The basic standpoint of the Sāṃkhya is dualism which admits *puruṣa* (spiritual being) and *prakṛti* (material principle) as the ultimate reality. According to the Sāṃkhya, final emancipation is attained by *viveka jñāna* (distinctive knowledge) which distinguishes *puruṣa* from *prakṛti*. Such knowledge, which is considered by modern minds to be mystical intuition, must be quite different from mundane knowledge. The dualism of the Sāṃkhya, however, inevitably causes a problem concerning what entity acquires distinctive knowledge, or, even in ordinary life, what entity recognizes the outer world before attaining emancipation. The Sāṃkhya admits two principles which are ultimately real, *puruṣa* and *prakṛti*, the first spiritual being that never touches the outer world although it is supposed to be a conscious being. The Sāṃkhya holds that a human being has sense organs and internal organs to cognize the outer world. But the sense organs and internal organs are derived from *prakṛti*, which is essentially material being. Neither organ, which work together in cognition of the outer world, has consciousness, because they are material. The conscious *puruṣa* is only a seer (*draṣṭṛ*) who stands apart from worldly affairs. Hence, as no other conscious principle is admitted, there occurs the problem of which entity is the knower of the outer world and attains knowledge for the final emancipation.

The *Yuktidīpikā* (*YD*),[1] one of the extant commentaries of the *Sāṃkhya-Kārikā* (*SK*), a compendium of the Sāṃkhya, discusses this problem in detail. In this paper I shall discuss the problem of the knower in the Sāṃkhya, examining the arguments in the *YD*.

We come across the problem first in the argument at the very beginning of the *SK* which mentions the necessity of the Sāṃkhya approach to emancipation. The first Kārikā runs as follows:

> *duḥkhatrayābhighātād tadapaghātake jijñāsā* / (*SK*1ab')
> As [a human being] suffers from three kinds of pain, there occurs the desire to know the way to eliminate them.

To the declaration of the Sāṃkhya, the author of the *YD* (*YDkāra*) introduces a view of an opponent who attacks the standpoint of the *SK* quoted above, which is as follows:[2]

> If you assume the existence of the desire for knowledge, does this desire belong to *puruṣa* or to *guṇa*? (*YD* p.16.8-9, Pandeya Edition p. 8.15-16)

Here the term *guṇa* seems to mean *buddhi*, an internal organ, which is the first evolute of *prakṛti* and hence made up of *guṇa* (material constituents). It is supposed to have the function of decision (*adhyavasāya*) about the object brought to it through sense-organs. The opponent continues the statement in more detail as below:

> The desire for knowledge cannot belong to *puruṣa*, because you maintain that *puruṣa* has no attributes. You don't admit that desire, hate, effort, pleasure, displeasure, merit, demerit, knowledge and latent impression are the attributes of self. (*YD*. pp. 16.9-17.2, Pandeya Edition p. 8.16-21)[3]
>
> On the other hand the desire for knowledge cannot belong to *guṇa*, because *guṇa* has no consciousness. It is not admittedly known that an unconscious being like a pot etc. desires to know the way of attainment of happiness and removal of calamity. Your *guṇa* is an unconscious being, because it is stated later that *pradhāna* is common, unconscious and productive (*SK*11b).

The opponent maintains that the consciousness of desire for knowledge occurs neither in *puruṣa* nor in *guṇa*. He further points out that the Sāṃkhya admits no principle other than *puruṣa* and *guṇa*. He concludes that there can be no good reason for consciousness to occur, and that the statement of the *SK* is not acceptable.

To this objection the *YDkāra* replies that the desire for knowledge occurs, not in *puruṣa* but in *buddhi*, and puts an end to the argument by stating that it can show that desire occurs in *buddhi* even though it has no consciousness.

The theme of the argument is the possibility of the existence of a being possessing consciousness in the framework of Sāṃkhya thought. The term *guṇa* is used to stand for *buddhi* which emanates from *pradhāna* and, therefore, is material. The opponent denies the possibility that material *buddhi* has the consciousness to desire knowledge. On the other hand *puruṣa,* a conscious being, is not considered to have the consciousness to desire knowledge. As a result, in Sāṃkhya theory, the opponent says, there cannot exist any being who desires knowledge of the Sāṃkhya way of emancipation. The Sāṃkhya must satisfy this objection. The Sāṃkhya has to ascribe such consciousness to *buddhi* as to desire knowledge, in order to keep puruṣa untouched by the material world, though *buddhi* is a material being born from the predominal material. In the Sāṃkhya theory, though *buddhi* is derived from material being, one of its functions comes to be similar to the conscious self of other schools, that is, Nyāya and Vaiśeṣika, which admit that the self has feelings and the will to desire or to hate. The next question, therefore, will be what in the Sāṃkhya is the relation between *puruṣa* and *buddhi,* as one of them, *puruṣa,* seems to be useless in the process of cognition, if *buddhi* plays the role of a sort of conscious being.

PURUṢA AND *BUDDHI*

The *YD* argues the relation between *puruṣa* and *buddhi* in its commentary on *SK*17 and *SK*37. I show below the argument by translating into English the relevant passages.

(I) The *SK* proves the existence of *puruṣa* in the 17th Kārikā by five reasons, one of which is:

> *puruṣo 'sti bhoktṛbhāvāt* / (*SK*17c)
> (A spiritual being exits, because [it is seen that] an enjoyer exists.)

Material beings which have no consciousness cannot enjoy external things. Therefore, there exists an enjoyer different from material beings. Food, for example, has its enjoyer. The enjoyer of external things is inferred to be different from material beings, and that is *puruṣa.*

The Sāṃkhya explains the process of enjoyment of external things by *puruṣa* in the way that an external object first is caught by sense-organs (*jñānendriya*) like eyes, and then the image of that object is brought to *buddhi* by which it is discerned, and *puruṣa* enjoys the discerned object. In the process the essential function of *buddhi* is expressed by the term *adhyavasāya* (discernment, decision). Regarding the process of enjoyment, there occurs the question of whether the discernment(*adhyavasāsya*) made by *buddhi* can be considered to be a conscious act or not, or what the difference is between discernment by *buddhi* and enjoyment by *puruṣa*. Starting with these questions, the *YD* argues in detail the essential character of *puruṣa* and *buddhi* and then the relation of both. The relevant argument is as below: (*YD* pp. 171.10-173.19, Pandeya Edition pp. 79.27-81.19)

> Opponent: Is there any difference or no difference in nature between discernment (*vyavasāya*) and consciousness (*caitanya*)?
>
> Proponent: <.....>(?) What then? As *buddhi* consists of three components, it is an object of cognition, though its essence is in concept. But the nature of (*puruṣa*'s) consciousness appears in accordance with the form of (*buddhi*'s) discernment. Likewise the followers of Vārṣaganya say, '*puruṣa* follows *buddhi* which exists as consciousness, because *puruṣa* is pervaded by the function of *buddhi*.' Moreover it has been said:
>
> > As *buddhi* appears in accordance with the form of the object, so does *puruṣa*. Therefore the knower who appears as *buddhi* is said to be like a jewel (*maṇivad*). (Verse A)
> >
> > Because it is a conscious being, *puruṣa*, which follows various functions of the mind (*manovṛtti*), obtains the form of *buddhi* which depends on the other (that is, *puruṣa*). (Verse B)
>
> Opponent: (If this is the case,) **as there is no difference in form between *puruṣa* and *buddhi*, one of them becomes useless.**[4] If the form of discernment appears in the same form of consciousness, you must admit only the discernment (of *buddhi*) or only the consciousness (of *puruṣa*). You should not assume the existence of two entities which have one and the same function. Or you should state that both have different forms. If discernment is different from consciousness, you must mention that one has a certain form and the other does not.
>
> Proponent: One who maintains that, as there is no difference in form, there is no difference in objects, must be asked, 'What then?' For you, is there a difference in form between the knowledge and its object or not?

Opponent: There exists no difference (in form of knowledge and its object). The reason is: **if the form (*ākāra*) of knowledge is different from that of its object, the object cannot be decided (by its knowledge)**, because the form of an object cannot be decided without appearance of the knowledge of the object. Suppose that the form of a cow is different from that of knowledge of a cow, then, as the form of knowledge of a horse cannot discern a cow, which has a different form from that of the horse, one cannot discern the form of knowledge of a cow by the form of knowledge of the cow that has a different form (from that of the cow). Hence there is no difference in form between knowledge and its object.

Proponent: Then it must be asked whether an object and knowledge of it are two different entities or one and the same. You maintain that they are different. Why? **Because they are in relation of one that is made known (*jñāpya*) and the other that makes known (*jñāpaka*).** Then we quote:

> Knowledge is different from its object in the sense that one is caught and the other catches, though both have the same form. In the same manner *puruṣa* is different from its illumination (*buddhi*).

You conclude that there is a difference between knowledge and its object by assuming the relation of the cognised (*grāhya*) and the cogniser (*grāhaka*), though there is no difference in form. In the same manner as you we conclude that *puruṣa* is different from the internal organ (*buddhi*).

Opponent: **That is not right because the relation of the cognised and the cogniser is not established.** In the case of the cow and knowledge of a cow, the relation of the cognised and the cogniser is established. But the same relation is not known in the case of *puruṣa* and the internal organ (*buddhi*). Hence your comparison cannot be applied.

Proponent: **Your point is not acceptable**, because **you took the other way**. First you said that it is one and the same entity where there is no difference in form. Now you maintain that it is not the same entity on the grounds of the relation of the cognised and the cogniser, even though there is no difference in form. This is not a consistent argument.

Opponent: **Your objection is impossible, because only knowledge is admitted as an existent entity**. It is knowledge that appears as the form of an object and the knower of the object when it is coloured by an object which comes to be internally existent.

But there is nothing which exists outside or cognises a form of being cognised. It is impossible for our standpoint that knowledge is different from its object because of the difference of the cognised and the cogniser.

Proponent: **That is not right, because of the difference of the doctrine**. The error that you have pointed out may occur in maintaining that external things exist. But we refute those who maintain that only knowledge is an object and, at the same time, its knower.

Opponent: **Even so, you fall into the error of the infinite regress of the object, because you admit that a knower of an object is again an object**. If a knower of an object too is considered to be an object to be discerned, *puruṣa*, a knower, has another knower, and that knower has another knower again. In this way there occurs an infinite regress. To avoid this error, you might say that *puruṣa* is not an object because of its nature of discernment. But then, you cannot assume that a final discerner (*puruṣa*) is different from discernment (*buddhi*).

Proponent: **It cannot be applied to *puruṣa* because of its being conscious**. The sense organs do not have consciousness because their essential nature is only grasping (objects). They are considered to be instruments for a being that has consciousness. The internal organ cannot perceive an object as such by itself, because of its being unconscious, even though it gains the form of an object by attaining the function of a sense-organ which can grasp the object. The internal organ, therefore, depends on *puruṣa* which is a conscious enjoyer. But *puruṣa* does not require another entity which perceives *puruṣa* itself, because it is an entity of being conscious. Therefore there never occurs an error of infinite regress.

Opponent: (If this is the case,) ***puruṣa* must be an entity which discerns because it is a conscious entity (*caitanya*)**. If *buddhi* has no consciousness, no function of discernment comes to it, like a pot (does not discern). And if *puruṣa* has the function of discernment (instead of *buddhi*), *buddhi* has no reason to exist.

Proponent: **It is not true. As *puruṣa* has the nature of being isolated, it comes to have no objection (in discernment)**. It will be pointed out later that the nature of *puruṣa* is pure. If *puruṣa* discerns, it has no obstacle (for discernment), as the result of which one who sleeps or gets drunk or is unconscious can decide the direction etc. But it is known by experience that such men have obstacles in discernment. Therefore the function of discernment does not belong to *puruṣa*. On the other hand, for those who maintain that the internal organ decides, such errors do not occur.

> Why? **Because the internal organ (*buddhi*) is made up of three qualities.** The internal organ is nothing but a specified condition of *sattva* etc, because causes (other than *sattva* and so on) are denied. In this situation when *sattva*, whose essential nature is discernment, is obstructed by other causes and comes to be secondary, and its faculty is made latent by the predominance of *tamas*, then the discernment (of *buddhi*) is obstructed.
>
> Opponent: How is it understood that things of this whole world are unconscious ?
>
> Proponent: Because they come into existence from the ultimate material being. In this world that which emerges from *prakṛti* has no consciousness, like threads and cloths. All emerge from *prakṛti*. Therefore they are unconscious. **If you say that it is not definite, because we have the sky as a counter example, we say, 'No', because of its not being accepted.** In our view the sky is not established to be a being which emerged from *prakṛti*. It therefore is correct that all existent beings don't have consciousness because they emerge from *prakṛti*. Moreover a being which has consciousness does not emerge from *prakṛti*, because they have different natures from each other. One highest principle (*prakṛti*) is not an enjoyer, because it has no consciousness. (If *prakṛti* is not an enjoyer) it comes to be stated properly that *puruṣa* exists because of the existence of an enjoyer.

(II) The relation of *puruṣa* and *buddhi* is again argued in the interpretation to the *SK*37 in the *YD*. The *SK*37 discusses the *puruṣa*'s enjoyment of objects and the role of *buddhi* in the cognition for emancipation. The *YD* does not lead a long argument on the interpretation of the Kārikā. But here we come across the view of the author of the *YD* on the relation of *puruṣa* and *buddhi* in relation to cognition. I translate the relevant passage (*YD*. p. 223.9-35, Pandeya Edition p. 117.5-25) below:

> Proponent:
> Because the internal organ (*buddhi*) makes it possible for *puruṣa* to enjoy all (*SK*37ab).
>
> (The criticism raised by opponents such as:) The ego-organ and think-organ have conceit and thinking respectively as their essential nature, not having the quality of discernment. Or it must be useless that *puruṣa* is connected with the function of organs which have no decisive objects. Or if *puruṣa* itself makes a decision, it must come to be a doer, as a result of which it becomes an impure entity for discernment. All criticisms have already been

answered. (cf.*SK*20) It is the internal organ *buddhi* that has discernment as its essential nature. Objects, which the function of *buddhi* reaches, are observed by *puruṣa* only because of their proximity to *puruṣa*. They don't disturb the indifference of *puruṣa*, and (enjoyment by *puruṣa* itself) does not come to be useless. This is the reason why the Kārikā (*SK*37ab) says 'Because the internal organ makes it possible for *puruṣa* to enjoy all.'

Opponent: Even if that is so, it is only objects, like sound, that are relevant and are made known to *puruṣa* by *buddhi*. There exist other objects of cognition whose feature is the difference between primary matter and *puruṣa*. It has been said that enjoyment begins with the perception of sound etc. and ends in the cognition of (the difference between) the *guṇa* and *puruṣa*. Therefore another organ which is responsible for cognition should be mentioned.

Proponent: There is no need to do so because it, on the other hand, discerns the subtle difference between primary matter and *puruṣa*. (*SK*37cd)

When the qualities of *sattva* such as virtue are supressed by the predominant darkness (*tamas*), *buddhi* decisively considers *guṇa* to be the self (*ātman*). But the *guṇa*s are supposed to exist both in primary matter and its evolutes; they depend on others, and help and are helped, being unconscious and impure.

Thereafter *buddhi* brings *guṇa*s to *puruṣa*. The *puruṣa*, following the image of *buddhi* which is coloured by the repetition of wrong knowledge and its latent influence, understands objects as shown by (*buddhi*). When the darkness is removed by the accumulation of virtue (*sattva*), and the nature of virtue is predominant step by step, the function of *buddhi* ceases to have wrong notion, making lucid discernment that *puruṣa* does not exist in primary matter or its evolutes, is independent, and neither helps nor is helped, being conscious and pure, which is the opposite of *guṇa*s. The difference between *guṇa* and *puruṣa* is 'subtle', because both have decisive nature. The term 'subtle' means deep or difficult to know.

ACTIONS OF *BUDDHI*

This is a rough sketch of two arguments on the relation of *puruṣa* and *buddhi* found in the *YD*. There remain in these arguments some portions whose significance is not so clear. Let us examine them.

The answers given by the *YDkāra* ('Proponent' in the translation) suggest that *buddhi* is considered to be a knower of the outer world. But why is it possible that a material entity derived from primary matter can have a conscious function? We need more clarification of the concept of *buddhi*. In the *YD buddhi* is referred to as an entity which has such actions or nature as 'function'(*vṛtti*), 'discernment' (*adhyavasāya*) and 'notion'(*pratyaya*) in the process of cognition of the outer world. I would like to examine these three concepts—function, discernment and notion—through which the concept of *buddhi* in the Sāṃkhya becomes clarified.

In the passages translated above, it is stated that the sense-organs, *manas* and *buddhi*, have function. I begin with the examination of the function of sense-organs. The Sāṃkhya preaches that sense-organs are derived from an internal organ called self-concept (*ahaṃkāra*), which is again derived from *buddhi*. Therefore sense-organs are material beings as well as other internal organs. Even if they are material beings, they have no definite form, unlike the material elements such as earth, water, fire, wind and sky. The internal organs are entities which have a kind of psychic energy. The sense-organs take over the same kind of energy from *ahaṃkāra*, so they are also entities of psychic energy.

The old theory of perception which is one of three ways to right knowledge admitted by the Sāṃkhya is defined thus: perception is the function of ears, etc.[5] The meaning of the definition is that perception is reaching and changing of the sense organ to the form of its object. That is to say, according to the Sāṃkhya theory of perception, the perception of outer objects is that a sense-organ reaches an outer object and takes its form. The taking of the form of the object is called the function. Taking over the old concept of function, in the argument where he discusses the nature of the sense-organs in relation to *prāpyakāritva*, the author of the *YD* mentions that the essential nature of the function of the sense organs is the change of the sense organ to the form of its object.[6]

We may conclude that the function of sense organs is the change to the form of the object perceived, and that it played an important role in the old perception theory of the Sāṃkhya. Turning our eye to *buddhi*, what is its function? In the verse quoted above, *buddhi* is considered to appear like the form of the object. The function of *buddhi*, therefore, is inferred to be the change to the form of the object. Both *buddhi* and sense-organs seem to have the same function of changing to the form of the object perceived. But do they have exactly the same function? The author of the *YD* explains the difference in the interpretation of the *SK*26 which treats *buddhīndriya* (sense-organs), as follows:[7]

> The internal organ cannot directly grasp external objects such as sound because it has no external function. It therefore needs other organs like ears, which can directly illuminate an external object. The internal organ grasps an external object through the canal of the sense organ.

The internal organ (*buddhi*) is considered to grasp the object not directly, but indirectly, in the sense-organ that has changed to the form of the object. Then the question arises: what is the situation in which *buddhi* functions in the sense-organ that has changed to the form of the object? In relation to this question we have to refer to 'notion' which is supposed to be the essential nature of *buddhi*. The author of the *YD* discusses the relation of notion of *buddhi* and the function of sense organs as follows:[8]

> A sense-organ attains the form of an object through contact with the object. This is the function of the sense-organ, which is nothing but grasping. And notion is discernment (*niścaya*) of the object by following the object and the function of the sense-organ. Notions are, for example, 'This is a cow', 'It is white', 'It is running', and so on.

In the following passage the *YDkāra* concludes that the function of sense organs is different from that of *buddhi* because the former has no notion. But here it can be pointed out that the *YDkāra* treats notion as synonymous with discernment (*niścaya* and perhaps *adhyavaāya*).

There then arise two questions. First, why is the term notion used synonymously with discernment, which has a more limited scope? Second, what is the relation between the notion 'This is a cow' and the function, which is the change to the form of an object?

MANAS AND *BUDDHI*

Hereafter I discuss these two questions by examining the function of *manas*. In the *SK manas* as an organ of desire[9] which does not play an important role in the process of cognition. It is situated on the same level as the sense of knowledge and the sense of action (*SK*27c). On the other hand the function of *manas* is referred to in the quoted Verse B. In Verse B *puruṣa* is explained as appearing according to the function of *manas* (*yathā yathā manovṛttiḥ puruṣo 'pi tathā tathā*). Further along in Verse A it is mentioned that the form of *puruṣa* is the same as that of *buddhi*. If we take these into consideration, in the earlier doctrine found in the quoted Verses A and B, both *manas* and *buddhi* are used to refer to almost the same concept. In the earlier doctrine *manas* is not situated under *buddhi* as in the *SK*, but both seem to be used without distinction. If, in the earlier doctrine, *buddhi* had been used synonymously with *manas*, *buddhi* must have the nature of the mind in general which *manas* usually means. Then its function is also something like the action of the mind which leads to the concept of notion.

Regarding the second question, I shall examine the relation of function and discernment. The *YD* states that discernment such as 'This is a cow' and the function of 'change to the form of an object' belong to *buddhi*. But how is it possible that these two belong to one and the same entity? They seem to have different and contradictory natures. The function itself does not have discernment, and there must exist another that discerns the function. On the other hand, it will be useless if there exists another entity which discerns the discernment. Therefore these two are considered to be of different and contradictory nature. Then how can these different and contradictory natures belong to one entity? A comparison of the earlier defintion of perception with the later one seems to give a clue.

As mentioned above, the earlier definition of perception in Sāṃkhya thought is that perception is the function of ears, etc. According to this definition, it is clear that *buddhi* has no role in the process of perception. On the contrary the definition of perception in the *SK* is that perception is a discernment of each object. Comparing these definitions, we find easily that there is no term of 'function' in the definition in the *SK*. It can be further pointed out that in the defintion of the *SK*, two organs, ears and *buddhi*, are used, while in the earlier definition only one organ is used. In the new defintion it is ambiguous which organ is responsible for perception. In the argument of the YD, the opponents raised a question about this problem. The *YDkāra*, answering opponents, declares that the function of sense-organs is more important (*mukhya*, *YD* p. 80.12, Pandeya Edition p. 36.25) and that the role of *buddhi* is only to remove doubt. This explanation is unique in that it does not follow the term in the *SK*, and that it makes the earlier theory important, which is not found in other commentaries of the *SK*. It can be inferred that the *YDkāra* tries to interpret the new definition of perception of the *SK* by using the terms and concept of the earlier definition which is however very different. As a result, in the *YD* there remain the two theories of perception, and hence the contradictory concepts, function and notion, are ascribed to one entity. Therefore the author of the *YD* treats the function found in the early definition as discernment in the new definition to harmonize the two different definitions.

Regarding the relation of the function of *buddhi* and that of sense-organs, the description of the *YDkāra* does not give us a lucid idea. The *YD* reads that *buddhi* grasps an outer object through the canal-like sense organs. This parable gives us the impression that he took the sense organ not to be potency but rather place. But as the sense-organ is derived from *ahaṃkāra*, it must be psychic energy like *buddhi*. Therefore the *YD* does not seem to give us a persuasive explanation of the difference between the function of *buddhi* and that of sense- organs. I infer the situation as follows. Taking the function of *manas* discussed in the previous section into consideration, the *YDkāra* perhaps has two kinds of function: one is used in the early definition of perception, and the other, like the function of *manas*, general function of the mind. Each function is so different from the other as to combine without contradiction in the explanation of the new definition of perception. The solution taken by the *YDkāra* is to treat sense organs as a place where the function of *buddhi* takes place.

ANOTHER ASPECT OF *BUDDHI*

I suppose that from the examination above, the process in which *buddhi* comes to have seemingly contradictory nature is now clear. I now discuss another aspect of *buddhi*.

If we observe the passage of the *YD* translated in the preceding section, we understand that *buddhi* is an entity that is responsible for cognizing the external world, obtaining discriminative knowledge or letting *puruṣa* obtain it. *Puruṣa* which can emancipate by this discriminative knowledge is supposed to be consciousness itself and thus eternal and pure. *Puruṣa* by nature transcends this world full of pain and dirtiness. The parable of the jewel in Verse A is used to show this nature of *puruṣa*. A jewel appears the some colour as a thing which is put near it, and then appears transparent when the thing is put far away. So too, *puruṣa* is influenced by *buddhi* which is near, but does not itself change. Though they are different entities, they appear the same. Vārṣagaṇya says that *puruṣa* is coloured by *buddhi*. This condition in which *puruṣa* is coloured by *buddhi* is one in which they cannot be distinguished. This very state is that of a human being as conceived by the Sāṃkhya. In this state *buddhi* is wrongly taken as *puruṣa* or *puruṣa* seems not to exist at all because it is hidden behind *buddhi*. This means that the essential existent mode of *puruṣa* that does not touch the outer world is made possible by the existence of *buddhi*. The role of *buddhi* in the Sāṃkhya system is considered to be a more important aspect in the emancipation theory than in the theory of cognition. By this role *buddhi* comes to be such that it knows the external world and at the same time it is negated in the discriminative knowledge of emancipation. In this aspect *buddhi* can be considered to be the ordinary self which is lower than the true self, *puruṣa*. As the ordinary self must be denied finally, *buddhi* must be included in a category essentially different from *puruṣa*, the only conscious entity in the Sāṃkhya.

CONCLUSION

I thus propose the following:

1 The early definition of perception in the Sāṃkhya is different from that of the *SK*. In the early definition *buddhi* does not play any role in the process of perception. In the *SK* it is *buddhi* which plays a decisive role.

2 The role of *buddhi* in the Sāṃkhya system is of primary importance in the theory of emancipation, in the sense that it guarantees the final stage of emancipation, that is, *puruṣa*'s essential nature of purity.

3 Last, I would refer to the view of the opponent(s).

(a) They maintain that the form of an object is the same as knowledge of the object. If they are different, they insist, knowledge cannot be connected with the object.

(b) The difference between the form of knowledge and the form of the object is in that the former is that which grasps and the latter is that which is grasped.

(c) External objects don't exist at all. Knowledge is the only real being which appears as the form of an object and knowledge of it. Knowledge and its object are different aspects of one and the same knowledge.

This way of thinking is nothing but a theory of *sākārajñānavāda* of the Yogācāra school of Buddhism. The *YD* refers in detail to the *anātmavāda* or *kṣanabhaṅgavāda* of Buddhism.[10] From these facts we may infer that one of the main opponents to the author of the *YD* is Buddhism at certain stage of development.

NOTES

1 The *Yuktidīpikā*, the most significant commentary of the *Sāṃkhyakārikā*, critically edited by A. Wezler and S. Motegi, Hamburg, 1998.

2 When I wrote this paper in Japanese 1984, no English translation had been published. In 1990 the first English translation from the *Yuktidīipikā* edited by R.C. Pandeya in 1967 (in this paper I refer to it as 'Pandeya Edition') was published by Dr. Shiv Kumar and Dr. D.N. Bhargava. The present paper contains a large portion of the English translation of the YD which was made in 1884, being now revised by comparison with the English translation of Dr. Shiv Kumar and Dr. D.N. Bharvaga. Cf. YUKTIDĪPIKĀ, Tr. Shiv Kumar and D.N. Bargava, Delhi, vol. 1 (1990), vol. 2 (1992).

3 Cf. *Vaiśeṣika Sūtra* 3.2.4, *Nyāya Sūtra* 1.1.10.

4 The portions written in boldface are *vārttikas*. Cf. *YD*, Introduction pp.XXII-XXIII.

5 *śrotrādivṛttiḥ pratyakṣam* (*YD* p.5.11, Pandeya Edition p.3.20-21).

6 *viṣayākārapariṇāmātmikā vṛttir* (*YD* p.203.28-29, Pandeya Edition p.103.26).

7 *antaḥkaraṇasya nāsti bahirvṛttir ity ato nālam etat sākṣāc chabdādīn arthān pratipattum / tasmāc chrotrādilakṣaṇam sākṣādbāhyaviṣayaprakā-śanasamartham k<a>raṇāntaram apekṣate /* (*YD* p. 197.18-22, Pandeya Edition p. 99.8-10).

8 ***viṣayasamparkāt tādrūpyāpattir indriyavṛtti<r> grahananam*** */ tathā viṣayendriyavṛttyanukāreṇa niścayo gaur ayaṃ śuklo dhāvatīty evamādiḥ pratyayaḥ /* (*YD* p. 203.4-6, Pandeya Edition p.103.9-10).

9 The *SK*27 defines *manas* as *saṃkalpakam atra manaḥ*. The *YD* interprets *saṃkalpakam* as *saṃkalpo 'bhilāṣa icchā tṛṣṇetyādy anarthāntaram.* (*YD* p.199.14, Pandeya Edition p.100.20).

10 Regarding *vijñaptimātra* theory, we come across a description of hell which is reminiscent of that of *Viṃśatikā* 3-4. (*YD* p. 219.1-6, Pandeya Edition p.115.7-12).

5

Bondage in Sāṃkhya*

KOKI ARUGA

In order to clarify the concept of bondage in Sāṃkhya, it is necessary to investigate the roles of the word *bandha* through its history. Many Sāṃkhya terms already played important roles before the formulation of Īśvarakṛṣṇa's classical Sāṃkhya system. We can find various views later referred to by those terms already in the epics or philosophical literature, and suppose therefore the pre-existence of some philosophical ideas of classical Sāṃkhya. However it is also a fact that the processes of development of such views are not clear. With regard to the word *bandha*, we are not provided so far with any clue for understanding the formulation of the bondage theory.

Many Sāṃkhya terms are used by individual Sāṃkhya teachers in the philosophical literature, but rarely in a systematic way. Accordingly there are many difficulties in interpreting such terms as parts of systems, since the authors have often given us their ideas only in fragmentary form. Therefore, in this paper, I will not make reference to 'proto-Sāṃkhya speculations'[1] but try to examine mainly the concept of *bandha* in the philosophical texts of the Sāṃkhya and Yoga traditions and how it is treated in the commentaries and other sources.

BANDHA AND *SAṂYOGA* IN THE *SĀṂKHYAKĀRIKĀ*

In *Sāṃkhyakārikā* (*SK*) 44 and 45, eight *bhāvas* ('dispositions') of the *buddhi* ('intellect') and their results are concisely mentioned. According to *SK* 44, *bandha* is described as follows:

dharmeṇa gamanam ūrdhvaṃ gamanam adhastād bhavaty adharmeṇa /
jñānena cāpavargo viparyayād iṣyate bandhaḥ //.

What is meant by the word *bandha* is the bondage that is the result of ignorance. Ignorance is one of the eight *bhāvas* of *buddhi*. We find in the latter half of this verse the contrast between *bandha* and *apavarga* ('liberation'). And then we may suppose that a person (precisely speaking, a subtle body) is liberated when he gets the knowledge of the twenty-five principles or the distinction between the *puruṣa* and the *prakṛti*, while he is in the state of bondage when he has ignorance. In our daily lives, we are, without such knowledge, in the state of bondage and thus have to suffer various pains. To avoid suffering, we have to proceed to acquire this knowledge.[2] Thus *bandha*, which is opposite to *apavarga*, conveys a negative and undesirable connotation.

In *SK* 62 and 63, Īśvarakṛṣṇa uses *bandha* ($\sqrt{}$ *bandh* in the following) with *mucyate* and *saṃsarati*.

> *tasmān na badhyate nāpi mucyate nāpi saṃsarati kaścit /*
> *saṃsarati badhyate mucyate ca nānāśrayā prakṛtiḥ //*
> *rūpaiḥ saptabhir eva badhnāty ātmānam ātmanā prakṛtiḥ /*
> *saiva ca puruṣārthaṃ prati vimocayaty ekarūpeṇa //*
>
> Therefore no (*puruṣa*) is bound, nor released, nor transmigrates; the *prakṛti*, in various forms, transmigrates, is bound and is released.
> By only seven forms the *prakṛti* binds herself by herself. And this very same (*prakṛti*) releases (herself) for the sake of the *puruṣa* by one form.

It is declared here that what transmigrates, is bound and released, is not *puruṣa* but *prakṛti*. These verses, which are to be construed with *SK* 20 and 21,[3] are intended to elucidate the real nature of the *prakṛti*. Judging from the usage of the word we are interested in and the context of these verses, we can ascertain that *bandha*($\sqrt{}$ *bandh* in the above) signifies nothing but bondage. Incidentally, in the above descriptions, we have to admit two levels of usage of *bandha*, i.e. the bondage of the *puruṣa* and the bondage of the *prakṛti*. The former is in reality not possible but the latter is real. Hence *bandha* is an expression of the state of the *prakṛti*. And here we find a similarity to the expression of the relation '*saṃyoga*' between *puruṣa* and *prakṛti*.

This *saṃyoga* is one of the most important but ambiguous ideas in the evolution theory. According to *SK* 21, the conjunction between the *puruṣa* and the *prakṛti* occurs due to a kind of teleological requirement. On the other hand, as we see in *SK* 19[4] and 62, it is illogical to assume that the *puruṣa*, who is free from action, has a conjunction with the *prakṛti*. As has been often pointed out,[5] there is a quite fundamental difficulty here that the *puruṣa*, in itself liberated and inactive, is united with the *prakṛti*.

In the commentaries, *saṃyoga* is given some interpretations or reconciliation. For instance, the author of the *Yuktidīpikā* (*YD*) elaborately introduces the viewpoint of *upacāra* and gives explanations in which *saṃyoga* is discussed.[6] In most commentaries the idea of *sannidhi* ('proximity') is used to explain what *saṃyoga* is.

Since *saṃyoga*, caused by unevenness of *guṇas*, brings about creation, its role is important in the evolution theory. Its purpose is liberation.[7] In this sense *saṃyoga* is positive and desirable.

Bandha and *saṃyoga* both have their roles in the theoretical aspects of Sāṃkhya. The concept of *bandha* represents the reality of our existence which is caused by ignorance. A practical factor for liberation is intended by mentioning *jñāna*. The concept of *saṃyoga* represents the theoretical aspect of the *puruṣa* and the *prakṛti*. It is combined with a kind of teleological requirement to accomplish the teleological evolution theory which is, at the same time, dependent on the *guṇa*-theory.

Thus Īśvarakṛṣṇa deals with them separately as a result of concise systematization of theories. Even so, fundamental problems remain.

BANDHA AND *SAṂYOGA* IN THE YOGA TEXTS

Patañjali, the author of the *Yogasūtra* (*YS*), and Vyāsa, a commentator on the *YS*, treat *bandha* and *saṃyoga* in slightly different ways. Although *ajñāna* causes *bandha* in Īśvarakṛṣṇa's view, it is said in the *YS* that *saṃyoga* is brought about by *avidyā* ('ignorance').[8]

> *svasvāmiśaktyoḥ svarūpopalabdhihetuḥ saṃyogaḥ* //(*YS* 2.23).
> *tasya hetur avidyā* //(*YS* 2.24)
>
> Conjunction (*saṃyoga*) is the cause of apprehending the true nature of the powers of the possessor and the possessed.
> Ignorance is its cause.

There is a difference in the respective terms for ignorance. In addition, if we pay attention to Vyāsa's commentary, it will be apparent that Vyāsa in many cases uses *darśana* ('knowledge') and *adarśana* ('ignorance') when he refers to *saṃyoga* and *bandha*.

When he comments on *YS* 2.23, Vyāsa says:

> *adarśanābhāvād eva bandhābhāvaḥ sa mokṣa iti / darśanasya bhāve bandhakāraṇasyādarśanasya nāśa ity ato darśanaṃ jñānaṃ kaivalyakāraṇam uktam* (*Yogabhāsya* (*YBh*) on *YS* 2.23)
>
> The absence of *bandha* comes only from the absence of *adarśana*. That is liberation. Where there is *darśana* there is destruction of *adarśana*, the cause of *bandha*; therefore *darśana*, or *jñāna*, is said to be the cause of isolation.

Thus *darśana* can be called *jñāna* and *adarśana* can be called *ajñāna*. Nevertheless what is important is that Vyāsa seems to use *bandha* and *saṃyoga* in the same meaning. In *YS* 2.25, *kaivalya* is explained.

> *tadabhāvāt saṃyogābhāvo hānaṃ tad dṛśeḥ kaivalyam* //(*YS* 2.25)
>
> From the absence of it (*avidyā*, or ignorance), the absence of conjunction comes; (it is) removal; it is isolation of the Seer (*puruṣa*).[9]

Vyāsa explains as follows:

> *ṭasyādarśanasyābhāvād buddhipuruṣasaṃyogābhāva ātyantiko bandhanoparama ity arthaḥ* (*YBh* on *YS* 2.25).
>
> From the absence of that *adarśana*, the absence of conjunction between *puruṣa* and *buddhi* comes; (it is) the ultimate cessation of *bandhana*; this is the meaning.

According to Vyāsa's description here, *bandha*(*-na*) and *saṃyoga* share the same meaning in the context of what is brought about by the absence of ignorance. The description '*adarśanābhāvād eva bandhābhāvaḥ sa mokṣa*' in *YBh* on *YS* 2.23, though it deliberately declares the content of the following *sūtras*, is to be connected with '*tadabhāvāt saṃyogābhāvo hānam tad dṛśeḥ kaivalyam*' in *YS* 2.25 and '*tasyādarśanasyābhāvād buddhipuruṣasaṃyogābhāva ātyantiko bandhanoparama*' in *YBh* on *YS* 2.25. Thus, we can say, *bandhābhāva* and *buddhipuruṣasaṃyogābhāva* are same.

Vyāsa's comment on *YS* 2.25 shows us his attitude towards precise interpretation. When he explains *saṃyogābhāva* in *YS* 2.25 with *buddhipuruṣasaṃyoga*, we have to remember that, in his clear statement, *bandha* and *mokṣa* exist in the intellect itself, and these terms while appearing to refer to the *puruṣa*[10] actually refer to the *buddhi*.

As we have seen above, *bandha* and *saṃyoga* are used equally, especially in the *YBh*. It is clearly described that *saṃyoga* or *bandha* is brought about by ignorance. On the other hand, a kind of teleological requirement of *saṃyoga* does not play an important role.[11]

THREE KINDS OF BONDAGE IN THE SĀṂKHYA TRADITION

In the history of Sāṃkhya and Yoga, Vyāsa is the earliest who referred to the division of the three kinds of bondage.[12] Īśvarakṛṣṇa never refers to it. However it is probable that it was included in the classical system of Sāṃkhya at an early stage.[13] Almost all of the commentaries, including Paramārtha's Chinese translation of the *Suvarṇasaptati* (*PS*) which must have been translated between AD 546 and 69, refer to it.[14]

However, little attention has been given to the interpretations of the three kinds of bondage.[15] Many scholars seem to follow Vacaspatimiśra's interpretation, which, it should be noted, is rather different from those in other commentaries on the *SK*.[16]

The *Gauḍapādabhāṣya* (*G*) presents a simple verse.

> *prākṛtena ca bandhena tathā vaikārikeṇa ca /*
> *dākṣiṇena tṛtīyena baddho nānyena mucyate //*

> A person who is bound by *prākṛta-bandha*, *vaikārika* (*-bandha*), or the third *dākṣiṇa* (*-bandha*), is not liberated by anything other (than knowledge).

Although different kinds of bondage are referred to slightly differently, there are common factors to their explanations. For the convenience of comparison we first show the explanations in the *Māṭharavṛtti* (*M*) and the *Tattvakaumudī* (*TK*).

1)*prākṛta*(*prakṛti*,*prākṛtika*)*-bandha* (*Pb*)

*Pb*1: *tatra prakṛtibandho nāmāṣṭāsu prakṛtiṣu paratvenābhimānaḥ* (*M* on *SK* 44).

Among them, it is called *prakṛtibandha* to think erroneously of (what has resolved) into the eight *prakṛtis* as the highest.

*Pb*2: *prakṛtilayaḥ prakṛtibandha ity ucyate* (*M* on *SK* 45).

Resolution into *prakṛtis* is said to be *prakṛtibandha*.

*Pb*3: *prakṛtav ātmajñānād ye prakṛtim upāsate teṣāṃ prākṛtiko bandhaḥ, yaḥ purāṇe prakṛtilayān praty ucyate*... (*TK* on *SK*

44).

> Those who worship *prakṛti* through knowledge of *ātman* (identified) with *prakṛti* have *prākṛta-bandha*, which is mentioned in a Purāṇa by reference to those who have resolved into *prakṛti*....[17]

The pattern *Pb*1 is found also in the *Sāṃkhya-Saptati-Vṛtti* (*V*1).[18] The *Jayamaṅgalā* (*J*) uses *paratattva* when it explains *prākṛtikabandha.*[19] But it does not refer to the eight *prakṛtis*. By the word *paratva* in *Pb*1, the state of being the highest or the final of resolution is intended. According to the *PS*, it is *prakṛtibandha* to regard what has resolved into the eight *prakṛtis* but not yet is liberated as liberated.[20] Therefore the explanation in the *PS* seems to correspond to *Pb*1.

The pattern *Pb*2 is, needless to say, directly based on '*vairāgyāt prakṛtilayaḥ*' in *SK* 45. It is found also in the *V*1. In *Pb*2, the *prakṛti* of *prakṛtilayaḥ* is construed in accordance with the *prakṛtis* in *Pb*1. This pattern reminds us of '*prakṛtilayānāṃ prākṛto bandhaḥ*' in Vācaspatimiśra's *Tattvavaiśāradī* (*TV*).[21] The *YD* refers to the eight *prakṛtis* and *laya.*[22]

In *Pb*3, Vācaspatimiśra connects *prakṛtilaya* with a Purāṇa and gives a different explanation of *prakṛtibandha*. The *Candrikā* (*C*) apparently follows him.[23]

2)*vaikārika* (*vaikṛtika*)-*bandha* (*Vb*)

*Vb*1: *vaikārikabandho nāma brahmādisthāneṣu śreyobuddhiḥ* (*M* on *SK* 44).

> It is called *vaikārikabandha* to regard (birth in) the regions of *Brahmā*, etc., as the best.

*Vb*2: *aiśvaryādinimitto bhogo vaikārika ity ucyate* (*M* on *SK* 45).

> Enjoyment caused by power, etc., is called *vaikārika* (-*bandha*).

*Vb*3: *vaikāriko bandhas teṣāṃ ye vikārān eva bhūtendriyāhaṅkārabuddhīḥ puruṣadhiyopāsate, tān pratīdam ucyate*...(*TK* on *SK* 44).

> Those who worship the various evolutes—i.e. gross elements, organs, ego and intellect—as the *puruṣa* have *vaikārika-bandha*. With regard to them it is said....[24]

The pattern *Vb*1 is found also in the *V*1.[25]

The pattern *Vb*2 is not found in the *V*1.[26] The reference to *aiśvarya*, etc., is characteristic in *Vb*2. The *J* also refers to *aiśvarya*. [27] The *YD* starts explaining *vaikārikabandha* just after '*aiśvaryād avighātaḥ*' of *SK* 45.[28] The explanation in the *YD* can more or less be looked upon as *Vb*2.[29] According to the *PS*,[30] those who live in the regions of Brahmā and other gods, have eight kinds of *avighāta* because they have eight kinds of *aiśvarya*, viz., *aṇimā*, *laghimā*, and so on. These eight kinds of *aiśvarya* are related to the *buddhi*. Thus they are not liberation but *vaikārikabandha*. This explanation in the *PS* can be looked upon as the same as *Vb*2.

In *Vb*3, Vācaspatimiśra gives a different explanation. The *C* follows Vācaspatimiśra.[31]

3)*dākṣiṇaka* (*dakṣiṇā*)-*bandha* (*Db*)

*Db*1: *dakṣiṇābandho nāma gavādidānejyānimittaḥ* (*M* on *SK* 44).

It is called *dakṣiṇābandha* that is caused by donation of a cow, etc., and sacrifice.

*Db*2: *yajñādibhir dakṣiṇābandha ity ucyate* (*M* on *SK* 45).

What is caused by sacrifice is called *dakṣiṇābandha*.

*Db*3: *iṣṭāpūrtena dākṣiṇakaḥ* (*TK* on *SK* 44).

By performing sacrifices, charities, etc., *dākṣiṇaka(-bandha)* is brought about.[32]

The pattern *Db*1 is found also in the *V*1.[33] The pattern *Db*2 seems to be a different expression of what *Db*1 states. The author of the *YD* explains *dakṣiṇābandha* when he comments on '*saṃsāro bhavati rājasād rāgāt*' in *SK*45.[34] He does not use either *gavādidānejyā* as in *Db*1 or *yajñādi* as in *Db*2. His explanation is characterized by *dṛṣṭānuśravikaviṣayābhilāṣa* .[35]

The *PS* refers to donation and a kind of sacrifice.[36] The *C* uses *vaidikakarma*.[37] Vācaspatimiśra uses *iṣṭāpūrta* in *Db*3. The *J* also uses *iṣṭāpūrta* in the explanation.[38]

Thus, on the one hand, the following are characteristic in Vācaspatimiśra's explanations of each *bandha*:

(1) It is *prakṛtibandha* to think of the *prakṛti* as the *puruṣa*.
(2) It is *vaikārikabandha* to think of the evolutes (*vikāras*) as the *puruṣa*.
(3) In the explanation of *dākṣiṇakabandha*, *iṣṭāpūrta* is used.

On the other hand, some other patterns can evidently be traced much earlier than *Pb*3, *Vb*3, and *Db*3, because they are found in the *PS*. The explanations in the *J* show a similarity, to some extent, to earlier patterns, while, as for *dakṣiṇābandha*, the explanation shows a similarity to *Db*3 in employing the expression *iṣṭāpūrta*. It is evident that the *C* follows Vācaspatimiśra.

Since the bondage theory, which consists of three kinds of bondage, is found in almost all the commentaries, it is possible to say that the commentators of the *SK* regard it as a doctrine of the Sāṃkhya philosophy. But it should be noted that the commentators introduce the bondage theory when they explain the results of the eight *bhāvas* of the *buddhi* under *SK* 44 and 45, and that Vācaspatimiśra gives distinctive explanations of the three kinds of bondage. The reason why he gives such explanations remains to be clarified.

BONDAGE THEORY OF SĀṂKHYA IN THE *TARKAJVĀLĀ*

There are some other materials that refer to the bondage theory of Sāṃkhya.[39] Among them, the most interesting description of the bondage theory of Sāṃkhya is found in the *Tarkajvālā* ascribed to Bhāviveka (Bhavya, Bhāvaviveka, 490-570 ?).[40] The three kinds of bondage are explained in Tibetan as follows:

*Pb*4: *raṅ bshin gyi ḥchiṅ ba shes bya ba ni lha daṅ / lha ma yin daṅ / mi daṅ / dud ḥgro la sogs pa rnams kyi lus gaṅ dag gshan daṅ gshan rnam pa sna tshogs kyi raṅ bshin du ḥgyur baḥi bdag ñid du ḥbyuṅ ba ste / bde ba daṅ / sdug bsṅal daṅ / rmoṅs paḥi bdag ñid kyi phyir daṅ / ṅar ḥdsin pa daṅ / de tsam daṅ / dbaṅ poḥi khyad par gyi mtshan ñid can yin paḥi phyir ro / ḥkhor ba na yul la sred pa ñid kyis skyes bu daṅ raṅ bshin la gcig pa ñid du rmoṅs pa yod la.*

It is the case of bondage of primordial matter that respectively various bodies of gods, demons, human beings, animals, etc., emerge as individuals on the variously differentiated primordial matter (*prakṛti*), because pleasure, pain and delusion individuate them and they have specific characteristics of ego, subtle elements and organs. In transmigration, due only to desire for sense objects, the *puruṣa* and the *prakṛti* are erroneously considered to be the same.[41]

*Vb*4: *ḥgyur baḥi ḥchiṅ ba shes bya ba ni rab tu byuṅ ba rnams blta bar ḥdod pas sgra daṅ / reg bya daṅ / ro daṅ / gśugs daṅ / dri rnams khyis dbaṅ poḥi ḥgyur bar byed paḥi phyir ḥchiṅ ba shes byaḥo.*

It is the case of bondage through evolution that renunciants are bound by transformation of organ due to sound, touch, taste, color and smell when they are trying to observe (them).

*Db*4: *de la re shig nor gyi ḥchiṅ ba shes bya ba ni khyim paḥam / tshaṅs par spyod paḥam / nags la gnas pa la sogs pa rnams ni nor rñed pas ḥchiṅ ba yin te / nor brgya rñed dam stoṅ rñed ces bya ba la sogs pas so.*

Among them, first, it is the case of bondage through wealth that householders, religious students, or hermits, etc., (in the Brahmanical stages) are bound by the acquisition of wealth (or reward). By a reward of one hundred or one thousand *paṇas* (or cows)[42] (they are bound), etc.

Compared with those we have examined in the preceding section, these explanations contain notable points: (1) the reference to the sameness of the *puruṣa* and the *prakṛti* is found; (2) the Brahmanical stages are clearly referred to in *Vb*4 and *Db*4; (3) there is no reference to eight *prakṛtis* as in *Pb*1. (4) *prakṛtilaya* as in *Pb*2 is not clearly mentioned; (5) there is no reference to *aiśvarya* as in *Vb*2; (6) bondage through wealth is brought about, in *Db*4, by the acquisition of wealth, etc.

Thus the explanations of bondage in the *Tarkajvālā* seem to be different from those in the commentaries on the *SK*. As we have seen previously, the commentators of the *SK* recognize that the three kinds of bondage should be associated with the doctrine of the eight *bhāvas* of the *buddhi*. However, in the *Tarkajvālā*, we can not find a connection between the three kinds of bondage and results of *bhāvas* of the *buddhi*.

The *Tarkajvālā* gives us a different viewpoint. According to it, this bondage theory is that advocated by a certain Sāṃkhya teacher.[43] In his view, it is the *puruṣa* who is really liberated from bondage. This view is clearly denied by Īśvarakṛṣṇa in *SK* 62. [44] If we followed the viewpoint given by the *Tarkajvālā*, we would have to suppose that the bondage theory originally belonged to a certain Sāṃkhya teacher's view and that the commentators on the *SK* introduced it into such a system as Īśvarakṛṣṇa's. However, there is no other material which confirms the credibility of this.

CONCLUSION

For purposes of showing the concept of bondage and how bondage is treated in the philosophical texts in the Sāṃkhya-Yoga tradition, we have referred to the descriptions of *bandha* and *saṃyoga* in the *SK* and the *YBh*. And it has become obvious that *bandha* and *saṃyoga* are treated as the same in the *YBh*. But, so far as Īśvarakṛṣṇa's treatment is concerned, they are not the same in the *SK*.

The commentators introduce the three kinds of bondage under *SK* 44 and 45 which describe the eight *bhāvas* of the *buddhi* and their results. Having examined some central explanations of the bondage theory, it has become obvious that not all explanations of the three kinds of bondage are systematically based on the doctrine of the *bhāvas*, and that, therefore, there is no need for us to regard the bondage theory as derived from such a doctrine. Another material the *Tarkajvālā* also refers to the three kinds of bondage. But it does not refer to the doctrine of the eight *bhāvas*.

The bondage theory in the *Tarkajvālā* is ascribed to a certain Sāṃkhya teacher, though it is not the same as those in the Sāṃkhya materials. However, there is no material available to confirm the interpretation of this text. The bondage theory of Sāṃkhya in the *Tarkajvālā* calls for further investigation.

NOTES

* Acknowledgement: This research was supported in part by a Grant-in-Aid for scientific research from the Ministry of Education, Science and Culture in 1998.

1 G. Larson, *Classical Sāṃkhyā*, 2nd revised edition, Delhi, 1979, p. 75.

2 See *SK* 1.

3 In *SK* 20, it is explained how the unconscious one appears to be conscious and the indifferent one appears to be the agent. In *SK* 21, the purpose of conjunction is described.

4 In *SK* 19, the *puruṣa* is said to be inactive.

5 Cf. A.B. Keith, *A History of the Sāṃkhya Philosophy*, 2nd edition, Delhi, 1987, pp. 86-7; Larson, *Classical Sāṃkhya*, p. 172.

6 Cf. R.C. Pandeya, *Yuktidīpikā*, Delhi, 1967, pp. 88-9.

7 Precisely speaking, *darśana* ('seeing') and *kaivalya* ('isolation') are the purposes. See *SK* 21.

8 As in the case of the *SK*, we sometimes have to face difficulty in examining the terms in the *YS*. I intend to follow Vyāsa's interpretations here. R.Z. Bodas, *The Yogasūtras of Patañjali with the scholium of Vyāsa and Vāchaspatimiśra*, Bombay Sanskrit and Prakrit Series No. XLVI, 2nd edition, Bombay, 1917 is used in this paper for the texts of the *YS* and the commentaries by Vyāsa and Vācaspatimiśra.

9 I here follow Vyāsa's commentary. See *YBh*, p. 97. Cf. *YBh*, pp. 88-91.

10 *YBh* on *YS* 2.18: *evaṃ bandhamokṣau buddhāv eva vartamānau puruṣe vyapadiśyete, sa hi tatphalasya bhokteti / buddher eva puruṣārthāparisamāptir bandhas tadarthāvasāyo mokṣa iti.*

11 Needless to say, a teleological tendency is also found. Cf. *YBh* on *YS* 2.18: *buddher eva puruṣārthāparisamāptir bandhas tadarthāvasāyo mokṣa iti.*

12 *YBh* on *YS* 1.24: *kaivalyaṃ prāptās tarhi santi ca bahavaḥ kevalinaḥ / te hi trīṇi bandhanāni cchittvā kaivalyaṃ prāptāḥ.*

13 Frauwallner thinks that the theory of the three kinds of bondage is to be traced to outside influences on the Sāṃkhya. E. Frauwallner, *Geschichte der indischen Philosophie*, Band 1, Salzburg, 1953, pp. 338-9.

14 In the *Sāṃkhya-Vṛtti* (*V*2), the portion of the commentary on *SK* 44 is missing. Accordingly it is impossible to know whether the *V*2 had any reference to the division of the same kinds of bondage.
The Sanskṛit texts used below are as follows:
E.A. Solomon, *Sāṃkhya-Saptati-Vṛtti* (V_1), Ahmedabad, 1973;
E.A. Solomon, *Sāṃkhya-Vṛtti* (V_2), Ahmedabad, 1973;
T.G. Mainkar, *Sāṃkhyakārikā of Īśvarakṛṣṇa with the Commentary of Gauḍapāda*, Poona, 1972;
V.P. Śarmā and S. Vaṅgīya, *Sāṃkhya-Kārikā of Śrīmad Īśvarakṛṣṇa with the Māṭharavṛtti of Māṭharācārya and the Jayamaṅgalā of Śrī Śaṅkara*, Chowkhamba Sanskrit Series No. 296, Varanasi, 1970;
G. Jha and H.D. Sharma, *The Tattva-Kaumudī*, Poona Oriental Series No. 10, Poona, 1934;
D. Śāstri, *Sāṃkhyakārikā, Saṭippaṇa-Sāṃkhyacandrikāṭīkopetā*, Haridās Sanskrit Granthamālā 132, Varanasi, 1953.

15 Only Frauwallner introduces the widespread view of the three kinds of bondage. Frauwallner, *Geschichte der indischen Philosophie*, p. 338. Chakravarti does not discuss the three kinds of bondage adequately when he refers to bondage. P. Chakravarti, *Origin and Development of the Sāṃkhya System of Thought,* 2nd edition, New Delhi, 1975, pp. 231-4; 323-4.

16 For example, see V.V. Sovani, *A Critical Study of the Sāṅkhya System*, Poona Oriental Series No. 11, Poona, 1935, p. 42; Mainkar, *Sāṃkhyakārikā of Īśvarakṛṣṇa*, p. 157.

17 Cf. Jha's translation. *TK*, An English Translation, p. 100: The 'Natural' bondage is that of those who worship Nature as the Spirit; with reference to such men, who are called 'Prākṛtika'('Merged into Nature'), it is said

in the Purāṇas....

18 *V*1, p. 59. E. A. Solomon summarizes *prakṛtibandha* as follows:(i) when one conceives the eight generative principles—the unmanifest, intellect, egoity, and the five subtle elements—as the highest (*prakṛtibandha*). See *Encyclopedia of Indian Philosophy* Vol. 4, pp. 203-4.

19 *J*, p. 102: *yeṣāṃ prakṛtir eva paratattvaṃ nānyat, teṣāṃ prakṛtivādināṃ prākṛtiko bandhaḥ.*

20 See *Taishō Shinshū Daizōkyō* Vol. 54, p. 1256a.

21 *TV*, p. 27.

22 *YD*, p. 125: *vairāgyād aṣṭasu prakṛtiṣu layaṃ gacchati, asāv ucyate prakṛtibandha iti.*

23 *C*, p. 33: *tatra prākṛtikaḥ ātmabuddhyā prakṛtyupāsananibandhano yathā....*

24 Cf. Jha's translation. *TK*, An English Translation, p. 101: The 'Evolutional' bondage is of those who worship the various evolutes of Nature,—as Spirit. With regard to them it is said....

25 *V*1, pp. 59-60.

26 It seems that there is a textual problem. The same is the case with *dakṣiṇābandha*. See *M*, p. 45 and *V*1, p. 60.

27 *J*, p. 102: *yeṣāṃ vikāra evaiśvaryalakṣaṇaḥ puruṣārtha iti, teṣāṃ vikāratvavādināṃ vaikāriko bandhaḥ.*

28 See also the *PS*, *Taishō* Vol. 54, p. 1256a-b.

29 The *YD* gives details of *aiśvarya*: *yad aṣṭaguṇam aiśvaryam aṇimādi prāg upadiṣṭaṃ tasmāt sve sve viṣaye 'vighāta utpadyate / tadabhiratir vaikāriko bandhaḥ* (p. 126).

30 See *Taishō* Vol. 54, p. 1256a-b.

31 *C*, p. 33: *vaikṛtika ātmabuddhyendriyopāsananibandhano yathā* ... .

32 Cf. Jha's translation. *TK*, p. 101: The 'Personal' bondage is due to *iṣṭāpūrta*(actions like charities, sacrifices, digging of tanks etc., done with the sole motive of personal gains hereafter).

33 *V*1, p. 60.

34 See also the *PS*, *Taishō* Vol. 54, p. 1256a.

35 *YD*, p. 125f.: *yo 'yaṃ dṛṣṭānuśravikaviṣayābhilāṣaḥ sa rāgaḥ / tatra dṛṣṭaviṣayarāgāt tatprāptinivartakaṃ karma karoti / tataś ca tatropapadyate / ānuśravikaviṣayābhilāṣād agnihotrādiṣu pravartate / tataś ca svargādiṣūpapattir bhavati / asau dakṣiṇābhandhaḥ.*

36 See *Taishō* Vol. 54, p. 1256a. It seems that the sacrifice referred here is *mahāyajña*.

37 *C*, p. 33: *dākṣiṇaḥ puruṣam ajānataḥ kāmanayā vaidikakarmānuṣṭhānanibandhano yathā....*

38 *J*, p. 102: *yeṣāṃ iṣṭāpūrtabhāvina eva divyaādivyamānuṣabhogāḥ puruṣārtha iti, teṣāṃ karmavādināṃ dakṣiṇābandhaḥ*. Cf. *TV*, p. 27: *dakṣiṇābandho divyādivyaviṣayabhogabhājām.*

39 In the *Sāṃkhyaprabodhadvātriṃśikā* attributed to Siddhasena, we can find a verse which refers to *bandha* and its division. However no details are mentioned there. See A.N. Upadhye, *Siddhasena's Nyāyāvatāra and Other Works*, Bombay, 1971, p. 149. Siddhasena's date is controversial. Cf. Ibid., pp. *3-*72.

40 *The Tibetan Tripiṭaka* Vol. 96, Peking edition, Tokyo-Kyoto, 1957, 257b. To some extent some Japanese scholars have contributed to the study of *Sāṃkhyatattvāvatāra* of the *Madhyamaka-hṛdaya-kārikā* and its commentary the *Tarkajvālā*. Z. Watanabe, 'Chūganshinju no Suron-ha' ('A Criticism of Sāṃkhya in the *Madhyamaka-hṛdaya-kārikā*'), *Shimizu Ryūzan Sensei Koki Kinen Ronbunshū* (*A Felicitation Volume for Dr. R. Shimizu on His Seventieth Birthday*), 1940, pp. 640-67; H. Hadano, 'Suron-ha ni okeru Gedatsu-ron to Suron-ge (The Moksha Theory in the Sāṃkhya School and the Sāṃkhyakārikā)', *Journal of Indian and Buddhist Studies* Vol. 1 No.1, Tokyo, 1952, pp. 164-71; N. Nakada, 'The Sanskrit text of the Madhyamaka-hṛdaya-kārikā and the Tibetan text of the Madhyamaka-hṛdaya-vṛtti-tarkajvālā (Part 1. Pūrvapakṣa)' and 'Chūganshinron no Ju Dai-roku-shō oyobi Ronri-no-honoo (The Sāṃkhya-philosophy described by Bhāvaviveka in his Madhyamakahṛdaya and his own commentary on it)', *The Bulletin of Tsurumi Women's Junior College* 6, 1973, pp. 145-85. For a Japanese translation of the whole text of the Sāṃkhya chapter in the *Tarkajvālā*, see M. Honda, *Sāṃkhya Tetsugaku Kenkyū* (*A Study of the Sāṃkhya Philosophy*), Part 1, Tokyo, 1980, pp. 129-66.

41 After introducing the three kinds of bondage, Bhāviveka starts the explanation of *Madhyamakahṛdayakārikā* 3 from this sentence.

42 Cf. *Db*1.

43 *The Tibetan Tripiṭaka* Vol. 96, 258a.

44 Hadano calls attention to the description of two kinds of liberation in the *Tarkajvālā*. The one is of the *puruṣa* and the other is of the *prakṛti*. The three kinds of bondage are introduced in the explanation of the former. Hadano suggests that the idea of the liberation of the *prakṛti* was developed in order to avoid the theoretical difficulty which is brought about by liberation of the *puruṣa*. His view is very interesting and calls for further consideration. Hadano, 'Suron-ha ni okeru Gedatsu-ron to Suron-ge', pp. 164-71.

6

Prasaṃkhyāna in the *Yogabhāṣya*[*]

KO ENDO

INTRODUCTION

In his *Meditation in Śaṅkara's Vedānta*[1], J. Bader observed that the deliberating practice of *parisaṃkhyāna* that Śaṅkara, author of the *Brahmasūtrabhāṣya* (*BSBh*), proposed in the *Upadeśasāhasrī Gadyabandha* (*USG*)3 was formulated from the *prasaṃkhyāna* detailed in the *Yogasūtra* (*YS*) and its commentary *Yogabhāṣya* (*YBh*). Although Śaṅkara rejects a claim of *prasaṃkhyāna* by an opponent in the *Upadeśasāhasrī Padyabandha* (*USP*)18, he utilizes 'the technique of *prasaṃkhyāna*' presented in *YBh* 'through casting it in a slightly different mould'.[2] Despite Bader's helpful discussion, it appears to me that the question raised by S. Mayeda regarding the difference between *parisaṃkhyāna* found in *USG* and the *prasaṃkhyāna* found in *USP*[3] still remains unanswered. Bader rightly pointed out the reason Śaṅkara and his disciple Sureśvara rejected the *prasaṃkhyāna*: *prasaṃkhyāna* 'might entail injunctions or imply a sense of agency' and 'the knowledge of reality does not arise through *prasaṃkhyāna*'.[4] However, the cause of confusion regarding the difference between *parisaṃkhyāna* and *prasaṃkhyāna* in the *Upadeśasāhasrī* is, I think, the definition of *prasaṃkhyāna* given by an opponent in Sureśvara's *Naiṣkarmyasiddhi* 3.90 (*tattvamasyādiśabdārthānvayavyatirekayuktiviṣayabuddhyāmreḍanam*), which Mayeda cites in his note that takes up the question of the difference between the two.[5] It is *parisaṃkhyāna*, not *prasaṃkhyāna*, that is supposed to have a close resemblance to *anvaya-vyatireka* in Śaṅkara's thought.[6] Therefore, the definition given by Sureśvara's opponent is very confusing. Since Bader does not make clear the similarity and difference between the two *prasaṃkhyānas* expressed in *YBh* and *USP*, his presentation of the similarity between the *prasaṃkhyāna* found in *YBh* and Śaṅkara's *parisaṃkhyāna* leads to a more puzzling situation.

In the history of Advaitavedānta, the role of meditation in the search for liberation was paraphrased as the role of action. This question about the action constituted a significant dispute among Advaitins.[7] If we knew the characteristics of the *prasaṃkhyāna* in Śaṅkara's thought more precisely, we would be a step closer to better understanding of his thought and Advaita philosophy. Since I am not an expert on Advaitavedānta, it is beyond my ability to discuss the problem of meditation in the intellectual history of Advaita, even that in Śaṅkara's thought. However, the examination of the *prasaṃkhyāna* found in *YBh* offers the key to the better understanding of meditation in Śaṅkara's thought as Bader showed. Therefore, I will attempt, pursuing Bader's discussion, to present a more detailed description of the *prasaṃkhyāna* found in *YBh*, further, on the basis of it, to consider briefly the characteristics of the *prasaṃkhyāna* and *parisaṃkhyāna* in the *Upadeśasāhasrī*, in an endeavour to clarify a puzzling situation.

PRASAṂKHYĀNA IN *YBH*

Before examining the characteristics of the *prasaṃkhyāna* expressed in *YBh*, a few remarks should be made concerning the meaning of *prasaṃkhyāna*. The word *prasaṃkhyāna*, in general, does not necessarily mean meditation. For example, we find the word in the *Nyāyabhāṣya* 4.2.2 used in the sense of the correct consideration to acquire right knowledge (*tattvajñāna*), especially right knowledge of the Self. It may mean the knowledge itself. According to the *Nyāyabhāṣya* 4.2.1, this right knowledge destroys wrong knowledge (*mithyājñāna*) that is the knowledge of the Self on the non-Self (*anātmany ātmagrahaḥ*) and that leads us to transmigration. Uddyotakara in his *Nyāyavārttika* 4.2.2 defines *prasaṃkhyāna* as the discriminating knowledge between the Self and the non-Self (*śarīrādiṣu naite ātmāna iti vyatirekadarśanam*). However, the explanation given by Vacaspatimiśra in the *Nyāyavārttikatātparyaṭīkā* 4.2.2 bears a different tone. Taking meditation into account, he interprets *prasaṃkhyāna* as right knowledge generated by meditative concentration (*samādhijaṃ tattvajñānaṃ*). Another example shows that the object of the knowledge does not necessarily concern the Self. Praśastapāda applies the word *prasaṃkhyāna* for the consideration of the six categories (*ṣaṭpadārtha*) of Vaiśeṣika philosophy, though this *prasaṃkhyāna* appears to be connected with yoga.[8] Therefore we may say that *prasaṃkhyāna* generally means correct consideration, in or not in meditation, to acquire right knowledge. Or it may mean acquired right knowledge also. In the system of Pātañjala-yoga, it is no doubt related to meditation.

Contrary to Bader's opinion that 'a more precise definition of *prasaṃkhyāna* is given in the *Yogasūtra*',[9] *YS* contains neither a definition of it nor any explanation of the word except a reference in the *sūtra* 4.29, which will be discussed later. This suggests that the word *prasaṃkhyāna* is not a technical term in the system of Pātañjala-yoga. J.H. Woods translates the word as 'elevation', which is followed by T.S. Rukmani,[10] while T. Leggett translates it as 'meditation practice'.[11] That the word *prasaṃkhyāna* means 'meditation practice' in Pātañjala-yoga, as translated by Leggett, is understood from *YBh* 2.11. There, the word '*dhyāna*' in *YS* 2.11, which does not mean the *dhyāna* in the eightfold Yoga but general meditation practice, is interpreted as *prasaṃkhyāna*.[12]

At the same time, *YBh* 2.11 tells us the remarkable characteristic of the *prasaṃkhyāna*: it attenuates, as if it burns, the activities of hindrance, or afflictions (*kleśa*) after they are weakened by the yoga of action (*kriyā-yoga*).[13] Then what kind of meditation is it? To put it briefly, it is, in the context of *YBh*, the meditation that culminates in making the mind nothing but the discriminative knowledge of the Self (*puruṣa*) from the *sattva* of the mind (*sattvapuruṣānyatākhyāti*).[14] Although these characteristics of the *prasaṃkhyāna* set forth in *YBh* were sketched by Bader,[15] two important points remain unexplored: the nature of meditation as burning fire and the nature of the knowledge produced by meditation. Focusing attention on these two points, I will now examine the characteristics of the *prasaṃkhyāna* in *YBh*.

Prasaṃkhyāna is considered to have power (*bala*). *YBh* 1.15 says it brings about its effect, such as detachment (*vairāgya*). One of the effects is, as has been mentioned above, the attenuation of the afflictions. *YBh* 2.2 explains it as follows: *kriyā-yoga* weakens the afflictions and *prasaṃkhyāna* attenuates the subtle forms of the afflictions.[16] From *YBh* 2.2 and 2.11, we understand that the gross forms of the afflictions are weakened by *kriyā-yoga* and the subtle forms of them, not easily attenuated by *kriyā-yoga*, are attenuated by *prasaṃkhyāna*. The attenuation means to make the afflictions incapable of production (*aprasavadharmin*), like burned seeds (*dagdhabīja*) incapable of germination. The power that effects the burning is phrased as 'fire (*agni*)'.

Here, the figurative expression of seed (*bīja*) is employed to picture the subtle form of the affliction. According to *YBh* 2.4, the subtle form is the form of mere potency (*śaktimātra*) that the afflictions take in their dormant state (*prasupta*, *prasupti*),[17] one of their four states.[18] The employment of these figurative expressions such as seed, germination, etc., in *YBh* is described by K.H. Potter as agricultural analogy.[19] Clearly the metaphor of seed is employed not only as a comparison between the production by the afflictions and the sprouting of seeds, but also because of the similarity of the afflictions' subtleness, their subtle form as the mere potency in the dormant state, to the minuteness of seeds. The analogy of seed is not a result of mere functional similarity. It also reflects the resemblance of physical images.

The same may be said of the figurative expressions for the power of *prasaṃkhyāna*, viz., fire or burning. This expression of fire is understood to indicate not only that the meditation makes things unproductive as fire does through burning, but also that it has a power resembling the power of fire, a power symbolized by heat. The heating power of meditation reminds us of the correspondence between yoga and *tapas* (self-castigation, asceticism).[20] *Tapas*, as is well known, originally means 'heat'. It is believed to bring about a magical power symbolized by heat. Although *tapas* is often applied toward perfection of rather secular objectives, not for spiritual purposes,[21] it seems reasonable to suppose that the author of *YBh* had in mind that *prasaṃkhyāna* has a magical power similar to that of *tapas*. Without *tapas*, reduction of the impurity (*aśuddhi*) caused by *karman* and the afflictions is impossible.[22] It is the magical power of heat that effects the reduction of the afflictions. After all, the portrayal of *prasaṃkhyāna* as burning fire connotes its ascetic nature. While *tapas* weakens the afflictions in gross form, it is *prasaṃkhyāna* having the ascetic power of heat that attenuates the afflictions in the subtle form, in a form like seed, which is difficult to be reduced by *tapas*.

Having observed the nature of *prasaṃkhyāna* as burning fire, we may now consider the nature of the knowledge produced by the meditation. *YS* mentions the word *prasaṃkhyāna* only once in 4.29, as mentioned earlier. *YS* 4.29 and *YBh* 4.29 tell us that a *yogin* who is indifferent to *prasaṃkhyāna* achieves the discriminative discernment (*vivekakhyāti*), i.e. the realization of the distinction between the Self (*puruṣa*) and the mind or the mind-body complex manifested from primordial matter (*prakṛti*). This state of mind grows into the concentration known as rain-cloud of virtue (*dharmamegha-samādhi*). What becomes apparent from these passages is that *prasaṃkhyāna* brings about discriminative discernment and that when the mind is completely filled with the discernment, it changes into the *dharmamegha-samādhi*. *YBh* 1.2 says the same.[23] In *YBh* 1.2, it is called the supreme *prasaṃkhyāna* that the mind is transformed into the discriminative knowledge of the Self (*puruṣa*) from the *sattva* (*sattvapuruṣānyatākhyāti*). Therefore, we can understand that *prasaṃkhyāna* is the meditation that brings about discriminative discernment (*vivekakhyāti*) and culminates in leaving the mind entirely occupied by discriminative discernment.

However, this discriminative discernment sometimes disappears and the mind becomes occupied instead by other ideas due to latent dispositions (*saṃskāra*) accumulated in the previous life, according to *YS* and *YBh* 4.27. *YBh* 4.28 says these latent dispositions also should be removed through burning in the fire of knowledge (*jñāna-agni*) just as the afflictions are attenuated by the fire of *prasaṃkhyāna*.[24] It appears that discriminative discernment must be realized through meditation again and again. Indeed, we find the recommendation of the repeating exercise of discriminative knowledge (*vivekadarśana-abhyāsa*) in *YBh* 1.12. Therefore, we may say that this meditation of discriminative knowledge is called *prasaṃkhyāna* in *YBh*. It may be worth pointing out that in *YBh* 4.28 the knowledge produced from *prasaṃkhyāna* also is thought to have the nature of heating power.

YBh 1.2 states that even this discriminative discernment should be restrained in the non-conscious concentration (*asaṃprajñātasamādhi*) where nothing is perceived. Consequently, we understand that discriminative discernment is knowledge which arises in the conscious concentration (*saṃprajñātasamādhi*) that is the lower state of the mind compared to the non-conscious concentration. According to *YS* 1.47, 48 and *YBh* on them, the knowledge that arises in the highest clarity (*vaiśāradya*) of conscious concentration is called *ṛtaṃbharā prajñā* (truth-bearing insight). *YBh* 1.49 says this insight works towards things not known by worldly means of knowledge, things such as the Self (*puruṣa*) or subtle material elements (*bhūtasūkṣma*). However, it must be remembered that the object of this knowledge or *ṛtaṃbharā prajñā* is, according to *YS* 1.49, different from the objects of inferential knowledge and scriptural knowledge. While the latter two have universals (*sāmānya*) as their objects, this knowledge has particulars (*viśeṣa*).[25] Since the epistemology of Pātañjala-yoga described in *YBh* 1.7 claims *viśeṣa* is an object of perception (*pratyakṣa*), one of the means of valid knowledge (*pramāṇa*), the *ṛtaṃbharā prajñā* is understood to be a result of yogic perception (*yogi-pratyakṣa*). Thus discriminative discernment also can be understood as the result of yogic perception.

Further, in the epistemology of Pātañjala-yoga, perception is the foundation of the other means of valid knowledge, viz., inference (*anumāna*) and verbal testimony (*āgama*).[26] Perception produces immediate knowledge while the others produce only mediate knowledge. Therefore, the knowledge about the Self produced by meditation is more direct compared to knowledge derived from the scriptures (*śruti*). Thus the discriminative discernment brought about from *prasaṃkhyāna* is more direct knowledge compared to knowledge derived from the scriptures. As a matter of course, yogic perception is regarded as superior to other means of valid knowledge in the system of Pātañjala-yoga.

From the above discussion, the following points become clear regarding the *prasaṃkhyāna* in *YBh* : it has the ascetic power of heat that attenuates the afflictions; it produces the discriminative discernment that is insight which arises in concentration (*samādhiprajñā*) and has particulars (*viśeṣa*) as its object; this knowledge is believed to be a comparatively superior knowledge to that derived from the scriptures.

PRASAṂKHYĀNA IN *USP*

Śaṅkara refuted the opponent who advocates *prasaṃkhyāna* in *USP* 18. As Halbfass points out, the *prasaṃkhyāna* in *YBh* seems to be adopted by several Vedāntins as a technique to realize the meaning of the Upaniṣadic *mahāvākya*.[27] Let us now examine the *prasaṃkhyāna* in *USP*.

The opinion of the opponent in *USP* 18.9-18 can be summarized as follows[28] : (1) Because the simple listening to the sacred texts, such as '*tat tvam asi*', does not give rise to the knowledge that leads to liberation, *prasaṃkhyāna* and the reasoning (*yukti*) are needed [9, 10, 15]. (2) The scripture must be enjoining action that produces the knowledge, and the action is *prasaṃkhyāna* [11, 16, 17]. (3) *Prasaṃkhyāna* is not incompatible with the knowledge so long as the latter is not firm, and it should be practised to gain intuitive knowledge (*anubhava*) of the Self [11, 12, 17, 18]. (4) The knowledge of the Self obtained from the scripture is negated by the latent dispositions (*saṃskāra*) arising from perception, because perceptual knowledge (*akṣaja-pratyaya*) having particulars (*viśeṣa*) as its object surely hinders scriptural and inferential knowledge (*śrutānumānajanman-pratyaya*) having universals (*sāmānya*) as their objects [13, 14].

Śaṅkara refutes this view on the ground that the Vedas do not give any injunction of action for knowledge leading to liberation.[29] For him, the knowledge of the identity of the Self (*ātman*) and *Brahman*, which destroys nescience (*avidyā*), is the only means to final release. Moreover, this knowledge can be derived only from the scriptures, not from action, because action is caused by nescience.[30] Therefore, the opponent's idea that *prasaṃkhyāna*, which is a kind of action, brings about the knowledge is not acceptable for him.

Why can the opponent claim that *prasaṃkhyāna* produces the knowledge of reality ? The answer lies in the last point of the above summarized opponent's opinion: Scriptural knowledge of the Self is negated by the latent dispositions engendered by perception, because perceptual knowledge hinders scriptural and inferential knowledge.[31] In *USP* 18.13-14, this portion of the opponent's idea is expressed in a somewhat abrupt way. Accordingly its contextual relation to the other portions is not entirely clear. However, we find the discussion about particulars and universals as the objects of knowledge in *BSBh* also. In *BSBh* 4.1.2, an antagonist to the opponent of Śaṅkara insists: (1) Inference and the scripture can produce only the knowledge of universals but not the knowledge of particulars. (2) Intuitive knowledge (*anubhava*) that has the particular as its object removes nescience. (3) Repetition (*āvṛtti*) of the knowledge acquired from the scripture is necessary because it produces intuitive knowledge.[32] The repetition (*āvṛtti*) means meditation (*upāsana*) or the profound meditation (*nididhyāsana*) expressed in the *Bṛhadāraṇyakopaniṣad* 2.4.5.[33] Here Śaṅkara clearly considers an opinion that meditation, or repetition of the knowledge acquired from the scripture, is necessary for direct perception of the Self because meditation produces the immediate, perceptual knowledge of the Self, while the hearing of the scripture brings about only a mediate knowledge. Therefore, although it is not explicitly mentioned by the opponent, the opinion in *USP* 18.13-14 has the following meaning: (1) Knowledge that has particulars as its object negates a contradicting knowledge with universals as its object because the former is immediate and the latter is mediate. (2) The scriptural knowledge of the Self, of which the object is the universal of the Self, is negated by contradicting ordinary perceptual experience. (3) The knowledge obtained from *prasaṃkhyāna* is not negated by ordinary perceptual experience because it is also a perceptual knowledge, the particular being its object. (4) Therefore, *prasaṃkhyāna* should be practised to obtain perceptual knowledge of the Self. Thus, *prasaṃkhyāna* is regarded as a technique to realize the meaning of the *mahāvākya*, to obtain perceptual knowledge about the Self. Further, from the similarity between *prasaṃkhyāna* and the repetition (*āvṛtti*) of the knowledge, which is also known as *upāsana*, one may say that the *prasaṃkhyāna* found in *USP* 18 is also meditative practice.

It is useful to recall that discriminative discernment, the knowledge produced by the *prasaṃkhyāna* in *YBh*, is also perceptual knowledge having particulars (*viśeṣa*) as its object. As mentioned earlier, it is the view maintained by *YS* 1.49 that the object of perceptual knowledge obtained from meditation is particulars, while that of inferential and scriptural knowledge is universals (*sāmānya*). With this idea, Pātañjala-yoga regards yogic perception as producing more direct knowledge compared to inference and the scriptures, and awards it a superior position in comparison with the others.

Therefore, with reference to the epistemological characteristics of the knowledge produced by *prasaṃkhyāna*, there is no doubt about the intimateness between the *prasaṃkhyāna* in *USP* 18 and that found in *YBh*. Both the *prasaṃkhyānas* are regarded as meditative practice which produces insight arising in concentration (*samādhiprajñā*) that is perceptual knowledge, or immediate knowledge. Precisely because it produces immediate knowledge, it is regarded as a superior means for the realization of the Self compared with the scripture. For Śaṅkara, who thinks the realization of the Self is possible only from the scripture, the insistence on such meditation is certainly unacceptable. According to him, perception (*pratyakṣa*) as a means of knowledge is fallacious.[34]

PARISAṂKHYĀNA IN *USG*

In *USG* 3, Śaṅkara teaches a deliberate practice called *parisaṃkhyāna*. It is 'described for seekers after final release, who are devoting themselves to destroying their acquired merit and demerit, and do not wish to accumulate new ones', 'for the sake of final release from those *karman*s'.[35] The following is a summary of his description. First, the discrimination between the Self and objects of perception, such as sound, form and colour, etc., is deliberated.[36] Next, the discrimination of the Self from one's body, sense organs, internal organs and objects of them is deliberated.[37] Further, the Self is deliberated as free from the results of action, being not affected by the change of the five material elements, free from the results of *karman* such as merit or demerit, on the basis of the scriptures and the reason that anything other than *ātman* does not exist.[38]

It is not easy to define what *parisaṃkhyāna* is. Mayeda says that 'it seems to be a kind of meditation which consists in recapitulating the conclusion which has been arrived at through one's previous study and discussion with a teacher'.[39] On the contrary, Vetter denies its being meditation and gives German rendering 'Betrachtung' to the word.[40] There exists, in this way, divergence of opinion even about the primary nature of *parisaṃkhyāna*. To give a full account of *parisaṃkhyāna* is not the purpose of the present study. Here, I would like to clarify, firstly, the difference between the *prasaṃkhyāna* in *USP* and *parisaṃkhyāna*; secondly, whether the latter is really a developed form of the *prasaṃkhyāna* found in *YBh*.

The discrepancy just mentioned seems to arise from the differences in the understanding of 'meditation'.[41] Śaṅkara describes *parisaṃkhyāna* as deliberation on the nature of one's Self, discriminating it from what is not the Self. This description leaves the impression that it is a kind of contemplating practice or meditation practice. However, *parisaṃkhyāna* seems not to be meditation if we follow the 'provisional definition' of meditation given by Bader: 'the concentration of the mind on a particular theme or object in preparation for the direct intuition of truth'.[42] For *parisaṃkhyāna* does not give rise to any direct knowledge of the Self. As we have seen, such meditation practice as *prasaṃkhyāna* that produces perceptual knowledge of the Self is refuted by Śaṅkara. At least we can be reasonably certain that *parisaṃkhyāna* is not the meditation which produces perceptual knowledge of the Self, although it appears to be a kind of contemplation or reflection. Thus, we may say the difference between the *prasaṃkhyāna* found in *USP* and *parisaṃkhyāna* lies in whether or not it generates perceptual knowledge in the form of *samādhiprajñā*. In *YBh* also, *prasamkhyāna* is regarded as meditation that produces perceptual knowledge. Consequently, Bader's claim that Śaṅkara formulated *parisaṃkhyāna* on the basis of the *prasaṃkhyāna* expressed in *YS* and *YBh* is open to question.

Let us briefly review Bader's view. He says Śaṅkara's explanation of *parisaṃkhyāna* 'bears a striking similarity to the concept of *prasaṃkhyāna*' found in *YS* and *YBh*. He illustrates the similarity with two points: the purpose of *parisaṃkhyāna*, 'to free one from the effects of karma' is similar to that of the *prasaṃkhyāna* in *YBh*, 'to remove the afflictions or hindrances (*kleśa-s*) to liberation'; Śaṅkara's explanation of ignorance, or nescience (*avidyā*), as the cause of faults (*doṣa*) is very similar to the notion of *avidyā* found in *YS* as the cause of the afflictions (*kleśa*). Further, he explains that Śaṅkara does not use the term *prasaṃkhyāna* with the intention of avoiding both the meditation insisted by the *jñānakarmasamuccayavādin* and the process not associated with the Upaniṣads, despite 'implicit approval of *prasaṃkhyāna*' expressed in *YBh*. Śaṅkara adopts another term, *parisaṃkhyāna*, derived from '*parisaṃkhyā*' that designates a type of Vedic injunction, the injunction that excludes forms of action, in the terminology of the Mīmāṃsā school. According to Bader, Śaṅkara thus modifies *prasaṃkhyāna*, which is an action as object-centred meditation, into a process of knowledge to destroy the false identification of the non-Self with the Self.[43] This transformation of meditation is well exemplified by the resemblance of *parisaṃkhyāna* to the method of reasoning '*anvaya-vyatireka*'.[44] Like *anvaya-vyatireka*, '*parisaṃkhyāna* involves the rejection of anything which does not agree with the ever-present, essential unity of Brahman and *ātman*'.[45]

The foundation of Bader's view is his observation of 'the striking similarity' between *parisaṃkhyāna* and the *prasaṃkhyāna* found in *YBh*. Although he supplies two illustrations of similarities, it appears to me that his opinion relies solely upon the similarity of aims. For the resemblance in the interpretations of nescience (*avidyā*) cannot also illustrate the similarity of the methods to destroy nescience.

As to the attenuation of afflictions by the *prasaṃkhyāna* expressed in *YBh*, we have studied its ascetic nature. It attenuates the afflictions by its magical power of heat. Does *parisaṃkhyāna* free the aspirant from the effects of *karman* directly in the same way by its power of burning heat? Śaṅkara does not explicitly explain how it brings the release from *karman*. *Parisaṃkhyāna* is described, as Bader points out, in the character of 'the way of knowledge' reminiscent of the reasoning *anvaya-vyatireka*. Then, at least *parisaṃkhyāna* should be understood to bring about its effect logically and not by the magical power of burning. In this respect, apparently, *parisaṃkhyāna* works against *karman* or against the afflictions very differently from the *prasaṃkhyāna* in *YBh*. Rather, this *parisaṃkhyāna* resembles the *prasaṃkhyāna* found in the *Nyāyabhāṣya* 4.2.2 in the sense that it is a logical deliberation.

From the above examination, it is clear that *parisaṃkhyāna* in *USG* differs from the *prasaṃkhyāna* in *YBh* in two respects: the former does not produce perceptual knowledge of the Self as the latter does; the former does not depend on magical power of heating as the latter does to free the aspirant from the effects of *karman*. To be sure, this does not negate the possibility that the *prasaṃkhyāna* in *YBh* is one source

Śaṅkara consulted to develop the idea of *parisaṃkhyāna.* Their names and aims are similar. Yet, the *prasaṃkhyāna* in *YBh* cannot be the only meditation exercised aiming at the destruction of the results of *karman* or to attenuate afflictions.[46] The resemblance of their names and aims is not a sufficient reason to suppose their direct connection. Therefore, it is doubtful that Śaṅkara's idea of *parisaṃkhyāna* is directly developed from the notion of the *prasaṃkhyāna* expressed in *YBh.*

I would like to mention, in passing, that Śaṅkara prescribes repetition of the scripture and reasoning (*śāstrayuktyabhyāsa*) in *BSBh* 4.1.2. This repetition is recommended for the person who cannot obtain intuitive knowledge (*anubhava*) of the Self from the hearing of the sentence '*tat tvam asi*' due to the obstruction regarding the meaning of the two terms in the sentence caused by ignorance (*ajñāna*), doubt (*saṃśaya*) and error (*viparyaya*). The exercise aims at the discernment of the sense of the words (*padārthavivekaprayojana*). This repetition appears similar to *parisaṃkhyāna* in the sense that it is performed without aiming at the intuition of the Self. In addition, although *parisaṃkhyāna* does not have the power of burning heat, this does not mean Śaṅkara excludes such power from his system of Vedānta. As has been pointed out by H. Nakamura,[47] the way the knowledge destroys *karman* is typically expressed as the burning out of the seeds of *karman* by knowledge (*jñānāt karmabījadāhaḥ*).[48] However, I am not competent to discuss in detail Śaṅkara's thought on the way of liberation. These are issues for future discussion.

SUMMARY

I would like to close by repeating several noteworthy points of comparison and contrast. The *prasaṃkhyāna* in *YBh* has the magical power of heating that attenuates the afflictions. It produces the discriminative discernment that is insight which arises in meditative concentration (*samādhiprajñā*) whose object is particulars (*viśeṣa*), and that is regarded as comparatively superior knowledge to that derived from the scriptures. The *prasaṃkhyana* in *USP* is meditative practice that produces the perceptual knowledge of the Self. In this respect, it resembles the *prasaṃkhyāna* expressed in *YBh. Parisaṃkhyāna* in *USG* does not produce perceptual knowledge of the Self. In this point, it differs from *prasaṃkhyāna* found in *USP* and *YBh.* Further, it also differs from the *prasaṃkhyāna* in *YBh* in that it does not have the ascetic power of heating to free one from the effects of *karman.*

TEXTS AND ABBREVIATIONS

BSBh: *Brahmasūtrabhāṣya. The Brahmasūtra Śāṅkarabhāṣya: With the Commentaries Bhāmatī, Kalpataru and Parimala* (2 vols. Parimal Sanskrit Series 1), K.L. Joshi ed., Delhi, 1996.

YBh: *Yogabhāṣya. Vācaspatimiśraviracitaṭīkāsaṃvalitavyāsabhāṣyasametāni Pātañjalayogasūtrāṇi: Tathā Bhojadevaviracitarājamārtaṇḍābhidhavṛttisametāni Pātañjalayogasūtrāṇi* (Ānandāśrama Sanskrit Series 47), K.S. Āgaśe ed., Puṇyākhyapattana, 2nd., 1919.

YS: *Yogasūtra*. See *YBh*.

UPG: *Upadeśasāhasrī Gadyabandha. Śaṅkara's Upadeśasāhasrī*, S. Mayeda ed., Tokyo, 1973.

USP: *Upadeśasāhasrī Padyabandha*. See *USG*.

NOTES

* I express my gratitude to Prof. Julian Gitzen, Aichi Bunkyo University, for correcting my English.

1 See review by Sengaku Mayeda in *Indo-Iranian Journal* 41,1 (1998)

2 J. Bader, *Meditation in Śaṅkara's Vedānta*, New Delhi, 1990, p.78.

3 S. Mayeda, *A Thousand Teachings*, Tokyo, 1979, pp. 196-97, n.13 and p.254, n.1. See also Bader, *Meditation in Śaṅkara's Vedānta*, p. 73.

4 Bader, *Meditation in Śaṅkara's Vedānta*, p. 77.

5 Mayeda translates it as 'mentally going over the meaning of such Śruti saying as 'Thou art That' and the reasoning based on the method of agreement and contrariety.' See Mayeda, *A Thousand Teachings*, pp. 196-97.

6 See Mayeda, *A Thousand Teachings*, p. 56 and Bader, *Meditation in Śaṅkara's Vedānta*, p. 79.

7 For the followers of *jñānakarmasmuccayavāda*, such as Maṇḍanamiśra, liberation is possible with Upaniṣadic knowledge assisted by ritual actions commanded by the Vedas. Śaṅkara refutes an assertion of *prasaṃkhyāna* in *USP*18.9-18, which is also ascribed to a *jñānakarmasamuccayavādin*. See Mayeda, *A Thousand Teachings*, pp. 88, 173-74. Such a view was strictly rejected by Sureśvara too. See *Naiṣkarmyasiddhi*, 3.89-91, 3.123-126. However, so far as meditation is concerned, later Advaitins gradually incorporated it in their way to liberation. See Iwao Shima, 'The Path Toward Release in the Advaita Vedānta School (Huni'ichigenrongakuha ni okeru gedatsu eno mich, in Japanese)', *Journal of Religious Studies* 60, 2 (no.269), 1986.

8 *Praśastapādabhāṣya*, text no. 315: *trayāṇām anyatamasya ... saṃnyasya svāni karmāṇi yamaniyameṣv apramattasya ṣaṭpadārthaprasaṃkhyānād yogaprasādhanaṃ pravrajitasyeti* [J. Bronkhorst and Y. Ramseier eds., *Word Index to the Praśastapādabhāṣya*: *A Complete Word Index to the Printed Editions of the Praśastapādabhāṣya*, Delhi, 1994, p. 65].

9 Bader, *Meditation in Śaṅkara's Vedānta*, p. 76.

10 J.H. Woods, *The Yoga-System of Patañjali*, Harvard Oriental Series 17, Delhi, rpt. 1977, p. 340. T.S. Rukmani, *Yogavārttika of Vijñānabhikṣu, vol.4 Kaivalyapāda*, New Delhi, 1989, p. 121.

11 T. Leggett, *Śaṅkara on the Yoga Sūtra-s*, Delhi, 1992, p. 410.

12 *YBh* 2.11: *kleśānāṃ yā vṛttayaḥ sthūlās tāḥ kriyāyogena(ṇa)* [*sic.*] *tanūkṛtāḥ satyaḥ prasaṃkhyānena dhyānena hātavyā* yāvat sūkṣmīkṛtā yāvad dagdhabījakalpā iti* / [p. 67]. *Though n.1 in the Ānandāśrama edition shows a variant reading, '*prasaṃkhyānena hātavyā*', the *Pātañjalayogaśāstravivaraṇa* (p. 142) also supports the reading '*prasaṃkhyānena dhyānena hātavyā*'.

13 *Kriyā-yoga*, Yoga of action, consists of 'self-castigation (*tapas*)', 'study (*svādhyāya*)' and 'devotion to the *Īśvara* (*īśvarapraṇidhāna*)'. It is practised 'for the cultivation of concentration (*samādhi*) and for the attenuation of the hindrances (*kleśa*)'. See *YS* 2.1 and 2. Here I have followed the translation of J.H. Woods.

14 *YBh* 1.2: *tad eva rajoleśamalāpetaṃ svarūpapratiṣṭhaṃ sattvapuruṣānyatākhyātimātraṃ dharmameghadhyānopagaṃ bhavati / tat paraṃ prasaṃkhyānam ity ācakṣate dhyāyinaḥ* / [pp. 5-6]. See also Bader, *Meditation in Śaṅkara's Vedānta*, p. 76.

15 Bader, *Meditation in Śaṅkara's Vedānta*, p. 43, pp. 76-77.

16 *YBh* 2.2: *sa hi kriyāyogaḥ ... sa hy āsevyamānaḥ samādhiṃ bhāvayati kleśāṃś ca pratanū karoti / pratanūkṛtān kleśān prasaṃkhyānāgninā dagdhabījakalpān aprasavadharmiṇaḥ kariṣyatīti* / [p. 58].

17 *YBh* 2.4: *tatra kā prasuptiḥ / cetasi śaktimātrapratiṣṭhānāṃ bījabhāvopagamaḥ /...prasaṃkhyānavato dagdhakleśabījasya saṃmukhībhūte 'py ālambane nāsau punar asti, dagdhabījasya kutaḥ praroha iti / ... satāṃ kleśānāṃ tadā bījasāmarthyaṃ dagdham iti viṣayasya saṃmukhībhāve 'pi sati na bhavaty eṣāṃ prabodha ity uktā prasuptir dagdhabījānām aprarohaś ca* / [pp. 59-60].

18 The other states are 'attenuated (*tanu*)', 'intercepted (*vicchinna*)' and 'sustained (*udāra*)'. See *YBh* 2.4. I followed the translation by Woods.

19 K.H. Potter, 'The Karma Theory and Its Interpretation in Some Indian Philosophical Systems' in W.D. O'Flaherty, ed., *Karma and Rebirth in Classical Indian Traditions*, Delhi (Indian ed.), 1983, pp. 245-47.

20 See M. Hara, *Tapas in the Mahābhārata* (*Koten Indo No Kugyo*, in Japanese), Tokyo, 1979, pp. 324-28.

21 M. Hara, *Tapas in the Mahābhārata*, pp. 385-413. See also M. Hara, 'Yoga to kugyo (in Japanese)' in G. Nagao, et al., eds., *Indo Siso* 3 (Iwanami Koza Toyo Siso, vol.7), pp. 196-97.

22 *YBh* 2.1: *anādikarmakleśavāsanācitrā pratyupasthitaviṣayajālā cāśuddhir nāntareṇa tapaḥ saṃbhedam āpadyata* [p. 57]. See also *YS* 2.31.

23 See *YBh* 1.2 cited in n. 13.

24 *YBh* 4.28: *yathā kleśā dagdhabījabhāvā na prarohasamarthā bhavanti tathā jñānāgninā dagdhabījabhāvaḥ pūrvasaṃskāro na pratyayaprasūr bhavati* / [p. 202].

25 *YS* 1.49: *śrutānumānaprajñābhyām anyaviṣayā viśeṣārthatvāt*. See also *YBh* 1.49.

26 See *Tattvavaiśāradī* 1.7 and *Pātañjalayogaśāstravivaraṇa* 1.7.

27 W. Halbfass, *Tradition and Reflection: Explorations in Indian Thought*,

Albany, 1991, p. 227.

28 This portion of *USG* has been already summarized by Vetter. See T. Vetter, *Studien zur Lehre und Entwicklung Śaṅkaras*, Publications of the De Nobili Research Library, vol. 6, Wien, 1979, pp. 102-3. Here I consulted Vetter's study and Mayeda's translation in his *A Thousand Teachings*, pp. 173-74.

29 See *USP* 18.19 and Bader, *Meditation in Śaṅkara's Vedānta*, p. 77, Halbfass, *Tradition and Reflection*, p. 227. See also H. Hatae, 'Śaṅkara's Criticism of the *Prasaṃkhyānavāda* (Śaṅkara no prasaṃkhyāna setsu hihan, in Japanese)', *Journal of Indian and Buddhist Studies* 30, 2, (1982). Bader and Halbfass supplement Sureśvara's opinion: such a practice does not produce the knowledge of reality.

30 See Mayeda, *A Thousand Teachings*, pp. 46-49, 84-87.

31 *USP* 18.13-14: *sad asmīti ca vijñānam akṣajo bādhate dhruvam / śabdotthaṃ dṛḍhasaṃskāro doṣaiś cākṛṣyate bahiḥ //13// śrutānumānajanmānau sāmānyaviṣayau yataḥ / pratyayāv akṣajo 'vaśyaṃ viśeṣārtho nivārayet //14//.*

32 *BSBh* 4.1.2: *athāpi syād yuktyā vākyena ca sāmānyaviṣayam eva vijñānaṃ kriyate, na viśeṣaviṣayam / yathā 'sti me hṛdaye śūlam ity ato vākyād gātrakampādiliṅgāc ca śūlasadbhāvasāmānyam eva paraḥ pratipadyate, na viśeṣam anubhavati —yathā sa eva śūlī, viśeṣānubhavaś cāvidyāyā nivartakas tatas tadarthā "vṛttir iti cet,* ... [p. 931].

33 *BSBh* 4.1.1: *pratyayāvṛttiḥ kartavyā / kutaḥ? asakṛdupadeśāt 'śrotavyo mantavyo nididhyāsitavyaḥ' ity evaṃjātīyako hy asakṛdupadeśaḥ pratyayāvṛttiṃ sūcayati* / [p. 929]; *api copāsanaṃ nididhyāsanaṃ cety antarṇītāvṛttiguṇaiva kriyā 'bhidhīyate* / [p. 929].

34 *USP* 18.7. See also Mayeda, *A Thousand Teachings*, pp. 172-3, and p. 196, n. 8.

35 *USG* 3.112: *mumukṣūṇām upāttapuṇyāpuṇyakṣapaṇaparāṇām apūrvānupacayārthināṃ parisaṃkhyānam idam ucyate /...tanmokṣārtham//* [p. 216]; translated by Mayeda in *A Thousand Teachings*, p. 251.

36 *USG* 3.115.[pp. 216-17]. See Mayeda, *A Thousand Teachings*, p. 252.

37 *USG* 3.116 [p. 217]. See Mayeda, *A Thousand Teachings*, p. 253.

38 *USG* 3.116 [pp. 217-18]. See Mayeda, *A Thousand Teachings*, p. 253.

39 Mayeda, *A Thousand Teachings*, p. 254, n. 1.

40 See Vetter, *Studien zur Lehre*, pp.77-78. Vetter translates *prasamkhyāna* as 'anhaltende Betrachtung'. See, ibid., p. 102.

41 While Mayeda regards the three chapters of *USG* correspond to *śravaṇa*, *manana* and *nididhyāsana* respectively, Vetter observes them as independent instructions of the way of liberation. Mayeda, *Śaṅkara's Upadeśasāhasrī*, Tokyo, 1973, p. 66, Vetter, *Studien zur Lehre*, pp. 77-78. This may be another reason for the discrepancy.

42 Bader, *Meditation in Śaṅkara's Vedānta*, p.32.

43 Ibid., pp. 77-79.

44 As to the characteristics of *anvaya-vyatireka* in Advaitavedānta, see G. Cardona, 'On Reasoning from *Anvaya* and *Vyatireka* in Early Advaita', in D. Malvania and N.J. Shah, ed., *Studies in Indian Philosophy: A Memorial Volume in Honour of Pandit Sukhlalji Sanghvi*, L.D.Series 84, Ahmedabad, 1981. See also Halbfass, *Tradition and Reflection*, pp. 132-

204. Cardona emphasizes that reasoning from *anvaya* and *vyatireka* is not a meditation but 'a mode of reasoning' against Mayeda's opinion that *anvaya-vyatireka* 'seems to be a meditational method rather than an exegetical method'. Cardona, 'On Reasoning from *Anvaya* and *Vyatireka*', p. 93, Mayeda *A Thousand Teachings*, p. 52 and 56. See also Halbfass, *Tradition and Reflection*, pp. 162-64. Nevertheless, the description of *parisaṃkhyāna* in *USG* gives us an impression of the proximity of *parisaṃkhyāna* with *anvaya-vyatireka* in the sense that both are applied to 'discriminate between what is and is not the self (Cardona, 'On Reasoning from *Anvaya* and *Vyatireka*', p. 87)'. It is not in the scope of the present study to discuss whether *anvaya-vyatireka* in Advaita is a meditation or not. However, it appears to me that the difference between Mayeda and Cardona arises, again, from their different understanding of the meaning of meditation. The reasoning is not necessarily a meditation but it may be applied in a deliberation about the nature of the Self.

45 Bader, *Meditation in Śaṅkara's Vedānta*, p. 79.

46 For example, Buddhist text *Abhidharmakośa* describes a process of meditation in which afflictions are attenuated. See *Abhidharmakośa-bhāṣya* 6.17, 6.27, etc.

47 H.Nakamura, *Śaṅkara No Siso* (in Japanese), Tokyo, p. 778.

48 *BSBh* 3.3.32 [p. 818]. See also *BSBh* 4.1.13 [p. 954]; 4.1.19 [p. 969]; *USP* 17.25.

7

Some Remarks on Jayanta's Writings: Is *Nyāyakalikā* his Authentic Work?*

HIROSHI MARUI

The date of Jayanta Bhaṭṭa, a unique Nyāya philosopher of Kashmir, has attracted scholarly attention especially in connection with that of Vācaspatimiśra. Although there is not yet a complete agreement among scholars about the chronological order of the two, Jayanta's date itself has been established as the latter half of ninth century.[1] With regard to the question of his writings, however, not much has been done so far. Certainly Jayanta is famous for his magnum opus, *Nyāyamañjarī*. In addition he is sometimes referred to as the writer of the philosophical drama, *Āgamaḍambara.* But it seems that he wrote other works as well.

This article[2] consists of two parts. First, we survey earlier studies and observations on his work. Then a careful investigation is undertaken as to whether he himself composed a digest of the Nyāya system named *Nyāyakalikā.*

For convenience we will use the following abbreviations for the main preceding studies or remarks on Jayanta's writings:

Frauwallner [1936] = E. Frauwallner, 'Beiträge zur Geschichte des Nyāya, 1. Jayanta und seine Quellen', *Wiener Zeitschrift für die Kunde des Morgenlandes* 43 (1936), pp. 263-78 (=*Kleine Schriften*, Wiesbaden, 1982, pp. 145-60).

Raghavan [1960] = V. Raghavan, 'Why was Jayantabhaṭṭa known as Vṛttikāra?', *Poona Oriental Series*, No.93 (1960), Professor P. K. Gode Commemoration Volume, pp. 173-4.

Steinkellner [1961] = E. Steinkellner, 'Die Literatur des älteren Nyāya', *Wiener Zeitschrift für die Kunde Süd- und Ostasiens* 5 (1961), pp. 149-62.

Gupta [1963] = B. Gupta, *Die Wahrnehmungslehre in der Nyāyamañjarī*, Walldorf, 1963. (Dissertation submitted to Rheinische Friedrich-Wilhelms-Universität, Bonn in 1962.)

Raghavan [1964] = V. Raghavan's introduction to the *Āgama-*

dambara, ed. by V. Raghavan and A. Thakur, pp. i-xxix.
Matilal [1977] = B.K. Matilal, *Nyāya-Vaiśeṣika* (= *A History of Indian Literature*, ed. J. Gonda, vol. 6, fasc. 2), Wiesbaden, 1977.
Potter [1977] = K.H. Potter, *Encyclopedia of Indian Philosophies*, vol. 2 : *Indian Metaphysics and Epistemology: The Tradition of Nyāya-Vaiśeṣika up to Gaṅgeśa*, Princeton and Delhi, 1977, pp. 341-3.

Frauwallner [1936] was the first to draw attention to the significance of the *Nyāyamañjarī* (=*NM*) for reconstruction of the history of Indian philosophy. At that time no texts other than *NM* and *Nyāyakalikā* (=*NKali*) had been published. But Frauwallner asserted that Jayanta must have written another book because Jayanta, in his view, sometimes refers the reader to 'another work' (*śāstrāntara*) when he enters into a discussion too detailed to be covered thoroughly in *NM*,[3] and he could not have meant thereby the small *NKali*. Moreover, Frauwallner noted that Jayanta is called 'a [new] commentator' (*[nava]vṛttikāra*) by himself and his son Abhinanda[4], and added that the commentary simply referred to *NM* or possibly to another (lost) work.

In the early 1960s new light was shed by V. Raghavan, E. Steinkellner and B. Gupta. They came to know of the *Āgamaḍambara* (=*ĀgamḌ*). Prof. Raghavan edited the text with A. Thakur, appending an introduction to it (= Raghavan [1964]). But the other two scholars, too, became acquainted with it before it was issued. Steinkellner, or perhaps Frauwallner, to whom he probably owed this information, seems to have been in contact with Raghavan when the latter was preparing the edition. B. Gupta utilized a photocopy of the manuscript of the Bhandarkar Oriental Research Institute.

The drama settled the question of *vṛttikāra*, for it contains a statement that Jayanta was given this second name because he wrote a commentary on grammar when he was young.[5] It is not a Nyāya work, as was formerly assumed, but undoubtedly a commentary on the *Aṣṭādhyāyī* (Steinkellner [1961] p. 159; Raghavan [1964] p. v),[6] the very first work of Jayanta (Raghavan [1964] p. v). In addition, *ĀgamḌ* shares several verses with *NM* and one of them is preceded by a statement which evidently shows that it is the words of Jayanta.[7] It is almost certain, then, that Jayanta wrote the play after *NM* (Raghavan [1964]).

It is interesting to note that Jayanta is one of the Naiyāyikas whom late Jaina scholars often quote (Gupta [1963] p. 19). Among others, one often comes across citations from Jayanta in Hemacandra's *Pramāṇamīmāṃsā*, Vādidevasūri's *Syādvādaratnākara* (Gupta [1963] p. 19; p. 16, fn. 32) and Prabhācandra's *Nyāyakumuda-candra*.

It is the *Syādvādaratnākara* (=*SyādVR*) that quotes from the '*Pallava*' of Jayanta (Steinkellner [1961] p. 159; Raghavan [1964] p. v[8]). Seven verses are cited, introduced by the phrase '*tathā ca sam-ācaṣṭa bhaṭṭajayantaḥ pallave*' (p. 64.1), six verses by '*tad api cātra plavate yad ajalpe jayantena pallave*' (p. 302. 13), and one verse by '*tad uktaṃ bhaṭṭajayantenāpi pallave*' (p. 780.7-8). Raghavan [1964] assumes that it is a moderate-sized metrical gloss on Gautama, and seems to understand '*Pallava*' as an abbreviation of '*Nyāyapallava*'.

The authorship of *NKali* is a subject of dispute, to be discussed in the following section of this paper.

Raghavan [1964] briefly deals with the order in which Jayanta wrote his works. According to him, it is : 1. *vṛtti* on *Aṣṭādhyāyī*, 2. *NKali*, 3. *(Nyāya)pallava*, 4. *NM*, and 5. *ĀgamḌ*. There seem to be good reasons to consider the *vṛtti* as his first work and to put *NM* before *ĀgamḌ*. But he does not give a reason for the sequence 2-3-4.

In conformity with Frauwallner [1936], Gupta [1963] thinks of several instances of the '*śāstrāntara*' in *NM* as a reference to another book of Jayanta which is lost (p. 16).[9] In the present writer's opinion, they refer not to another work, but to a 'System' other than the Nyāya: the Mīmāṃsā system in particular, and the system of Pāṇini's grammar in one instance.[10]

It seems that practically no advance in research has been made since the early 1960s. Potter [1977] gives a fairly good account of Jayanta's writings, largely based on Gupta [1963]. It also reports (p. 342) that P.V. Kane credits Jayanta with the authorship of several lost works on dharma,[11] but regrettably lacks reference to the 'Pallava' and the problem of '*śāstrāntara*'.

Matilal [1977] may be good for a beginner as it is easy to read and presents an interesting picture of Jayanta. But it is even less informative in regard to his writings.

In short the following five questions still remain to be settled.

(1) Is *NKali* an authentic work of Jayanta, or a later compilation?
(2) What sort of book is the *Pallava* that is quoted in *SyādVR*? Is it different from *NM*?[12]
(3) The question of '*śāstrāntara*' remains.[13]
(4) Can the works on Dharmaśāstra mentioned by Kane really be

attributed to the same Jayanta?
(5) The sequence of his writings.

Let us now devote the rest of this paper to the first question.

THE AUTHORSHIP OF THE *NYĀYAKALIKĀ*

NKali begins with an opening benedictory verse (*maṅgala*) dedicated to Śiva and then quotes the *Nyāyasūtra* I.1.1, which declares that the true knowledge of sixteen 'categories' (*padārtha*) will lead to the attainment of liberation. In the rest of the book each of them is defined, divided and briefly explained. Finally, *NKali* ends with these words:

ity etad + + + + +
ṣodaśapadārthatattvaṃ bālavyutpattaye/
ajātarasaniṣyandam anabhivyaktasaurabham/
nyāyasya kalikāmātraṃ jayantaḥ paryadīdṛśat//
(It is not clear what the series of the symbols '+' stands for.)

Steinkellner [1961] says, 'the published Nyāyakalikā is not a work of Jayanta, but a later compilation out of sentences of Jayanta', and adds that he depends on V. Raghavan for this assertion. But we do not find any such view in Raghavan [1964], who seems to take it for granted that *NKali* was written by Jayanta himself. How do we learn, then, what grounds were intended for denying the attribution of *NKali* to Jayanta?

It is only to Gupta [1963] that we could turn in this connection. He says:

> E. Steinkellner behauptet unter Berufung auf V. Raghavan, daβ die Nyāyakalikā eine später verfaβte Kompilation von Jayantasätzen sei (Siehe 'Die Literatur des älteren Nyāya' WZKSO, Bd.V, 1961, S.159,4). Wollte man aber aufgrund der zahlreichen wörtlichen oder sinngemäβen Entsprechungen die Nyāyakalikā als 'eine späte Kompilation von Jayantasätzen' betrachten, so wäre man gleichermaβen berechtigt, auch daran zu zweifeln, daβ das Āgamaḍambara von Jayanta verfaβt sei, was aber wohl doch zu weit ginge. Zudem läβt sich bei einer genauen Kenntnis der Jayantatexte beobachten, daβ er häufig eigene Formulierungen wörtlich oder sinngemäβ wieder-aufgreift. Auβerdem spricht auch folgende Tatsache dafür, daβ das Buch von Jayanta selbst abgefaβt wurde. Vādideva Sūri, der in seinem Buch 'Syādvādaratnākara' oft seitenlang Jayanta zitiert, führt hierbei auch solche Sätze an, die nicht in der Nyāyamañjari, wohl

aber in der Nyāyakalikā zu finden sind, z.B. ....(p. 16, fn. 32)

It is evident from this passage that in Gupta's understanding, the existence of many verbal or semantic parallels between *NM* and *NKali* provided the reason for denying Jayanta's authorship of *NKali*. Having this in mind, Gupta set out the following counter-arguments:

(1) If the very existence of many parallels in *NKali* with *NM* meant the later compilation of it, the same argument could be applied in the case of *ĀgamḌ* which has common verses with *NM*.[14] Thus, you would also be justified in casting doubt on Jayanta's authorship of the drama. But that would be going too far.
(2) A closer study of Jayanta's writings reveals that he frequently repeats his own expressions verbally or semantically. (Therefore, it is quite possible for him to use the same or similar phrases in *NM* and *NKali*.)
(3) Vādideva Sūri often quotes from Jayanta over many pages in his *SyādVR*,[15] and in some of these cases one comes across those sentences which occur not in *NM* but in *NKali* only. This fact speaks for Jayanta's authorship of *NKali*.

But one can counter again the first and second arguments by saying that they are also not strong enough to establish the authenticity of *NKali* as Jayanta's treatise. They only lead one to the conclusion that it may or may not be by Jayanta.

On the other hand, we must carefully examine the third argument before we can evaluate it. Gupta simply shows the number of each corresponding page and line of *SyādVR* and *NKali* where one finds common phrases or sentences.

First, there are five instances in *SyādVR* in which the editor identified quotations from *NM*. Four of them are introduced by a phrase which explicitly states that Jayanta said so: '*uktaṃ caitad ... jayantenāpi*' (p. 593.3-4), '*tathā ca ... agādi jayantena*' (p. 976.19), '*yat tu jayanto jagāda*' (p. 1115.1-2), and '*yac coktam anenaiva (=jayantenaiva)*' (p. 1115.7). The other is preceded by the words '*tad uktam*' (p. 597.1).

We have already noted three instances of quotation from the '*Pallava*' of Jayanta in *SyādVR*, though the editor of the text understood the 'Pallava' to be another name of *NM*.[16]

The passages that Gupta adduces as implicit evidence for Jayanta's authorship of *NKali* belong to the context (*SyādVR*, pp. 970.20-975.17), the purpose of which is to present the Naiyāyikas' concepts of the sixteen categories beforehand in order to criticize them. Below we will survey an agreement and disagreement of this context of *SyādVR* with *NKali* and *NM* concerning description of each category.

The definition of each of the first three categories, *pramāṇa*,[17] *prameya*,[18] and *saṃśaya*,[19] is nearly the same as that of *NM* and is quite different from that of *NKali*. On the other hand, corresponding *Nyāyasūtras* are cited for enumeration of the twelvefold *prameya* as well as for the definitions of the fifth and eleventh *prameyas*, whereas there is a marked agreement on the definitions of some of the other *prameyas* between *SyādVR* and *NKali*.[20] It may be added in this connection that *SyādVR* contains a relatively detailed reference to the difference in explanation of the *saṃśaya* between the '*bhāṣyakāra*' and the '*vārttikakāra*' (pp. 912.17-913.17).

Two definitions are offered of *prayojana*.[21] The first is exactly the same as the one in *NM*. The other one is nothing but *NS* I.1.24. The description of *dṛṣṭānta* contains *NS* I.1.25 which defines it, and an extract from the *Nyāyabhāṣya* on the sūtra. Moreover, two other definitions or explanations of the category are given.[22] They show partial similarity to *NM* and *NKali* respectively.

As for *siddhānta* (p. 973.2-17), it is defined exactly as in *NM*,[23] whereas six lines of explanation (p. 973.9-12; 15-17) completely agree with relevant portions of *NKali* (p.9.8-14). It may be worth noting that *NS* I.1.28 quoted there shows a reading peculiar to the sūtra transmitted in *NM* and nowhere else.[24]

With regard to *avayava*,[25] *tarka*[26] and *nirṇaya*,[27] there is a predominant verbal agreement with *NKali*, except for the *NS* I.1.32 which enumerates five divisions of *avayavas* and the definition of '*avayava*' which is substantially the same as *NM*. The definitons of *vāda*, *jalpa* and *vitaṇḍā*,[28] on the other hand, show almost complete agreement not with *NKali*, but with *NM*.

The description of *hetvābhāsa*,[29] again, presents striking similarities to *NKali* (p. 14.5-10, 18-20, 24-25; p. 15.14-17; pp. 15.21-16.1), though the first sentence also occurs in *NM*. The definition of *chala* (p. 975.9) agrees with that of *NM*,[30] but the example (p. 975.10-12) is rather similar to that of *NKali* (p. 16.11-13).

With regard to *jāti*, however, *SyādVR*[31] has very little in common with *NKali* or *NM*. The last category *nigrahasthāna* is defined in *SyādVR* in just the same words as in *NM*.[32]

Thus, the relevant passages of *SyādVR* show an outstanding correspondence with *NM* and *NKali*. Judging from this fact, it is highly probable that both books were sources for the author of

SyādVR in this passage; and if it is the case, it will suggest that the two texts have a close relationship of some kind, perhaps even common authorship. But this is not certain.

On the other hand, it may be important to note that none of those corresponding portions in *SyādVR* give any indications of quotation from Jayanta such as an introductory phrase 'as is said by Jayanta'. Nevertheless, it does not preclude the possibility that they are citations from Jayanta, because the absence of indications of quotation can be explained by too general a character of the descriptions of categories to treat as quotations from any particular source.

In short, Gupta [1963] is very important in that it draws our attention to the problem of authorship of *NKali* and also to the existence of many parallel passages between *SyādVR* and *NKali*.[33] But his arguments for Jayanta's authorship of *NKali* are far from conclusive. They invite new questions instead.

PURSUIT OF SOLUTION

Can we now give a definite answer to our question? In the present circumstances that may be difficult, but I think it is possible for us to take a further step by preparing a foundation for a future decision. My humble contribution here would be to supply, or suggest paying attention to, the following information and consideration.

1. *NM* and *NKali* share exactly the same benedictory *śloka*.[34] Is that evidence for or against the common authorship of the two texts? Before we can offer a decisive answer, we must investigate other relevant matters. Is it possible that the same author uses the same *maṅgala* verse for two different works, or can it mean that a different writer borrows the benedictory verse from *NM* in order to make *NKali* look like a book of Jayanta? Moreover, to what extent should we take into account the possibility of a different authorship for a *maṅgala* verse and the text that follows?

Thus the situation is not very simple. At any rate, if *NKali* is his true work, I don't think it very probable for Jayanta himself to put the same *maṅgala* at the head of his two different books because it would go against the poet in him.

2. The title '*Nyāyakalikā*' occurs in Guṇaratna's commentary on Haribhadra's *Ṣaḍdarśanasamuccaya*[35]:

eṣāṃ (* =*naiyāyikānāṃ*) *tarkagranthā nyāyasūtrabhāṣyanyāya-*

vārttikatātparyaṭīkātātparyapariśuddhinyāyālaṃkāravṛttayaḥ krameṇākṣapādavātsyāyanodyotakaravācaspatiśrīudayanaśrī-kaṇṭhābhayatilakopādhyāyaviracitāḥ 54000 *pramitāḥ* (BI ed. omits: *pramitāḥ*)/ *bhāsarvajñapraṇīte nyāyasāre 'ṣṭādaśa ṭīkāḥ, tāsu mukhyā ṭīkā nyāyabhūṣaṇākhyā tenaiva racitā* (BI ed. omits: *tenaiva racitā*) *nyāyakalikā jayantaracitā/ nyāyakusumāñjali-tarkaś ca/* (*ṢDSamuc*, p. 138.4-7; the present writer's additional remarks are enclosed in parentheses.)

Formerly some scholars such as Vidyābhūṣaṇa read the '*nyāya-kalikā jayantaracitā*' as one of the 'eighteen commentaries on *Nyāya-sāra*' (*nyāyasāre 'astādaśa ṭīkāḥ*), asserting that Jayanta is posterior to Bhāsarvajña.[36] But later it turned out that *NKali* is not a commentary on *Nyāyasāra* but an independent small treatise of Nyāya system, insofar as the printed *NKali* is concerned. In addition, it would be syntactically more natural to interpret the '*nyāyakalikā*' as the beginning of a new sentence.[37]

Moreover, the former explanation is contradicted by Prof. Slaje's decision in favour of Jayanta's precedence to Bhāsarvajña on the basis of his comparative analysis of the contents of discussion of *NM* and *Nyāyabhūṣaṇa* concerning four selected topics. He has clearly shown that Jayanta's arguments represent former stages than those of Bhāsarvajña in those contexts.[38]

Furthermore, the following passage in Rājaśekhara's *Ṣaḍdarś-anasamuccaya* is also favorable to the latter interpretation:

jayantācāryaracito nyāyatarko 'tidustaraḥ/
anyas tūdayanācāryo granthaprāsādasūtrabhṛt//
bhāsarvajño nyāyasāratarkasūtravidhāyakaḥ/
nyāyasārābhidhe tarke ṭīkā aṣṭādaśa sphuṭāḥ//
nyāyabhūṣaṇanāmnī tu ṭīkā tāsu prasiddhibhāk/
(*ṢDSamuc-Rj*, p. 10.3-7)

The '*jayantācāryaracito nyāyatarko*' evidently corresponds to '*nyāyakalikā jayantaracitā*' in the former text. The '*nyāyatarka*' in the latter case is mentioned as an independent book. Therefore, it might safely be said that the same is the case with the '*nyāyakalikā jayantaracitā*'.

But it is rather improbable that such a short work as the printed *NKali* is mentioned in a doxography, no matter how often Jayanta is quoted by Jaina scholars of later periods.[39] Accordingly, the '*jayantācāryaracito nyāyatarko*' is most probably the *NM*. What about the '*nyāyakalikā jayantaracitā*' then?

If it referred to the printed *NKali*, it would make a strong evidence for Jayanta's authorship of *NKali*, but then one would have to explain why Guṇaratna mentioned such a small book instead of the magnum opus. On the other hand, if it was originally meant to refer to a different work by Jayanta, or rather *NM*, and if the wording became somehow altered in a course of time, it may provide no evidence for or against.

The situation is again not very simple.

3. The assertion by Gupta [1963] that *NKali* is not Jayanta's work but a later compilation of his sentences, is based on *NKali*'s similarity to the relevant parts of *NM*. A closer look will reveal, however, that the similarity is not very great. For instance, when we compare *NKali*'s definitions and short explanations of the sixteen Nyāya categories with those of *NM* in the passage that shows a remarkable correspondence to *SyādVR* (*NM*, I, pp. 17-18), complete agreement occurs only in the definition of *hetvābhāsa*,[40] and considerable similarities show themselves with *tarka*, *chala* and *jāti*.[41] But with regard to the other twelve categories, divergence is much more prominent than agreement and sometimes there is even a total difference in expression.[42] Consequently one must reexamine the very basis for this assertion.

Likewise we need to cast a critical eye on Gupta's observation that Jayanta frequently repeats his own expressions verbally or semantically. Apart from semantic repetition, I do not think that he would just repeat the same expressions very often. It is true that *ĀgamḌ* shares four and a quarter verses with *NM*, but as far as I can see, when in *NM* he refers to what he has already stated, he usually changes his expressions. As a poet, he does not seem to like the bare repetition.

In other words, in case one should find too great a similarity in expression, it would constitute proof against Jayanta's authorship of *NKali*. Otherwise we will obtain no positive evidence for or against it. But in any case we would still have to make a more careful comparison between *NKali* and *NM* as a whole in order to determine the true extent of parallelism between the two.

4. In spite of all this, one will incline, perhaps with good reason, toward affirmation of his authorship of *NKali*, when one notes this description of Jayanta by Raghavan:

> The imagery of the tree, its foliage, buds and flowers is a favourite of Jayanta; not only has he called his three Nyāya

works after the bud, the sprout and the bunch of flowers, *kalikā pallava* and *mañjarī*, but the whole Nyāya Śāstra is described by him as a mighty fruit-laden tree whose expanse is difficult to comprehend in full ... (Raghavan [1964] p. viii, n. 1)

For Jayanta's description of the whole Nyāya Śāstra as a giant tree, one may refer to the introductory part of *NM* (Vol. I, p. 3. 11-12):

akṣapādapraṇīto hi vitato nyāyapādapaḥ/
sāndrāmṛtarasasyandaphalasandarbhanirbharaḥ//

Am I the only person who obtains the impression that this verse is probably composed by the same writer of the last verse of *NKali* ('*ajātarasaniṣyandam* ...', quoted above,? Or again, should we take into account the possibility of a rather elaborate camouflage by another writer who tried to make it look like a Jayanta's writing?

At any rate, if it is true that Jayanta wrote all three books, 'The bud of Nyāya', 'The sprout of Nyāya', and 'The bunch of flowers of Nyāya', it may be natural to suppose that he struck on and devised, to a certain extent, the idea of this trilogy fairly early in life. But the idea of trilogy itself presupposes Jayanta's authorship of *NKali*. Can we not escape the vicious circle, then?

Here I would like to mention again the result of my study of the '*Pallava*' which will be published in a separate article in the near future. On the testimony of *SyādVR*, I concluded in the article[43] that Jayanta must have written another book on Nyāya system named [*Nyāya-*]*pallava*' in addition to *NM*. If this is correct, it will undoubtedly strengthen the plausibility of the idea of a trilogy.

CONCLUSION

Although we do not yet have sufficient evidence to form a final decision about the authorship of *NKali*, we may safely conclude for the time being as follows. There is a good probability that Jayanta wrote the *NKali* as one of his trilogy of Nyāya system. The author of *SyādVR* knew the trilogy from which he freely quoted. But the opening benedictory verse in the printed text of *NKali* was perhaps composed by another person.

TEXTS AND ABBREVIATIONS

ĀgamḌ: *Āgamaḍambara, otherwise called Ṣaṇmatanāṭaka of Jay-anta Bhaṭṭa*, ed.V.Raghavan and A. Thakur, Mithila Institute Series, Ancient text No.7, Darbhanga, 1964.

Nkali: *Nyāyakalikā* of Jayantabhaṭṭa, ed. Ganganatha Jha, The Princess of Wales Sarasvati Bhavana Texts 17, Varanasi, 1925.

NM: *Nyāyamañjarī* of Jayantabhaṭṭa, 2 Vols, ed. K.S. Varada-charya, Mysore, 1969, 1983.

NM(KSS) : *Nyāyamañjarī* of Jayantabhaṭṭa, ed. by Sūrya Nārāyaṇa Śukla and Madhvācārya, Kashi Sanskrit Series 106, 2nd. ed., Varanasi, 1971.

NS: *Nyāyasūtra*.

NS(Ruben): *Die Nyāyasūtra's*. Text, Übers., Erl., und Glossar, von W. Ruben, Abhandlungen für die Kunde des Morgenlandes 18,2, Leipzig, 1928.

ṢDSamuc: *Ṣaḍdarśanasamuccaya* of Haribhadra Sūri, with the commentaries *Tarkarahasyadīpikā* of Guṇaratnasūri and *Laghuvṛtti* of Somatilaka Sūri and an Avacūrṇi, ed. by M.K. Jain, Jñānapīṭha Mūrtidevī Granthamālā: Sanskrit Grantha 36, Ahmedabad, 1969.

ṢDSamuc(BI): *Ṣaḍdarśanasamuccaya* of Haribhadra Sūri, with Guṇa-ratna's commentary *Tarkarahasyadīpikā*, ed. L. Suali, Bibliotheca Indica 167, reprint, Calcutta, 1986.

ṢDSamuc-Rj: *Ṣaḍdarśanasamuccaya* of Rājaśekhara, ed. Haragovinda Dasa and Becara Dāsa, Yaśovijaya Jaina Granthamālā 17, Varanasi,1911/12 (Vīrasaṃvat 2438).

SyādVR: *Syādvādaratnākara* of Vādideva Sūri, 2 Vols., reprint, Delhi, 1988.

NOTES

* I express my deepest gratitude to Prof. A. Wezler for his kindness in reading through the draft of this article and giving me various valuable suggestions. I strongly feel that his constant guidance and encouragement constitute the very essence of the present study. My special thanks also go to Prof. K. Preisendanz. I owe it to her that I was able to revise the earlier paper in several areas. She is for me the Mount Everest of Nyāyaśāstra standing high above, toward which my eyes are drawn in admiration.

1 The most important contribution toward settling Jayanta's date was made by P. Hacker in 'Jayantabhaṭṭa und Vācaspatimiśra, ihre Zeit und ihre Bedeutung für die Chronologie des Vedānta', *Beiträge zur indischen Philologie und Altertumskunde, Walter Schübring zum 70. Geburtstag*, Hamburg, 1951, pp. 160-9 (also in: *Kleine Schriften*, Wiesbaden 1978, pp.110-19). With respect to the chronological order of the two philosophers, Prof. W. Slaje produced a very good survey of the

relevant previous studies in: 'Untersuchungen zur Chronologie einiger Nyāya Philosophen', *Studien zur Indologie und Iranistik*, 11/12 (1986), pp. 245-77.

2 The greater part of the present study was already published in my paper (in Japanese), 'Some Remarks on the Works of Jayanta Bhaṭṭa', *Hokkaido Journal of Indological and Buddhist Studies*, No. 11 (1996), pp. (1)-(20). But some revision and a slight enlargement are made in this paper besides minor changes in arrangement and presentation. Above all, one might note these three differences. First, I make a brief reference to two relevant studies I have done in the meantime, though I basically exclude them from the following survey of previous studies on Jayanta's works. See notes 8 and 10. Second, here I pay more attention to arriving at a conclusion, no matter how tentative it may be. Third, notes are enlarged by providing further information and showing much more Sanskrit texts.

3 Frauwallner ([1936] p. 270) adduces three instances, giving the page number according to the Vizianagram Sanskrit Series, no. 8, 1895. The corresponding pages of the Mysore edition are: *NM*, vol. I, p. 682.17, p. 690.11; vol. II, p. 69.2. B. Gupta ([1963] p. 16) evidently supports his view on the '*śāstrāntara*', but the present writer has a different opinion. See notes 9 and 10 below.

4 *NM*, vol. II, p. 718.5-6: *vādeṣv āptajayo jayanta iti yaḥ khyātas satām agraṇīḥ anvartho navavṛttikāra iti yaṃ śaṃsanti nāmnā budhāḥ/*. Abhinanda mentions his father Jayanta in the introduction to his *Kādambarīkathāsāra* (in *NM*(KSS), Bhūmikā, p. 5.24-26): *putraṃ kṛtajanānandaṃ sa (= Kāntaḥ) jayantam ajījanat/ vyaktā kavitvavaktṛtvaphalā yasya sarasvatī//10// vṛttikāra iti vyaktaṃ dvitīyaṃ nāma vibhrataḥ/*

5 *ĀgamḌ*, Act I, p. 2.22-23: *adya cātrabhavataḥ śaiśava eva vyākaraṇavivaraṇakaraṇād vṛttikāra iti prathitāparanāmno bhaṭṭajayantasya ...*; see Raghavan [1960].

6 Cf. A. Wezler, 'Zur Proklamation religiös-weltanschaulicher Toleranz bei der indischen Philosophen Jayantabhaṭṭa', *Saeculum*, XXVII, Heft 4, pp. 329-47 (esp. p. 340, n. 31).

7 *ĀgamḌ*, Act IV, pp. 88.19-89.4:

ata eva hi bālakaver avalokitasakalaśāstrasārasya/
sūktam idaṃ tattvavido bhraṣṭabhrānter jayantasya//53//
nānāvidhair āgamamārgabhedair ādiśyamānā bahavo 'bhyupāyāḥ/
ekatra te śreyasi saṃpatanti sindhau pravāhā iva jāhnavīyāḥ//54//

Thus the verse 54 is regarded as a good saying by Jayanta, and exactly the same one occurs in *NM*, vol. I, p. 640.20-21. Cf. Wezler, 'Zur Proklamation religiös-weltanschaulicher Toleranz bei der indischen Philosophen Jayanta', p. 340, n. 31.

8 For the details of '*Pallava*' fragments in *SyādVR*, Raghavan refers readers to his paper, 'Works and Authors cited in Śrīdeva's Syādvādaratnākara', *Journal of the Kalinga Historical Research Society* I, pp. 255-64. Since this article is not available to me, I am not sure whether the fragments he had traced are exactly the same as the three

instances that the editor of *SyādVR* marked with bold letters. But insofar as those three are concerned, all the fragments are in verse, though the source is named simply '*Pallava*' instead of '*Nyāyapallava*'.

9 He adds a fourth instance: *NM* (KSS), p. 45.10 = *NM*, vol. I, p. 129.2. Cf. Steinkellner [1961] p. 159.

10 For more details, see my paper (in Japanese): 'Does Jayanta Refer to His Own Work as "*śāstrāntara*" in the *Nyāyamañjarī*?', *Journal of Indian and Buddhist Studies*, XLVII, No. 2 (1999), pp. (42)-(48).

11 P. V. Kane, *History of Dharmaśāstra*, vol. I, pt. II, Poona, 1975 (rev. ed.), pp. 1180-81.

12 Although the editor of *SyādVR* understood the 'Pallava' to be another name for *NM*, I think it is almost certain that the *Pallava* is different from *NM*. For details, see my article (in Japanese): 'Fragments of Jayanta Bhaṭṭa in Some Jaina Philosophical Literature and the Identification of His *Pallava*', to be published in the Felicitation Volume for Prof. Junsho Kato on his Sixtieth Birthday (in press).

13 I discuss this in the paper mentioned in note 10.

14 They are identified in Raghavan [1964] pp. xxvi-xxvii.

15 The relevant page numbers of those quotations from Jayanta by Vādideva Sūri that have been identified by the editor of *SyādVR* are given above or below in the present paper. It should be added, though, that Gutpa's expression '(Vādideva Sūri) quotes from Jayanta over many pages' is a slight exaggeration.

16 *SyādVR*, p. 64, n. 1: *adhunā mudritāyāṃ nyāyamañjaryām idaṃ nopalabhyate/ nyāyamañjary eva pallavasaṃjñayā śrīvādidevasūribhiḥ saṃmanyate/*. Yet in my view the *Pallava* is different from *NM*. See note 12 above.

17 p. 970.22: *arthaparicchittisādhanaṃ pramāṇam*. Cf. *NM*, vol. I, p. 17.13: *arthaparicchittisādhanāni pratyakṣādīni pramāṇāni/*; *NKali*, p. 9-10: *pramīyate 'neneti pramāṇam/ pramīyata iti pramā pramitiḥ pratītiḥ upalabdhiḥ jñānaṃ janyate ity arthaḥ/*

18 p. 971.1: *tatparicchedyam ātmādi dvādaśavidhaṃ prameyam/*. Cf. *NM*, vol. I, p. 18.1: *tatparicchedyam ātmādi prameyam/*; *NKali*, p. 4.17: *pramāṇaviṣayo 'rthaḥ prameyam/*.

19 p. 971.15: *nānārthavimarśaḥ saṃśayaḥ/*. Cf. *NM*, vol. I, p. 18.2: *nānārthāvamarśaḥ saṃśayaḥ/*; *NKali*, p. 8.6-7: *viśeṣasmṛtihetor dharmasya grahaṇād viśeṣasmṛteś ca jāyamānaḥ kiṃsvit iti vimarśaḥ saṃśayaḥ/*.

20 For *pravṛtti*, see *SyādVR*, p. 971.7: *vāṅmanaḥkāyavyāpāraḥ subhāśubhaphalapravṛttir*(read:*-phalaḥ pra-*)*ity ucyate*; *NKali*, p. 7.9-10: *vanmanaḥkāyavyāpāraḥ śubhāśubhaphalā* (*-phalaḥ*?) *pravṛttir ity ucyate/*. For *doṣa*, see *SyādVR*, p. 971.8: *puruṣasya karmasu pravartayitāro rāgadveṣamohā doṣāḥ/*; *NKali*, p. 7.11-12: *puruṣasya karmasu pravartayitāro rāgadveṣamohāḥ* (*-mohā doṣāḥ*?). For *pretyabhāva*, see *SyādVR*, p. 971. 8-9: *de hendriyādisaṃghāta sya saṃghātāntaragrahaṇaṃ pretyabhāvaḥ/*; *NKali*, p. 7.14-15: *dehendriyādisaṃghātasya prāktanasya tyāge na saṅghātāntaragrahaṇaṃ pretya-bhāvaḥ/*

21 p. 972.17-20: *hitāhitaprāptiparihārau tatsādhanaṃ ca prayojanam* (=*NM*, vol. I, p. 18.3), '*yam artham adhikṛtya pravartate tat*

prayojanam' (*NS* 1.1.24). *NKali*, p. 8.19: *yam artham adhikṛtya puruṣah pravartate tat prayojanam/*.

22 pp. 972.20-973.2: *pratibandhāvaraṇasthānaṃ dṛṣṭāntaḥ/ .../ teṣāṃ sādhyasādhanādhikaraṇatvena tadrahitatvena vā buddhisāmya-viṣayo 'rtho dṛṣṭāntaḥ/*. Cf. *NM*, vol. I, p. 18.4: *hetoḥ pratibandhāvadhāraṇaṃ dṛṣṭāntaḥ/*; *NKali*, p. 8.22-24: *vādiprativādinoḥ sādhyasādhanadharmādhikaraṇatvena tadrahitatvena vā prasiddho 'rtho dṛṣṭāntaḥ/ sa ca nyāyasya pratibandhagrahaṇasthānam iti pṛthag upadiśyate/*.

23 *SyādVR*, p. 973.2-3 = *NM*, vol. I, p. 18.5: *pramāṇato 'bhyupagamyamānaḥ sāmānyaviśeṣavān arthaḥ siddhāntaḥ/*.

24 *NS* 1.1.28 as transmitted in *NM* (vol. II, p. 545.15) and *SyādVR* (p. 973.4) reads: *sarvatantrāviruddhaḥ svatantre* (for '*tantre*') *'dhikṛto 'rthaḥ sarvatantrasiddhāntaḥ*. See *NS*(Ruben), p. 10.

25 pp. 973.17-974.10: *parārthānumānavākyaikadeśabhūtā avayavāḥ/ tathā ca sūtram .../ tatra sādhyadharmaviśiṣṭasya dharmiṇo nirdeśaḥ pratijñā/ yathānityaḥ śabda iti/ liṅgavacanaṃ hetuḥ/ yathā kṛtakatvād iti/ dṛṣṭāntavacanam udāharaṇam/ .../ sādharmyavaidharmyodāharaṇānusāreṇa tatheti na tatheti vā sādhyadharmiṇi hetor upasaṃhāra upanayaḥ/.../ hetvapadeśena punaḥ sādhyadharmopasaṃharaṇaṃ nigamanam/ .../*. Cf. *NM*. vol.I, p. 18.6: *parārthānumānaikadeśabhūtāḥ pratijñādayo 'vayavāḥ/*; *NKali*, pp. 9.16-13.4: *sādhanīyasyārthasya yāvatā vākyena parasmai pratipādanaṃ kriyate tasya pañca bhāgāḥ pratijñādayo 'vayavāḥ/ pratijñā hetur udāharaṇam upanayo nigamanam iti/ tatra sādhyadharmaviśiṣṭasya dharmiṇo nirdeśaḥ pratijñā/ .../ liṅgavacanaṃ hetuḥ/ .../ .../ dṛṣṭāntavacanam udāharaṇam/ .../ sādharmyavaidharmyodāharaṇānusāreṇa tatheti na tatheti vā sādhyadharmiṇi hetor upasaṃhāra upanayaḥ/ .../ hetvapadeśena punaḥ sādharmyopasaṃharaṇān(sic.) nigamanam/ .../*.

26 p. 974.10-7: *avijñātatattve dharmiṇy ekatarapakṣānukūlārthadarśanena tasmin sambhāvanāpratyaya ūhas tarkaḥ/ yathā .../ puruṣaniścayahetūnāṃ ca śiraḥpāṇyādiviśeṣāṇām apratibhāsāt/*. Cf. *NM*, vol. I, p. 18. 7-8: *sandigdhe 'rthe 'nyatarapakṣānukūlakāraṇadarśa-nāt tasmin sambhāvanāpratyayas tarkaḥ/*; *NKali*, p. 13.5-12: *avijñātatattve dharmiṇi ekatarapakṣānukūlārthadarśanena tasmin sambhāvanāpratyayarūpa ūhas tarka ucyate/ yathā .../ puruṣaniścaya-hetūnāṃ ca śiraḥpāṇyādiviśeṣāṇām apratibhāsāt/*.

27 p. 974.17: *pakṣapratipakṣaviṣayasādhanopalambhaparīkṣayā tadanyatarapakṣāvadhāraṇaṃ nirṇayaḥ/*. Cf. *NM*, vol. I, p. 18.9: *sādhanopalambhajanmā tattvāvabodho nirṇayaḥ/*; *NKali*, p. 13.15-6: *pakṣapratipakṣaviṣayasādhanopālambhaparīkṣayā tadanyatarapakṣāvadhāraṇaṃ nirṇayaḥ/*.

28 p. 974.18-9: *vītarāgakathā vastunirṇayaphalā/ vādo* (read:*-phalā vādaḥ/*) *vijigīṣukathā puruṣaśaktiparīkṣaṇaphalā jalpaḥ/ jalpaviśeṣo vitaṇḍā/*. Cf. *NM*, vol. I, p. 18.10-12: *vītarāgakathā vastunirṇayaphalā vādaḥ/ vijigīṣukathā tu puruṣaśaktiparīkṣaṇaphalā jalpaḥ/ tadviśeṣo vitaṇḍā/*; *NKali*, p. 13.18-24: *vādo nāma vītarāgayoḥ pakṣapratipakṣaparigrahapūrvakaḥ pramāṇatarkapūrvakasādhanopālambhaprayo-*

ge kriyamāṇe ekapakṣanirṇayāvasāno vākyasamūhaḥ/ .../ sa eva pakṣapratipakṣaparigraho vijigīṣayā prayuktaḥ chalajātinigrahasthānaprayogabahulo jalpaḥ/ svapakṣasādhanopanyāsahīno jalpa eva vitaṇḍā bhavati/.

29 pp. 974.19-975.9: *ahetavo hetuvad ābhāsamānā hetvābhāsāḥ/ hetoḥ pañcalakṣaṇāni pakṣadharmatvādīni/ teṣām ekaikāpāye pañca hetvābhāsā bhavanty asiddhaviruddhānaikāntikakālātyayāpadiṣṭaprakaraṇasamāḥ/ tatra pakṣadharmatvaṃ yasya nāsti so 'siddhaḥ/ .../ sapakṣe sattvaṃ yasya nāsti vipakṣe cāsti sa sādhyaviparyayasādhanād viruddhaḥ/ .../ vipakṣād aparicyutaḥ pakṣasapakṣayor vartamāno hetuḥ savyabhicāritvād anaikāntikaḥ/ .../ pratyakṣāgamaviruddhaḥ kālātyayāpadiṣṭaḥ/ .../ viśeṣāgrahaṇāt prakaraṇe pakṣe saṃśayo bhavati — nityaḥ śabdo 'nityo veti/ tad eva viśeṣāgrahaṇaṃ bhrāntyā hetutvena prayujyamānaṃ prakaraṇasamo hetvābhāso bhavati/ .../.* Cf. *NM*, vol. I, p. 18.13: *ahetavo hetuvad ābhāsamānāḥ hetvābhāsāḥ/*; *NKali*, pp. 14.5-16.1: *ahetavo hetuvad avabhāsamānāḥ hetvābhāsāḥ/ hetoḥ pañca lakṣaṇāni pakṣadharmatvādīni uktāni/ teṣām ekaikāpāye pañca hetvābhāsā bhavanti/ asiddhaviruddhānaikāntikakālātyayāpadiṣṭaprakaraṇasamāḥ/ tatra pakṣadharmatvaṃ yasya nāsti so 'siddhaḥ/ .../ sapakṣe sattvaṃ yasya nāsti vipakṣe vṛttir asti sa sādhyaviparyayasādhanatvād viruddho bhavati/ .../ vipakṣād aparicyutaḥ pakṣasapakṣayor vartamāno hetuḥ savyabhicāritvād anaikāntiko bhavati/ .../ pratyakṣāgāmaviruddhaḥ kālātyayāpadiṣṭaḥ/ .../ viśeṣāgrahaṇāt prakaraṇe pakṣe saṃśayo bhavati—nityaḥ śabdo 'nityaḥ śabdo veti/ tad eva viśeṣāgrahaṇaṃ bhrāntyā hetutvena prayojyamānaṃ prakaraṇasamo hetvābhāso bhavati/ .../.*

30 *SyādVR*, p. 975.9 = *NM*, vol. I, p. 18.14: *arthavikalpair vacanavighātaś chalam/.* Cf. *NKali*, p. 16.8-9: *parasya vadato 'rthavikalpopapādanena vacanavighātaḥ chalam/.*

31 p. 975.12-14: *vādyabhipretavastupratiṣedhārthasamartho jāyamāno hetupratibimbanaprāyaḥ prasaṃgo jātiḥ/ .../.* Cf. *NM*, vol. I, p. 18.15: *hetupratibimbanaprāyaṃ pratyavasthānaṃ jātiḥ/*; *NKali*, p. 17.1-2: *samyag hetau hetvābhāse vā prayukte jhaṭiti taddoṣatattvāpratibhāse tu pratibimbanaprāyaṃ kim api pratyavasthānaṃ jātir ity ucyate/.*

32 *SyādVR*, p. 975.14-15 = *NM*, vol. I, p. 18.16: *satyavastvapratibhāso viparītapratibhāsaś ca nigrahasthānam/.* Cf. *NKali*, p. 21.22: *vipratipattir apratipattiś ca nigrahasthānam* (=*NS* 1.2.19).

33 It may be true that Wright rightly criticizes Gutpa [1963] on some points, but on the whole he is a little too harsh. Gupta [1963] deserves higher evaluation and more attention even today. Review by J. C. Wright, *Bulletin of the School of Oriental and African Studies*, 27 (1964), p. 638.

34 *NM*, vol. I, p. 1.= *NKali*, p. 1: *namaḥ śāśvatikānandajñānaiśvaryamayātmane/ saṅkalpasaphalabrahmastambhārambhāya śambhave//* (The printed text of *NKali* reads '*saṅkalpasakalabrahma-*', but it should be emended as given above). The reading '*saphala*' is also attested by Cakradhara. *Nyāyamañjarīgranthibhaṅga* (L. D. Series 35, Ahmedabad 1972), pp. 1-2. Kaviraj already pointed out that the two texts share the

same opening benedictory verse. G. Kaviraj, *The History and Bibliography of Nyāya-Vaiśeṣika Literature*, The Princess of Wales Sarasvati Bhavana Studies (Reprint Series No. 2), Varanasi 1982 (repr.), p. 129, n. 103.

35 In my earlier paper I used only the edition of Bibliotheca Indica. I would like to express my gratitude to Prof. K. Preisendanz, Wien for her kind suggestion that one should check the other edition.

36 For instance, Vidyabhusana, *A History of Indian Logic (Ancient, Medieval and Modern Schools)*, Delhi 1971 (orig., Calcutta 1921), p. 371.

37 See Yogīndrānanda's preface ('*prāgbandha*') to the *Nyāyabhūṣaṇa* of Bhāsarvajña, ed. by himself, Varanasi 1968, pp. 13-14; Matilal [1977] p. 93. Cf. A. Thakur's introduction to the *Ratnakīrti-nibandhāvaliḥ (Buddhist Nyāya Works of Ratnakīrti)*, Tibetan Sanskrit Works Series III, 2nd rev. ed., Patna 1975, p. 18.

38 W. Slaje, 'Untersuchungen zur Chronologie einiger Nyāya-Philosophen'(see n. 1), p. 274.

39 It is interesting that Jayanta seems to have been 'favoured' almost exclusively by Jaina scholars in the sense that he is frequently quoted or referred to by them. On the other hand he is seldom quoted in later Nyāya literature as far as I know. In addition, Jayanta has never been reported to be quoted by Buddhists. For the problems of citations from Jayanta's works in Jaina philosophical literature, see my separate paper mentioned in note 12.

40 See note 29.

41 See notes 26, 30, 31.

42 For instance, compare the definitions of *pramāṇa, prameya, saṃśaya* or *nigrahasthāna*. See notes 17, 18, 19, 32.

43 See note 12.

8

Liberation in Early Navya-Nyāya*

TOSHIHIRO WADA

INTRODUCTION

The main concern of Navya-nyāya or 'New Logic', which begins in the eleventh century,[1] is epistemology as well as logic. It inherits its ontological framework from the Vaiśeṣika school[2] and fundamental theories in logic and epistemology from the classical or old (*prācīna*) Nyāya school and the Vaiśeṣika school. There is no significant difference in the concept of liberation (*mokṣa*, *mukti*) between the Navya-nyāya, and the Old Nyāya and Vaiśeṣika, and most scholars of these schools defined liberation in negative terms such as termination (*nivṛtti*) and absence (*abhāva*).[3] It is also a fact that Navya-nyāya developed technical terms such as 'delimitor' (*avacchedaka*) and 'describer' (*nirūpaka*) related to logic and analysis of relations and 'epistemic qualifier' (*prakāra*) and 'objectness' (*viṣayatā*) related to epistemology. Using these terms, Navya-nyāya scholars tried to formulate correct definitions of various philosophical concepts and satisfactory logical theories.

It is regrettable to some extent that they not pay more attention to liberation than philosophical or logical concepts and theories and that they did not use their technical terms to define the concept of liberation. However, for this task Navya-nyāya scholars such as Śaśadhara and Gaṅgeśa employ one technical term, i.e. *samānādhikaraṇa* (sharing a locus with). This term is not necessarily peculiar to Navya-nyāya, but the frequent use of it is a feature of the Navya-nyāya literature. Similarly we can find the Navya-nyāya terminology in the discussion of liberation. It would be meaningful to examine the concept of liberation in Navya-nyāya and to analyze its terminology in the discussion of liberation. I will focus on one of the early Navya-nyāya scholars, Śaśadhara (12 c. A.D.), and his work the *Nyāyasiddhāntadīpa* (*NSD*), and briefly refer to the consolidator[4] of this school, Gaṅgeśa (14 c.

A.D.) and his *Tattvacintāmaṇi (TC)*. I will also examine the connection between the definitions of liberation formulated by the two.

OLD NYĀYA-VAIŚEṢIKA AND NEW NYĀYA

We can say that the frequent use of relation is a feature of the Navya-nyāya literature, and as a result, this school creates new technical terms, some of which have been mentioned above, to identify relation. First, let us see how Navya-nyāya frequently uses relation to define various concepts. An example of this is the definition of substance. It is possible to infer the definition in the period of classical Nyāya-Vaiśeṣika from the statement about the properties of substances in the *Padārthadharmasaṃgraha* of Praśastapāda (550-600 A.D.), who enumerates five characteristics of substance as follows: (1) the relation with substanceness (*dravyatva*), (2) producing effect in itself, (3) possessing qualities, (4) being not destroyed by its cause and effect, and (5) possessing particulars (*viśeṣa*).[5] According to Śrīdhara (10 c. A.D.) and Udayana (11 c. A.D.), the second characteristic means that a substance is an inherent cause (*samavāyikāraṇa*) of qualities (*guṇa*) and actions (*karman*) possessed by itself.[6] Hence, this characteristic presupposes the existence of quality and action. Since, according to Śrīdhara, the fourth characteristic helps differentiate sound (*śabda*) and action from substances,[7] it cannot be a substantive definition. Thus, among the five characteristics provided by Praśastapāda, all except the fourth seem to be the substantive definitions[8] of substance. In any case, in these four characteristics, substance is defined with the help of the concept expressed in absolute general terms[9] such as 'substanceness', 'quality', 'action', and 'particular'.

Udayana, on the other hand, formulated four definitions of substance in the *Lakṣaṇāvalī*, and one of them consists only of relative general terms: a substance is an entity (*x*) that possesses an inhering [entity (*y*)] which has [an entity] for inhering [in itself (*y*)] (*samavetasamavetasamavetam*).[10] Here the definition consists of only the relative general term 'inhering' (*samaveta*).[11] Naturally Udayana provides other definitions which include absolute general terms, but his above-mentioned definition clearly reveals the characteristics of the Navya-nyāya method of description. Thus, Navya-nyāya gradually developed a tendency to use terms expressive of relation in the analysis of various concepts.

Next we will see how Navya-nyāya employs technical terms such as 'delimitor' and 'describer' to analyze relation. Let us take up the statement 'pot-maker is the cause of pot' (*kumbhakāraḥ kumbhasya kāraṇam*). Since this statement does not include a definite or indefinite particle to 'pot-maker' (*kumbhakāra*) and 'pot' (*kumbha*), we do not know the quantity of these two terms. As a result, no one can determine in which case this statement is valid. In other words, the statement does not necessarily refer to a cause and effect relationship (*kārya-kāraṇabhāva*) between some pot-maker(s) and some pot(s), some pot-makers and all pots, all pot-makers and some pots, or all pot-makers and all pots.

The present section is not intended to provide a detailed exposition of delimitor and describer,[12] and so I will confine my remarks to their fundamental function. A delimitor for 'pot-maker' indicates its quantity, and a delimitor for 'pot' indicates the quantity of 'pot'. If 'pot-maker' in the above statement means all pot-makers, Navya-nyāya regards pot-maker-ness (*kumbhakāratva*) residing in them as the delimitor of causeness (*kāraṇatā*) residing in them. In other words, pot-maker-ness is assumed to confine causeness to all pot-makers. If 'pot-maker' means a particular person, Navya-nyāya regards particular-pot-maker-ness (*tatkumbhakāratva*) residing in him as the delimitor of causeness residing in him.

Causeness in the present case is considered as the relation of 'pot' to 'pot-maker'.[13] The relation is a particular one and is different from the causeness between carpenters and the houses built by them. Otherwise, when a pot-maker is producing a pot, he would simultaneously build a house because he possesses the causeness to a house. Hence, causeness must differ in pot-makers and carpenters. To differentiate causeness in the two cases, Navya-nyāya specify it by means of the quantification of the relatum (i.e. 'pot-maker') by delimitor. If pot-maker-ness becomes the delimitor of causeness, all pot-makers will be relatum of the relation of causeness. To put it another way, Navya-nyāya identifies this relation as causeness which has all pot-makers for its relatum.

Now let us suppose that the statement means that all pot-makers are the cause of all pots and refrain from referring to the delimitor of effectness (*kāryatā*) residing in 'pot' in order to simplify our discussion. Then, the relation of causeness can be illustrated as that which has all pots, for its relatum. Navya-nyāya takes all pots, or another relatum of this relation, for the describing factor of the relation, and gives this relatum the designation of describer (*nirūpaka*). Thus, the relation will be called the causeness described by all pots (*sakalaghaṭanirūpita-kāraṇatā*).

Finally, the statement will be analyzed as the causeness delimited by pot-maker-ness and described by all pots (*sakalaghaṭanirūpita-kumbhakāratvāvacchinnakāraṇatā*).[14] This is the Navya-nyāya method of description of relation, and this method permeated other schools of philosophy, rhetoric, and so forth.

ŚAŚADHARA ON LIBERATION

The *Nyāyasiddhāntadīpa*[15] (*NSD*) of Śaśadhara shows the frequent use not only of relation but also of technical terms such as delimitor,[16] while the author does not seem to frequently employ describer.[17] In view of that frequent use, we can say that his Sanskrit text possesses the characteristic of the Navya-nyāya method of description. This text includes the Chapter on Liberation (*muktivāda*),[18] in which Śaśadhara criticizes the concept of liberation in other schools such as Mīmāṃsā, Sāṃkhya, and Nyāya, and arrives at his own conclusion. However, we will limit ourselves to a looking at Śaśadhara's analysis of the Nyāya concept of liberation and his conclusion.[19]

The View of the Opponent

Śaśadhara makes the opponent appear and begin his discussion of the definition formulated by the Nyāya school: the absolute termination of suffering (*atyantakī duḥkhanivṛtti*).[20] This definition is given by Udayana.[21] The opponent presents the alternative of the interpretation of termination (*nivṛtti*) in the definition: destruction (*dhvaṃsa*) or other varieties of absence (*abhāva*). If we take the first alternative, the termination of suffering means the destruction of suffering. Suffering, then, can be divided into two: produced and non-produced (i.e., coming in the future). The destruction of produced suffering cannot be achieved by effort (*yatna*), and hence people do not behave in order to obtain such destruction. This claim may not be readily intelligible. Effort is a kind of quality (*guṇa*) in the ontological framework of Vaiśeṣika, and it is determination in the mind (exactly speaking, in a soul [*ātman*]) to bring about action. On the other hand, desire (*icchā*), which is also a kind of quality, cannot directly bring about action, because we can imagine a case in which we want, for instance, to drink some water but do not or cannot drink for some reason. Thus, effort cannot directly destroy or overcome suffering, and so the claim of the opponent is logically true. However, it is tricky, because we can also say that suffering can be overcome by some action. While neglecting this possibility, Śaśadhara lays great emphasis on it in his answer to the opponent, which will be referred to in the latter part of the present section. If the termination of suffering means the destruction of non-produced suffering, no one can overcome suffering which has not yet come into being. Hence, whether suffering is a produced or non-produced phenomenon, the concept of the termination of suffering cannot hold good for the definition of liberation.

If we take the second alternative, the termination of suffering means the prior absence (*prāgabhāva*), constant absence (*atyantā-bhāva*), or mutual absence (*anyonyābhāva*) of suffering. The opponent alleges that this alternative does not hold true, because any absence in the above sense cannot be a human goal. We can infer the reason for this in the following manner. No one can produce prior and constant absence.[22] Mutual absence, on the contrary, can be produced. For example, when a potter makes a pot, he simultaneously produces the mutual absence of another pot (or the difference from another pot) in this pot. However, it would not be necessary to deliberately produce the mutual absence of suffering, since such an absence exists in any entity (including souls) other than suffering. From this it follows that everyone possesses such an absence at all times and that all people would be liberated from the time of their birth. Hence, if 'termination' in the definition means mutual absence, the termination of suffering cannot become a human goal (*puruṣārtha*). If 'termination' is interpreted as prior or constant absence, liberation which cannot be obtained by any person cannot constitute a human goal.

Next the opponent discusses how to interpret 'absolute' (*atyantikī*) in the definition. He denies the possibility of interpreting it as an occurrent not simultaneously with suffering which shares a locus with [the occurrent] (*samānādhikaraṇaduḥkhāsamānakālīna*). He says that this is because there is no proof for the existence of the termination of suffering which does not occur simultaneously with suffering that shares a locus with the termination. Here 'locus' stands for a soul (*ātman*). According to the opponent, even if the termination of some suffering occurs in a particular soul, another suffering can simultaneously spring in the *same* soul[23] in daily life.

The foregoing discussion presupposes the idea that liberation can be defined in negative terms. If liberation, on the contrary, is described by a positive term such as happiness (*sukha*), it will be a human goal.

Anticipating this, the opponent notes the possibility of interpreting liberation as a kind of happiness, but denies this possibility because he follows the traditional Nyāya-Vaiśeṣika view that happiness does not continue forever and thus invariably produces suffering.[24] In this sense, happiness cannot be a human goal, and so tradition cannot designate as liberation anything that is not a human goal.

The opponent anticipates a counterview: people aim at happiness occurrent simultaneously with 'liberation while living' (*jīvanmukti*), but ultimate liberation (*paramamukti*) will be achieved another way. The advocate of this view insists that whatever the definition of 'liberation' may be, liberation should be accompanied by happiness which can become a human goal. The opponent points out two defects in this view. Once people obtain happiness occurring with 'liberation while living', they will not pursue further liberation, or ultimate liberation, which may be in the form of the destruction of suffering. Furthermore, a person, or a soul, who has achieved 'liberation while living',[25] does not possess attachment (*rāga*) to anything and so does not pursue even happiness. This means that a person who has achieved 'liberation while living' does not pursue happiness. After thus objecting to this counterview, the opponent seeks the definition of ultimate liberation. He reports seven main definitions, all of which are formulated in terms of destruction. Hence, they may have been espoused by various scholars in Nyāya-Vaiśeṣika. These definitions are as follows:[26] the destruction of suffering which does not simultaneously occur with suffering which shares a locus [with the destruction] (*samānādhikaraṇaduḥkhāsamānakālīnaduḥkhadhvaṃsa*), the 'destruction of suffering' which is the object of knowledge which does not generate inertia (*saṃskārājanakasākṣātkāraviṣayaduḥkhadhvaṃsa*), the 'destruction of suffering' which does not generate [inertia] (*ajanakaduḥkhadhvaṃsa*), the destruction of all specific qualities of a soul[27] (*sakalātmaviśeṣaguṇadhvaṃsa*), the destruction of all suffering (*sakaladuḥkhadhvaṃsa*), all destruction of suffering (*duḥkhadhvaṃsamātra*), and the 'destruction of experience' caused by the absence of unseen force (*adṛṣṭābhāvahetukānubhavadhaṃsa*). The opponent negates the validity of all these definitions.

The View of Śaśadhara

Śaśadhara does not deny all the definitions of liberation examined by the opponent. Śaśadhara emphasizes that even if the destruction of all types of suffering cannot be achieved by effort (*yatna*), one can accomplish it by yoga practice. He seems to mean that effort causes action (*karman*), or yoga practice, and then that such practice can terminate all suffering. Then, he answers the opponent on major points.

Śaśadhara states that people do not behave properly for the sake of the destruction either of produced suffering or of non-produced suffering. Here he points out that it is not significant to examine the definition by classifying suffering into two groups. He continues: people behave to halt the transmigration (*saṃsāra*) of souls. Recognizing this, people figuratively refer to the cause of suffering as suffering. Every science (*śāsta*) teaches that human endeavour makes possible the eradication of the cause of suffering, and so Śaśadhara has not yet presented his own definition of liberation.

There is an interesting sentence suggesting the inclination of Śaśadhara to one of the definitions of liberation mentioned by the opponent. Śaśadhara states that the state of being the destruction of suffering is not pervaded by the state of being an occurrent simultaneously with suffering which shares a locus [with the destruction] (*tathā ca na duḥkhadhvaṃsatvaṃ samānādhikaraṇaduḥkha-samānakālīnatvavyāpyam*).[28] This statement includes a technical term in Indian logic, i.e. 'pervaded' (*vyāpya*), and the meaning of the suffix -*tva*, but we will interpret it in a simpler way. It means that the destruction of suffering is not always an occurrent simultaneous with suffering which shares a locus with the destruction. To put it differently, there is the destruction of suffering that is an occurrent not simultaneous with suffering which shares a locus with the destruction, which was refused by the opponent for the definition. This view was set forth in the case of the opponent's interpretation of the word 'absolute' (*atyantakī*) in the definition. This is the only case in which Śaśadhara refers to the refused concrete definition. Since he does not explicitly mention his own definition of liberation, that statement seems to be his favorite definition. Therefore, we can infer that he defined liberation as the destruction of suffering which occurs not simultaneously with suffering which shares a locus with the destruction (*samānādhikaraṇa-duḥkhāsamānakālīnaduḥkhadhvaṃsa*).[29]

Śaśadhara alleges that the destruction of suffering can be a human goal, but that happiness is not always a human goal.[30] To uphold this, he illustrates an example in which a man in a state of overexhaustion does not pursue even happiness but wishes the removal of over-exhaustion. Moreover, he points out that if liberation is in the form of happiness, the liberated person will experience enjoyment (*bhoga*) which in turn will lead the person to the transmigration of souls (*saṃsāra*). This result contradicts the view that a liberated person will never be subjected to such transmigration. Śaśadhara thus argues that liberation cannot be defined as a kind of happiness.

Then, he mentions the definitions of 'liberation while living' and ultimate liberation. The former liberation is defined as the knowledge of truth caused by unseen force caused by yoga practice (*yogajādṛṣṭa-janyatattvasākṣātkāra*), and the latter as the destruction of wrong knowledge which is embedded [in a soul] and is accompanied by specific qualities sharing a locus (i.e. the soul) with the destruction (*samānādhikaraṇaviśeṣaguṇāvacchinnasavāsanamithyājñānadhvaṃsa*). Let us number these definitions (1) and (2) respectively.

The difference between the two definitions does not lie in the fact that definition (1) involves 'the knowledge of truth' and that definition (2) involves 'the destruction of wrong knowledge'. This is because, immediately after these two definitions, Śaśadhara mentions the knowledge of truth and the destruction of wrong knowledge as features common to both types of liberation. Rather, we should note the expression 'which is accompanied with specific qualities' in definition (2). Since this definition has 'destruction' for the last part, it means that liberation is the state of being devoid not only of wrong knowledge but also of all specific qualifies of souls such as cognition (*buddhi*), happiness (*sukha*), suffering (*duḥkha*), etc.[31] Definition (1), on the other hand, does not tell us anything about these qualities, so it implies that liberation while living is the state of being possessive of them. This outcome accords with Śīdhara's statement that a liberated person (*jīvanmukta*) who has realized the truth of the soul continues to act, whereas a person who remains only within the Self, who is approaching liberation, and who has almost stopped action, does not.[32] Without specific qualities of soul, a person cannot behave. The existence of the specific qualities can function as a criterion by which the two kinds of liberation are differentiated. Therefore, the main difference between the two kinds of liberation is as follows: a soul in liberation while living possesses specific qualities of souls, while a soul in ultimate liberation possesses none.

Furthermore, he provides three features common to both kinds of liberation: the destruction of wrong knowledge continuing in a soul (*savāsanamithyājñānadhvaṃsa*), the absence of the prior absence of the knowledge of truth (*tattvasākṣātkāraprāgabhāvaviraha*), and the absence of the prior absence of merit (or virtue) caused by yoga practice (*yogajadharmaprāgabhāvaviraha*). Here it may be necessary to explain the absence of the prior absence of x. That the prior absence of x exists in y means that x is absent in y but will necessarily come into existence in y. Hence, that the absence of the prior absence of x exists in y means that it is not true that x is absent in y but will necessarily come into existence in y. In other words, the absence of the prior absence of x implies that x is present in y and will never disappear in y. The double negation seems to be used in the present case to emphasize the certainty of the existence of x in the future as well as at the present moment. The second and third common features, meanwhile, signify the certain existence of the knowledge of truth and merit caused by yoga practice respectively.

GAṄGEŚA ON LIBERATION

We have seen various issues of liberation discussed by Śaśadhara. Among them, I took particular notice of the definition of liberation. To clarify the connection between his and Gaṅgeśa's definitions, I will explain Gaṅgeśa's definition in this section.

Gaṅgeśa defines liberation in the first part of the Muktivāda[33] of the *Tattvacintāmaṇi* as follows: final beatitude (*apavarga*) [i.e. liberation] is the 'destruction of suffering' which does not occur simultaneously with the prior absence of suffering which shares a locus [with the destruction] (*samānādhikaraṇaduḥkhaprāgabhāvāsahavṛtti-duḥkhadhvaṃsa*).[34] To understand what this definition means, let us suppose that suffering does not exist at time 1; suffering takes place at time 2; suffering ceases at time 3. At time 1 there exists the prior absence of suffering, and this absence disappears at time 2. In this supposition, 'that (destruction) which does not occur simultaneously with the prior absence' in the definition applies to the destruction of suffering which occurs at time 3. If no suffering appears after time 3, this destruction at time 3 persists forever. And since no suffering comes into existence after time 3, there is no prior absence of suffering after time 3, and the destruction at time 3 satisfies the condition in the definition that destruction should not simultaneously occur with prior absence. Therefore, the definition means that if all suffering ceases in a person and no suffering is experienced after this cessation, the person is liberated (*mukta*).

The purpose of 'which shares a locus with' (*samānādhikaraṇa*) in the definition is to mention that the prior absence and the destruction should occur in one and the same soul. If absence occurs in distinct souls, the destruction of suffering will not be liberation. Let us assume that the prior absence of suffering exists in soul 1 at time 1, and that the destruction of suffering happens in soul 2 at time 2. In addition, let us suppose that soul 2 experiences another suffering at time 3. These suppositions tell us that neither soul 1 nor 2 is liberated. Soul 1 will certainly have suffering sometime after time 1, since it possesses the prior absence of suffering at time 1. Soul 2 also has suffering at time 3. Nevertheless the definition of liberation will apply to the 'destruction of suffering' in soul 2 if the definition does not incorporate 'which shares a locus with'.

Let us test the definition which does not incorporate this expression. It will run as follows: the 'destruction of suffering' which does not occur simultaneously with the prior absence of suffering (*duḥkha-prāgabhāvāsahavṛttiduḥkhadhvaṃsa*). The 'destruction of suffering' which occurs in soul 2 at time 2 does not simultaneously take place with the 'prior absence of suffering' which occurs in soul 1, because soul 1 possesses the prior absence at time 1. All the conditions stated in the definition have been met, and thus the definition applies to the destruction of suffering possessed by soul 2 which is not yet liberated. This is a defect in that the definition applies to that to which it should not apply, i.e. the defect of over-application.

If the expression is restored to the definition, it will not apply to the destruction possessed by soul 2. The definition prescribes that the destruction should share a locus with the prior absence. The destruction of suffering occurs in soul 2, while the prior absence of suffering occurs in soul 1. Both destruction and prior absence do not have one and the same soul for the locus. Hence, the full definition cannot apply to the destruction of suffering, and thus the expression saves the definition from the defect of over-application.

CONCLUSION

We can infer Śaśadhara's inclination in defining liberation. He seems to bear in mind the following definition: the destruction of suffering which occurs not simultaneously with suffering which shares a locus with the destruction (*samānādhikaraṇaduḥkhāsamānakālīnaduḥkha-dhvaṃsa*). This definition resembles Gaṅgeśa's definition: the 'destruction of suffering' which does not occur simultaneously with the prior absence of suffering which shares a locus with the destruction (*samānādhikaraṇaduḥkhaprāgabhāvāsahavṛttiduḥkhadhvaṃsa*). In this point, we can find the continuity between Śaśadhara and Gaṅgeśa, and this continuity corroborates the result of past research on the relationship between them.[35]

The definitions of two types of liberation given by Śaśadhara inherit the traditional view on liberation conceived by Śrīdhara, and others. Śrīdhara differentiates them by acting or not acting after liberation. Instead of referring to action, on the other hand, Śaśadhara classifies those two types by having recourse to the specific qualities of the soul. His use of 'specific quality' enables him to employ the term 'delimited' (*avacchinna*) in the definition of ultimate liberation. He means 'accompanied' by 'delimited', and 'an accompanying entity or entities' by 'delimitor' (*avacchedaka*) which is expected by 'delimited'. His use of both terms in this meaning does not accord with the later Navya-nyāya terminology, but it is certain that accompanying and accompanied entities share a locus with each other. This feature is important to 'delimitor' and 'delimited' in the later terminology.[36]Thus, Śaśadhara's text clearly shows the initial stage of the Navya-nyāya terminology.

When Śaśadhara points out the three features common to both kinds of liberation, he always uses two absences to express double negation and seems to emphasize the certainty of the existence of the entity in question. His use of double negation reminds us of a Navya-nyāya feature: reversing all quantified statements by the use of two negatives.[37] The present examples of Śaśadhara are not necessarily related to all quantified statements, but we may say that Navya-nyāya makes the frequent use of double negation.

We have made clear that although Navya-nyāya inherits the traditional view on liberation, the Muktivāda of Śaśadhara's *NSD* reveals Navya-nyāya terminology. The connection between his and Gaṅgeśa's Muktivādas is an issue for further inquiry.

NOTES

* I wish to thank Prof. Brian Burke-Gaffney, Nagasaki Institute of Applied. Science and Technology, for correcting my English.

1 I have followed Goekoop on how to divide the history of Indian logic into three periods: old Nyāya, Buddhist logic, and new Nyāya (Navya-nyāya). (C. Goekoop, *The Logic of Invariable Concomitance in the Tattvacintāmaṇi*, Dordrecht, 1967, p. vii.) I have agreed with Dineshchandra

Bhattacharya in marking the start of New Nyāya with Udayana flourishing in the eleventh century. (D. Bhattacharya, *History of Navya-Nyāya in Mithilā*, Darbhanga, 1958, p. 1.) Bimal K. Matilal also considers that *Navya-nyāya* began with Udayana (B.K. Matilal, *Nyāya-Vaiśeṣika*, Wiesbaden, 1977, pp. 101ff.) Some modern scholars regard Gaṅgeśa as the founder. (S.C. Vidyabhusana, *A History of Indian Logic*, Delhi, 1970, p. 405; D.H.H. Ingalls [see the following paragraph of this footnote]; Karl H. Potter and Sibajiban Bhattacharyya, eds., *Encyclopedia of Indian Philosophies Volume VI: Indian Philosophical Analysis Nyāya-Vaiśeṣika from Gaṅgeśa to Raghunātha Śiromaṇi*, Delhi, p. 3.) On the origin of Navya-nyāya, I am writing an article. Ingalls reports that Gaṅgeśa designates his own teachings as the New Nyāya, that is, as distinguished from the Old Nyāya that begins with the *Nyāyasūtras* and has for its great teachers like Udayana and so on. Furthermore, Ingalls states that because of the originality of Raghunātha's work, many Indians use the term Navya-nyāya only of him and his followers. (D.H.H. Ingalls, *Materials for the Study of Navya Nyāya Logic*, Cambridge [MA], 1951, p. 5.) Potter and Bhattacharyya point out that the term 'Navya-nyāya' is used in two senses: Nyāya-Vaiśeṣika literature which was written from the time of Gaṅgeśa onwards, and the literature which includes certain technical terms. This implies that this term can be employed to mean Nyāya-Vaiśeṣika literature which appeared from the time of Gaṅgeśa onwards but did not contain the technical terms. (Potter and Bhattacharyya, eds., *Encyclopedia of Indian Philosophies Volume VI*, pp. 3-4.)

2 Navya-nyāya scholars before Raghunātha Śiromaṇi (c. 1510) followed the theory of the seven categories of Vaiśeṣika: substance (*dravya*), quality (*guṇa*), action (*karman*), generic property (*sāmānya* or *jāti*), particular (*viśeṣa*), and absence (*abhāva*). In his *Padārthatattva-nirūpanam*, Raghunātha eliminated space (*ākāśa*), time (*kāla*), and direction (*diś*) in substance, number (*saṃkhyā*), distinctness (*pṛthaktva*), remoteness (*paratva*), proximity (*aparatva*) in quality, particular, and so on from the list of category, and added eight new categories to the list. For his revision of the categorical list, see Karl H. Potter, *The Padārthatattvaniūpaṇam of Raghunātha Śiromaṇi*, Cambridge (MA), 1957, pp. 10-15. However, his list did not survive in tradition. On the other hand, we know from Raghunātha's *Tattvacintāmaṇidīdhiti* that some Navya-nyāya scholars considered counterpositiveness, locusness, locuslessness, and relationness as independent categories. (*viṣayatā-tattvādivat pratiyogitvādhikaraṇatvatattvasambandhatvādayo 'pi atiriktā eva padārthā ity ekadeśihaḥ. Tattvacintāmaṇidīdhiti* included in *Gādādharī* (2 vols.) edited with the *Dīdhiti* of Raghunātha Śiromaṇi on the *TC* by Vindhyeśvarī Prasāda Dvivedī, Vāmācaraṇa Bhatācārya, Rāma Śāstri, and Ḍhuṇḍirāja Śāstrī [second edition revised by Kīrtyānanda Jhā and Satkāriśarmā Vaṅgīya,] Varanasi, 1970, p. 371,19-20.)

3 I owe my understanding of the concept of liberation in the old Nyāya and Vaiśeṣika schools to the following two papers written in Japanese: Keiichi Miyamoto, 'Nyāya Vaisheshika ryoha no gedatsukan' (Remarks on the Nyāya-Vaiśeṣika Conception of Liberation), *Gedatsu* (Liberation),

Buddhist Thought 8, Kyoto, 1982, pp. 327-52, and Hiroshi Marui, 'Indo ronrigakuha no gedatsukan ni tsuite' (Remarks on the Nyāya Conception of Liberation), *Musashino joshi daigaku bukkyō-bunka kenkyūjo kiyō* 7 (*Annals of the Musashino Women's University Institute of Buddhist Culture*), 1988, pp. 31-46. Marui's paper refers to the study on religious aspects in Nyāya and Vaiśeṣika by G. Oberhammer and D.H.H. Ingalls, and interestingly introduces Bhāsavajña's view on liberation, which differs from the traditional view.

4 On the position of Gaṅgeśa in the history of Navya-nyāya, there are three main views. For these views, see note 1.

5 *pṛthivyādīnāṃ navānām api dravyatvayogaḥ svātmany ārambhakatvaṃ guṇavattvam kāryakāraṇāvirodhitvam antyaviśeṣavattvam. PDhS*, p. 20, 14-16.

6 *Nyāyakandalī* (included in *Prasastapāda Bhāshya with the Commentary Nyayakandali* edited by V.P. Dvivedin, Delhi, 1984), p. 21,2-3: *svātmany ārambhakatvam* iti. *svasamavetakāryajanakatvam ity arthaḥ. Kiraṇāvalī* (included in *Praśastapādabhāṣyam with the Commentary Kiraṇāvalī of Udayanācārya* edited by J.S. Jetly, Baroda, 1971), p. 23,6-7: *svātmany ārambhakatvam svasamavetakāryakāritvaṃ samavāyikāraṇatvam ity arthaḥ*.

7 *Nyāyakandalī*, p. 21,4-10: *kāryakāraṇāvirodhitvam. guṇo hi kvacit kāryeṇa vināśyate yathādyaḥ śabdo dvitīyaśabdena kvacit kāraṇena vināśyate yathāntyaḥ śabda upāntyaśabdena karmāpi kāryeṇa vināśyate yathottarasaṃyogena dravyāṇi tu na vināśyante nāpi kāraṇeneti kārya-kāraṇāvirodhīni nityānāṃ kāraṇavināśayor abhāvād eva kāraṇenāvināśaḥ anityadravyāṇāṃ kāraṇavināśayoḥ sambhave 'pi kāraṇena na vināśaḥ kiṃ tv anyeneti vivekaḥ*.

8 Definition (*lakṣaṇa*) in Indian philosophy may be given in the form of a sentence or by pointing out the property which exists only in the definienda (*lakṣya*). For the concept of definition, see Toshihiro Wada, *Invariable Concomitance in Navya-Nyāya*, Delhi, 1990, pp. 99-104.

9 The antonym of absolute general term is relative general term. See note 11.

10 *Lakṣaṇāvalī* (included in Musashi Tachikawa, *The Structure of the World in Udayana's Realism,* Dordrecht, 1981), p. 56, no. 12.

11 Other instances of this term are 'cause', 'effect', 'father', 'son', and so on. On relative and absolute general terms, see Bimal K. Matilal, *The Navya-Nyāya Doctrine of Negation*, Cambridge (MA), 1968, p. 31; Wada, *Invariable Concomitance in Navya-Nyāya*, p. 67.

12 For a detailed discussion of delimitor and describer, see Wada, *Invariable Concomitance in Navya-Nyāya*, pp. 66-98.

13 Causeness indicates the 'direction' of the relation: from 'pot' to 'pot-maker'. Navya-nyāya does not have a term directly expressive of direction and instead uses counterrelatum (*pratiyogin*) and baserelatum (*anuyogin*) to refer to direction. Direction is considered from counterrelatum to baserelatum. On this point, see Wada, *Invariable Concomitance in Navya-Nyāya*, pp. 66-8. The relation whose direction is from 'pot-maker' to 'pot' is named effectness (*kāryatā*).

14 If the delimitor of effectness is introduced in the present analysis, the statement will mean the causeness delimited by pot-maker-ness and described by the effectness delimited by potness (*ghaṭatvāvacchinna-kāryatānirūpitakumbhakāratvāvacchinnakāraṇatā*). In the present paper, I do not discuss why the meaning of statement can be relation.

15 Included in Śaśadhara's *Nyāyasiddhāntadīpa with the Ṭippana of Guṇaratnasūri* edited by Bimal K. Matilal, Ahmedabad, 1976.

16 Śaśadhara quite often uses 'delimitor' in the Vyāptivāda of the *NSD*, and therein (p. 68, 24) defines it as *samaniyata*; *x* is the *samaniyata* of *y* if *x* always shares a locus with *y* and *y* also always shares a locus with *x*. According to *Nyāyakośa* (edited by B. Jhalakikar, Poona, p. 957), *samaniyatatvam* is defined as *vyāpyatve sati vyāpakatvam*.

17 This term is found at least once in the *NSD* (p. 13,1), and it appears to be used as in the later terminology.

18 *NSD*, pp. 33-8.

19 His analysis and conclusion are provided in *NSD*, pp. 35,22-38,6.

20 The portion of the opponent starts on p. 35,22 and continues to the end of p. 36.

21 *niḥśreyasaṃ punar duḥkhanivṛttir atyantikī. Kiraṇāvali*, p. 5,4. This reference is provided by Miyamoto, 'Remarks on the Nyāya-Vaiśeṣika Conception', p. 349, n.29.

22 Prior absence has no beginning but an end, because it exists till the time of the appearance of its counterpositive (*pratiyogin*). (*Tarkasaṃgraha* [included in *Tarkasaṃgraha of Annaṃbhaṭṭa* edited with the author's *Dīpikā* and Govardhana's *Nyāyabodhinī* by Yashwant Vasudev Athalye and Mahadev Rajaram Bodas, Poona, 1974], p. 62,12.) A counterpositive is that whose existence is negated. Constant absence exists eternally. (*Tarkasaṃgraha*, p. 62,14-15.) No one can produce these two varieties of absence.

23 If liberation is the termination of suffering which occurs in the locus of suffering, no suffering should occur after the termination.

24 For the traditional view, see M. Hiriyanna, *Outline of Indian Philosophy*, Bombay, 1983 (1st edn: 1932), pp. 263ff. The *Nyāyabhāṣya* (p. 231,4-6) states: *neṣṭam aniṣṭenānanuviddhaṃ sambhavatīti iṣṭam apy aniṣṭaṃ sampadyate, aniṣṭahānāya ghaṭamāna iṣṭam api jahāti, viveka-hānasyāśakyatvād iti.* (*Nyāyabhāṣya* included in *Nyāyadarśanam* edited with Vātsyāyana's *Bhāṣya*, Uddyotakara's *Vārttika*, Vācaspati Miśra's *Tātparyaṭīkā*, and Viśvanātha's *Vṛtti* by Taranatha Nyaya-Tarkatirtha and Amarendramohan Tarkatirtha, Calcutta, 1936 [reprint in Kyoto, 1982].)

25 A soul is an eternal entity in Nyāya-Vaiśeṣika, and it is possible that a soul is liberated after the death of the body. Hence, it is not necessarily redundant to say that a person, or a soul, obtains liberation while living.

26 Precisely speaking, the *NSD* states the definitions of the state of being ultimate liberation (*paramamuktitva*), or ultimate-liberation-ness, and not the definitions of ultimate liberation. Hence, each definition has the suffix *-tva*. To facilitate our discussion, I have removed this suffix from *paramamuktitva*, and the meaning of the suffix from the translation of the definitions.

27 According to *Tarkasaṃgraha* p. 59,6 (*buddhyādayo 'ṣṭāv ātmamātraviśeṣaguṇāḥ*), the eight qualities particular to souls are cognition (*buddhi*), happiness (*sukha*), suffering (*duḥkha*), desire (*icchā*), aversion (*dveṣa*), effort (*prayatna* or *yatna*), virtue (*dharma*), and vice (*adharma*). Inertia (*saṃskāra*) has three varieties, one of which is impression (*bhāvanā*). This variety resides in a soul, but the other two do not. Hence, it is not true that all inertia resides in a soul.

28 *NSD*, p. 37,13-14.

29 The *Maṇikaṇa* (p. 58,14-16) introduces this definition as a traditional one: "*sa ca ātyantiko duḥkhadhvaṃsaḥ. ātyantikatvaṃ ca svasamānādhikaraṇaduḥkhāsamānakālīnatvam. ... ity sampradāyaḥ.*"

30 *NSD*, p. 37,15-18.

31 On specific qualities of souls, see n. 27.

32 *Nyāyakandalī*, p. 285,13-16: ... *sphuṭīkṛtātmatattvasyāpi jīvanmuktasya tāvat karmāṇi bhavanti yāvad yātrānuvartate ātmaikapratiṣṭhasya tv abhyarṇamokṣasya parikṣīṇaprāyakarmaṇaḥ tāni naśyanty eva bahiḥ saṃvittivirahāt.*

33 *TC*, pp. 2055-83. Sibajiban Bhattacharyya provides a summary of this chapter in Potter and Bhattacharyya, eds., *Encyclopedia of Indian Philosophies Volume VI*, pp. 235-8, but it covers till *TC* p. 2066.

34 *paramaprayojanan tv anumānasyāpavargaḥ, "ātmā vā are śrotavyaḥ mantavyo nididhyāsitavyaḥ (sākṣātkarttavyaḥ)" iti śruteḥ. sa ca samānādhikaraṇaduḥkhaprāgabhāvāsahavṛttiduḥkhadhvaṃsaḥ*. *TC*, p. 2055,3-6.

35 On the connection between Śaśadhara and Gaṅgeśa, see D. Bhattacharya, *History of Navya-Nyāya in Mithilā*, pp. 89ff; B.K. Matilal, Introduction in Śaśadhara's *Nyāyasiddhāntadīpa with the Ṭippana of Guṇaratnasūri*, pp. 10-11; J. Vattanky, *Gaṅgeśa's Philosophy of God*, Madras, 1984, p. 123; V.N. Jha, *The Philosophy of Injunctions*, Delhi, 1987, p. 5.

36 On this feature, see Wada, *Invariable Concomitance in Navya-Nyāya*, pp. 83, 91.

37 On this feature, see D.H.H. Ingalls, 'The Comparison of Indian and Western Philosophy', *Journal of Oriental Research* 22, 1952, p. 7.

9

Universals and Particulars in the Early Vaiśeṣikas

KEIICHI MIYAMOTO

The terms *sāmānya* and *viśeṣa* are used quite technically in the later Vaiśeṣika texts. But they are sometimes technical and sometimes non-technical in the *Vaiśeṣikasūtra (VS).* So we should investigate the usage of the terms in *VS*, and try to clarify the true intention of the Sūtrakāra on whether the particular universal (*sāmānya-viśeṣa*) is an independent category or not. For, while it is an independent category in the *Daśapadārthī (DP),* it is not so in the *Praśastapādabhāṣya (PBh).* Besides we shall investigate the usage of the terms in *PBh* because Praśastapāda seems to use them freely in some places in spite of his rigid definition of them.

UNIVERSALS AND PARTICULARS IN *VS*[1]

Non-technical Usages

To begin with we shall enumerate all of the cases in which the terms *sāmānya* and *viśeṣa* are not used technically.

The term *sāmānya* which appears in *VS* 1.1.17, 22[2], 24[3], 29[4]; 2.1.6[5], 7[6] means merely 'common' (=*samāna*), and therefore is not a technical term. *VS* 1.1.17, for example, runs as follows:

> *dravyaguṇakarmaṇāṃ dravyaṃ kāraṇaṃ sāmānyam* (Substance is a common cause of substance, quality and action.).

The term *viśeṣa* in *VS* 1.2.18[7] means 'particular' in the non-technical sense. What is existent (*bhāva=sat*) is not manifold because there are found no particular marks by force of which it appears manifold.

The term *viśeṣa* in *VS* 2.2.9[8], 15[9] means 'particular' in a non-technical sense. Time appears manifold by force of particular action such as beginning. Space appears manifold by force of particular action such as performing dedication to gods in the east.

The term *sāmānya* in *VS* 2.2.19[10] which explains why a doubt (*saṃśaya*) occurs means 'common feature', and the term *viśeṣa* in the same sūtra means 'uncommon feature'. A doubt occurs when one sees only common features and does not see an uncommon feature.

The term *sāmānya (sāmānyato dṛṣṭa)* in *VS* 2.1.16[11], 3.2.7[12] means 'generarity' or 'commonness'.

The term *viśeṣa* in *VS* 2.2.26[13] means 'something particular'. We have a doubt as to whether sound is a substance, a quality or an action because something particular such as being grasped by the ears is found in a thing of the same kind (quality) as well as in another thing (substance or action).

The term *sāmānya* in *VS* 2.2.43[14] which explains why repetition of words occurs means 'similarity'. Repetition of words occurs because of their similarlity, not because of their being eternal.

The term *viśeṣa* in *VS* 3.2.14[15] means 'difference'. We do not recognize the difference between Yajñadatta's cognition and Viṣṇumitra's cognition in spite of the difference between their bodies.

The term *viśeṣa* in *VS* 4.1.4[16] means 'special'. Non-eternity is a special state of negation of eternity.

The term *viśeṣa* in *VS* 4.2.5[17], 6[18] means 'special'. Atoms are said to produce a body by force of special merit. By seeing special effects such as grasshoppers we cognize that there are beings which are not born from the womb.

The term *viśeṣa* in *VS* 5.1.8[19], 9[20], 10[21] means 'particular' in the non-technical sense. There occurs neither upward movement nor zigzag movement when there are no particular shakings. There occurs particular shaking by force of particular mental effort. A particular shaking produces a special throwing to a distant place.

The term *viśeṣa* in *VS* 5.1.16[22] means 'many kinds of'. The fact that there occur many kinds of connection non-simultaneously in an arrow proves that there are plural actions.

The term *viśeṣa* in *VS* 5.2.2[23], 4[24] means 'an unordinary case'. In an unordinary case an action of the earth (earthquake) is produced by an unseen thing. In an unordinary case the fall of water (rain) is produced by an unseen thing.

The term *viśeṣa* in *VS* 6.2.16[25] means 'different'. A different desire occurs from different birth. For example herbivorous animals have a desire to eat grass.

The term *viśeṣa* in *VS* 7.1.16[26] means 'particular' in the non-technical sense. A large thing is produced by plurality of its causes, by largeness of its causes or by a particular collection of its causes.

The term *viśeṣa* in *VS* 7.1.18[27] means 'excellence'. A secondary expression about a thing that this is small(er) or large(r) occurs from existence of excellence or from non-existence of excellence.

The term *viśeṣa* in *VS* 8.17[28] means 'difference'. Water (tongue) is the cause of the cognition of taste. Fire (eyes) is the cause of the cognition of colour. Wind (skin) is the cause of the cognition of touch. For there is difference among taste, colour and touch in the cognitions of taste, colour and touch.

The term *viśeṣa* in *VS* 9.13[29], 22[30] means 'special'. A direct cognition of soul is produced by a special connection of soul with mind. Memory is produced by a special connection of soul with mind and by impression.

The term *viśeṣa* in *VS* 10.2[31], 11[32] means 'difference'. Pleasure and pain are different because of difference of their causes, namely desired things and undesired things and because of their mutual contradiction. Difference among cognitions about a head, about a back, about a belly and about a hand is due to their difference.

Technical Usages

The most important argument about universals and particulars in a technical sense is found in *VS* 1.2.3-6. These sūtras are as follows:

> *sāmānyaṃ viśeṣa iti buddhyapekṣam.* 3 [Cognition] that [this is] a universal or that [this is] a particular is caused by cognition [of concomitance or exclusion].
>
> *bhāvaḥ samānyam eva.* 4 Existence (=*sattā,* being existent) is a pure universal.
>
> *dravyatvaṃ guṇatvaṃ karmatvaṃ ca sāmānyāni viśeṣāś ca.* 5 Substanceness, qualitiness and actionness are universals as well as particulars.
>
> *anyatrāntyebhyo viśeṣebhyaḥ.* 6 [Substanceness and so on] exclude ultimate particulars.

According to the above argument the Sūtrakāra seems to assume three types, namely universal (=being existent), particular universal and particular (=ultimate particular). That is, the Sūtrakāra seems to admit these three types as three independent categories.

A Chinese commentary on the *Nyāyapraveśaka* contains a very interesting episode. According to it at first Ulūka (=Kaṇāda) declared six categories, namely substance, quality, action, large existence (perhaps '*mahābhāva'=sattā),* universal-particular (*sāmānyaviśeṣa*), inherence. It may be that the concept of universal-particular contains so-called particular universal such as substanceness, earthness, potness and so on as well as ultimate particular. But Pañcaśikhin, Ulūka's deciple, denies the concept of large existence though he affirms the concept of universal-particular.

Unfortunately the conclusion of the dispute between them is not conveyed. Yet we may be permitted to guess that Ulūka amended his system of categories. He renamed large existence as '(pure) universal' and divided universal-particular into particular universal and (ultimate) particular. Traces of this can be found in *VS* 1.2.4-6. Besides, the Sūtrakāra does not use even the term *padārtha* (category). Therefore we cannot tell which items he enumerates as categories. Such an ambiguity resulted in appearence of two systems, one of ten categories and another of six. The latter came to be the orthodox version from the time of Praśastapāda.

Now, another four sūtras indicate that a particular universal (*sāmānyaviśeṣa*) is without doubt treated by the Sūtrakāra as an independent category. Those sūtras are as follows:

> *sad anityaṃ dravyavat kāryaṃ kāraṇaṃ sāmānyaviśeṣavad iti dravyaguṇakarmāviśeṣaḥ.*(*VS* 1.1.7) There is no difference among substance, quality and action as to that they are existent, non-eternal, effects, causes, and possess particular universals.

In this case '*sat*' is nothing but '*sattāvat*'. Besides it is only eternal substances that possess ultimate particulars. Thus '*sāmānyaviśeṣa*' in this case is determined as 'particular universals'.

> *sāmānyaviśeṣābhāvāc ca.* (*VS* 1.2.11) [Being existent (*sattā*) is neither a substance, a quality nor an action.] Because there are not particular universals [in a being existent].

It is obvious that '*sāmānyaviśeṣa*' in this case does not contain *sattā.* Besides ultimate particulars do not exist in qualities and actions.

> *sāmānyaviśeṣābhāvena ca.* (*VS* 1.2.13) [Substanceness is not a substance.] Because there are no particular universals [in substanceness].

sāmānyaviśeṣābhāvena ca. (*VS* 1.2.15) [Qualitiness is not a quality.] Because there are no particular universals [in qualitiness].

sāmānyaviśeṣābhāvena ca. (*VS* 1.2.17) [Actionness is not an action.] Because there are no particular universals [in actionness].

The meaning of above three sūtras is quite obvious. Incidentally, the terms *sāmānya* and *viśeṣa* in *VS* in a technical sense have a kind of 'sway' in two sūtras.

sāmānyaviśeṣeṣu sāmānyaviśeṣābhāvāt tata eva jñānam. (*VS* 8.5) Because there are no universals and [ultimate] particulars in universals and [ultimate] particulars cognitions of universals and [ultimate] particulars are produced by it (a contact) only.

In this case the term *sāmānya* means a being existent (=a pure universal) as well as particular universals, namely substanceness and so on. Therefore the term *viśeṣa* means ultimate particulars only.

sāmānyaviśeṣāpekṣaṃ dravyaguṇakarmasu. (*VS* 8.6) [Cognitions] of substances, qualities and actions are caused by a [pure] universal and particular [universals].

It is only eternal substances that possess ultimate particulars. That is, no qualities, no actions and no non-eternal substances possess ultimate particulars. Therefore the term *viśeṣa* in this case does not mean ultimate particulars, but particular universals. And therefore the term *sāmānya* in this case should mean a pure universal (being existent) only.

UNIVERSALS AND PARTICULARS IN *DP*[33]

DP inherited quite fathfully *VS* which declares division into three categories, namely a pure universal (a being existent), particular universals and ultimate particulars. We shall quote Candramati's definitions of the above three categories. First, the definition of universal:

What is the category of universal? It is a being existent (=the highest universal). (*kaḥ sāmānyapadārthaḥ? satteti.*) [66]

What is a being existent? That which is inherent in all the categories of substance, quality and action, is perceived by all the sense organs, and is the cause of the expression and cognition, namely, '[This is] *sat* (existent)' as to substances, qualities and actions is called a being existent. (*kā sattā? yā sarvadravyaguṇakarmapadārthasamavetā sarvendriyagrāhyā yo dravyaguṇakarmasu sadabhidhānajñānahetuḥ saiva sattety ucyate.*) [67]

Second, the definition of particular:

> What is the category of particular? That which is eternal, exists in [eternal] substances, has one substance as its locus, is the cause of the cognition, namely, '[This is] excluded from that (any other thing)' and is as well the cause of the cognition, namely, 'This is represented as it is' is called the category of particular.(*ko viśeṣapadārthaḥ? yo nityo dravyeṣu vartamāna ekadravyāśritas tadvyāvṛttibuddhihetur etadvyaktibuddhihetuś ca sa eva viśeṣapadārtha ity ucyate.*) [68]

Another explanation of particular:

> A particular exists in [eternal] substances, has one [eternal] substance as its locus, is the cause of the cognition, namely, '[This is] excluded from any other [substance], is as well the cause of the cognition, namely, 'This is represented as it is,' is the cause of the names 'ether' and so on being present in ether, space and time, is eternal, is a non-product, is without quality, action and part, inheres in those [categories of entities] whose exceptions are a being existent, potentialities, non-potentialities, particular universals and particulars, and is plural.(*viśeṣo dravyeṣu vartamāna ekadravyāśrito 'nyavyāvṛttibuddhihetur etadvyaktibuddhihetur ākāśadikkāleṣu vartamāna ākāśādisañjñāhetur nityo 'kāryo nirguṇo niṣkriyo nir-avayavo 'nyatra sattāśaktyaśaktisāmānyaviśeṣaviśeṣebhyaḥ samaveto 'nekaḥ.*) [238]

The claim that particulars are the causes of the names 'ether' and so on is quite unique. This claim is found only in *DP*.
Third, the definition of particular universal:

> What is the category of particular universal? Substanceness, qualitiness and actionness, and those such as earthness, colourness, upward-movementness and so on which are inherent in the same thing as the former ones [are inherent in] are called the category of particular universal.(*kaḥ sāmānyaviśeṣapadārthaḥ? dravyatvaguṇatvakarmatvāni tathā tadekārthasamavāyini pṛthivītvarūpatvotkṣepaṇatvānīty evamādīni sāmānyaviśeṣapadārtha ity ucyate.*) [72]

> Substanceness: That which is inherent in all of the substances, is the cause of the expression and cognition, namely, '[This is] a substance' with reference to all of the substances, does not exist in qualities and actions, and is perceived by eyes and skin is called substanceness. (*dravyatvam iti yad sarvadravyasamavetaṃ sarva-*

dravyeṣu dravyābhidhānapratyayahetur guṇakarmasv avartamānaṃ cakṣuḥsparśanagrāhyaṃ tad eva dravyatvam ity ucyate.) [73]

Qualitiness: That which is inherent in all of the qualities, is the cause of the expression and cognition, namely, '[This is] a quality' with reference to all of the qualities, does not exist in substances and actions, and is perceived by all of the sense organs is called qualitiness.(*guṇatvam iti yad sarvaguṇasamavetaṃ sarvaguṇeṣu guṇābhidhānapratyayahetur dravyakarmasv avartamānaṃ sarvendriyagrāhyaṃ tad eva guṇatvam ity ucyate.*) [74]

Actionness: That which is inherent in all of the actions, is the cause of the expression and cognition, namely, '[This is] an action' with reference to all of the actions, does not exist in substances and qulalities, and is perceived by eyes and skin is called actionness. (*karmatvam iti yad sarvakarmasamavetaṃ sarvakarmasu karmābhidhānapratyayahetur dravyaguṇeṣv avartamānaṃ cakṣuḥsparśanagrāhyaṃ tad eva karmatvam ity ucyate.*) [75]

Earthness and so on are [to be explained] in the same way as above. (*pṛthivītvādīni caivam eva.*) [76]

DP contains no confusion or ambiguity of usage of the terms *sāmānya, viśeṣa* and *sāmānyaviśeṣa.* It is probable that it inherited quite faithfully the divison into three categories found in *VS* 1.2.4-6.

UNIVERSALS AND PARTICULARS IN *PBh*[34]

Praśastapāda maintains that there are two categories, universal and particular, and defines the universal as divided into the highest (*para*) and lower (*apara*). The highest universal is nothing but a being existent (*sattā*). Lower universals are, for example, substanceness, qualitiness, actionness and so on. Therefore the particular denotes ultimate particular only. Thus his definition of universal and particular is very simple and clear though it is a little far from that in *VS.* It is likely that he averted a possible confusion in the expression '*sāmānyaviśeṣa*' because such an expression can be interpreted in two ways, as 'a pure universal and an ultimate particular' as well as 'a particular universal.'

Yet in spite of his clear definition he frequently uses the terms *sāmānya* and *viśeṣa* in an untechnical sense or ambiguously. It is so tiresome to enumerate all of such cases that we shall investigate only the compounds '*sāmānyaviśeṣa.*'

[235] For it (a direct cognition) is produced about categories of

substances and so on. At first a mere observation of an essence about three kinds of large substances is produced by their possessing [substances] which possess many substances, by emerged colors, by a light, by contact of four things (soul, mind, sense organ and object), and by the presence of a set of causes such as a merit and so on. [Next] a direct cognition 'A white cow which exists, is a substance, is a piece of earth and possesses horns walks' is produced by that contact of soul with mind which is caused by qualifiers such as *sāmānyaviśeṣa,* substances, qualities and actions.[35]

In this case it is obvious that *sāmānya* denotes the highest universal (*sattā*) only while *viśeṣa* denotes particular universals such as substanceness, earthness, whiteness and cowness. The term *viśeṣa* in this case cannot denote ultimate particulars. For qualities and actions do not possess them. This is a fundamental rule for the Vaiśeṣikas.

> [243] Here a direct cognition in the form of a mere observation of the essence about *sāmānyaviśeṣa* is the instrument of cognition, categories of substances and so on are the objects of cognition, a soul is the cognizer, and cognitions whose objects are substances and so on are the cognitions as results.[36]

In the case where the expression 'substances *and so on'* exists the term *viśeṣa* cannot mean ultimate particulars. For neither qualities nor actions possess ultimate particulars. Therefore in this case the term *viśeṣa* means lower universals, while *sāmānya* means the highest universal.

> [244] In the case where a cognition of *sāmānyaviśeṣa* is produced a direct cognition in the form of an unseparated mere observation (=contact) is the instrument of cognition. There is no other instrument of cognition in this case because such a direct cognition is not an effect [of another thing or of any kind of cognition].[37]

In this case *viśeṣa* can be an ultimate particulars while *sāmānya* means the highest universal as well as lower universals (=particular universals). This case is the same with *VS* 8.5. But when we take paragragh [243] into consideration and regard the compound *sāmānyaviśeṣa* as means the same thing both in [243] and in [244], we are obliged to admit that *sāmānya* means nothing but the highest universal, while *viśeṣa* means lower universals.

Thus, though Praśastapāda declared a new definition of universal and particular, his usages of the terms universal and particular are sometimes inconsistent with his own definition.

CONCLUSION

The terms *sāmānya* and *viśeṣa* are used both in the non-technical sense and in a technical sense in *VS.* But in a technical sense the Sūtrakāra seems to maintain three categories, a pure universal (a being existent), pariticular universals and ultimate particulars though he does not use the term 'category' (*padārtha*). Candramati, the author of *DP,* inherited this classification quite faithfully, and used the terms without ambiguity. Praśastapāda put the pure universal and the particular universal into one category, the universal. But he sometimes deviated from his own definition. This means that Candramati is far more rational than Praśaspatāda. Yet, though the true reason is not yet clear, Praśastapāda's system came to achieve orthodoxy while that of Candramati came to be forgotten completely among Vaiśeṣikas.

In my opinion the Sūtrakāra intended to assume at least eight kinds of categories, namely substance, quality, action, (pure) universal (*sāmānya*), particular universal (*sāmānyaviśeṣa*), (ultimate) particular (*viśeṣa*), inherence and negation (*pratiṣedha* or *abhāva*). If so, we can say that Candramati inherited the earliest Vaiśeṣika system very faithfully. This tells also that Candramati flourished very early, perhaps from the latter half of the fourth century to the early fifth century.

NOTES

1 The sūtrapāṭhas are based on *Vaiśeṣikasūtra of Kaṇāda with the Commentary of Candrānanda* (G.O.P. No.136).
2 *dravyāṇāṃ dravyaṃ kāryaṃ sāmānyam.*
3 *asamavāyāt sāmānyaṃ karma kāryaṃ na vidyate.*
4 *kāraṇasāmānye dravyakarmaṇāṃ karmākāraṇam uktam iti.*
5 *sarpirjatumadhūcchiṣṭānāṃ pārthivānām agnisaṃyogād dravyatā 'dbhiḥ sāmānyam.*
6 *trapusīsaloharajatasuvarṇānāṃ taijasānām agnisaṃyogād dravatā'd-bhih sāmānyam.*
7 *salliṅgāviśeṣād viśeṣaliṅgābhāvāc caiko bhāva iti.*
8 *kāryaviśeṣeṇa nānātvam.*
9 *kāryaviśeṣeṇa nānātvam.*
10 *sāmānyapratyakṣād viśeṣāpratyakṣād viśeṣasmṛteś ca saṃśayaḥ.*
11 *sāmānyato dṛṣṭāś cāviśeṣaḥ.*
12 *sāmānyato dṛṣṭāś cāviśeṣaḥ.*
13 *tulyajātīyeṣv arthāntarabhūteṣu ca viśeṣasyobhayathā dṛṣṭatvāt.*
14 *saṃkhyābhāvaḥ sāmānyataḥ.*

15 *na tu śarīraviśeṣād yajñadattaviṣṇumitrayor jñānaviśeṣaḥ.*
16 *anityam iti ca viśeṣapratiṣedhabhāvaḥ.*
17 *dharmaviśeṣāt.*
18 *kāryaviśeṣāt.*
19 *nodanaviśeṣābhāvād nordhvaṃ na tiryag gamanam.*
20 *prayatnaviśeṣān nodanaviśeṣaḥ.*
21 *nodanaviśeṣād udasanaviśeṣaḥ.*
22 *iṣāv ayugapat saṃyogaviśeṣāḥ karmānyatve hetuḥ.*
23 *tad viśeṣenādṛṣṭakāritam.*
24 *tad viśeṣenādṛṣṭakāritam.*
25 *jātiviśeṣāc ca rāgaviśeṣaḥ.*
26 *kāraṇabahutvād kāraṇamahattvāt pracayaviśeṣāc ca mahat.*
27 *aṇu mahad iti tasmin viśeṣabhāvād viśeṣābhāvāc ca.*
28 *tathāpas tejo vāyuś ca rasarūpasparśajñāneṣu rasarūpasparśaviśeṣād iti.*
29 *ātmanya ātmamanasoḥ saṃyogaviśeṣād ātmapratyakṣam.*
30 *ātmamanasoḥ saṃyogaviśeṣāt saṃskārāc ca smṛtiḥ.*
31 *iṣṭāniṣṭakāraṇaviśeṣād virodhāc ca mithaḥ sukhaduḥkhayor arthāntarabhāvaḥ.*
32 *śiraḥ pṛṣṭam udaraṃ pāṇir iti tadviśeṣebhyaḥ.*
33 Paragraph numbers and a reconstructed Ssnskrit text are based on K. Miyamoto, *The Metaphysics and Epistemology of the Early Vaiśeṣikas* [Appendix], Pune: Bhandarkar Oriental Research Institute, 1996.
34 The text and paragraph numbers are based on J. Bronkhorst and Y. Ramseier, *Word Index to the Praśastapādabhāṣya,* Delhi: Motilal Banarsidass Publishers, 1994.
35 *Tad dhi dravyādiṣu padārtheṣūtpadyate. Dravye tāvat trividhe mahaty anekadravyavattvodbhūtarūpaprakāśacatuṣṭayasannikarṣād dharmādisāmagrye ca svarūpālocanamātram. Samānyaviśeṣadravya-guṇakarmaviśeṣaṇāpekṣād ātmamanaḥsannikarṣāt pratyakṣam utpadyate ---- sad dravyam pṛthivī viṣāṇī śuklo gaur gacchatīti.*
36 *Tatra sāmānyaviśeṣeṣu svarūpālocanamātraṃ pratyakṣaṃ pramāṇam, prameyā dravyādayaḥ padārthāḥ, pramātā"tmā, pramitir dravyādiviṣayaṃ jñānam.*
37 *Sāmānyaviśeṣajñānotpattāv avibhaktam ālocanamātraṃ pratyakṣaṃ pramāṇam asmin nānyat pramāṇāntaram asti aphalarūpatvāt.*

10

The Impermanence of *Śabda* in Classical Vaiśeṣika*

YASUTAKA MUROYA

INTRODUCTION

Sound (*śabda*) is a specific quality (*vaiśeṣikaguṇa*) of ether (*ākāśa*),[1] an eternal, all-pervasive substance. At the same time, sound is non-eternal. This is proven not only in the *Vaiśeṣikasūtra* (*VS*), *Nyāyasūtra* (*NS*), and *Nyāyabhāṣya* (*NBh*), but also by Uddyotakara, a great Naiyāyika scholar. On the other hand, Praśastapāda, who is said to have systematically completed the Vaiśeṣika system of category, does not appear to take the position that sound is *anitya* (non-eternal). In his *Padārthadharmasaṃgraha* (*PDhS*), PraZastapAda only claims that it is momentary (*kṣaṇika*), as if to avoid dealing with the concept of 'non-eternal',[2] and makes no explicit attempt to prove such an attribute. On the contrary, he tries to indirectly discuss the impermanence of sound by clarifying the relationship between ether and sound, and reinforcing the categoric framework of substance and quality.[3] From the temporal point of view, he explains that sound is not existent so long as the substance as a substratum continues to exist (*ayāvaddravyabhāvitva*),[4] similar to the relationship between *ātman* and *buddhi*.[5] The corresponding permanent relationship between substance and quality is described in *VS* VII.1.4: *pṛthivyāṃ rūparasagandhasparśā dravyānityatvād anityāḥ.*[6] Praśastapāda transforms this older way of thinking about the relationship between substance and its peculiar quality into the newly expressed compound *yāvaddravyabhāvitva*, while he uses *ayāvaddravyabhāvitva* specifically to refer to the relationship between ether and sound or between *ātman* and *buddhi* without any clear proof. As for the spatial relationship, sound and cognition are each existent as a part (*pradeśavṛtti*) of the ubiquitous substances, ether and *ātman*.

Praśastapāda's mysterious statements about sound and ether, both of which are fundamentally identical and ontologically related in an inseparable way (*ayutasiddha*), might be caused by his keen awareness of such contradition as one being eternal and the other non-eternal. Praśastapāda's definite and proof-indifferent description may suggest his intention to solve the contradiction authoritatively. The Mīmāṃsā and Sāṃkhya regard the generation of sound not as production (*utpatti*) but as manifestation (*vyakti/abhivyakti*).[7] It is also assumed that Praśastapāda is quite familiar with the view that sound is a controversial matter with other schools since at least the compilation of the *VS*,[8] and then feels the necessity to steadily shape sound as the category quality. The present paper investigates the process of theoretical transformation by Praśastapāda by observing the physical aspects of the genesis and impermanence of sound.

Although Praśastapāda proves the presence of ether more elaborately than does the *VS* II.1.20-25, he does not refer to the topic of doubt or *saṃśaya* as to whether sound is a substance, quality or motion, as described in VS II.2.25, nor does he take up proof for the controversial theme. Why does he make any implicit mention of the argument and establish the category of quality sound mainly in relation to ether? More specifically, why is it that while other Nyāya and Vaiśeṣika authorities make use of the term *anitya* of sound, Praśastapāda only uses the term *kṣaṇika* for sound, as might be seen from the table below?[9]

Table: Terminology in the Sound Theory

	an	K	śj	st(I)	v	st(II)	s/v
VS	○		○				
NS	○			○			
**TS(V)*			○	○	○		○
**TS(B)*		○	×	×	×	×	×
NBh	○		○	○			○
**DA*	○		○				○
PDhS	[Q1]	○	○	○	○		[Q2]
NV	○		[○]	○		○	○
ŚV		○	[○]	○			○
CV	○		○	○			
Vyo	○	△	○	○	○		
NK	○	△	○	○	○		
Kir	○	[?]	○	○	○		
NVTṬ	○		○	○			○

an=*anitya*; k=*kṣaṇika*; śj=*śabdaja*; st(I)=*saṃtāna* I; v=*vīcī*; st(II)=*saṃtāna*II; s/v=*saṃskāra/vega*; V=Vaiśeṣika; B=Buddhist

Does Praśastapāda have any reasonable motive to dismiss the usage of the concept of disposition (*saṃskāra*) or momentum (*vega*) in the theory of sound, while some Nyāya scholars such as Vātsyāyana, and the Harivarman's opponents, most presumably earlier Vaiśeṣika school, in the **Tattvasiddhi* (**TS*) refer to momentum on the sound theory, as could be seen from the table above?

TWO TYPES OF *SAṂTĀNA* IN *NV*

Like Vātsyāyana, Uddyotakara describes the theory of sound transmission (*saṃtāna*) which is first terminologically introduced in the *NS*. There seem to be two possible interpretations of the process of the sonic propagation expounded by Uddyotakara. The first explanation (*saṃtāna* I[10]) is also employed by Vātsyāyana and the later Vai-śeṣika commentators, and the other is more theoretically and deeply developed by Uddyokatara. The former is also known for the *śabdaja* theory mentioned in the *VS*.

> *NV* on *NS* II.2.13: 596, 9-13 *tatrādyaḥ śabdaḥ saṃyogavibhāga-hetukaḥ. tasmāc chabdāntarāṇi kadambagolakanyāyena sarvadi-kkāni tebhyaḥ pratyekam ekaikaḥ śabdo mandataratamādinyāyen-āśrayāpratibandham anuvidhīyamānaḥ prādur asti. tato 'ntyasyātimāndyāc chabdāntarotpattiśaktivighātaḥ, yena kenacit pratibandhād bhavatīti. ataḥ śabdasaṃtānocchedaḥ. tatra yaḥ karṇaśaṣkulīmantam ākāśadeśaṃ prāpnoti, sa upalabhyate, netara iti. tasmād aindriyakatvam. tac cānyathā na yuktam iti. ato 'nitya iti.*
>
> Then, the first sound is brought about by conjunction and disjunction. From that [sound], other sounds are [produced] in all directions, [just] like the filaments of the *Kadamba* flower. From those [sounds] each sound appears in each direction by the diminishing gradation [of sound] insofar as there is no obstacle [to sound]. Then, as the last sound becomes extremely feeble, the destruction of the efficiency to produce another sound is brought forth, if any obstacle comes forth. Thus sound succession is destroyed. With regard to this [process], if one [sound] reaches a [particular] place in ether, namely the ear-cavity, the [sound] is perceived, not vice versa. Therefore sound is perceived by the [auditory] sense, and otherwise it [would] not be justified. Thus [sound] is non-eternal.

The characteristic of the Uddyotakara's first theory is reified by the term 'the first sound' (*ādya-śabda*), which is produced by conjunction and disjunction. He also appears to think that if sound is part of ether (*ākāśadeśa*), identified as the audible organ (*karṇaśaṣkulīmant*), he could do with the sound propagation as the issue of point or place (*pradeśa*), which might imply one of the attributes of sound, '*pradeśavṛtti*'.[11]

The second theory of sound succession (*saṃtāna* II) is based mainly on the theory of disposition (*saṃskāra*) which is theoretically introduced by Vātsyāyana.[12]

> *NV* on *NS* II.2.36: 634, 7-10 *atha ghaṇṭāsthaḥ saṃskāraḥ pāṇi-saṃśleṣān nivartate, tathāpi kathaṃ śabdasaṃtānoccheda iti? --- na brūmo ghaṇṭāsaṃśleṣaḥ śabdān ucchinattīti, api tu pāṇi-ghaṇṭāsaṃśleṣāt tadvṛttisaṃskāraḥ sparśavaddravyasaṃyogavi-rodhitvān nivartate.*
>
> (Objection) If disposition residing in the bell disappears because of the contact of the hand [with it], then how can the destruction of sound succession be brought about? (Answer) We do not claim that the contact with the bell destroys [many] sounds, but that disposition residing in that [bell] disappears because [the disposition is] obstructed by the conjunction with the tactile entity by way of the contact of the hand with the bell.

Until the vibration of the bell comes to an end by the contact of the hand with it (*pāṇighaṇṭāsaṃśleṣa*), there have been a series of many sounds which plural dispositions or momenta (*vega*), inherent in the bell and being continually produced, give birth to.[13] It is emphasized in Uddyotakara's comprehensive explanation about the second type of sound succession that disposition, referred to as the cause of sound production (*śabdotpattikāraṇa*), is existent in the vibrating bell (*ghaṇṭāstha/-vṛtti*)[14] which has a different foundation (*ādhāra*) from sound, and that their foundations are different from each other even if they are in a causal relationship.

Why did Vātsyāyana and Uddyotakara employ the theory of disposition in interpreting the sound succession? Was it insufficient to classify the cause of sound production into three older patterns of cause as seen in *VS* II.2.36? We could make two assumptions about these questions. One might be related to the three causes of sound production as expounded in *VS* II.2.36. The concept of the third cause 'produced from sound' (*śabdaja*) is not present in the Vaiśeṣika list of categories, though the other two causes are respectively listed as the important subdivisions of categorical quality (*guṇa*). During the course of the theoretical and categorical systematization of the classical Vaiśeṣika, there might have been an increasing demand for classifying the theory of *śabdaja* into the orthodox system of category.

The second reason is concerned with the peculiar characteristics of disposition. It is stated as a basic element enabling motions to be generated successively, as described already in the *VS*.[15] Moreover, Vātsyāyana and Uddyotakara might have assumed that as disposition is 'a temporal existence' (*kadācidbhāva*),[15] they could coherently describe the process of sound production and destruction, and theoretically prove the impermanence of sound. They might have been worried that it is hardly sufficient to explain the production stated in *NS* II.2.36 only in terms of the conjunction of the hand with a bell (*pāṇighaṇṭā-saṃśleṣa*), for the purpose of giving a more systematic and consistent explanation to the disappearance of the sound which has reached and touched the sense of hearing.[17]

Another possible reason is that those authors might have assumed that if the plurality of disposition could lead to the concept of the plural sound individuals (*anekaśabda*),[18] they could provide a theoretical basis for the gradation theory of pitch or tone (*mandataramandatamā-dibhinnarūpa*).[19] On the other hand, Praśastapāda does not mention the numerable disposition. The reason might be that if there is number (*saṃkhyā*) or a numerical attribute in disposition, that would be incompatible with the fact that both disposition and number are qualities and they cannot possess each other, as stated in the authoritative definition of *VS* I.15: [quality] does not possess any quality (*aguṇavat*).[20]

More ontologically interesting and epistemologically problematic is the last presumable reason. It is explicitly argued especially by Uddyotakara that disposition, which is called 'the cause of sound production' (*śabdotpattikāraṇa*), has a different substratum (*vaiyadhi-karaṇya*) from sound. Why is it necessary for him to emphasize the argument of the different substrata of disposition and sound? There might have been some schools that regard the substratum of sound as the sound source such as a bell, and they are the biggest opponents for the doctrine of auditory perception of the Nyāya and Vaiśeṣika, that is, the Sāṃkhya and Buddhist, which we will see in the later section. According to the former's epistemology, the auditory sense moves out towards and contacts the sound source as its object. Then the sound, which is inherent in its source, is perceived.[21] In the meanwhile, the Nyāya and Vaiśeṣika hold the theory of *prāpyakāritva* being applicable even to the perception of color and sound, according to which theory the substratum of sound is confined only to and identified with a part of ether (*ākāśadeśa*) and sound is transmitted through ether, reaching the auditory sense.[22] The biggest difference in their substrata between disposition and sound consists in the matter of whether their basis is tactile (*sparśavat*) or not. The substratum of sound is intangible and all-pervasive (*asparśavyāpidravyāśraya*),[23] and the principle is already stated in *VS* II.2.24 and *NS* II.2.38.[24] On the other hand, in his authoritative and categoriological work, Praśastapāda points out that the substratum of disposition is what is formed (*mūrtimat*).[25] Therefore, the claim that both disposition and sound are inherently existing in the same substratum would be incompatible with the categorical system of the Nyāya and Vaiśeṣika, who might be keenly aware of the persistent way of explaining how sound can be produced from sound source, which is ontologically different in its substratum from that of sound.

SAṂTĀNA DESCRIBED IN NYĀYA AND VAIŚEṢIKA COMMENTARIES

Of the two types of theory of sound succession presented by Uddyotakara, the theory of disposition is not expounded by the later Vaiśeṣika commentators on Praśastapāda's *PDhS.*[26] On the contrary, by commenting on *kāryakāraṇobhayavirodhitva* through which Praśastapāda refers to sound succession in an indirect way in his *PDhS*, they employ the theory of the first type of succession which the earlier Nyāya authors had already adopted.[27] The problematic compound *kāryakāraṇobhayavirodhitva* is assumed to be originally related to the destruction of substance, quality and motion in *VS* I.1.11-13.

The commentators did not decidedly state that the compound refers to the succession, but instead established the three kinds of sound, and explained the production and destruction of sound. At the same time, their ways of describing are not identical, especially with regard to the intermediate sound (*madhya-śabda*). Moreover, such an interpretation of sound destruction leads directly to the undetermined matter of how to translate *ubhaya* of the *dvandva* compound *kāryakāraṇobhaya-virodhitva* in the *PDhS.*[28]

In his *Nyāyakandalī* (*NK*), Śrīdhara claims that an intermediate sound is destroyed both by the effect and causal sounds.[29] His interpretation is based on the understanding which is the same as that of Candrānanda.[30]

On the other hand, Vyomaśiva does not make any mention of the vanishing process of the last sound as Śrīdhara, though he explains that an intermediate sound is destroyed only by its effect sound.[31] Vyomaśiva's interpretation of *ubhaya* is different from and more intelligible than that of Śrīdhara.[32]

Prior to the theory of Uddyotakara, the cause of sound destruction (*vināśakāraṇa/śabdābhāva/saṃtānoccheda*) was described in such expressions as 'contact with the efficient cause of the hand' (*NS: pāṇini-mittapraśleṣa*), 'conjunction with the obstructing object' (*NBh: pratighātidravyasaṃyoga*), 'being obstructed by the conjunction with the tactile object' (*NV: sparśavaddravyasaṃyogavirodhitva*), and 'contact of the hand with a bell' (*NV: pāṇighaṇṭāsaṃśleṣa*).[33] As there seems to have been no theory before Uddyotakara that the very last sound is destroyed by the preceding one, it might lead us to assume that Śrīdhara may have tried to solve the problem of the interpretation of the controversial compound *kāryakāraṇobhaya* by thinking of the destruction by the preceding sound before the last sound (*upāntya-śabda*). But his idea is incompatible with the earlier way of understanding the compound as mentioned above. On the other hand, Vyomaśiva, naturally knowing the older comprehension of the compound, might appear to have chosen not to adopt the later Vaiśeṣika standardized theory.

Vācaspati Miśra, one of the greatest commentators at the last stage of the classical Nyāya and Vaiśeṣika, avoids the matter of the interpretation of *kāryakāraṇobhaya* as 'unestablished' (*aniyama*), probably observing the controversial situation.[34]

SAṂTĀNA IN **TS*

The epistemology, based on the theory of *prāpyakāritva* in the **TS* of Harivarman (訶梨跋摩) (Taisho 32 No. 1646; Chin. Tr. by Kumārajīva 鳩摩羅什 in 411-12), is significant in that it holds the theory of disposition as the cause of the sound production which is expounded by the opponent (who is assumed to be the earlier Vaiśeṣika[35]) for the following reasons. The refutation in 聞聲品第五十 in the **TS*[36] is based on the theory of the three types of sonic production mentioned in *VS* II.2.36; moreover, the name of Vaiśeṣika (衛世師) is referred to in the phrase 然則衛世師經一切皆壞.[37] This assumption suggests the possibility that theVātsyāyana's theory of disposition is developed not only inside the Nyāya but under some influence of the Vaiśeṣika, and especially, introduced directly from the Vaiśeṣika. The theory of disposition is also stated in the other Vaiśeṣika text, Candramati's **Daśapadārthī* (**DA*) (or **Daśapadārthaśāstra*).[38] If the **DA* was composed between 450 and 550 as suggested by Frauwallner,[39] we could conclude from this evidence that the Vaiśeṣika made use of disposition in explaining the sound production, and that most probably Praśastapāda, who is thought to have flourished around the sixth century, might be the first scholar to dismiss the usage of the concept of disposition from the Vaiśeṣika theory of sound.

In the **TS*, the Vaiśeṣika theory that the preceding sound produces another sound in a successive way（相續 **saṃtāna*) like a wave is criticized.[40] It is the momentariness (念念滅 **kṣaṇika*) of sound that is taken up by Harivarman as the antithesis against this theory.[41] The fundamental Buddhist idea is that what is existent is momentary and it cannot be produced by any other thing and is destroyed just after its production.[42] If one sound could not be produced, depending on its preceding sound, the sound succession might be inevitably disappeared. What is enumerated as momentary in the the **TS* is mind and other mental factors (諸心意識), and motions (業 **karman*).[43] Surprisingly enough, this position is quite similar to that of Praśastapāda.[44]

As the criticism by Harivarman might contain some points which are not proclaimed by the Vaiśeṣika as an opponent, it would lead us to a misunderstanding of the original and real Vaiśeṣika thought, while his descriptions are very useful for reconstructing the earlier Vaiśeṣika thought. Harivarman's standpoint in criticizing the opponent's sound theory is based on the Vaiśeṣika's three main categories, such as substance, quality and motion. For example, if the sonic succession is considered to be the movement of sound individuals, this identification with individual objects would be contrary to the definition that quality cannot possess any motion (以諸求那無作業故).[45]

We can see another instance of Harivarman's criticism in the following passage in terms of motion and momentum as a kind of disposition.

> T. 32 270b2-9 又同業故。聲與同相。如說雖聲求那滅與業同。... 汝分別。從初業勢。更生後業。如是亦應從初聲生勢。從勢生後諸業。是中無有異。

[It is] also because [the sound succession would] be the same as the

> motion. . . . According to your theory, momentum is produced from the first motion, and the following motions are produced [from the momenta]. Just like this [case of motion], momentum will be produced from the first sound, and the following many motions are produced from the momenta. In this [explanation], there is no difference [between the theory of the production of motions and that of sounds].

If sound succession is produced from momentum (勢 **vega*), sound itself — more correctly, sound succession — is motions (聲與業同相), as motions are produced from momenta, which are the cause of the successive motions. Actually this is contrary to the Vaiśeṣika theory of sound. The theory of momentariness of sound might be effective only when the classical Vaiśeṣika makes an attempt to ward off the same attributes as those of motions which must be limited to a substance, an ontologically independent object, and to confine sound to the category of quality so that sound may lose the objectivity of a concrete entity.

CONCLUSION

It can be said that much of his description might be influenced by the thought already stated by preceding Nyāya and Vaiśeṣika scholars such as Vātsyāyana and so on. Moreover, he does not refer to disposition in the section dealing with sound, on which much emphasis is given as a basic causal factor for explaining the process of sound transmission by the Nyāya authors such as Vātsyāyana and Uddyotakara. As we have already seen in the previous section, this might result from such a background as the controversial status of disposition in sound theory which attracted a serious criticism from the Buddhists as seen in the **TS*. Another more possible and internal reason might be that he is quite aware that even if the theory of disposition could reasonably and mechanically explain the process of sound succession and confine sound as a quality only to ether as its substratum, there might still be much difficulty in establishing the relationship between disposition and sound in a categorical framework. To avoid this theoretical problem, he instead seems to have adopted a peculiar and new concept of momentariness, borrowing from the Budddhist theory of sound which could steadily and provisionally be installed into the categorical system of quality, and then employing the inductive method of *pariśeṣa*.[46] On the other hand, in spite of severe criticisms toward the theory of sound transmission by the Buddhist as seen in the **TS*, Praśastapāda adopted the theory which had been arranged in a more and more theoretical way through the arguments with other opponents ever since the *NS*. We can assume the reason for the employment of the theory of sound succession in such a way as the Vaiśeṣika epistemology of auditory perception inevitably requires the direct contact of sound with the audible organ, which is known as the *prāpyakāritva* theory, while in the Buddhist epistemology there is no need for such a direct contact because of their theory of *aprāpyakāritva*.

NOTES

* An earlier form of this paper first appeared in 'The Noneternality of *śabda* in Vaiśeṣika Philosophy' (in Japanese), *Journal of Indian and Buddhist Studies* 47-1 (1998), pp. 463-5.

1 *PDhS* (Ed. J. Bronkhorst and Y. Ramseier, Delhi, 1994) [89] *rūpa-rasagandhasparśasnehasāṃsiddhikadravatvabuddhisukhaduḥkhecchādve-ṣaprayatnadharmādharmabhāvanā**śabdā vaiśeṣikaguṇāḥ***. Cf. W. Halbfass, '*Ākāśa*: The Elusive Element' in *The Perception of the Elements in the Hindu Tradition (La perception des éléments dans les traditions hindoues,* ed. by M. Burger and P. Schreiner, Bern, 1999, pp. 159-80, esp. pp. 163-7.

2 *PDhS* [10] *ākāśātmanāṃ **kṣaṇikai**kadeśavṛtti**viśeṣaguṇavat**tvam*. Cf. also *PDhS* [320, 1-3].

3 Sound is not enumerated as quality in *VS* I.1.5. *VS* (Baroda, 1961; GOS) II.2.25 raises the question of whether it is a substance, quality, or motion. The fact that Praśastapāda describes sound in a quite different section from the other four cognitive objects, and moreover in the last section of the quality suggests that sound is given a special status. On sound as not originally a quality in the early Vaiśeṣika, see J. Bronkhorst, 'Studies on Bhartṛhari, 5: Bhartṛhari and Vaiśeṣika,' *Bhartṛhari*, Delhi, 1994, pp. 75-94 (=*AS/ÉA* 47, 1992: 75-94): 80-87 ; M. Nozawa, ' "vaishēshika-sūtora" no futatsu no sō,' *Indo-shisōshi kenkyū*, 7 (1995), pp. 72-84 ('Two Layers in the *Vaiśeṣikasūtra', Studies in the History of Indian Thought*): 76. In particular, the former points out that *śabda* is originally a substance and wind (*vāyu*) itself.

4 *PDhS* [115] *śeṣāṇām **ayāvaddravyabhāvitvaṃ** ceti*. On other occurrences, see *NV* (Calcutta, 1936-94; repr. Kyoto, 1982) 612, 6-7 *kāryākāśa-saṃyogo vipratipattiviṣayaḥ, **na yāvaddravyabhāvI,** avinaś-yadādhāratve, kriyāvaddravyavṛttitve saty aprāptipratidvandvitvāt, mūrtimaditara-saṃyogavat. ; Candrānandavṛtti* (*CV*) 16, 12-13 on *VS* II. 2.2; ibid., 16, 15 on *VS* II.2.3.

5 For the explicit argument in the Nyāya texts, see, for example, *NBh* on *NS* III.2.42: 881, 1-3 *anityāyāṃ ca buddhāv **utpannāpavargitvāt** kālāntarā-vasthānāc **cānityānāṃ** saṃśayaḥ. kim **utpannāpavargiṇī buddhiḥ śabda-***

***vat**, āhosvit kālāntarāvasthāyinī kumbhavad iti. utpannāpavargiṇīti pakṣaḥ parigṛhyate.* In this passage, *anitya* is para-phrased by the compound *utpannāpavargin*, which means 'the destruc-tion of what is produced', and it is made clear that sound and cognition are the two major controversial matters in those days. For the occurrence of *apavarga* meaning destruction or disappearance, see *VS* II.2.29; *Vākyapadīya* (Wiesbaden, 1977) III.9.27; *Laṅkāvatārasūtra* (Ed. B. Nanjio, Kyoto 1923) 221, 1-3.

6 Cf. *VS* VII.1.9 *anityeṣv anityā dravyānityatvāt.*

7 On the concept of manifestation in Sāṃkhya school, see the paper of the present author, '*satkāryavāda* ronshōni okeru *abhivyakti* to *pariṇāma*,' *Indo-shisōshi Kenkyū*, 8 (1996), ('*Pariṇāma* and *Abhivyakti* in the Sāṃkhya Argument for *Satkāryavāda*,' *Studies in the History of Indian Thought*): 42-63; on that concept in Nyāya and Vaiśeṣika schools, see, in particular, M. Nozawa, 'abhivyakti (kengen) nitsuite,' ('On *abhivyakti* (manifestation)') *Hokkaido Journal of Indological and Buddhist Studies*, vol. 6, 1991, pp. 91-105.

8 For summary of the differences among some major schools, see W. Ruben, *Die Nyāyasūtra's*, Leipzig, 1928, p. 192[15].

9 All further references and discussions on the occurrences of the relevant phrases in the table will be shown later.

10 Cf. B. Seal, *The Positive Sciences of the Ancient Hindus*, London, 1915, pp. 156-8.

11 For the earlier occurrence of 'place of ether' which explains the propagation of sound and the sound perception, see *Śābarabhāṣya* (Ed. Kāśīnāth Vāsudev Abhyaṅkar, Poona, 1976: ĀSS) (*ŚBh*) 81, 5-82, 3 *evaṃ śabde 'pi vyāmohād anavadhāraṇaṃ deśasya. yadi śrotraṃ saṃyoga-vibhāgadeśam āgatya śabdaṃ gṛhṇīyāt tathāpi tāvad anekadeśatā kadācid avagamyeta. na ca tatsaṃyogadeśam āgacchati. pratyakṣā hi karṇaśaṣkulī taddeśā gṛhyate. vāyavīyāḥ punaḥ saṃyogavibhāgā apraty-akṣasya vāyoḥ* ***karṇaśaṣkulīpradeśe*** *prādurbhavanto nopalabhyanta iti nānupapannam. ata eva vyāmoho yan nānādeśeṣu śabda iti.* ***ākāśadeśaś*** *ca śabda iti.* For another type of sound propagation based on the concept of part of ether, see *NV* 606, 10-13.

12 For the general explanation of the sound theory based upon disposition in the *NBh*, see Ruben, *Nyāyasūtra's*, p. 193[160]. Cf. also Seal, *Positive Sciences*, pp. 159-61.

13 For the occurrence of *vega, see NV* 633, 4-7 *kutas tadutpattiḥ? pāṇisaṃśleṣam apekṣamāṇāt karmaṇaḥ. pāṇighaṇṭāsaṃśleṣāt pāṇigata**vegā**pekṣād ghaṇṭāyāṃ karma. tatkarma pāṇyabhighātam apekṣamāṇaṃ vibhāgasamakālaṃ* ***saṃskāraṃ*** *karoti. sā calanty ādhyatmikaṃ vāyum upagṛhṇāti. sā ca vāyunābhihatā punaḥ karma karoti. tataś ca karmaṇā saṃskāraḥ. saṃskāreṇa punaḥ karma. punar vāyūpagraha ityevam-ādinyāyena* ***saṃskāra*** *utpadyata iti.*

14 *NV* 630, 4-631, 5 (6 times); 632, 4-6 (twice); 634, 7-10 (once).

15 *VS* V.1.17 *nodanād ādyam iṣoḥ karma karmakāritāc ca* ***saṃskārād*** *uttaraṃ tathottaram uttaraṃ ca.* For other similar examples of a flying arrow mentioned in this sūtra, see *NBh* 634, 1-6 (on *NS* II.2.36); *NV* 636,

11-637, 10 (on *NS* II.2.38).

16 *NV* 632, 6-8 *ghaṇṭāstham utpattikāraṇaṃ* ***kadācic*** *chabdān utpādayati, kadācin neti nityavat prasaṅgaḥ. na prasaṅgaḥ* ***kadācidbhāvāt****: śabdānām utpattikāraṇaṃ ghaṇṭāvṛtti tat* ***kadācid bhavati kadācidbhāve 'pi sati saṃtānavṛtti****.* For the occurrence of *kadācit* in the context of auditory perception, see *ŚBh* 81, 5-8. See also W. Halbfass, *On Being and What There Is*, Albany, 1992, p. 212.

17 Cf. *NV* 636, 7-8 *kathaṁ* ***anyatra vartamānasya pāṇighaṇṭāsaṃśleṣo nivartaka*** *iti? na, uktottaratvāt. uktottaram etat. kāraṇābhāvād anya-śabdānutpādaḥ.*

18 *NV* on *NS* II.2.38: 636, 10-637, 10 *yo 'yaṃ* ***saṃskāraḥ śabdakāraṇatvena*** *samadhigataḥ, sa kim eko 'neko veti saṃdihyate.* ***anekaḥ saṃskāra iti tattvaṃ****, śabdabhedāt. kāraṇabhede sati kāryabhedo dṛṣṭaḥ. yasyaikaḥ saṃskāraḥ tasyeṣoḥ pātaḥ prāpnoty agatvaiva yāvad gantavyam iti. athāpratibadhyamāne saṃskāre dravyaṃ gacchati, na kadācit pātaḥ prāpnoti. tasmād* ***anekaḥ saṃskāraḥ****.*

19 *NV* 632, 8-9 *tasmān nimittabhedānuvidhāyinaḥ śabdāḥ kadācid bhavanti. saṃtānavṛttitvāc ca* ***mandataramandatamādibhinnarūpānuvidhāyinaṃ*** *śabdam utpādayantīti. tac ca kāraṇaṃ saṃskāra iti.* On the difference of this theory from that of the Vaiśeṣika, see *NVTṬ* 637, 14-5 *yasya ca vaiśeṣikasyaikaḥ saṃskāras tasyeṣoḥ pātaḥ prāpnoti.* We can note here that according to Vācaspati Miśra's understanding, one and indivisible disposition is the peculiar theory for Vaiśeṣika.

20 On the presumable contradiction of the sound theory stated by Vatsyā-yana with the Vaiśeṣika definition of quality, see G. Jhā, *The Nyāyasūtras of Gautama, with Vātsyāyana's Bhāṣya and Uddyotakara's Vārttika, translated into English*, repr. Kyoto, 1983, vol. II, 388 fn.

21 On the classical definition of the epistemology of the Sāṃkhya, see *Sāṃkhyakārikā* (Ed. A. Wezler and Sh. Motegi, *Yuktidīpikā. The Most Significant Commentary on the Sāṃkhyakārikā*, Stuttgart, 1998) (*SK* and *YD*) 5c *prativiṣayādhyavasāyo dṛṣṭam; YD* 5, 11-2 *śrotrādivṛttiḥ pratyakṣam.* Cf. P. Chakravarti, *Origin and Development of the Sāṃkhya System of Thought*, Calcutta, 1975[2], pp. 171-3; M. Hattori, *Dignāga, On Perception, being the Pratyakṣapariccheda of Dignāga's Pramāṇa-samuccaya from the Sanskrit fragments and the Tibetan versions*, Cambridge, 1968, pp. 148[5.1]. In the *YD*, it is stated that sense organs are made up of self-consciousness (*āhaṃkārika*) and are all-pervasive (*vyāpaka*), so they can be modified according to the forms of their objects (*viṣayākārapariṇāma*) for the purpose of perceiving them: *YD* 203, 28-30 *āhaṃkārikāṇāṃ tu teṣāṃ [indriyāṇāṃ]* ***vyāpakatvād viṣayākārapari-ṇāmātmikā vṛttir*** *vṛttimato 'nyā sati sambhavaty evety suvacaṃ* ***prāpyakāritvam****.* For further reference to this passage, see *Nyāya-mañjarī* (Ed. S.N. Śukla, Varanasi, 1971, part II, 29, 5-10); *Ślokavārttika* (ChSS, Benares, 1898-9) (*ŚV*) (*pratyakṣa*) 43cd-44 *sāṃkhyādīn vā vinirjitya* ***prāptapakṣo*** *'tra dūṣyatām // tayoś [śrotracakṣuṣoś* in v. 40] *ca* ***prāpyakāritvam*** *indriyatvāt tvagādivat /* ***kecit*** *tayoḥ* ***śarīrāc ca bahirvṛttiṃ*** *pracakṣate //; Nārāyanatīrtha* (in *ŚV*) 147, 7-8... ***kecid iti. sāṃkhyās*** *tāvad āhaṃkārikayoḥ śrotracakṣuṣor vṛttiḥ* ***śarīrād vinir-***

***gatyā**rthaṃ gṛhṇātīti manyante*. Cf. Chakravarti, *Sāṃkhya System*, pp. 176[2], 177; K. Preisendanz, 'On *ātmendriyamanorthasannikarṣa* and the Nyāya-Vaiśeṣika Theory of Vision,' *BIS* 4/5, 1989, pp. 141-213, esp. pp. 170-1. The theory that a sensory organ reaches a cognitive object and can perceive it is also mentioned and criticised by Śabarasvāmin in his commentary on *Mīmāṃsāsūtra* I.1.15: *ŚBh* 81, 5-7 *yadi śrotraṃ saṃyogavibhāgadeśam āgatya śabdaṃ gṛhṇīyāt, tathāpi tāvad anekadeśatā kadācid avagamyeta. na ca tatsaṃyogadeśam āgacchati.*

22 See, for example, *NV* 596, 12-3; *NVTṬ* 636, 15-8 ***prāpyakāritvam indriyāṇāṃ** vyavasthitaṃ prāk. ghaṇṭādyāśrayaḥ śabdo na śrotraṃ prāpnoti. evaṃ hi prāpnuyād **yadi ghaṇṭā karṇaśaṣkulīm āgacchet**, karṇaśaṣkulī vā ghaṇṭām. na cāhaṃkārikam indriyaṃ vyāpīty uktam. tasmāc **chabdādhāro niḥsparśo vyāpī cākāśaḥ, tadādhāraḥ śabdaḥ śrotram āyāti saṃtānavṛttyeti** yuktam.*

23 *NBh* on *NS* II.2.38: 636, 2-4 *yad idaṃ nākāśaguṇaḥ śabda iti pratiṣidhyate. ayam anupapannaḥ pratiṣedhaḥ. **rūpādisamānadeśasyāgrahaṇe** śabdasaṃtānopapatter **asparśavyāpidravyāśrayaḥ** śabda iti jñāyate **na kampasamānāśraya** iti.* In his commentary *NVTṬ*, Vācaspati Miśra mentions that the opponent of the argument is the Sāṃkhya school: *NVTṬ* 635, 20 ***saṃprati sāṃkhyaḥ** pratyavatiṣṭhate: kampasamānāśrayasyeti.*

24 *VS* II.2.24 *kāraṇaguṇapūrvakaḥ kārye guṇo dṛṣṭaḥ, kāryāntarāprādurbhāvāc ca śabdaḥ sparśavatām aguṇaḥ.*; *NS* II.2.38 *asparśatvād apratiṣedhaḥ.*

25 *PDhS* [303, 1-2] *tatra vego **mūrtimatsu pañcasu dravyeṣu** nimittaviśeṣāpekṣāt karmaṇo jāyate.*

26 On the explanation by Vācaspati Miśra, see *NVTṬ* 606, 14-9. He emphasizes that the succession of sound is not the movement of part of ether, but rather is likely to be applied to the sound source and the points of space (*viśiṣṭadigdeśāvasthitaśaṅkhādiprabhavaśabdasaṃtāna*) in order to preserve the concept of *śabdasaṃtāna.*

27 *NBh* on *NS* II.2.35: 628, 10-629, 2 *tatra kāryaḥ śabdaḥ kāraṇaśabdaṃ niruṇaddhi, pratighātidravyasaṃyogas tv **antyasya** nirodhakaḥ. dṛṣṭaṃ hi tiraḥpratikuḍyam antikasthenāpy aśravaṇaṃ śabdasya, śravaṇaṃ dūrasthenāpy asati vyavadhāna iti.*

28 Cf. S. Bhaduri, *Studies in Nyāya-Vaiśeṣika Metaphysics*, Poona, 1947 (repr. 1975), p. 181.

29 *NK* (SGDOS; Delhi 1984) 288, 16-8 *ādyaḥ śabdaḥ svakāryeṇa virudhyate. antyaḥ svakāraṇenopāntyaśabdena virudhyate. antyasya vināśakāraṇasyābhāvāt. madhyavartinas tūbhayathā virudhyante.*

30 *CV* on *VS* I.1.12: 4, 22 *virodhina **ādyamadhyāntyaśabdāḥ kāryobhayakāraṇaiḥ** [yathāsaṃbhavam].*

31 *Vyomavatī* (CSS; Benares 1924-31) 650, 2-4 *tad evam anityatve vyavasthite vināśakāraṇam āha: kāryakāraṇobhayavirodhīti. **ādyaḥ śabdaḥ kāryeṇa** virudhyate. **antyas** tu kāraṇaṃ viruṇaddhi. **madhyagatās** tu kāryeṇa virudhyante, kāraṇaṃ ca virundhantīti.*

32 On the fact that Śrīdhara's interpretation is more obedient to the Praśastapāda's theory than that of Vyomaśiva, see H. Isaacson, *Materials*

for the Study of the Vaiśeṣika System, 1995 (Diss., Leiden), 188-9[24].

33 These expressions are originally from *NS* II.2.36 ***pāṇinimittapraśleṣāc*** *chabdābhāve nānupalabdhiḥ*.

34 *NVTṬ* 596, 21-4 *tato 'ntyasyātimāndyād iti. nāntyaḥ śabdāntaram ārabhate, na kevalam asau svakāraṇaṃ śabdaṃ nāśayati, kiṃtu so 'pi svakāraṇena śabdena nāśyate, tad idam anayoḥ kāryakāraṇavirodhitvam. ādyas tu kāryeṇaiva nāśyate* ***madhyānāṃ tv aniyama*** *iti*.

35 For the refutation against 勢 (**vega*), see T. 32 270b2-29.

36 T. 32 269c9-270c8.

37 T. 32 270c1-2.

38 See, for example, 成實論, T. 54 1265a18-21 聲有三種一合二離生三聲生。合生者觸實合勢用俱有觸實空處合爲因。離生者有觸實離勢用俱有觸實空處離爲因。聲生者有觸實合離勢用待無障空處聲爲因。For the reconstructed Sanskrit text and translation of this passage, see K. Miyamoto, *The Metaphysics and Epistemology of the Early Vaiśeṣikas*, Pune, 1996, pp. 193-4 [156-159].

39 E. Frauwallner, 'Candramati und sein Daśapadārthaśāstra,' *Studia Indologica*, Salzburg, 1955, p. 80 = *Kl. Schr.*, p. 217.

40 T. 32 270a2-3 問曰。從聲相續生聲求那。如水中波。名爲聲去。In his commentary on Vasubandhu's *Abhidharmakośabhāṣya* (Ed. P. Pradhan, Patna, 1975[2]) (*AKBh*) Yaśomitra refers to the Vaiśeṣika school as holding the theory that one cognition (*buddhi*) or sound can be destroyed by another cognition or sound: *Abhidharmakośavyākhyā* (Ed. W. Unrai, Tokyo, 1971) II 346, 29-30 *yas tu manyata iti* ***vaiśeṣikāḥ*** *pūrvā buddhir uttarayā buddhyā utpannayā vināśyate. anyā tu buddhiḥ pūrvayā buddhyā vināśyate. evaṃ śabdo 'pi vācyaḥ*.

41 T. 32 270a19-21 又聲念念滅故不生異聲[.] 不見念念滅法[.]能有所生.是故聲不生異聲 = *Satyasiddhiśāstra* (Ed. N.A. Sastri, Baroda 1975; GOS) I 136, 8-9 *śabdaś ca* ***kṣaṇika****tvān na śabdāntaram utpādayati. na hi paśyāmaḥ* '***kṣaṇika****dharmaḥ kasyacij janaka' iti. ato na śabdaḥ śabdāntaraṃ janayati.* For the occurrences in which the term *kṣaṇika* is translated into Chinese phrase 念念滅, though I have not affirmed the actual case in the Kumārajīva's translations, who is also the translator of **TS*, see some few occurrences in the Chinese translations of *Abhidharmakośa* by Paramārtha (眞諦) and so on: for example, T. 29 No. 1559 204b26 譬如燈雖念念滅由相續得至餘處 = *AKBh* 129, 19-20 *tadyathā pradīpaḥ kṣaṇiko 'pi saṃtatyā deśāntaram* . . . = T.29 No.1558 (Tr. Xuan zang 玄奘) 47c12 譬如燈焔雖刹那滅而能相續轉至餘方。

42 Cf. *AKBh* 193, 2 *ko 'yaṃ kṣaṇo nāma. ātmalābho 'nantaravināśī. so 'syāstīti kṣaṇikam*. On the cause of the general production after the theory of momentariness, see Th. Stcherbatsky, *The Central Conception of Buddhism and the Meaning of the Word "Dharma"*, 1923 (Repr. Delhi 1970), 38: 'A cause for the Buddhists was not a real cause but a preceding moment, which likewise arose out of nothing in order to disappear into nothing.'

43 T. 32 280b8-9 又聲業相續念念滅相。於中生知。故知心念念滅。

44 On *buddhi, see PDhS* [4, 10] *ākāśātmanāṃ* ***kṣaṇikai****kadeśavṛttiviśeṣaguṇavattvam*; on *karma*, see *PDhS* [68, 4-5] *ekadravyavattvaṃ* ***kṣaṇika-***

tvaṃ *mūrtadravyavṛttitvam aguṇavattvaṃ* . . . ; [69, 10].

45 T. 32 270a1-2 又聲是求那。是故不去。以諸求那無作業故。*PDhS* [3, 4] *guṇādīnāṃ pañcānām api nirguṇatva**niṣkriyatve***. ; [18, 1-2] *rūpādīnāṃ guṇānāṃ sarveṣāṃ guṇatvābhisambandho dravyāśritatvaṃ nirguṇatvaṃ* ***niṣkriyatvam***. ; *NV* 594, 16-595, 6 *śrotraṃ tāvan na śabdadeśam upagacchati, amūrtatvāt. yad amūrtaṃ tan niṣkriyaṃ, yathā rūpādi. amūrtaṃ cākāśam, tasmān* ***niṣkriyam*** *iti*. ; 596, 7-8 *tasmād akriyāvattvād ākāśaṃ na gacchati, śabdo 'pi na gacchati,* ***niṣkriyatvād*** *eva*. On the assumption that early Vaiśeṣika does not consider quality as 'having an action', see Preisendanz, 'On ā*tmendriyamanorthasaṃnikarṣa*', pp. 158-9. For the similar critisism that a sound cannot produce another sound because of its immobility, see *śabdanityatā* chapter in *ŚV*: 91cd ***ārambhakatvaṃ śabdasya niṣkriyasyā****pramāṇakam*.

46 See *PDhS* [323] ; *NV* 596, 6-9.

11

Change of View on *Apūrva* from Śabarasvāmin to Kumārila*

KIYOTAKA YOSHIMIZU

In the Bhāṭṭa school, *apūrva* was considered to be a kind of disposition (*saṃskāra*). Man was supposed to go to heaven by virtue of the *apūrva* accumulated in his self (*ātman*) by means of Vedic sacrifices. As far as the existent Mīmāṃsā literature is concerned, in his commentary on the *Mīmāṃsāsūtra* (*JS*) 2.1.5: '*codanā punar ārambhaḥ*' Śabarasvāmin introduced the notion of *apūrva* as an intermediary between the ephemeral session of a sacrifice and its result in the future. On the other hand, he explicitly rejects the hypothesis that the physical act of offering would endure by its transposition in the *ātman* (*ŚBh* 2: 372,3-373,1). In this paper, I will examine the nature of *apūrva* described by Śabara in his commentary on later sections (*JS* 2.2, 7 and 9) in order to find what is implied in his brief words on *JS* 2.1.5. Later I will elucidate how Kumārila estimated the various views on the nature of *apūrva* advocated in his times, and thereby clarify his own idea about how *apūrva* plays a role within the structure of a sacrifice.

APŪRVA AND PARTICULAR SACRIFICES

Śabara regards the first Pāda of the second Adhyāya including *JS* 2.1.5 as an introduction (*upodghāta*) to the next Pāda (*ŚBh* 2: 336,2-3). In *JS* 2.2 and 2.3 one investigates what are the characteristics of a Vedic sentence by which it is entitled 'the impelling-injunction' (*codanā*)[1] of an act of offering within the complex text. Although the term '*apūrva*' does not appear in the sūtras of the second and the third Pāda,[2] in each section Śabara qualifies the act of offering prescribed exclusively by an impelling-injunction as 'something not preceded' (*a-pūrva*)[3]. He further contrasts the impelling-injunction with a restatement (*anuvāda*) which refers to an act of offering already prescribed by another injunction.[4]

Insofar as the manner of offering at the sacrificial altar is concerned,

Śabara finds the originality (*apūrva*) of an act of offering in its oblation and the deity to which it is offered. This combination of oblation and deity is called its 'form' (*rūpa*). The reason why a Vedic sentence is called the impelling-injunction (*codanā*) of an act of offering is that it prescribes a particular form that distinguishes it from others.[5] By the phrase 'making *apūrva*' in this context,[6] Śabara refers to performing an act of offering in strict accordance to the prescribed form. The term '*apūrva*' is not used here to mean a kind of potency left by the sacrifice.

The term '*apūrva*' appears frequently again at the beginning of the commentary on *JS* 7. Śabara addresses the following question at first: What is the purpose of the prescription (*dharma*) of each element in a sacrifice: Is it to accomplish the act of offering in general (*yaji*) or to accomplish an *apūrva* (*ŚBh* 5: 375,1-2)? The term '*yaji*' in the first alternative consists of the root √*yaj* with the suffix iK and denotes the general form common to all the acts of offering.[7] Śabara devotes most parts of his commentary in justifying the second alternative[8] and he reveals some aspects of *apūrva* not argued in *JS* 2.1.1-5.

In accordance with the traditional notion of *apūrva* traced back to *JS*[9] and even to Śrautasūtras,[10] Śabara distinguishes a particular (*viśeṣa*) from the universal (*sāmānya*) in a group of sacrifices by contrasting *apūrva* with *yaji*. For that purpose, he modifies the two alternatives in the above question as follows: Is the prescription of each element in a sacrifice related to the sacrifice in general (*yāgamātra*) or a particular kind of sacrifice (*yāgaviśeṣa*) (*ŚBh* 5: 379,9-10)? By means of specifying the ritual elements such as deity, oblation, etc., one can perform a particular sacrifice which has a particular name such as '*darśapūrṇamāsa*', '*jyotiṣṭoma*'. It is this particular sacrifice that Śabara relates to *apūrva*.[11] Even within the impelling-injunction: '*darśapūrṇamāsābhyāṃ svargakāmo yajeta*' the root √*yaj* of the verb means an act of offering in abstract form (*sāmānya*) whereas the noun '*darśapūrṇamāsa*' refers to this same act (*sāmānādhikaraṇya*) as a concrete way (*viśeṣa*) of offering at a new or a full moon day.[12] Each rite in a sacrifice is performed for the purpose of contributing to such an *apūrva* and not to the general form of sacrifice, just as one dyes clothes not for the sake of the clothes, but for the sake of a particular person, the man or woman who wears them (*ŚBh* 5: 384,14-17).

APŪRVA IS NOT A DISPOSITION

Kumārila has recourse to daily experiences caused by a certain disposition (*saṃskāra*) as an analogy of the Vedic *apūrva*. He says that the daily activities such as cultivation of soil, ingesting ghee, studying, etc., leave in the soil or in the performer a disposition, which continues to be accumulated so as to finally produce a result (*TV* 2: 365,15-17). In Śabara's Bhāṣya on Adhyāya 7, however, it is the opponent that resorts to an analogy of ingesting ghee and sesame oil in order to justify his view that the sacrificial act will endure even after it is out of sight (*ŚBh* 5: 383,15-17). Although he does not use the term '*saṃskāra*', Śabara rejects this analogy definitively. According to him, ingesting sesame oils etc., has only a tentative effect that calms the disturbance of the circulatory system (*ŚBh* 5: 384,20-24). Although Śabara admits that there is a ritual act which leaves in the performer a certain disposition,[13] he does not accept that the act of offering causes an inner change which would be called '*apūrva*' in the sacrificer.[14]

APŪRVA AS A *CAUSA FINALIS*

Generally speaking, adherents of an ideal consider it their purpose to be accomplished in the future. At the same time, we can say that the ideal guides them to right behavior because the ideal has been instilled into their mind by another adherent or by its originator. Śabara also states that *apūrva* plays the roles both of purpose and cause when one performs the detailed procedure for an offering. We can find this statement in his Bhāṣya on *JS* 9.1.1 which is the beginning of the chapter on modification (*ūha*). On the assumption that a man performs each details of a ritual in order to realize *apūrva* by offering, as was ascertained in *JS* 7.1, Śabara now asks about the cause which urges the sacrificer to perform the details. At first, the opponent denies the possibility of *apūrva* being the cause, because nothing can be both a cause (*nimitta*) working at present and a purpose (*prayojaka*) to be accomplished in the future (*ŚBh* 6: 62,3-6). Śabara rejects this view and maintains that an *apūrva*, once revealed by the impelling-injunction, requires a detailed procedure for its realization (*ŚBh* 6: 62,12-16).

By virtue of the optative ending of the verb '*yajeta*', the impelling-injunction '*darśapūrṇamāsābhyāṃ svargakāmo yajeta*' urges the hearer to undertake the sacrifice. Śabara regards *apūrva* here as the meaning of the optative ending[15] and thereby indicates the inseparability of *codanā* from *apūrva.*[16] What the *codanā* of the new and full moon sacrifices reveals is the distinct ideal, not shared by other sacrifices. Because of this distinctiveness, it comes to be required by the *apūrva* to perform a programmed series of many subsidiary rites, e.g. preparing a particular oblation and eulogizing a particular deity by chanting *mantras.* If *apūrvas* of Vedic sacrifices are ideals of action, they have been ever present in the mind of a sacrificer since he learned the Vedas in his student days. He tries to perform the whole program of a sacrifice periodically in order to realize the *apūrva* in accordance with the Aryan tradition. By recourse to a simile of a garden and a gardener,[17] Śabara maintains that *apūrva* has already been established as an ideal of action in the Aryan society before an individual takes part in preserving the tradition as a sacrificer.

QUOTATION OF *JS* 2.1.5 IN THE SEVENTH ADHYĀYA

To discern the structure of Śabara's Bhāṣya on *JS* 2.1.5 with the help of our foregoing examinations, it is also worthwhile paying attention to the first section[18] of *JS* 7.4 where Śabara quotes *JS* 2.1.5[19] together with *JS* 2.3.14 and 6.1.3 as the sūtras indispensable for the argument of this section.

Here Śabara extracts the impelling-injunction (*codanā*) from an aggregate of injunctions by calling it the 'chief-injunction' (*vidhyādi, lit.* 'the beginning of injunctions'), and compares it with other injunctions called 'appended-injunction' (*vidhyanta, lit.* 'the end of injunctions'). In the mind of a person who has learned the whole text of the Vedas, all injunctions are arranged in a hierarchical order. As soon as the impelling-injunction has prompted the person to undertake the sacrifice, the appended-injunctions are set in motion (*pravarteta*) (*ŚBh* 5: 431,24-432,4).

The 'appended-injunctions' taken into account here prescribe how to prepare the oblation to be offered in the main offerings.[20] Because it is necessary for the impelling-injunction to be assisted by the appended-injunctions, the person prompted by the impelling-injunction can 'realize the specified *apūrva*' (*viśiṣṭāpūrvanirvṛtti*) by an offering after he has prepared proper oblations by following the 'appended-injunctions'. As mentioned earlier, as well as *JS* 2.3.14 which distinguishes an offering from others by specializing its oblation, Śabara quotes *JS* 2.1.5 at the beginning of this section. We can therefore safely say that the meaning of '*apūrva*' discussed by Śabara in *JS* 2.1.5 does not differ from the distinctive form of each particular sacrifice investigated from the beginning of *JS* 7.[21]

PARAPHRASE AND ARGUMENT IN THE APŪRVĀDHIKARAṆA

Now we are in a position to analyse Śabara's commentary on *JS* 2.1.5. Let us quote the beginning by numbering each phrase:

> (1) *katham punar idam avagamyate 'asti tad apūrvam' iti. ucyate: codanā punar ārambhaḥ. (2) codanety apūrvaṃ brūmaḥ. (3) apūrvaṃ punar asti, (4) yata ārambhaḥ śiṣyate 'svargakāmo yajeta' iti. (5) itarathā hi vidhānam anarthakaṃ syāt. (6) bhaṅgitvād yāgasya. (7) yady anyad anutpādya yāgo vinaśyet, phalam asati nimitte na syāt.*

When modern scholars read this paragraph, they have generally understood (4) and (5) to form a proof of the existence of *apūrva* asserted in (3). What is meant by '*itarathā*' in (5) is: 'if there were no such thing as *apūrva*', i.e. negative assumption of (3). Then, if the phrase '*ārambhaḥ śiṣyate*' in (4) has the same meaning as '*vidhānam*' in (5) in the passive, (4) and (5) form a proof of *arthāpatti*, from which (3) logically results after the conditional (5) is justified by the argument beginning from (7) onwards.

What is called '*vidhānam*' in (5) is the function of the optative verb '*yajeta*' in the impelling-injunction '*svargakāmo yajeta*' to prompt the hearer to offer some oblation into the sacrificial fire (cf. the definition of '*yajati*' in *JS* 4.2.27). If we, however, pay enough attention to the usage of the term '*ārambha*' in *ŚBh*,[22] we can safely say that the term '*ārambha*' in (4) refers to undertaking the whole procedure of a sacrifice beginning from the first preparatory rite prescribed by a subsidiary injunction. This first preparatory rite is different from the act of offering prescribed (*vidhāna*) by the verb '*yajeta*' of an impelling-injunction as illustrated in (5). Taking into consideration the fact that (4) and (5) do not refer to the same action, we cannot but think it impossible that (4) and (5) form an *arthāpatti* proof which would confirm (3) logically. From this it follows that (4) alone is enough to give the reason for (3), since the subordinate clause '*yataḥ* ...' ends before (5). Because all three words of *JS* 2.1.5 appear in (3) and (4), it must be a paraphrase of *JS* 2.1.5 that Śabara intends by (3) and (4).

In the first section of *JS* 2.1, namely, 2.1.1-4, it is argued that among words used in an impelling-injunction it is only the verb such as '*yajeta*' that turns the hearer towards the *apūrva* of a sacrifice.[23] But such a verb, which is common to all impelling-injunctions, cannot by itself indicate the *apūrva* definitely (*ŚBh* 2: 340,9-341,1: *na ... sākṣād apūrvasya vācakaḥ*) because *apūrva* is the original pattern of offering which differs from one offering to another. In the next section, Śabara asks (1) how to recognize such a definite *apūrva*. This question is answered by *JS* 2.1.5, which Śabara glosses by (3) and (4) taking the contextual relation among the whole injunctions of a sacrifice into account. Though it is the optative ending of '*yajeta*' in the *codanā* that makes the hearer aware that there should be something unique (*apūrva*) in an offering prescribed in a Vedic chapter, it is only the whole injunctions from the beginning of the chapter that shows what it is and how to accomplish it. *JS* 2.1.1-5 is thus forming an introduction (*upodghāta*) to the next Pāda (*JS* 2.2).

In the argument from (5) onwards, Śabara additionally elaborates an indirect proof of the existence of *apūrva* by eliminating the possibilities of the efficacy of a sacrifice without the help of *apūrva*.[24] As a result of this argument, the role of intermediary is added to the traditional notion of *apūrva*. It does not, however, directly give an answer to the question raised in (1) because what is ascertained by this argument is the common nature of all *apūrvas* actualized by main offerings of all kinds of sacrifices, whereas what is asked in (1) is the way of knowing the individual *apūrva* particular to the act of offering in a sacrifice.

KUMĀRILA'S REFUTATION OF *APŪRVA* AS A SEPARATE BEING (*VASTVANTARA*)

Compared with his Apūrvādhikaraṇa of the *Tantravārttika* (*TV*), one may find it strange that Kumārila says nothing about the *apūrva* as a potency (*śakti*) of the individual self (*ātman*) in his *Ślokavārttika* (*ŚV*). Although he argues about many topics in ontology and epistemology by recourse to the notion of *śakti*,[25] he mentions only one *śakti* of the self, namely, the capacity of knowing (*ŚV* Ātman k.67-73: *dhī, buddhi, jñāna*). He suggests barely just once that *apūrva* might be regarded as *śakti* of the act of offering or as that of its result[26] (*ŚV* Codanā k. 199).

In the Codanāsūtra-chapter on *JS* 1.1.2, Kumārila enumerates five theories about what *dharma* is (k. 195-196). According to the three commentators, Umbeka, Sucarita and Pārthasārathi, the first four theories were held by other schools outside the Mīmāṃsā, whereas the last one, namely '*dharma* is that which was not born before (*apūrvaj-*

anman)', was advocated within the Mīmāṃsā school. On account of the rivalry against the inner opponent, Kumārila strongly criticizes only the last theory. He abbreviates '*apūrvajanman*' just to '*apūrva*' and accuses the opponent of regarding *apūrva* as a separate being (*vastvantara*) that is neither the act of offering nor the result (k. 197) because the opponent would thereby abandon the direct assertion of the Vedas (*śrutatyāga*) and assume something not asserted in it (*aśrutakalpanā*) (k. 198). In his foregoing assertion (k. 191), Kumārila has maintained that only the substance (*dravya*), quality (*guṇa*) and act (*karman*), namely, empirical constituents of a sacrifice characterized by Vedic injunctions are what is called '*dharma*'. By reducing the *apūrva* to a kind of *śakti*, Kumārila demonstrates that the causality between a sacrifice and its result will be completed within this and the next life of an individual person without the intervention from the transcendent reality.[27]

Kumārila's critical attitude towards the transcendent *apūrva* is reflected also in the *Tantravārttika*. In his Apūrvādhikaraṇa an opponent demonstrates at full length that the assumption of *apūrva* would contradict the Vedas and the efficacy of a sacrifice can be satisfactorily explained without assuming *apūrva*. At the beginning of the refutation, Kumārila points out that the opponent imagines as if *apūrva* is something corporeal (*vigrahavad iva*) (*TV* 2: 364,4). In order to get rid of this misunderstanding, he argues that the *apūrva* which realizes the efficacy of a sacrifice exists as a *śakti* inhering in a substratum (*āśraya*), which is nothing but the permanent self (*ātman*) (*TV* 2: 369,8). By characterizing the rejected *apūrva* as 'corporeal' and the approved *apūrva* as '*śakti*', Kumārila denies the possibility that *apūrva* could exist independently of any substratum. With 'corporeal *apūrva*', Kumārila expresses in other words the *apūrva* that was called a 'separate being' (*vastvantara*) in the Codanāsūtra of *ŚV*, where he also stated that one cannot refer just to *śakti* by the word denoting an existent (*bhāva*) in which the *śakti* inheres (k. 200).[28]

TWO COMPETING THEORIES OF *APŪRVA*

In the last part of the Apūrvādhikaraṇa of *TV*, Kumārila considers how *apūrva* contributes to formation of the unity of a sacrifice. Because one should offer many oblations at intervals in the course of a sacrifice, it is necessary to explain how the acts of offering cooperate in realizing the result of the sacrifice. Kumārila presents two theories in his times.

'Some scholars' (*kecit*) hold the following theory (*TV* 2: 370,10-

16): Because all *apūrvas* of subsidiary offerings (*aṅgāpūrva*) which precede the main offerings as well as those of succeeding subsidiaries have been set in operation (*pracalitāvastha*) once the sacrifice commenced (*prakrama*), each act of primary offering (*pradhāna*) accomplishes its own *apūrva* assisted by all the subsidiary *apūrvas*. Just like a special kind of sacrificial grass (*ātithyābarhis*)[29] used repeatedly in a series of subsidiary offerings at the Soma sacrifice, the subsidiary *apūrvas* do not cease their operations even if one of the primary offerings has accomplished its *apūrva*. It is possible for the *apūrva* of a succeeding subsidiary offering to contribute to forming the *apūrva* of the primary offering performed at present because it is absolutely determined (*ekāntāvadhāraṇa*) to perform the former in the near future, just as, the 'some scholars' *(kecit)* say, one cannot but clean dishes when mealtime is drawing near. The mealtime in the near future prompts one to clean the dishes. Although subsidiary future *apūrvas* can thus work for a primary offering at present, we should actually perform them later because the primary *apūrvas* do not complete their operation (*nāpavṛjyante*) to bring about the result if any subsidiary offerings are omitted in the session.

This theory of 'some scholars' may be traced back to the traditional view of Mīmāṃsā as presented in earlier that a transcendent *apūrva* urges the hearer of a Vedic injunction to undertake the process of sacrifice. Because the 'some' believe that each *apūrva* of offerings has always been there as a *causa finalis*, they insist that once the sacrifice commenced all *apūrvas* world have been set in operation (*pracalitāvastha*). It therefore becomes possible to offer a primary oblation in order to give actuality to the primary *apūrva* with the help of subsidiary *apūrvas* including those to be actualized in the near future.[30]

Without offering criticism of the 'some', Kumārila turns to the presentation of the second view held by 'others' (*anye*) as follows (*TV* 2: 370,16-24): By each act of subsidiary offering alone, one *apūrva* is formed without assistance by other *apūrvas*. The act of primary offering also forms its *apūrva* assisted neither by the subsidiary *apūrvas* of the preceding offerings nor by the *apūrvas* of succeeding ones. At the primary offering, however, only the *apūrva* accumulated in the oblation during the course of its preparation contributes to forming the primary *apūrva*. When all *apūrvas* have been accomplished individually in this way, all the secondary *apūrvas* cease to operate after having helped the primary ones to form the final *apūrva* which will continue till the result of the sacrifice is realized.

According to this theory of 'others', we do not have to suppose that *apūrvas* have already had the transcendent existence before one performs the corresponding act of offering because until the end of a sacrifice there is no opportunity for cooperation among *apūrvas*. Contrary to the earlier mentioned 'some', the scholars called 'others' do not rely on the traditional view of the transcendent *apūrva*. They concentrate on explaining the mechanism of a sacrifice empirically as far as possible without postulating the existence of an ideal structure preceding the life of individual persons. Although Kumārila does not say directly, we can consider that he stands definitely by the 'others' because he replies voluntarily to a question posed to the 'others' as to why the *apūrvas* cannot cooperate until the end of a sacrifice.[31]

In addition to this, another question to the 'others' now arises (*TV* 2: 371,13-14): In the case of the new and full moon sacrifices, the same secondary offerings are made on a day of the full moon as well as on the following day of the new moon, while the main offerings characteristic either of the two sacrifices are made in the middle of the secondary offerings. If we accept the theory of 'others', we may conceive a doubt about the necessity of repeating the subsidiary offerings on the day of the new moon because the subsidiary *apūrvas* accomplished at the preceding full moon sacrifice are supposed to continue until the end of the sacrifice, namely, until the end of the new moon sacrifice. To resolve this problem, Kumārila draws the following conclusion (*TV* 2: 371,17-22): At the end of a full moon sacrifice, the *apūrvas* of the primary offerings cease to operate after having caused one *apūrva* representative of the full moon sacrifice with the assistance of the subsidiary *apūrvas*. At the end of the following new moon sacrifice, another *apūrva* is formed in the same way, and then the two *apūrvas*, representative of the two sacrifices, bring about the final *apūrva* which in turn brings the result in the future.

In this way, Kumārila intensified the unity of the new moon sacrifice and the unity of the full moon sacrifice respectively by postulating one representative *apūrva* at the end of each. Because at the end of a full moon sacrifice the subsidiary *apūrvas* cease to exist after having contributed to the formation of the representative *apūrva*, the sacrificer has to repeat them in the following new moon sacrifice. With this conclusion, Kumārila has adapted the theory of 'others' because he admits that the *apūrva* representative of each sacrifice is formed 'in exact accordance to the theory mentioned above' (*TV* 2: 371,18-19: *pūrvoktenaiva nyāyena*), namely, by the simultaneous cooperation of subsidiary *apūrvas* at the end.

KUMĀRILA'S INCLINATION TO VEDĀNTA

Although Kumārila supports and adapts the new theory of 'others' (*anye*) with regard to the function of *apūrva*, he tries to include the traditional theory of 'some' (*kecit*) by modifying the ontological status of *apūrva*. At the end of the Apūrvādhikaraṇa, Kumārila handles the question whether an *apūrva* manifests itself (*abhivyakti*)[32] from its latent state or originates (*utpatti*) entirely from the offering. The former view corresponds to the theory of 'some', while the latter to that of 'others'.

Kumārila justifies the origination theory at first. According to him, the origination of *apūrva* bears a close parallel to the process of understanding the meaning of a sentence because in both cases a kind of disposition (*saṃskāra*) occurs at each section of the whole, i.e. a sacrifice or a sentence, and this is accumulated so as to achieve the final effect (*TV* 2: 371,23-24). Far from refusing the manifestation theory, however, Kumārila maintains that the individual self (*ātman*) fulfills the role of substratum (*āśraya*) for the manifestation of *apūrva*. He says: Although the self of every individual person has been by nature equipped with *apūrvas* of all offerings, only the person who performs a sacrifice makes the *apūrva* manifest itself (*TV* 2: 372,5-7). Furthermore, he even presents a Vedantic statement: Although the individual self has the capacity for acquiring all (*sarvāvāptisamartha*) by nature, its realization is hindered by certain impediments (*pratibandha*), which will be removed by means of sacrifices (*TV* 2: 372,10-11).

Until the time of Śabara, Mīmāṃsā scholars believed that the unity of a sacrifice composed of many offerings is guaranteed by the syntactical and contextual unity of Vedic injunctions.[33] This belief was strengthened by the theory of *apūrva* as a permanent ideal which, once revealed from the impelling-injunction (*codanā*), urges a person to undertake (*ārambha*) a programmed series of rites that culminates in the act of offering. By the time of Kumārila, a considerable number of scholars have paid much attention to the efficacy of offerings that were to be completed in the individual life. By regarding *apūrva* as a *śakti* inhering in the individual self and by giving a detailed justification in the Apūrvādhikaraṇa, Kumārila succeeded in demonstrating the certainty about the personal retribution by means of sacrifice. At the same time his innovation resulted in an estrangement of *apūrva* from the Vedic revelation because *apūrva* now lost its existence outside the indi-vidual person. In order to make the immanence of *apūrva* in an individual theoretically sure as well as to prove his pure orthodoxy, Kumārila now turns to the view of man propounded in Vedānta, namely, the hermeneutics of the last part of the Vedas, i.e. Upaniṣads.[34] The mentioned statement of the omnipotence of the self suggests Kumārila's inclination to Vedānta, which culminates in another statement presented in a fragment from his later work, the *Bṛhaṭṭīkā*,[35] that the liberation is achieved by combination of wisdom and practice (*jñānakarmasamuccaya*) .

TEXT AND ABBREVIATIONS

ĀpŚS: *Āpastambaśrautasūtra*. 3vols, [Bibliotheca Indica 92] 2nd ed., New Delhi 1983.
DP: **Daśapadārthī*. See Miyamoto 1996, Appendix.
JS: *Mīmāṃsāsūtra*. See *ŚBh*.
MBhD: *Mahābhāṣyadīpikā*. Fasc.IV, Bhandarkar Oriental Research Institute Post-Graduate and Research Department Series 28, Poona 1987.
NM: *Nyāyamañjarī*. Vol.1, University of Mysore Oriental Research Institute Series 139, 1983.
ŚBh 1-7: *Śābarabhāṣya*. In: *Mīmāṃsādarśanam*. Ānandāśrama Sanskrit Series 97, pt. 1: 1976; pt. 2: 1981; pt. 3-7: 1971-4.
ŚBh(F): *Śābarabhāṣya* on *JS* 1.1.1-5. In Frauwallner's ed. : *Materialien zur ältesten Erkenntnislehre der Karmamīmāṃsā*. Wien 1968.
ŚV: *Ślokavārttika*. Prāchyabhārati Series 10, Varanasi 1978.
TS : *Taittirīyasaṃhitā*. *Indische Studien* 11; 12, repr. Hildesheim 1973.
TV: *Tantravārttika*. See *ŚBh*.
YD: *Yuktidīpikā*. Vol. 2, tr. by Sh. Kumar and D.N. Bhargava, Delhi 1992.

NOTES

* This article consists of summaries of my recent studies on *apūrva* from 1995 to 1999, by which I would like to shift the prevalent perspective of modern scholars (including Yoshimizu 1997: 61-62; 97-98) who have, oriented by the Bhāṭṭa tradition, characterized Śabara as a predecessor of the 'anthropocentric' view of Kumārila. I would like to express my deepest thanks to Prof. Francis X. Clooney, who kindly read through my manuscript to correct my English and gave me valuable suggestions.

1 It is mentioned frequently in *JS* 2 that the Vedic sentence to be identified in each section is the *codanā* of an offering. Cf. 2.2.6; 10; 16; 17; 2.3.5; 6; 22; 2.4.10; 25. By translating '*codanā*' literally, I distinguish it from injunctions (*vidhi*) in general.

2 Except *JS* 2.2.23, where Śabara glosses '*apūrva*' as '*apūrvayoḥ yāgayoḥ*' (*ŚBh* 3: 93,5-6)

3 Cf. *ŚBh* 3: 18,4-5; 32,3; 37,2; 65,4: *apūrvayoḥ karmaṇoḥ vidhātārau*. Cf.

also *ŚBh* 3: 49,3; 53,11-12; 68,2-3; 69,2; 71,2-3; 90,4.

4 Cf. *ŚBh* 3: 22,1; 24,2; 36,3; 50,7; 53,9; 65,3-4; 69,2-3; 71,3.

5 *ŚBh* 3: 32,4-6: 'By means of another sentence ["*yad āgneyo 'ṣṭākapālo 'māvāsyāyāṃ paurṇamāsyāṃ cācyuto bhavati*" (*TS* 2.6.3.3)] we will understand the form [of the new and full moon sacrifices] such as "there should be [an oblation] on eight potsherds for Agni on a day the full moon". It is the act of offering called "full moon sacrifice" that has such a form as : The deity is Agni, the substance (oblation) is a cake.

6 *ŚBh* 3: 4,3: *apūrvasya bhāvanā*; 5,1: *apūrvaṃ sādhayanti*.

7 Cf. *Vārttika* 8 (on Pāṇini 3.3.108): *ik kṛṣyādibhyaḥ; the Mahābhāṣya* (ed. Kielhorn, Pune 1985) 1: 293,7-8.

8 The main subject of *JS* 7 is the transference (*atideśa*) of the details of a basic sacrifice (*prakṛti*) into a modified one (*vikṛti*). The Mīmāṃsā school regards the transference as an exceptional case to a general principle that all the ritual elements prescribed in a chapter of the Vedas are attached to a particular sacrifice which is the subject of that chapter. In a case where there is a passage giving warrant for transference in the chapter on a modified sacrifice, this general principle is restrained. With the question raised by Śabara here and his justification for the second alternative, he is aiming to make sure this general principle. Although 'the whole of the project is carried out without reference to *apūrva*' (Clooney 1990: 229) in *JS* 7.1.1-12, Śabara does not deviate from the original context of *JS* because the '*apūrva*' in Śabara's second alternative corresponds to the '*codanā*' mentioned in the Siddhānta-sūtras of *JS* 7.1.3; 7.

9 I agree with the following comment on *JS* 10.7.33 by F.X. Clooney: 'An ectype is *apūrva*, distinct from the archetype, only by virtue of some new element not found in the archetype' (Clooney 1990: 233).

10 Cf. *ĀpŚS* 24.4.15 on the relation between *prakṛti* and *vikṛti*: *prakṛteḥ pūrvoktatvād apūrvam ante syāt*; Caland 1969: 398.

11 *ŚBh* 5: 377,10-12: *iha punar yajiviśeṣasaṃbandhena dharmā vidhīyante ... viśiṣṭayajisaṃbaddha evāpūrve bhavitum arhanti, na sarvatreti.*

12 Cf. *ŚBh* 5: 379,20-21; 381,11-12; 382,3-4.

13 Cf. *ŚBh* 2: 389,8-10 on causing *saṃskāra* by carrying a fire round a person (*paryagnikaraṇa*) and *ŚBh* on *JS* 3.7.6 about cutting the hair and beard of a sacrificer at the Jyotiṣṭoma. In the Mantrādhikaraṇa, an opponent maintains that an *apūrva* is caused by uttering a mantra (*ŚBh* 2: 57,8-11). This objection is refuted by Śabara immediately.

14 Śabara's assertion '*yāgo' pūrvasya dātā, puruṣaḥ pratigrahītā*' (*ŚBh* 4: 552,4) does not imply that the yāga causes an *apūrva* as a *saṃskāra* in the sacrificer, because it presupposes that there is already an *apūrva* which the offering gives and the sacrificer receives.

15 Cf. *ŚBh* 6: 62,15: *pratyayārthena*. The ending of a transitive verb (*karmaśabda*) in a sentence indicates the efficient-force (*bhāvanā*) of a person who intends to realize what he wishes for. In the case of an injunction the verb urges the hearer to employ his *bhāvanā*. Cf. *ŚBh* 3: 3,2-3; 2: 340,3-4. Although the sacrificer aims to attain heaven in the future, what he actually accomplishes at the sacrificial altar is the *apūrva*, the original form of a sacrifice as prescribed by the Vedas. Insofar as the inner structure of a sacrifice is concerned, Śabara regards *apūrva* as the

direct object of *bhāvanā* (*ŚBh* 5: 381,7; 6: 67,5: *apūrvabhāvanā*; 5: 17,7: *apūrvasya bhāvaḥ*; 2: 340,7-8; 5: 425,7: *apūrvaṃ kṛtvā*; 5: 384,18: *akṛtvā^apūrvam*; 6: 82,10: *apūrvaṃ kriyate*), and he admits that the optative ending (*liṅ*) of the verb in a *codanā* makes *apūrva* noticed (*jñāpitam*) (cf. *ŚBh* 3: 169,1-2: *todā liṅā nāpūrvaṃ jñāpitaṃ bhavet. tatrāpūrvajñāpanavacanaḥ śabda uparudhyeta*; Yoshimizu 1996).

16 In some sections where *JS* refers to impelling-injunction (*codanā*), Śabara insists on its inseparability from *apūrva* by the statement: '*codanā ity apūrvaṃ brūmaḥ*' (*ŚBh* 2: 358,16; 4: 596,2; 5: 384,10-11). Since the *codanā* is a kind of Vedic sentences that reveals an offering and urges the hearer to undertake it (cf. *ŚBh(F)* 16,9; *ŚBh* 2: 336,5), this statement of identification would be meaningless if the word '*apūrva*' means a kind of disposition that would exist physically independent of Vedic words.

17 *ŚBh* 6: 62,19-63,2: 'For example, the garden is both the purpose and the cause of hiring a gardener. On the ground of the presence of a garden (*ārāme sati*), wages are paid to him. Wages are distributed (v.l.: *vetana-saṃbandhaḥ*) to him so that he will maintain the garden (*ārāmaṃ rakṣayitum*). Therefore only the *apūrva* is both the purpose and the cause of preparatory acts.' The owner of a garden hires a gardener in order to maintain the beauty of the garden. But the gardener does not create a completely new garden in a desert. The garden has already been there before he sets about working in it. In this simile the owner of a garden is compared to the eternal Vedas having no human origin, the garden to the *apūrva* which is the ideal of sacrifice revealed in the Vedas, the gardener to the individual person who is urged by the Vedas to perform the sacrifice, and the wages of gardener to the result such as heaven which the sacrificer receives as the reward.

18 Śabara considers the subject of this section as finding a proper procedure (*itikartavyatā*) for an optional sacrifice (*kāmyakarman*), which would be the answer to the question how to realize an *apūrva* by means of that optional offering (cf. *ŚBh* 5: 425,18-19). With regard to an optional sacrifice prescribed just by the impelling-injunction (*codanā*): 'One who wishes splendor of *brahman* should offer porridge to Sūrya' (*ŚBh* 5: 424,9 ≒ *TS* 2.3.2.3) without any details given, Śabara begins to discuss how to perform this sacrifice as the realization of an *apūrva*. Because there is an injunction of a special fore-offering (*prayāja*): 'At each fore-offering, one offers one *kṛṣṇala* piece of gold' (*ŚBh* 5: 428,4 ≒ *TS* 2.3.2.3) in this section of the Veda, Śabara regards this porridge sacrifice for Sūrya as a modified type (*vikṛti*) of the new and full moon sacrifices and justifies the transfer of details from them.

19 *ŚBh* 5: 425,4-6: *idam api coktaṃ, yajir apūrvaṃ sādhayati. tataś cāpūrvāt kālāntare phalaṃ bhavatīti 'codanā punar ārambha' ity atra.*

20 *ŚBh* 5: 432,4-8: 'In case of the Veda, "One should perform a sacrifice (*yajeta*) named 'new and full moon sacrifices'" is the chief-injunction [of the new and full moon sacrifices]. The appended-injunctions are, on the other hand, the entire *brāhmaṇa*-portions dealing with the rice oblation except the injunctions of main offerings. Accompanied by these, the chief-injunction prompts the person to realize the specified *apūrva* (*viśiṣṭā-pūrvanirvṛtti*). Therefore the former is the appended compared with the

latter. In the same manner, "One should perform the sacrifice named 'Soma sacrifice'" is the chief[-injunction of the Soma sacrifice]. The *brāhmaṇas* dealing with *soma* plant are, on the other hand, the appended[-injunctions of it]'.

21 This interpretation of *apūrva* is also justified by the last argument in the Apūrvādhikaraṇa (*ŚBh* 2: 378,3-379,3), which concludes that the capacity of referring to *apūrva* is ascribed only to the verb in an injunction so as to make it sure that one should perform the act of offering exactly as prescribed without replacement (*pratinidhi*) by another form, whereas one can replace the material (*dravya*) for the oblation if the proper one is not available.

22 In his commentary on the third section of *JS* 6.2, Śabara deals with the way of performing an optional sacrifice (*kāmyakarman*). The impelling-injunction of a periodical sacrifice (*nityakarman*) prompts the hearer to undertake (*ārambha*) the sacrifice periodically. In case of optional sacrifices whose results are secular and differ from each other, the hearer should therefore choose the appropriate sacrifice which realizes the result he needs in his present life. For this reason, the impelling-injunction of it does not prompt him to undertake it, but to complete the sacrifice which he has already undertaken by his own choice (*ŚBh* 5: 231,2-8). From this instance it follows: When one has just undertaken a sacrifice, one is engaged not in the act of offering oblation, but in the first step towars it. The next instance is quoted from *JS* 11.1.8-10: The impelling-injunction of the new and full moon sacrifices does not only prompt the hearer to offer the oblation of this sacrifice, but also requires other injunctions prescribing the fore-offering, etc., as subordinate rites. In order to justify that the impelling-injunction can have such a double-function, Śabara says: In the impelling-injunction only the activity (*vyāpāra*) of sacrifice is prescribed, but it is not asserted directly how to carry it out; on the other hand, a series of rites such as rekindling the sacrificial altar (cf. *ĀpŚS* 1.1.2) are prescribed in proximity (*saṃnidhi*) of it; it is therefore appropriate to suppose that the impelling-injunction requires injunctions of the whole activity which begins (*ārambha*) with rekindling the sacrificial altar (*ŚBh* 7: 13,4-8).

23 As regards the function of the optative ending in an injunction, see note 15.

24 On the structure of the argument after (7) see Clooney 1990: 227-228. Instead of *arthāpatti* as it has been often so called (e.g. Yoshimizu 1997: 98) as Kumārila did, we had better call this argument an old-type of *pariśeṣa*, which eliminates all possibilities for the position of the opponent but still needs a positive proof for one's own position. Instead of a positive inference about the existence of *apūrva*, Śabara has recourse to the function of words of the *codanā* as summarized in (4). As regards the old-type of '*pariśeṣa*', see Frauwallner 1958: 231 and Oberhammer et al. 1996: 158. In *ŚBh* 5: 183,17-21, Śabara refuses an opponent who maintains that the effectiveness of a sacrifice is proved by an *arthāpatti* based on the validity of the Vedic statement.

25 Cf. *ŚV* Codanā k. 47-48; Pratyakṣa k. 224; Śūnya k. 253; Anumāna k. 110; Ākṛti k. 15-18; 31-32; 42.

26 Cf. also *ŚV* Citrākṣepaparihāra k. 8-9ab.

27 Following *ŚV* Codanā k. 195, Jayanta Bhaṭṭa summarizes the views on *dharma* held in other schools outside the Nyāya (cf. Halbfass 1991: 334 n. 46; Bronkhorst 1994: 384). He classifies the Mīmāṃsā factions into three: the former Mīmāṃsakas (*NM* 664,6: *vṛddhamīmāṃsaka*; 664,16: *jarajjaiminīya*) who regard *dharma* as the *apūrva* without substratum (*NM* 664,15: *nirādhāra*), *śābarāḥ* who say *dharma* is nothing but the act of offering, etc., (*yāgādi*) and, finally, the Prābhākaras who hold the *niyoga*-theory. Among them, the view of *śābarāḥ* seems to be based on *ŚV* Codanā k.191. Even in *TV*, Kumārila distinguishes the *dharma* characterized by a *codanā* from *apūrva* by calling *dharma* the means of accomplishing *apūrva* (*TV* 2: 337,8: *apūrvasādhana*). Although Śabara says '*yajati-śabdavācyam eva dharmaṃ samānanti*' (*ŚBh(F)* 20,11) quoting the *Ṛgveda* 10.90.16 (or *TS* 3.5.11.5), he does not limit '*dharma*' to empirical constituents of a sacrifice as Kumārila does. On the contrary, he identifies the *dharma* with *apūrva* when he draws a conclusion '*tasmād ekam apūrvam*' (*ŚBh* 2: 337,3) of the argument whether from an injunction one knows so many *dharmas* as the number of words constituting the injunction or just one *dharma* in all. Although Jayanta describes Kumārila as the legitimate successor of Śabara, we may call Śabara not so much '*śābara*' as a 'former Mīmāṃsaka'.

28 The reason why Kumārila did not say much about the *apūrva* approved as a *śakti* in *ŚV* may be explained as follows. In the *ŚV* where Kumārila resorts to *śakti* as a solution to ontological or epistemological problems, he always assigns the means of knowing *śakti* to *arthāpatti* (indispensable assumption), cf. *ŚV* Śūnya k. 254; Arthāpatti k. 3-6; k.47-49; Ākṛti k. 26; k. 41-42; Sambandhākṣepaparihāra k. 28-29; k. 141; Śabdanityatā k. 44; Vākya k. 112; k. 122; k. 160. In the Apūrvādhikaraṇa of *TV*, he declares that the means of knowing *apūrva* is only *śrutārthāpatti*, namely, an indispensable assumption based on [Vedic] words (*TV* 2: 364,15). In the Arthāpatti chapter of *ŚV*, however, he divides *arthāpatti* into *dṛṣṭārthāpatti* and *śrutārthāpatti* based on the difference in its object to be known. In contrast to the *dṛṣṭārthāpatti* where one assumes a certain matter indispensable for explaining an observation (*dṛṣṭa*), one assumes a means of knowing (*pramāṇa*), namely words, when one applies *śrutārthāpatti* after having heard some words (*śruta*) which needs supplement (k. 2cd). Kumārila spends most of the section on *śrutārthāpatti* (k. 51-78) in proving that *śrutārthāpatti* refers just to words (*śabdagocarā*), but not to the matter denoted by them (*arthagocarā*). In *ŚV* Arthāpatti k. 87, Kumārila adduces three examples of *śrutārthāpatti* from Mīmāṃsā exegesis (cf. *JS* 1.3.1-2; 3.2.3-4; 4.3.10-12), in all of which a word or an injunction is assumed. In order to keep consistency of the classification of two kinds of *arthāpatti* in *ŚV*, Kumārila had probably to refrain from assuming *apūrva* such as the *śakti* inhering in the self based on a *śrutārthāpatti* from Vedic injunction because such an assumption would be a kind of *arthagocarā*. It might be influenced by the Sāṃkhya proof of *śakti* inhering in the 'unmanifest'(*avyakta*) by means of inference that Kumārila applies *arthāpatti* to find out a *śakti* inhering in its substratum. Cf. *YD* (on k. 15: *śaktitaḥ*) 79,30-31: *kasmāt, sāmānyatodṛṣṭāntāt siddheḥ*.

See also *DP* (on **śaktipadārtha*) 179,3: **dravyaguṇakarmasamaveto 'nvayavyatirekādhyām... avadhṛtaḥ*; Miyamoto 1996: 115-135.

29 Namely, *aśvavāla*-grass used in *ātithyeṣṭi*, *upasad* and *agnīṣomīya*. Cf. *JS* 4.2.29-30; Caland-Henry 1906-07: 28; 53-60; 67-71; 78.

30 This theory of 'some' presents another similarity to Śabara's view. Both admit that all primary *apūrvas* are equally contributory to the future result without postulating one final *apūrva* accomplished by means of them. Cf. *ŚBh* 7: 6,2-3; 7,14-15 on *JS* 11.1.1. The *paramāpūrva* referred to by Śabara in case of Jyotiṣṭoma is not the final single *apūrva* of a sacrifice as Kumārila postulates. It is a primary *apūrva* formed by each primary offering, i.e. *soma* offering by means of cup (*graha*) (*ŚBh* 6: 92,1-4) and contrasted to the *aṅgāpūrva* formed by subsidiary offerings such as *dīkṣaṇīyā* (*ŚBh* 6: 68,3; 68,6).

31 Kumārila explains as follows why it is necessary for the *apūrvas* of primary offerings as well as for those of subsidiary offerings to operate simultaneously at each level: By means of *arthāpatti* which requires a minimum of assumptions (cf. *ŚBh* 3: 2,3-6), we need to postulate just one final *apūrva* for realizing the result. Because the offerings are performed at intervals, it is necessary for the *apūrva* of each offering to last for a while and to operate simultaneously with others to cause one common effect (*TV* 2: 371,5-10). As examined earlier, Śabara and even Kumārila in his *ŚV* did not apply *arthāpatti* in order to recognize an *apūrva*. We may say therefore that Kumārila speaks here voluntarily in defense of the theory of 'others'.

32 The manifestation theory of *apūrva* must have already been prevalent before the time of Kumārila because it is referred to by some scholars in the sixth century such as Uddyotakara in the *Nyāyavārttika* 1.1.7 (cf. Akamatsu 1991: 386-387) and Bhāviveka in the *Madhyamakahṛdaya* 9. 10; 55 (cf. Kawasaki 1992: 376; 384). Uddyotakara's opponent insists that *apūrva* manifests itself in individual persons. As pointed out by Bronkhorst [1994: 383], Bhartṛhari also presents a Mīmāṃsaka view that *dharma* manifests itself by sacrifices such as *agnihotra* (*MBhD* 25,24-26). On identification of *dharma* with *apūrva* in the traditional Mīmāṃsā, cf. note 27.

33 In *JS* 11.1, the basis for the cooperation of subsidiaries is ascribed to the unity of words prescribing them, which is called in *JS* 11.1.1: *ekaśabdābhisaṃyoga*; 8: *tācchabdya*; 16: *ekaśrutitva*; 25: *aikaśabdya*; 56: *ekaśabdopadeśa*. Cf. also *ŚBh* 5: 102,22-25 (on *JS* 4.4.34 about the distinction between primary and secondary offerings).

34 Mesquita [1994: 457] pointed out that the state of *ātman* after liberation described in *ŚV* (Sambandhākṣepaparihāra k. 107: *abhāvātmaka*) is close to the view of the Nyāya school. Harikai [1990: 140-141] identified the passages from the *Chāndogyopaniṣad* which Kumārila cites in the Vyākaraṇādhikaraṇa of *TV* to afford testimony about the realization of omnipotence by means of knowing *ātman*.

35 Cf. Harikai 1989: (71); Mesquita 1994: 464-479. Mesquita investigates also Jaimini's view on liberation (1994: 451-452).

REFERENCES

Akamatsu, A. 1991 (jp = a study in Japanese) A Study of the *Nyāyavārttika* (2) --- on *Apūrva* ---, in: *Essays in Honor of Dr. Shoren Ihara on his Seventieth Birthday*, Fukuoka: 377-398.

Bronkhorst, J. 1994 Bhartṛhari and Mīmāṃsā. In: *Studies in Mīmāṃsā, Dr. Mandan Mishra Felicitation Volume*, Delhi: 371-388.

Caland, W. 1969 *Das Śrautasūtra des Āpastamba aus dem Sanskrit übersetzt, 16.-24. und 31. Buch* [Amsterdam 1928].

Caland, W. et Henry, V. 1906-07 *L'agniṣṭoma, Paris.*

Clooney, F.X. 1990 *Thinking Ritually. Rediscovering the Pūrva Mīmāṃsā of Jaimini*, Publications of the De Nobili Research Library 17, Vienna.

Frauwallner, E. 1958 Die Erkenntnislehre des klassischen Sāṃkhya-Systems, *Wiener Zeitschrift für Kunde Süd- und Ostasiens* 2: 84-139.

Halbfass, W. 1991 *Tradition and Reflection. Explorations in Indian Thought*, Albany, N.Y.

Harikai, K. 1989(jp) Quotations from the *Bṛhaṭṭīkā* in the *Nyāyasudhā*, *Journal of Indian and Buddhist Studies* 37-2: (68)-(74).

Harikai, K. 1990(jp) *The Hermeneutics of Classical India — A Study of Arthavāda and Mantra of the Mīmāṃsā School*, Fukuoka.

Kawasaki, Sh. 1992(jp) *A Study of the Omniscient Being (sarvajña) in Buddhism*, Tokyo.

Mesquita, R. 1994 Die Idee der Erlösung bei Kumārilabhaṭṭa, *Wiener Zeitschrift für die Kunde Südasiens* 38: 451-484.

Miyamoto,K.1996 *The Metaphysics and Epistemology of the Early Vaiśeṣikas,* Bhandarkar Oriental Series No.28, Pune.

Oberhammer, G.; Prets, E.; Prandstetter, J. 1996 *Terminologie der früheren philosophischen Scholastik in Indien*. Bd. 2, Wien.

Yoshimizu,K.1996 The Means of Knowing *Apūrva* in Śabarasvāmin's Bhāṣya, *Journal of Indian and Buddhist Studies* 45-1,(10)-(14).

Yoshimizu, K. 1997 *Der 'Organismus' des urheberlosen Veda. Eine Studie der Niyoga-Lehre Prabhākaras mit ausgewählten Übersetzungen der Bṛhatī*. Publications of the De Nobili Research Library 25. Wien.

12

Reconstructing the *Dharma-abhivyakti-vāda* in the Mīmāṃsā Tradition*

KEI KATAOKA

This paper attempts to reconstruct the Mīmāṃsā *apūrva*-theory which I suggest might be referred to as '*dharma-abhivyakti-vāda*'[1] (the theory of *dharma*-manifestation). Halbfass has pointed out that the *apūrva*-theory is refuted by Uddyotakara in *Nyāyavārttika* on *Nyāyasūtra* 1.1.7,[2] a portion of which has been translated into Japanese and investigated further by Akamatsu.[3] For Akamatsu it is not clear what Uddyotakara regards as the Mīmāṃsakas' position on *apūrva*, i.e. what form of the *apūrva*-theory was dominant after Śabarasvāmin and before Kumārila. Yudhiṣṭhira Mīmāṃsaka,[4] with reference to the relevant portions which I will investigate below, attributes this form of *apūrva*-theory to Bhartṛhari and Bhartṛmitra, but does not clarify its content. Bronkhorst,[5] apparently relying on Yudhiṣṭhira Mīmāṃsaka, also refers to and translates the same passages, but he too does not comment on the theory. Ikari,[6] who is mainly concerned with understanding the Vedic thought-world, presents three aspects of action: a latent form of action, once made manifest through human performances, remains effective as an invisible substance. Ikari does not refer to our passages, but his exposition of this Vedic model is important for our *dharma-abhivyakti-vāda* as providing a prototype.

SOURCES

1 Bhartṛhari (AD 450-510)

Bhartṛhari, a grammarian who is said to have used an older Mīmāṃsā source[7] (probably Bhavadāsa's vṛtti, written in the first half of the fifth century[8]) than the *Śābarabhāṣya* (first half of the sixth century)[9], mentions the Mīmāṃsā theory in his discussion of *dharma*.

Svavṛtti on *Vākyapadīya* I.136: *tatra kecid ācāryā manyante. na prakṛtyā kiñcit karma duṣṭam aduṣṭaṃ* (ed. *dṛṣṭam adṛṣṭaṃ*) *vā. śāstrānuṣṭhānāt tu kevalād dharmābhivyaktiḥ, śāstrātikramāc ca pratyavāyayogaḥ. yeṣām eva hi brāhmaṇavadhādīnāṃ viṣayāntare pātakatvaṃ, teṣām eva viṣayāntare prakṛṣṭābhyudayahetutvaṃ śāstreṇa vidhīyata iti.* VP 224.5-8.

* Following an emendation by Yudhiṣṭhira (Yudhiṣṭhira 1987: 31). cf. Vṛṣabhadeva (VP 224, n.6): *na dṛṣṭo nādṛṣṭaḥ*] ed. ; *na dṛṣṭāntaduṣṭāḥ* variant

On this point some teachers think: No action is either impure or pure by nature. But dharma becomes manifest only through following scriptures, and negative consequences attach [themselves to a person] as a result of [that person's] transgressing scriptures. For scripture prescribes one and the same action of killing a Brahmin and the like (i.e. drinking wine, etc.) as a cause of downfall in one context as well as a cause of the greatest elevation [i.e. rebirth in heaven] in another context.[10]

The expression '*abhivyakti*' is used to explain the phenomenon that something eternal becomes perceptible in a certain case and not in other cases.[11] For example, the phoneme /g/, which is considered eternal in Mīmāṃsā, manifests itself and becomes audible through actual sounds (*dhvani, nāda*), which in this system correspond to conjunctions and disjunctions among wind-atoms.[12] The eternal cow-ness (*gotva*) of individual cows becomes manifest through individuals (*vyakti*) and makes us realize: 'this is a cow'.[13] Likewise the eternal dharma manifests itself through each ritual performance (*karman*).

The same idea is also referred to in another work by Bhartṛhari, the *Mahābhāṣyadīpikā,* together with more details and a metaphor. The relevant portion pointed out by Yudhiṣṭhira (1984: 392; 1987: 34) is translated by Bronkhorst (1989).

Mahābhāṣyadīpikā : *avasthita eva dharmaḥ. sa tv agnihotrādibhir abhivyajyate. tatpreritas tu phalado bhavati. yathā svāmī bhṛtyaiḥ sevāyāṃ preryate phalaṃ praty* ... . MBhD 25.25-26.

Dharma remains forever. But it is manifested by an *agnihotra* offering or the like. Urged by such (*agnihotra*), however, it gives a fruit. For example, a master is urged to [give] fruit by servants when they serve.... (my translation)

This passage refers to the idea that the dharma, although eternal, urged by individual performances (*tat-prerita*) such as the *agnihotra* offering, becomes manifest (*abhivyajyate*) and functions as a fruit-giver (*phalada*). While in the above-mentioned passage of the *Vākyapadīya* the eternality of dharma is inferred from the expression '*abhivyakti*', here dharma is clearly qualified as eternal and 'remains forever' (*avasthita eva*). Furthermore the *agnihotra* offering is personified as that which urges the eternal dharma. A reluctant master, urged by servants, gives them fees. Likewise the unchanging dharma, urged by daily performances of *agnihotra,* is forced to give fruits.

2 Bhāviveka (AD 490-570)

In the sixth century Bhāviveka criticized other schools in his *Madhyamaka-hṛdaya-kārikā*. He refers to the *dharma-abhivyakti-vāda* as an opponent's view in the chapter called *Mīmāṃsā-tattva-nirṇaya-avatāra*. (Edited and translated into Japanese by Kawasaki (1992: 409, 376), and into English by Lindtner (1997: 96). The answer from the Buddhist side is given in k. 55.)

> *Madhyamaka-hṛdaya-kārikā* IX, k.10:
> *apūrvo 'pi kriyāvyaṅgyaḥ, kriyā mokṣe 'pi sādhanam/*
> *somapānādikā, vidvān nirjayed antakaṃ yayā//*[14]
>
> And *apūrva* is manifested by a [ritual] act. A [ritual] act such as drinking soma [=soma sacrifice], etc., is also a cause of liberation. Through that [ritual act] the wise man conquers death.

The idea is that *apūrva* or 'a new thing' is manifested (*vyaṅgya*) through ritual acts, such as drinking soma (*somapānādikā kriyā*). It should be noted that the manifested element here is called '*apūrva*' instead of dharma. In the surviving Bhāṭṭa[15] and Prābhākara[16] sources, *apūrva* is interpreted as 'new to our knowledge' or 'new information', not 'new in origination' or 'newly born'.

What then is meant by saying that *apūrva* is manifested through acts? Is it to be interpreted from the viewpoint of epistemology, in such a way that *apūrva*, which is newly cognized through the Vedas, is manifested through ritual acts? Or should we interpret it from the viewpoint of ontology, in such a way that the eternal dharma is newly manifested in this world through individual acts such as daily *agnihotra*s?

3 Uddyotakara (first half of the seventh century)

The relevant portion of the *Nyāyavārttika* is translated into Japanese and analysed by Akamatsu (1991). Therefore in the following I pick up only the passages which are important for the reconstruction of the *dharma-*

abhivyakti-vāda.

> *Nyāyavārttika* on *Nyāyasūtra* 1.1.7:
> a. *nityam apy apūrvaṃ yo 'bhivyanakti tasya phalam, abhivyaktyarthā ca kriyā. abhivyaktyarthatvāc ca na kriyālopa iti. yena yad abhivyajyate tasyaiva tat phalapradātṛ bhavatīti dṛṣṭam.* NV 55.15-17.
>
> Although *apūrva* is [one and] eternal, [only] the person who makes [it] manifest has [its] fruit. And ritual act is [done] for the sake of manifestation. And because it is [done] for manifestation, ritual act is not left unperformed. [For] it is seen that whatever is manifested gives its fruit only to the one who manifests it.

As seen before, the eternal *apūrva* is manifested through acts (*kriyā*) and gives its fruit to humans. Eternal as it is, however, *apūrva* gives its fruit only to the particular person who made it manifest. Individual ritual acts aim at manifestation (*abhivyakty-artha*). In this way their efficacy or purposefulness is guaranteed through the following sequence: ritual acts, manifested *apūrva* and fruit. This theory avoids undesired consequences such as that ritual acts would not be performed (*kriyā-lopa*).

> b. *svargāpūrvadevatādiṣūpadeśo na prāpnoti, atīndriyatvāt. yadi sākṣātkaraṇam arthasyāptiḥ, svargāpūrvadevatādīn na kaścit paśyatīti tatpratipādako vyavahāro na syāt. tasmād āptaś cāsāv upadeśaś ceti yuktam, nāptasyopadeśa iti.* NV 54.17-20.
>
> [Opponent:] [Vedic] instruction does not hold good for (*prāpnoti*) heaven, *apūrva,* deities and so forth, because they are beyond perception. If the obtaining (*āpti*) of an object is directly perceiving it [as the *Nyāyabhāṣya* interprets it], verbal usage about them would not be possible, since no one sees heaven, *apūrva,* deities and so forth. Therefore it is proper [to interpret the compound '*āpta-upadeśa*'] as 'reliable instruction' [as a *karmadhāraya*], not 'instruction of the reliable' [as a *ṣaṣṭhī-tatpuruṣa*].

With regard to the compound *āpta-upadeśa* in the Sūtra, the opponent interprets it as a *karma-dhāraya* or 'reliable instruction' instead of as a *tat-puruṣa,* 'instruction of those who reached the object'.[17] In this interpretation the opponent presupposes that *apūrva* is imperceptible (*atīndriya*), like heaven and deities (cf. *Madhyamaka-hṛdaya-kārikā* IX, k.5). Being beyond the reach of the senses, *apūrva* cannot be reached by anyone, so there is no 'person who has reached it' (*āpta*). Therefore the opponent insists that a *tat-puruṣa* interpretation is impossible.

Furthermore *apūrva,* as well as heaven and deities, is considered to be an object of Vedic instruction. As *apūrva* is regarded as imperceptible, it can be said to be qualified further as an object of Vedic instruction only.

> c. *kaḥ punar atra nyāyaḥ svargādayaḥ kasyacit pratyakṣā iti. brūmaḥ. sāmānyaviśeṣavattvāt kasyacit pratyakṣā iti. āśritatvāt. *yad āśritaṃ tat kasyacit pratyakṣam iti. parārthatvāt. yat parārthaṃ tad api kasyacit pratyakṣam iti. vastutvād āgamaviṣayatvāc ca. yad vastu yac ca parasya kathyate, tat kasyacit pratyakṣaṃ dṛṣṭam, yathā ghaṭādaya iti. anityatvāt kasyacit pratyakṣā iti.* NV 55.3-7. **yad*] Calcutta ed. ; *yad yad* Thakur ed.
>
> [Opponent:] But what is the ground for [your declaration] that heaven and so forth are visible to someone?
> [Siddhāntin:] We answer. (1) [They are] visible to someone because they have certain generic properties. (a) Because of resting [in a locus]: everything that rests in a locus is visible to someone. (b) Because of being for others: everything that is for others also is visible to someone. (c) Because of being real and the object of authoritative speech: it is experienced that everything that is real and that is communicated to others, e.g. pots, etc., is visible to someone. (2) [They are] visible to someone because they are non-eternal.

In order to show that from the Nyāya point of view *apūrva* must be perceptible to someone, Uddyotakara refers to their common properties (*sāmānya*), i.e. *āśritatva, parārthatva* and *vastutva*cum*āgamaviṣayatva*, together with another, *anityatva.* Besides *vastutva* and *āgamaviṣayatva*, which could be admitted even by the Mīmāṃsaka, the opponent who insists that *apūrva*, etc., are imperceptible to anyone is supposed to admit the opposite properties, i.e. *an-āśritatva, a-parārthatva* and *nityatva.* In fact the last-mentioned property *nityatva* is admitted in the following argument by the opponent in relation to *abhivyakti.* As is seen from another and later source (Jayanta), *an-āśritatva* is also confirmed.[18]

> d. *athāpīdaṃ syāt. ekam apy apūrvaṃ vyañjakabhedānuvidhānād bhinnam iva bhavati. ... nanu ca khaḍgādibhedān mukhabhedaḥ tadanuvidhānād dṛṣṭaḥ.* NV 56.7-10.
>
> Further the following is also possible: *apūrva,* although one, takes form as if different according to the difference of its manifesters. ... [Opponent:] Due to the difference of [the reflecting surfaces], such as a sword, we find that [the appearance of the reflection of] the

face differs in accordance with that [difference of reflectors].

Uddyotakara attacks the *apūrva*-theory after first distinguishing two possibilities, i.e. whether it is one or plural. The opponent who holds that *apūrva* is one explains that the one *apūrva* appears as many, through many manifesters in the same way that one face is reflected in many surfaces. Considering this, and other examples, such as one eternal phoneme /g/ which manifests itself through many sounds, it is appropriate to assume that the eternal *apūrva* was regarded as one rather than many.

4 Kumārila Bhaṭṭa (AD 600-650)

Kumārila, discussing 'what is dharma' or 'what is the referent of the word "dharma"' in his subcommentary on *Jaiminisūtra* 1.1.2, criticizes the idea that dharma is 'something newly born (*apūrva-janman*)'.

> *Ślokavārttika codanā*, vv.195-6b:
> *antaḥkaraṇavṛttau vā vāsanāyāṃ ca cetasaḥ/*
> *pudgaleṣu ca puṇyeṣu nṛguṇe 'pūrvajanmani//*
> *prayogo dharmaśabdasya na dṛṣṭo....* / SV 78.5-7.
>
> We do not find the word '*dharma*' applied [in ordinary usage and the Vedas] to the activity of the internal organ (as in Sāṃkhya), the disposition of the mind (as in Buddhism), virtuous souls (as in Jainism), a quality of *ātman* (as for the Vaiśeṣikas) or 'something newly born' (as in Mīmāṃsā). [Therefore these are not really *dharma*.]

As already mentioned, the surviving traditions of the Bhāṭṭas and Prābhākaras interpret *apūrva* to mean 'something epistemologically new' or 'something never cognized through other means of cognition than Vedic instructions' (*mānāntarāvedya*). According to the view refuted by Kumārila in this passage, however, *apūrva* is interpreted as something ontologically new, i.e. a newly born thing. Kumārila's commentator Sucaritamiśra (Kāśikā 160.19-22), after identifying the opponent to be 'one group of Mīmāṃsakas' (*mīmāṃsakaikadeśinaḥ*), clarifies the ontological interpretation of *apūrva*: it is that which did not exist before ritual acts (*tad dhi na karmaṇaḥ pūrvaṃ jāyata eva*) and which is produced by them (*kṛte karmaṇi tanniṣpatteḥ*).

5 Jayanta Bhaṭṭa (latter half of the ninth century)

Jayanta, commenting on *Nyāyasūtra* 1.2.57, tries to protect the authority of the Vedas from the Nyāya position. In this context he discusses 'what dharma is'. In criticizing other schools, Jayanta presupposes Kumārila's position and gives more details. Jayanta calls the view of '*apūrva* as something newly born' (*apūrva-janman*) that of 'the old Mīmāṃsakas' (vṛddha-mīmāṃsakāḥ) as opposed to the views of the followers of Śabara and Prabhākara. (Part of the relevant portion was pointed out by Yudhiṣṭhira (1984: 393; 1987: 35) and translated by Bronkhorst (1989: 113).

> *Nyāyamañjarī* on *Nyāyasūtra* 1.2.57: *vṛddhamīmāṃsakāḥ yāgādikarmanirvartyam apūrvaṃ nāma dharmam abhivadanti. yagādikarmaiva śābarā bruvate. vākyārtha eva niyogātmā apūrvaśabdavācyaḥ, dharmaśabdena ca sa evocyata iti prābhākarāḥ kathayanti....svargayāgāntarālavartinaś ca sthirasya nirādhārasyāpūrvasya niṣpramāṇakatvāt jarajjaiminīyapra-vādo 'py apeśalaḥ.* NM 664.6-16.
>
> The old Mīmāṃsakas maintain that that unprecedented thing (*apūrvaṃ nāma*) that is accomplished through acts such as sacrifice, should be [accepted as] *dharma*. Those who follow Śabara maintain that dharma is only ritual action such as sacrifice itself. The Prabhākara school says that what is denoted by the word '*apūrva*' is nothing but the sentence-meaning which is a command, which again is denoted by the word '*dharma*'. ... And the [so-called] *apūrva* which exists between sacrifice and heaven, remains for some time and is without locus, lacks any proof of its existence. Therefore the statement of the old Mīmāṃsakas is either not correct. (my translation)

Jayanta explains the *apūrva-janman* mentioned by Kumārila as 'that unprecedented thing that is accomplished through acts such as sacrifice' (*yāgādikarmanirvartyam apūrvaṃ nāma*). In other words, Jayanta explains *janman* as accomplishment by sacrifice, etc. Jayanta confirms that the *apūrva* mentioned by Kumārila is ontologically, not epistemologically new. Furthermore, the view which Jayanta identifies as that of 'the old Mīmāṃsakas (vṛddha-mīmāṃsaka, jaraj-jaiminīya)' seems, or at least is believed by him, to precede Śabara and Prabhākara, in view of the order in which he mentions the three positions.

This *apūrva* or 'new thing' stands between (or connects) sacrifice and heaven (*svarga-yāga-antarālavartin*) and remains for some time (*sthira*). In other words, it is grasped as that which is accomplished through sacrifice, remains for some time and gives its fruit to the agent. The Bhāṭṭas[19] and Prābhākaras[20] also accept this character of *apūrva* positing it as a connector which guarantees the efficacy of ritual acts. But the *apūrva* which Jayanta mentions here does not have a locus (*nirādhāra*). It is different from Kumārila's *apūrva* which is 'just a latent force of sacrifice' (*yāgādeḥ śaktimātrakam*) or 'just a latent force of an animal or the like' (*paśvāder* [*śaktimātrakam*]) and from the *ātmaśakti* usually accepted by the Bhāṭṭas.[21] This quality of 'having no locus' was already suggested by Uddyotakara.

One still hesitates, however, to understand *apūrva-janman* as simply 'something newly manifested', because in some cases 'production' (*janman, niṣpatti, nirvṛtti*) is contrasted with 'manifestation' (*abhivyakti*).[22] To recapitulate:

i. According to the 'old Mīmāṃsakas' who preceded the followers of Śabara and Prabhākara, dharma is not sacrifice, etc., themselves, but a new thing which is accomplished through them.
ii. Although it remains for some time as a fruit-giver after sacrifice, it does not have any locus such as the *ātman* or sacrifice.

6 Siṃhasūrigaṇi

Siṃhasūrigaṇi, a commentator on the *Nayacakra* of Mallavādin, refers to a Mīmāṃsā view as that of an opponent. He paraphrases *apūrva* as 'different from the seen' (*adṛṣṭa*) and a 'particular dharma' (*dharma-viśeṣa*). Furthermore, he records the view of 'some Mīmāmsakas' that dharma is nothing but ritual acts themselves, which is in fact identical with Śabara's position.

> *Nyāyāgamānusāriṇī* on *Dvādaśāraṃ Nayacakram*, vidhividhyara: a. *na pūrvo 'pūrvo, 'dṛṣṭo dharmaviśeṣaḥ.... viśeṣaśabdāt parasparaviśiṣṭābhir yajñasaṃsthābhir agniṣṭomādibhir iṣṭibhiś cā-bhivyaktavyā apūrvā* (*-vyā apūrvā*] em.; *-vyāpūrvā* ed.) *api viśeṣyante dravyamantradevatādiviśiṣṭābhiḥ*. .NC 140.23-141.5.
>
> *Apūrva* is what was not before, i.e. a specific *dharma* which is different from the seen. ... By the word 'specific' [in Mallavādin's *apūrva-viśeṣa*] is intended the following: the *apūrva*s manifested through sacrifice-types, i.e. *agniṣṭoma*, etc., and *iṣṭis,* which are qualified mutually by each other, are themselves qualified by those [sacrifice-types] which are [again] qualified by [their respective] material, mantras, deities and so forth.

In this passage, *apūrva* is paraphrased as 'different from the precedent' (*na pūrvaḥ*) and further explained as 'a particular dharma which is different from the seen' (*adṛṣṭo dharmaviśeṣaḥ*). Although this *apūrva* looks at first glance like 'an epistemologically new thing', i.e. 'a new thing cognized only through the Vedas', it can be interpreted as an 'ontologically a new thing' if one considers the meaning of 'a particular dharma' (*dharmaviśeṣa*): a dharma, which is qualified through ritual acts which are again qualified variously through their materials and mantras, becomes a particular dharma different from the seen, and is called *adṛṣṭa.* It is not new in the sense that it is cognized only through the Vedas, but new and different from the seen in the sense that it is a particular thing newly manifested in a certain situation.

The description here seems to be parallel to the structure of the relationship between *sāmānya, viśeṣa* and *vyakti.*[23] The eternal dharma could be regarded as *sāmānya,* a particular dharma which manifests itself being qualified in a certain situation as *viśeṣa,* and the individual situations which qualify one *sāmānya* as *vyakti.* In other words, the one eternal dharma, when manifested through individual acts that are qualified by each other as well as by their materials, mantras and deities, is at the same time qualified by those same individual acts. One eternal universal 'cow-ness', when manifested through individual cows, is qualified by individual cows which consist of various parts.[24] In the same way, one eternal dharma, when it is manifested through individual ritual acts and appears as a particular, is qualified through the ritual acts which consist of various elements. The way in which dharma is qualified is similar to that of *bhāvanā,* as posited by Śabara and the Bhāṭṭas, which functions as a core element in ritualanalysis and is regarded as qualified by various elements in the way that a white canvas may be qualified.[25] That is to say, the role of *bhāvanā* as a core element in the *bhāvanā*-theory of Śabara and his followers is replaced by *apūrva* (or dharma) in the *dharma-abhivyakti-vāda.*

> b. *mā bhūd yajñasaṃjñāyāḥ kriyāyā eva dharmatvaṃ, yathā kaiścin mīmāṃsakair evaṃ vyākhyāyate 'yajñena yajñam ayajanta devās, tāni dharmāṇi prathamāny āsan'* (*Ṛgveda* 1.164.50; 10.90.16) *iti. kiṃ kāraṇam. tasminn arthe pratyakṣata evānityāyāḥ kriyāyā anantaraṃ phalasambandhādarśanāt kriyāvaiphalya-doṣaprasaṅgāc ca.* NC 141.5-7.

> One should not say that it is an act that is called 'sacrifice' which is *dharma*, in the way that [is held by] those Mīmāṃsakas who interpret in this way the sentence 'The gods sacrificed sacrifice through sacrifice. Those were the first *dharmas*'. Why? Because if that is the meaning [of '*dharma*'], its connection with the fruit is not seen immediately after the act, which is visibly transient, and because of the undesirable consequence that the act may lack fruit

[and therefore becomes useless].

Furthermore, if one identified dharma with ritual acts, as Śabara did, the direct connection between dharma and its fruit would become impossible, because dharma, being transient, cannot remain until the arising of the fruit. Consequently it would become useless to perform ritual acts, because they would not be the means of attaining their fruit. On the other hand, if one follows the *dharma-abhivyakti-vāda,* dharma is able to bring its fruit directly when it is manifested through individual acts and becomes 'a new thing'. In this way the direct connection between dharma and its fruit is guaranteed.

Simhasūri also refers to the exegesis of Vedic passages in accordance with the *dharma-abhivyakti-vāda.*

> c. *agnihotram iti dharmaḥ kriyābhivyaṅgya ucyate. kārye kāra-ṇopacārād agnihotrābhivyaṅgyo 'gnihotram iti. tataḥ 'agnihotraṃ dharmaṃ, juhuyād bhāvayet, svargakāmaḥ' ity eṣa vākyārtho nirdoṣa iti.* NC 141.7-9.
>
> The word '*agnihotra*' refers to *dharma* manifested through act. What is manifested through *agnihotra* is called '*agnihotra*' through the secondary application to the result of [a word which strictly speaking refers to] the cause. Then the meaning of the sentence '*agnihotraṃ juhuyāt svargakāmaḥ*' could be interpreted without any faults as 'One who wishes heaven should realize *dharma*' (*dharmaṃ bhāvayet svargakāmaḥ*).

To sum up,

i. The Vedic passage '*agnihotraṃ juhuyāt svargakāmaḥ.*' can be paraphrased: 'one who wishes heaven should realize dharma, which is manifested through the *agnihotra* offering'.
ii. This interpretation enables one to interpret the expression *svargakāmaḥ* and the accusative in *agnihotram* naturally; unlike Śabara who analysed it in an unnatural way.
iii. It shows clearly the position that dharma, not heaven, is the purpose (*karman*) of the principal ritual action, and the thing to be accomplished (*sādhya*).

It may be noted that *apūrva* as a particular dharma manifested through acts is called a *kārya* and can be the object of '*bhāvayet*'. It is possible, therefore, to construe the *apūrva-janman* mentioned by Kumārila as equivalent with 'a newly manifested thing'. That is to say, *janman* could be interpreted as manifestation and not production in a strict sense.

Furthermore, Siṃhasūri presents the *dharma-abhivyakti-vāda* as his main *pūrva-pakṣa*, though he is also aware of Śabara's opposing '*yāgādi*=dharma' theory. We may assume then that the *dharma-abhivyakti-vāda* was the mainstream theory in the Mīmāṃsā tradition at that time.

CONCLUSION

Chronology: This theory must go back to the latter half of the fifth century, since Bhartṛhari knew it. The way in which it was referred to by Bhāviveka and Siṃhasūrigaṇi allows us to conjecture that it was dominant in the Mīmāṃsā tradition in their time. We may be justified in concluding from Kumārila's criticism that its dominance was not surpassed even in his day. Jayanta's expressions '*jaraj-jaiminīya*' and '*vṛddha-mīmāṃsaka*', in contrast with '*śābara*' and '*prābhākara*', suggest that he believed that it predated Śabarasvāmin.

Content: The eternal dharma which is always there (*avasthita eva*) becomes manifest (*abhivyakta*) through actual ritual performance (*kriyā, karman*) such as *agnihotra-homa* and *soma-yāga*. Instead of '*dharma-abhivyakti*' we also find the expression '*apūrva-abhivyakti*'. Kumārila and Jayanta use instead of *abhivyakti* the words *janman* and *nir-√vṛt* respectively. With the help of Siṃhasūrigaṇi we can construe 'newly-born' (*apūrva-janman*) as meaning a certain special dharma yet unseen (*adṛṣṭo dharmaviśeṣaḥ*), which, in being manifested by the actual performances, is also qualified by them. Uddyotakara sums it up thus: '*apūrva,* although one, takes form as if different, according to the difference of its manifesters' (*ekam apy apūrvaṃ vyañjakabhedānuvidhānād bhinnam iva bhavati*).

From the ontological point of view, the eternal dharma corresponds to *sāmānya*; the actual performances, which function as manifesters, correspond to *vyakti*; and the manifested dharma or *apūrva* to *viśeṣa*. Man is also seen as a manifester, according to Uddyotakara. From the point of view of Vedic exegesis, the passage '*agnihotraṃ juhuyāt svargakāmaḥ*' might be paraphrased thus: 'One who wishes heaven should realize dharma, which is manifested through *agnihotra-homa*'. This manifested *apūrva* is without locus (*nirādhāra*), remains for some time (*sthira*) and brings fruit (*phalada*). Although it is one and eternal, and so might be expected to be common to all people, it brings its fruit only to specific persons because it is they who manifest it.

Relationship with the System: If one admits, like Śabara, that dharma is nothing but ritual acts such as sacrifices, dharma would be transient and non-eternal. In the *dharma-abhivyakti-vāda,* on the other hand, the eternality of dharma is not compromised. This enables one to explain easily the eternality of the three concepts referred to in the second sūtra, i.e. *codanā* (Vedic instructions), *dharma* and the relationship between them (*codanā→lakṣyalakṣaṇasambandha→dharma*). This is important for the *tarkapāda* section, the aim of which is to show that dharma is cognized through the Vedas in a way that is without faults. For the three items are all eternal and lack human agents that might introduce error. Furthermore, unlike Śabara's theory, according to which *apūrva* intervenes between dharma (=ritual acts) and its fruit, the *dharma-abhivyakti-vāda* guarantees the direct causal relation between dharma and its fruit.

Thus *abhivyakti-vāda,* which is resorted to to explain why the eternal thing works at some particular time and not at another, functions as a device which guarantees the eternality of dharma as well as its causal character. Two direct relations, between *codanā* and dharma and between dharma and *phala,* are stressed in this theory, so that the second sūtra may be interpreted straightforwardly: '*codanā-lakṣaṇo 'rtho dharmaḥ*' states that Vedic instructions are the means to cognize dharma, which in turn is a direct cause of the good (*śreyaskara*) and thus becomes a desirable thing (*artha*). As a topic of discussion, it may have developed from commenting on the second sūtra, since Kumārila criticized it while expounding the second sūtra.

In Vedic exegesis the *dharma-abhivyakti-vāda* allows more natural interpretations than those of Śabara. Two specific features can be pointed out in particular: first that it interprets dharma as an aim of action (*karman*) as indicated by the accusative in '*agnihotram*', and secondly that it allows natural analysis of *svargakāmaḥ*, instead of interpreting the word as expressing that *svarga* is an aim of *bhāvanā.*

TEXT AND ABBREVIATIONS

A: *Mīmāṃsādarśanam,* Subbhāśāstrī ed., Poona, 1929-34.

F: E. Frauwallner, *Materialien zur ältesten Erkenntnislehre der Karma-mīmāṃsā,* Graz-Wien-Köln, 1968.

Kāśikā: *Mīmāmsā Slokavārtika with the Commentary Kasika of Sucaritamiśra,* K. Sāmbaśiva Sāstrī ed., Trivandrum, 1990.

MBhD: *Mahābhāṣyadīpikā of Bhartṛhari,* Fascicle IV, Āhnika I, J. Bronkhorst ed., Poona, 1987.

NC: *Dvādaśāraṃ Nayacakram,* Part I, Muni Jambūvijayaḥ ed., Bhāvnagar, 1966.

NM: *Nyāyamañjarī of Jayantabhaṭṭa,* Vol. 1, K.S.Varadacharya ed., Mysore, 1969.

NV: *Nyāyabhāṣyavārttika of Bhāradvāja Uddyotakara,* Anantalal Thakur ed., New Delhi, 1997.

PP: *Prakaraṇa Pañcikā of Sri Śālikanātha Miśra with Nyāya-siddhi,* A. Subrahmanya Sastri ed., Varanasi, 1961.

SV: *Ślokavārttikam,* Dvārikādāsa Śāstrī ed., Varanasi, 1978.

VP: *Vākyapadīya of Bhartṛhari,* K.A. S. Iyer ed., Poona, 1966.

YD: *Yuktidīpikā,* Vol. 1, A. Wezler and S. Motegi ed., Stuttgart, 1998.

NOTES

* This papar was presented on 4 November 1998 at Wolfson College, Oxford, at the seminar 'Body, Mind and Religion in India', while I was there as Michael Coulson Junior Research Fellow.

1 This word '*dharma-abhivyakti-vāda*' is not found in the original Sanskrit texts.

2 W. Halbfass, 'Karma, *Apūrva*, and "Natural" Causes', *Karma and Rebirth in Classical Indian Traditions*, Wendy Doniger O'Flaherty ed., Berkeley/Los Angeles/London, 1980, p. 282: 'a pre-Kumārila version of the theory of *apūrva,* basically amounting to the idea of a substrateless and impersonal power which is invoked and manifested by the sacrificial performance, was already discussed and refuted by Uddyotakara in his *Nyāyavārttika* on Sūtra 1.1.7.'

3 A. Akamatsu, 'Uddyotakara no Shiso __NV Kenkyū (2), Apūrva wo Megutte__' [A study of the *Nyāyavārttika* (2), Uddyotakara on *apūrva*], *Ihara Shôren Hakushi Koki Kinen Ronbun shū,* 1991, pp. 377-98.

4 Yudhiṣṭhira Mīmāṃsaka, *Saṃskṛta Vyākaraṇa-śāstra kā Itihāsa*, Bhāga I, Bahālgaṛh, 1984; 'Śāstrāvatāra-mīmāṃsā', *Mīmāṃsā-śābara-bhāṣyam,* Yudhiṣṭhira Mīmāṃsaka ed., Prathamo Bhāgaḥ, Bahālgaṛh, 1987.

5 J. Bronkhorst, 'Studies on Bhartṛhari, 2, Bhartṛhari and Mīmāṃsā', *Studien zur Indologie und Iranistik,* Vol. 15, 1989, pp. 101-17.

6 Y. Ikari, 'Rinne to Gô' [*Saṃsāra* and *karman*], *Iwanami Kôza, Tôyô Shisô Dai Rokkan, Indo Shisô* 2, Tokyo, 1988, p. 298.

7 J. Bronkhorst, 'Studies on Bhartṛhari', p. 114.

8 F 101; E. Franco and K. Preisendanz, 'Bhavadāsa's Interpretation of Mīmāṃsāsūtra 1.1.4 and the Date of the Nyāyabhāṣya', *Berliner Indologische Studien,* vol. 8, 1995.

9 E. Frauwallner, *Geschichte der indischen Philosophie*, II, Salzburg, 1956, p. 23; H. Nakamura, *Shoki Vedānta Tetsugaku shi* [The early history of Vedānta philosophy], Vols. 1-4, Tokyo, 1981, pp. 189-90.

10 Cf. A. Akamatsu, *Koten Indo no Gengo Tetsugaku* [An annotated Japanese translation of the *Brahmakāṇḍa* of the *Vākyapadīya.*], Vol. 1, Tokyo, 1998, p. 226.

11 Cf. *Śābarabhāṣya* on *Jaiminisūtra* 1.1.13: *atrāpi yadi śakṣyāmo nityatām asya vispaṣṭaṃ vaktuṃ tato nityapratyayasāmarthyāt kadācid upalam-*

bhaṃ kadācid anupalambhaṃ dṛṣṭvā kiṃcid upalambhasya nimittaṃ kalpayiṣyāmaḥ. tac ca saṃyogavibhāgasadbhāve sati bhavatīti saṃyogavibhāgāv evābhivyañjakāv iti vakṣyāmaḥ. 'In this case too, if we can clearly show its (=*śabda*'s) eternality, then because of the fact that we cognize [it as] eternal, after experiencing that [it is] perceived at some time and not perceived at another time, we assume some cause of perception. And on the basis that [perception] arises when there are conjunction and disjunction, we can say that it is conjunction and disjunction which make [*śabda*] manifest.'

12 Cf. *Śābarabhāṣya* on *Jaiminisūtra* 1.1.13: *vāyavīyāḥ saṃyogavibhāgā vāyvāśritatvād....* 'Conjunctions and disjunctions of winds, because they are located in winds...'. A 78.4-5.

13 A. Akamatsu, 'Kotoba wa Eien na Mono ka Tsukuri dasareta Mono ka __ Bhartṛhari no Baai__(2)' [Are *śabda*s eternal or artificial? __A case study of Bhartṛhari__(2)], *Tetsugaku Nenpô* (Kyūdai Bungaku bu), Vol. 55, 1996, pp. 10-11.

14 C. Lindtner, 'Bhavya on Mīmāṃsā', *Studia Indologiczne*, Vol. 4, 1997, p. 96.

15 Even Śabara is aware of an interpretation according to which *apūrva* is something epistemologically new. *Śābarabhāṣya* on *Jaiminisūtra* 9.1.3: *tad api hy apūrvaṃ śabdād evāvagamyate. astīti na prāk śabdād anyena pramāṇenopasaṃkhyāyate.* A 1646.11-13. 'For that *apūrva* also is understood only through speech. It is not shown that it exists by other means of knowledge before speech.' Kumārila begins the opponent's view in the *apūrva-adhikaraṇa* presupposing the interpretation that *apūrva* is something epistemologically new or not known before. *Tantravārttika* on *Jaiminisūtra* 2.1.5: *tasmāt sarvapramāṇāpūrvatvād anvarthanāmaivāsadrūpam apūrvaṃ pratipattavyam.* A 390.13-14. 'Therefore, *apūrva,* which is indeed appropriately named, should be construed [literally] as non-existence, because it is *apūrva* or unknown to all [other] means of knowledge.'

16 *Prakaraṇapañcikā vākyārthamātṛkā* II, v. 25: *kriyādibhinnaṃ yat kāryaṃ vedyaṃ mānāntarair na tat/ ato mānāntarāpūrvam apūrvam iti gīyate//* PP 441. 3-4. 'The *kārya* or what should be done, which is different from acts, etc., is not known through other means of knowledge [than the Vedas]. Therefore it is called *apūrva,* because it is unknown to other means of knowledge [than the Vedas].'

17 It might be improper to attribute this view only to Mīmāṃsā, because the *karmadhāraya*-interpretation is also seen in one of the traditional interpretations on *Sāṃkhyakārikā* 5 '*āptaśrutir āptavacanan tu*'. *Yuktidīpikā* on *Sāṃkhyakārikā* 5d: *āptā cāsau śrutiś ca āptaśrutiḥ.* YD 87.5.

18 As for *a-parārthatva* (not being for others), in other words, *pradhānatva* (being primary), which is supposed to be related with the *śeṣa* or subsidiary element defined as *parārtha* in *Jaiminisūtra* 3.1.2, the present article will not discuss it because it is not crucial for the reconstruction of the *dharma-abhivyakti-vāda.*

19 Kumārila, however, emphasizes that *apūrva* or latent force is not a separate entity from its locus, namely the sacrifices or their fruit, considering the

position of *śakti* in his ontology and the relation between sacrifice and its fruit. *Ślokavārttika codanā,* v. 199: *tasmāt phale pravṛttasya yāgādeḥ śaktimātrakam/ utpattau vāpi paśvāder apūrvaṃ na tataḥ pṛthak//* 'Therefore *apūrva* is just a latent force of, for example, sacrifices, which act towards the attainment of their fruit, or [just a latent force] of an animal or the like, which [acts] towards the attainment of its birth; it is not separate from them.' *Tantravārttika* on *Jaiminisūtra* 2.1.5: *yāgād eva phalaṃ tad dhi śaktidvāreṇa sidhyati/ sūkṣmaśaktyātmakaṃ vā tat phalam evopajāyate//* A 395.11-12. 'For the fruit which [arises] only from sacrifice is realized through power [of sacrifice]. Or that which has a subtle power as its nature comes to arise as nothing but the fruit.'

20 *Prakaraṇapañcikā vākyārthamātṛkā* II, v. 24ab: *tad dhi kālāntarasthānāc chaktaṃ svargādisiddhaye/* PP 440.22. 'For it (=*kārya*) is capable of accomplishing heaven and so forth because it remains until the time [of its fruit].'

21 *Tantravārttika* on *Jaiminisūtra* 2.1.5: *saiva ca puruṣagatā kratugatā vā yogyatā śāstre 'sminn apūrvam ity apadiśyate.* A 394.10-11. 'And the same compatibility, whether it lies in person or ritual, is called *apūrva* in this system [i.e. Mīmāṃsā].'

22 Cf. *Śābarabhāṣya* on *Jaiminisūtra* 1.1.12, A 75.11-76.3.

23 Cf. A. Akamatsu, 'Uddyotakara no Shiso', p. 386.

24 Cf. *Śābarabhāṣya* on *Jaiminisūtra* 1.1.3-5, *vṛttikāra*: *atha gaur ity asya śabdasya ko 'rthaḥ. sāsnādiviśiṣṭākṛtir iti brūmaḥ.* F 40.13-14. '[Question:] Then what is the referent of the word 'cow'? [Answer:] We answer that [it is] the *ākṛti* or general form, qualified by the dewlaps and so forth.'

25 Cf. K. Kataoka, 'Naraseru no Kaishaku gaku' [Mīmāṃsā theory of causal action: Śabara's concept of *bhāva, kriyā* and *bhāvanā.*], *Indo Tetsugaku Bukkyôgaku Kenkyū,* Vol. 3, 1996, pp. 47-60.

13

Historical Perspective of Vedānta Philosophy

SHOUN HINO

INTRODUCTION

As in the case of any religion, there is a history of God-man conflict in Hinduism. The divine being, i.e. 'the sacred', and the human being, i.e. 'the profane', are opposed to each other and exist in the relationship of each negating the other. 'The profane', through negating itself, wishes to become 'the sacred' or to become one with it. On the other hand, 'the sacred', through negating 'the profane', wishes to reveal itself. Here, in this context, the keywords are: the effort to secure 'the sacred' on the part of 'the profane' is the religious practice, and the revealing of 'the sacred' is its becoming the divine or attaining the grace of 'the sacred'.

M.Weber maintains that there are various types of religions in accordance with ways of liberation; i.e. to get released 'from where (*wovon*)' and to be lead 'whereto (*wozu*)'. This can be said thus; in accordance with how to understand the religious structure of 'the sacred' and 'the profane', the religious practices; i.e. the contents of effort to liberation or means to achieve liberation, is variously claimed.

'The sacred' and 'the profane' can be divided into two types according to their mutual relationship. The first is the one in which the two are remote from each other: 'the sacred' transcends 'the profane' and both are essentially distinct. On the other hand, the second type is where both are close to each other, sometimes overlapping and the equality in essence between the two is emphasized. An example of the former type is Calvinism in Christianity and of the latter are the religions which have arisen in India.

In the first category, 'the sacred' and 'the profane' are the creator and the created that is burdened by the original sin respectively, and both are considered to be wholly different. Then the 'sacred' God is beyond the 'profane' human beings and is 'the transcendental principle'. Since there is a gap between them which makes it impossible for them to meet each other in any way, or makes it impossible for 'the profane' to become divine by means of solution of individual religious practice, the only possible is to consider this world as the stage for the purpose of materializing God's glory desired by the God itself, to have the feeling of being the 'instrument of God' supported by the God, to act for the God's will and to ascertain liberation by the grace of the God **through** the deed based on a lifetime attitude of austerity-in-the-world. Therefore, this type of religion is called the 'instrument type of religion' or the 'grace type of religion'. In this type of religion, the more is transcendent or superior is of 'the sacred', the more emphasized is the meaninglessness of intelligence on the part of human beings. And then it is said, 'Because unreasonable, I believe'; thus what is demanded is faith in God based on 'sacrifice of intellect'.

In the latter case, 'the sacred' and 'the profane' are emphasized as being equal, and the two are overlapping or 'the sacred' is described as existing as 'the immanent principle'. In this type the 'profane' human being is **possessed of** liberation by nature, and is therefore not the 'instrument of God' but the 'vessel of God'. Accordingly, here 'the profane' who is possessed of 'the sacred' in itself as the 'vessel of God' is: to be **against** its own deed in the world, to minimize its own acts and to endeavour to reveal 'the sacred' being hidden in the depth by negating itself, i.e. to try to make itself divine. This is called the 'vessel type' or 'self-reliance type' corresponding to 'instrument' or 'grace' respectively. Religions in India belonging to this type have essential equality of 'the sacred' and 'the profane' as their basic understanding. Understanding this equality will reveal why various religions have grown in India and why it is called the showroom of religions. M. Weber maintains that India is a typical country which tries to secure the meaning of life or the view of the world in its literal sense through knowledge only, and 'knowledge' (gnosis), which is the centre of means to liberation, has shades, i.e. Sāṃkhya and Vedānta. The former is realistic dualism and the latter is absolute monism wherein the 'sacred' universal principle (=Brahman) and the 'profane' individual principle (=Ātman) are identical.

Hindu theology acknowledges the authoritativeness of Vedic scriptures and believes that they are not composed by any human individual but are what was heard by seers (hence called Śruti) and therefore permanent. The Vedānta school agrees on the authoritativeness of the Śrutis and maintains that the Upaniṣads convey this ultimate truth. The Śruti is not always systematically presented and, time and again, contains some things which appears as mutually contradictory. And though quite a few Vedānta teachers came before Śaṅkara (eighth century), it was he who founded the Advaita school of Vedānta taking recourse to his Advaita theory (=Absolute Monism). It is, like Yoga, the religion of vessel-type, which maintains that negating 'the profane' by one's own individual religious practice helps reveal 'the sacred' within oneself. On realizing the knowledge of the oneness of the universal spiritual principle Brahman and the individual Ātman, and nullifying one's own 'profane' human existence (=the individual self), one becomes the 'sacred' Brahman. It is the knowledge-oriented liberation theory in which 'knowing is but becoming'.

KNOWLEDGE-ORIENTED LIBERATION

Śaṅkara maintains that 'knowing one (thing, viz., the soul), one knows all' (*ekavijñānena sarvavijñānam*) and to know this soul is achieving liberation. This soul, viz., Reality, is the unlimited Brahman. Śaṅkara's doctrine is the monism of the realistic Brahman. The 'sacred' Brahman is only real, and 'the profane' is all, in reality, non-existent; it is only pseudo-real.[1] This is the standpoint of the ultimate reality; but, from the viewpoint of daily practice, 'the profane' exists as 'the real'. Therein the daily verbal activities and sensual/spiritual functions are carried out and the human being, desirous of liberation (*mumukṣu*), carries out religious practices. The 'profane' human beings endeavour to abandon all their daily activities in this sphere in order to secure liberation. Thereby they want to nullify their own existences which are 'the profane'. And then knowing that 'the profane' own self is in reality the 'sacred' Brahman, they themselves become 'the sacred'.

Śaṅkara in keeping with such an assertion puts emphasis on Upaniṣadic sentences, the so-called Mahāvākyas, like *tat tvam asi* (*Chāndogyopaniṣad* 6.8.7), *aham brahmāsmi (Bṛhadāraṇyakopaniṣad* 1.4.10) which suggest the identity of the Brahman and the Ātman, and, regarding the theory of liberation, takes up sentences attaining like *brahma veda brahmaiva bhavati* (*Muṇḍakopaniṣad* 3.2.9), *brahmavid āpnoti param* (*Taittirīyopaniṣad* 2.1.1), *vidyayā 'mṛtam aśnute* (*Īśo-paniṣad* 11) which declares that to know the Brahman is to become the Brahman, i.e. liberation.

Śaṅkara maintains that *tat tvam asi* among the Mahāvākyas is the concise declaration of the truth of all Vedic scriptures. (So is *aham brahmāsmi* also.)

The Mahāvākya, *tat tvam asi* is repeated at the end of each section between *Chāndogyopaniṣad* 6.8 and 6.16. In this, the Upaniṣadic sage Uddālaka Aaruṇi instructs the absolute reality of the Brahman, and adopting particular illustrative similes for establishing the identity of the Brahman and the Ātman within one, he concludes: 'This all is of the nature of it'. It is real and the Ātman. O, Śvetaketu, that you are. The sole ultimate real, the Brahman is the primary cause, and that only is the reality and nothing else is real. That is to say, 'the sacred' is only real and 'the profane' is false. A pot or a plate, for instance, are originally clay and are thus only transformations of the same. Here transformation is the expression of the words (*vācārambhanaṃ vikāro nāmadheyam*) and therefore false, and similarly this all 'profane' being evolved from the Brahman is the transformation and expressible in words. And by the latter part of the citation 'That is the Ātman.... That you are', that ultimate Brahman is identical with the Ātman (the individual self)—that is then being identified with Śvetaketu, an individual being which is possessed of a body, etc.

This is demonstrated also by the simile of *mahākāśa* and *ghaṭākāśa: mahākāśa*, which is prevalent even in the universe, and *ghaṭākāśa*, which is ether in a pot, are originally one and the same (*ekarasa*). But ether is delimited by the existence of the pot; *mahākāśa*, ether in the universe, looks differentiated from *ghaṭākāśa*, ether in the pot. Similarly, the Brahman prevailing in the universe is but one and the same; however, being delimited by the body and the aggregate of sense-organs (produced due to ignorance) are considered to be differentiated from each other. By means of breaking the pot, ether in the pot is being permeated in ether in the universe and there is *ekarasa* ether. Or, by nullifying the aggregate of organs and body which differentiates the individual being from the one-in-all Brahman, the Ātman, on realizing its oneness with the Brahman, becomes one with it.

The word *tvam* signifies the individual human body, being an aggregate together with sense-organs. But the aggregate of the body and the sense-organs, which are individualizing factors, are pseudo-existent and do not have reality, but the individual self (=Ātman, the inner self) which is hidden in the depth of their (so-called) existence alone exists. Therefore, what is signified by the word *tvam* is this real Ātman. This Ātman and the Brahman, which is signified by the word *tat,* are linked by the word *asi* conveying the identity.

LIBERATION BASED ON KNOWLEDGE-ORIENTED BHAKTI

The gnosis-oriented liberation theory has been overlapped by the current of *bhakti*-oriented liberation theory. It is the process of the personification of the 'sacred' ultimate reality and the 'vessel-type' religion gets more influenced by the 'instrument-type' one. It is at the same time changing the process of the contents of *bhakti*.

For Śaṅkara, the 'sacred' Brahman is absolutely the abstract principle but *bhakti* needs the object to which the act of *bhakti* is directed at and 'the sacred' has necessarily become personified. For Rāmānuja (eleventh century) and Madhva (thirteenth century), 'the sacred' is the transcendental personified God Viṣṇu. According to Weber, Calvinism has the personified God as its idea of God and the religion of gnosis-oriented liberation has non-personified existence as its idea of God. In the instrument-type of Calvinism, liberation, endowed by the grace, presupposes the complete nullification of human self-reliant effort in front of God. Therein 'the sacrifice of intellect' is demanded. On the other hand, the preaching of the three Vedānta teachers (viz., Śaṅkara, Rāmānuja and Madhva), having the essential understanding of the oneness of 'the sacred' and 'the profane', assert the vessel-type of meditative life, being away from the world. And Śaṅkara tries to have the mystical union with 'the sacred' negating 'the profane', and Rāmānuja and Madhva consider the transcendent personified Viṣṇu as 'the sacred', and thereby appear to show the affinity to the liberation based on 'religion of faith'.

Here *bhakti* retains the tinge of gnosis which is highly estimated by Advaita. Then *bhakti* has characteristics of the religious practice on the part of 'the profane'. We find, in Rāmānuja, the tinge of self-reliance-type of religion which plans to get liberated by means of religious practice of *bhakti* on the part of 'the profane', and in Madhva the absoluteness of Viṣṇu is more emphasized and therefore the liberation owing to the God is more talked about and the significance of *bhakti* becomes less important; it becomes more like the grace-type of religions and appears closer to Calvinism.

Vedānta had arisen as Brahmavāda, holding the Brahman as the real and ultimate being, and Śaṅkara established its absolute singleness as Advaita, i.e. it is one without a second. In his means to liberation gnosis is highly emphasized. In Rāmānuja or Madhva, the notion of *bhakti* is introduced and incorporated in that gnosis. Basically both these Vedānta Acāryas focused their religious activities in south India at different times and from different standpoints, but in the same religious faith, i.e. firm devotion to God Viṣṇu. They had a significant mission to establish the theology of *bhakti* in conflict with the tradition of gnosis in Vedānta or Śaṅkara's Advaita.

The teaching of Rāmānuja is Viśiṣṭādvaitavāda. It is the theory of one who is qualified by attributes and is yet without a second, i.e. Lord Viṣṇu. In reality the Brahman alone exists but, in daily dealings, the Brahman, the individual self and the phenomenal world are components of the universe. These three are in the following relationships: at the time of creation of the world, the Brahman permeated into the individual selves and the material world and has become the inner essence as immanent principle, viz., the inner controller (*antaryāmin*). This inner controller (viz., the Brahman) has something qualifying, viz., the individual selves or gross things. This qualified Brahman is one with the individual self and the material world.

Rāmānuja says *tat tvam asi* signifies the same case relationship. *Tvam* and *tat* ontologically signify one and the same entity. *Tat* is 'the Brahman which is the cause of the world, the origin of all virtues and faults'. *Tvam* is 'the Brahman in the form of the inner controller of the individual self, i.e. the Brahman, qualified by the individual self, being existent as the inner essence of the individual self. This Brahman is the transcendental personified God, Viṣṇu and 'the sacred'; the individual self and the material world are 'the profane'.

Thus, in reality, 'the sacred' Brahman alone exists, but, in practical world of parity, the Brahman is regarded as the immanent principle of 'the profane' world and, as a result, the *ekarasa* Brahman is expressed by the words of 'the identity in reality' of the sacred and the profane. Obviously, this is the type of religion which permeated 'the sacred' in the vessel (=a body) of an individual self and the material world. But Rāmānuja was not like Śaṅkara. He did not differentiate 'the sacred' from the vessel by means of falsity (i.e. non-existence) of the body, viz., the vessel. He recognized these three, viz., the Brahman, the individual self and the material world (the sacred and the profane) as real and tried to reveal the Brahman in there. Therefore, the Brahman is the creator from the viewpont of the individual self and the material world and is thus endowed with transcendence and personality. Ontologically, he maintains the identity in reality of the sacred and the profane but, from the viewpoint of liberation, 'the profane' is relieved by the grace of personified God Viṣṇu. His theory is the combination of Śaṅkara and Calvinism.

In the theory of grace of Calvinism 'the profane' man leads a life of austerity-in-the-world and promotes and develops the world as the stage of God's glory. This is the way to ensure the God's grace, viz., being selected by God. Hindu theism has its origin in 'this Ātman is not obtained by the teaching, nor by intelligence, nor learning the scripture. It is obtained only by a man this whom (God, Ātman) selects. To him the Ātman is manifested.' (*Kaṭhopaniṣad* 2.23).

Rāmānuja, interpreting this, says, 'the man with *bhakti* is the one to be selected by the highest being; therefore, (the highest one) is obtained by him. This is the meaning of the scripture.' It is when a man is selected by God and begotten grace that the profane has secured *bhakti*.

Bhakti is not something to be begotten but something to acquire. Therefore, *bhakti* is a means of individual religious practice and not merely awaiting God's grace, and further various practice to be equipped with. *Bhakti* is nothing and it consists in the individual religious practice as a means to liberation. The resulting acquisition of *bhakti* is the time when God bestows grace on an individual and manifests himself in him, i.e. the time of being liberated.

Such *bhakti* is affectionate, absorbing and the special knowledge which deprives one of concern to others totally. *Bhakti* is 'special knowledge' and is not mere knowledge, i.e. knowledge differentiating the inner controller from the individual self. Or the word 'knowledge' here means the meditation which has risen above in the form of *bhakti*. This *bhakti* which is the ultimate form of meditation; it is devotion, viz., unexcelled meditation which is the state of direct experiencing God. For Rāmānuja this 'knowledge' is nothing but meditation and, moreover, the ultimate form of meditation, i.e. that of the nature of this is the immediate means to liberation or meditation having arisen above the form of *bhakti*.

The religion of Rāmānuja, being based on the fundamental understanding of identity of the sacred and the profane, maintains the liberation as coming through the grace of Viṣṇu. And therein *bhakti* is the means of acquiring liberation. But that *bhakti* (according to Rāmānuja) is doubtful in respect of its difference from the gnosis of Śaṅkara as far as the contents are concerned. Holding the personified God and being inclined to the instrument type of religion but having the idea of *bhakti* supporting grace, it does not go away from the vessel type as far as the religious practice is concerned.

In the teaching of Madhva, the Brahman and God Viṣṇu are considered to be identical and the triad, viz., the Brahman, the individual self and the material world, is differentiated within itself. He declares that the 'sacred' Viṣṇu and the 'profane' individual self and the material world are ever different existential entities and, therefore, his view is held as dualism. But from the viewpoint of the sacred and the profane, the sacred Viṣṇu and the profane individual self have mutually similar nature. Or in that the profane is created from the sacred and that the profane depends on the sacred, both the sacred and the profane are understood to be identical in reality. But, due to the insistence on the difference between the sacred and the profane, the distance between them is considered much farther as compared to that with Śaṅkara or Rāmānuja; it is the result of greater emphasis on Viṣṇu's transcendence and absoluteness, when compared with that in Rāmānuja.

The view of Madhva in respect of *tat tvam asi* is also unique. In common parlance, the *Chāndogya* sentence *sa ātmā tat tvam asi* is understood as *sa ātmā tat tvam asi*, '... the Ātman. That you are', but Madhva interprets it as *sa ātmā atat tvam asi* '... Not that you are'. The profane 'individual self' expressed by *tvaṃ* and the sacred 'Brahman' expressed by *tat* are distinct from each other. In the sentences *tat tvam asi* 'That you are', and *aham brahmāsmi* 'I am the Brahman', both the Brahman and the individual self, expressed by *tvam* and *aham*, are of similar nature. And 'are' or 'is' does not indicate ontological sameness. They are understood so by the means of secondary sense of the sameness. In the sentence 'He is a lion', a man's bravery is understood like that of a lion, and the sentence means 'He is brave as a lion is'. Similarly, on the basis of indescribability, excellence, eternity of the Brahman and the individual self, 'You are (like) that', *tat tvam asi* 'That you are' is understood as 'You are like that' (*tadvat tvam asi*) or 'You belong to it' (*tadadhīnaḥ tvam asi*).

Madhva understands *bhakti* as the 'love of God' which is firm and unshaken, beyond all, knowing the greatness of the highest God Viṣṇu. Knowledge and *bhakti* are being promoted in the course of mutual association. Through *bhakti* when a being is unattached to itself in the case of hearing, meditation, 'the knowledge of the greatness of God' (i.e. indirect knowledge) arises. From this knowledge arises as the immediate knowledge, which means that one realizes God directly and experiences God manifested just in meditation. From this immediate knowledge, *bhakti* arises the direct cause of liberation. This is the highest *bhakti* (*paramabhakti*) in later times. In the course of meditative life of austerity-in-the-world, *bhakti* is to be equipped with the individual religious practice, in the view of Madhva.

According to Śaṅkara, religious practice is preached for nullifying the activities, in order that one realizes the profane as false. But, in Madhva's opinion, the viewpoint of that 'profane' self is reality because Viṣṇu transcends the self and is quite far away from the profane; we know 'it is great' and try to improve the 'profane' self in order to get itself delighted by such 'sacred'. Here in the improvement of the profane we should notice the parallel between Calvinism and Madhva.

In the case of Rāmānuja, liberation is ensured by one who is equipped with the ultimate form of meditation, i.e. *bhakti*, but in the case of Madhva there is no word at all suggest that man is liberated by *bhakti* or something of the kind—it is repeatedly stated that one is liberated only by the transcendent God Viṣṇu and not by any other means. Compared with Rāmānuja, to become 'the sacred' on the basis of understanding the oneness of 'the sacred' and 'the profane' is hardly referred to by Madhva, and more stressed is the liberation of 'the profane' by the power of 'the sacred', i.e. by the endowing of the grace by Viṣṇu who has chosen to grant it.

LIBERATION BASED ON LOVE-ORIENTED *BHAKTI*

Bhakti is characterized by the religion of the elite and is practiced only by the monks in the monasteries. On the other hand, *bhakti* emphasizing the aspect of love is supported by the masses and stresses the immense love of God and His grace. We notice the division into two directions in the school of Rāmānuja (after his time). There occurred the monkey-cat discussion. The monkey runs away with the baby monkey when it clings to the mother's neck at the time of crisis. The cat runs away holding the neck of its kitten by its teeth. The former, the monkey-theory, is close to that of Rāmānuja, which demands the effort on the part of the baby monkey. This is supported by Vaḍagarai School of north India. The latter, the cat-theory, demands no effort on the part of human beings and relies on the grace of God. This is supported by Teñgalai School of south India which stresses the importance of Prapatti or dependence on the God's grace.

The *bhakti* movement was prevalent in south India for several centuries. The Āḷvārs talked about the Viṣṇu stories and sang the ardent love for Viṣṇu and the pleasure derived from it. The Nāyanārs sang the *bhakti* of Śiva. And *Bhāgavata Purāṇa* established this *bhakti* as religious thought. Then, later, this Purāṇa had been translated into various regional languages and together with it spread this *bhakti* thought into various parts of the country. In this process of expansion and variegation of *bhakti*, based on its infusion into local-regions as well as its prevalence among masses, some of them are seen to have been influenced by Islam.

From the discussions so far it can be gathered that *bhakti* is that which is directed by human beings to God. Incidentally, *viraha bhakti* finds a mention in the *Bhāgavata Purāṇa.* The tronger the love or inclination human beings have towards God, the more do they realize their own incapability to be one with God, accept the futility of their of effort on their own part and that there is the rigid distinction between themselves and God. Therefore human beings do not look upon *bhakti* as a means but consider it as their goal. In short, there is giving up of making an effort and therein *bhakti* is not a means but an object. This is called *viraha bhakti*[2] (which later on develops into *prapatti),* that gives up the notion of union with God through human effort and the complete surrender of one's liberation to God. This is a landmark in the course of the development of *bhakti* in that the initiative of liberation was entrusted by individual beings to God.

As a contrast to this *viraha bhakti*, we find *tāntric bhakti* which arose with Tantricism as a backdrop. These two *bhakti*s are similar in propagating their affirmation of 'this world'. This is the presupposition of the religion of the masses and the ultimate mode of religion in the sense that it signifies the state of the liberation while a being is alive in this world. And, moreover, these are two sides of the same coin. In other words, they show the culmination of the two types of religion mentioned so far, i.e. 'grace type' and 'self-reliance type'. That is to say: In this very world the 'profane' individual human being is united with 'the sacred'. *Viraha bhakti* takes the form of the grace of God from above. *Tāntric bhakti* takes the form of becoming-God on the part of human individuals from below.

In the case of the former, individual existence is nullified and the meaningfulness of human endeavour is lessened. On the contrary, the world is the development of power (*śakti*) of God and the grace of God is the development of the divine power. Therefore, to surrender oneself to the divine power and to enjoy the world which is the grace of the God—this is what is all about. Here the notion 'the individual is the vessel' which is of essential significance is totally lost and is understood to be something like the 'grace type'.

On the other hand, in *tāntric bhakti*, the 'profane' individual existence is always emphasized as the subject of loving God. And through proper rituals one is united with God.[3] The 'profane' individual can become, as it were, the 'sacred' God. If we consider it as becoming God in the world by a self-reliant endeavour on the part of 'the profane', it is nothing but what is advocated by the liberation theory of self-reliance type of religious practice based on 'vessel type' of religion. In the Advaita Vedānta 'the sacred' is the unlimited Brahman, and 'the profane', the vessel; it requires an endeavour to negate oneself to reveal 'the sacred' in the depth of oneself. And in *tāntric bhakti* the 'profane' human beings are taken to be really existent as apart from God, since is affirmed the real existence of the world. And moreover 'the sacred' is not the unlimited Brahman but the personified God-idea like Śiva or Viṣṇu. It is quite at variance with Śaṅkara's Advaita.

Our discussion begins with the setting of two opposites, Advaita (negation of the world, non-personified reality, vessel-type) and Calvinism (affirmation of the world, personified God, instrument-type). In the case of *viraha bhakti*, the personified God Viṣṇu becomes the divinity of high absoluteness which is remote from 'the profane' and shows similarity to Calvinism. And *tāntric bhakti* maintains the personified God and the affirmation of the world, and at the same time 'vessel-type'. Further, in accepting the personified God, it naturally talks about grace.

In the Advaita 'the sacred' is the Brahman and 'the profane' is to be negated. Here the world developed from Śiva's *śakti* is taken as real and Śiva as 'the sacred' and it is never to be negated. The phenomenal world and Māyā (=*śakti*), its origin, are all real.

In the *tāntric bhakti*, the transcendental principle Śiva develops himself and becomes the world as a result of the elevation of his absoluteness. In this sense the world/human beings is the vessel. Only ascetic practice is required to wipe away the dirt attached to the body. As regards grace, the world itself is the grace of God. The final stage of ascetic practices in the course of the ritual, i.e. on the occasion of securing the same power as God Śiva having the form of Guru who endows the power on a devotee, is also the grace. Compared with self-reliant asceticism, in a general way, the grace of Śiva is arranged. Thus it is the vessel type having the significance of grace in its core part of it. Also it maintains personified God despite being as it were the vessel-type. It is the complete mixed type of the vessel and grace types. Thus, the type retaining the original Advaita character, i.e. the religion of the elite, was established while maintaining the affirmation of the world.

We have got two types on the standpoint of affirming the world, *viraha bhakti* (in which the human is liberated through the grace of God) and *tāntric bhakti* (in which the human becomes God). These two are classified into the grace-type and the self-reliance type respectively. But it is sometimes two viewpoints of one and the same liberation, viz., from above (=God) or from below (=the human). It depends on how we understand the personified God.

Finally we shall see two examples, viz., Caitanya and Ramakrishna, to this effect. Caitanya lived in fifteenth century in Bengal. He advocated the ardent love for and faith in Rādhā-Kṛṣṇa. He says the world is real and permanent. The human in the world only depends on Kṛṣṇa. *Bhakti* towards Kṛṣṇa is the revelation of God. He did kīrtana, sang and danced for Kṛṣṇa and was united with Him in trance. Takashima maintains in his article that this is the unification of two movements of Tantricism and Hindu *bhakti*.[4] And Dasgupta claims in *Hindu Mysticism* that he (=Caitanya) is the embodied being of love like Rādhā or the *gopi*s who loved Kṛṣṇa.[5] Ramakrishna lived in nineteenth century in Bengal. For him God is only real and it is important to experience God directly. This real Brahman sometimes takes the form of Jesus or Allah as well as Hindu Godesses and Gods like Kālī, Śiva, Kṛṣṇa or Rāma. He himself experienced those Gods one after another and at the same time advocated 'the love of cat'.[6]

NOTES

1 This is the reason why Śaṅkara's Advaita is called *vivartavāda*.

2 M. Tokunaga, '*bhakti*—Kami eno Shin'ai to Kie' ('*bhakti*—love and devotion to God'), *Iwanami Koza Toyo Shiso* 7, *Indo Shiso* 3, Tokyo, 1989, pp. 222-226.

3 J. Takashima, 'Tantorizum' ('Tantricism'), *Iwanami Koza Toyo Shiso* 6, *Indo Shiso* 2, Tokyo, 1988, p. 135.

4 Ibid., p. 128.

5 J. Takashima, *Yoga to Hindu Shinpishugi (Yoga and Hindu Mysticism)*, (Japanese translation of S. Dasgupta's *Hindu Mysticism*), Tokyo, 1979, pp. 164-169.

6 Y. Nara, *Rāmakurishuna (Ramakrishna), Jinrui no Chiteki Isan* 53, Tokyo, 1983, p. 41.

14

Sarvajñātman's Theory of Definition

HIROYUKI SATO

The *Brahma-sūtra*, a text of aphorisms of the Vedānta school, declares that *Brahman* is the cause of the origin, maintenance and dissolution of the universe[1] while the Advaita school defines *Brahman* as Existence (*sat*), Consciousness (*cit*) and Bliss (*ānanda*).[2] Being a branch of the Vedānta school, the Advaita school must respect the definition of *Brahman* given in the *Brahma-sūtra*. This, however, placed the Advaita school into a difficult position in determining whether *Brahman* is the cause of the origin, etc., of the universe, or Existence, etc. In order to resolve this dilemma, the Advaita school accepted two kinds of definition, viz., the essential definition (*svarūpalakṣaṇa*) and the accidental definition (*taṭasthalakṣana*).[3] Hence, the cause of the origin, etc., of the universe is interpreted as the accidental definition while Existence, etc., is interpreted as the essential definition of *Brahman*.

I have already published an article on these two kinds of definition.[4] On the other hand, according to Sarvajñātman's *Saṃkṣepa-śārīraka*[5] the definition is divided into three kinds. Although he interprets the definition of *Brahman* given in the *Brahma-sūtra* as accidental definition[6] like other Advaita philosophers, prior to this interpretation he does not propose the three kinds of the definition as a special topic but as a very general topic. He does not explain in detail his theory of centered divisions of definition. Nevertheless, his explanation is significant in Indian philosophy. In the present paper an analysis will be given of Sarvajñatman's theory of definition.

DIVISION OF DEFINITION

It is very rare for an Indian philosopher to divide definitions. Since Indians who have a strong inclination for dividing did not show any concern for dividing definitions, it may be concluded that they did not recognize any other kinds of definition except the one definition.

Sarvajñātman, however, divides the definition into three kinds.

> It is well known in this ordinary practice that the definition of the definiendum (*lakṣya*) is of three kinds: (1) the essential definition (*svalakṣaṇa*), (2) the qualifying definition (*viśeṣaṇa*) and (3) the accidental definition (*upalakṣaṇa*) of it(=definiendum).[7] I will define these three kinds of definitions separately. May you understand it![8]

It is open to question whether the three kinds of definition are really 'well known in this ordinary practice' or not. Some literature of the Advaita school divides the definition into two kinds: the essential definition and the accidental definition,[9] but, so far as I know, there is not other literature which divides the definition into three kinds that included the qualifying definition.[10] As stated at the beginning of this paper, it is for the sake of interpreting the definition of *Brahman* given in the *Brahma-sūtra* that the Advaita school divides the definition. Although Sarvajñātman also divides it for the same reason, his intention of dividing it into three kinds exists in making use of this idea to interpret the general topics rather than the special topic (i.e. *Brahman*). He regards the essential definition and the accidental definition as the definition of *Brahman* but not the qualifying definition.[11] In other words, two definitions are sufficient for defining *Brahman*, but three definitions are necessary for interpreting the general topics. Therefore, when other Advaitins divided it into two kinds, they were not neglecting the qualifying definition nor did they think that the qualifying definition is included in the essential definition or the accidental definition.

GENERAL DEFINITION OF THREE KINDS OF DEFINITION

After dividing the definition Sarvajñātman discusses his understanding of the general definition, which is common to the earlier-mentioned three kinds of definition and constitutes his answer to the question, 'What is definition?'.

> It is held that the definition is known to occur in the definiendum (*lakṣayārtha*) and indicates it as entirely being differentiated from the other entity (=non-definiendum). This is the general definition of three kinds of definition.[12]

According to this explanation, the common factors or necessary condition for the three kinds of definition can be as follows:

[A] Occurring in the definiendum.
[B] Entirely differentiating the definiendum from the non-definiendum.

First, let us examine [A]. This factor may be requested so that the definition does not suffer from the defect of non-application (*asaṃbhava*) which is non-occurrence in all class of the definiendum and so that the definition applies to the definiendum.[13] But 'occurring in the definiendum' does not necessarily mean 'occurring in all class of the definiendum'. For example, if we define a cow by tawny color, this definition will fall into the defect of narrow-application (*avyāpti*) because it occurs only in a part of the class (= a tawny cow) of the definiendum including a black cow, etc. This definition, however, does not suffer from the defect of non-application because a tawny cow surely exists. In other words, the definition such as the tawny color of a cow meets the factor that the definition occurs in the definiendum even if it does in a portion of the definiendum. In the same way, 'occurring in the definiendum' does not mean 'non-occurring in the non-definiendum' because tawny color occurring in a portion of the definiendum (=cow) is applied to the non-definiendum (e.g. a tawny horse). Hence this factor means only that the definition is free from the defect of non-application, that is to say, this factor means that it does not always apply to all class of the definiendum, but does not mean that it is also free from the defects of narrow-application and over-application (*ativyāpti*).

The definition, however, can be free from the defect of over-application by [B], since the adverb 'entirely (*niḥśeṣatas*)' is added to the word 'differentiating' in it. If Sarvajñātman only stated 'differentiating the definiendum from the non-definiendum', it is not clear whether 'differentiating from all the non-definiendum' is meant or 'differentiating from a portion of the non-definiendum'. When we define a cow by a horn, for instance, although it will fall into the defect of over-application since it is also applied to an antelope which is a portion of the non-definiendum, it differentiates a cow from a rabbit which is another portion of the non-definiendum. Contrary to this, when the adverb 'entirely' is added to the word 'differentiating', [B] means 'differentiating from all the non-definiendum'[14] by which the definition can be free from the defect of over-application.

As mentioned earlier, although the definition is free from the defect of non-application by [A] and the defect of over-application by [B], it cannot be free from the defect of narrow-application by [A] or [B]. Therefore, Sarvajñātman must regard even the properties fallen into the defect of narrow-application as the definition since he does not give any factors to be free from the defect of narrow-application. In other words, according to him, it is the necessary and sufficient condition for the definition that some properties are at least occurring in a portion of the definiendum and non-occurring in all the non-definiendum.

The first angle to divide the definition is 'the way in which the definition occurs in the definiendum' in [A]. Based on this angle, a name such as the essential definition is given. The second angle is 'the way in which the definition entirely differentiates the definiendum from the non-definiendum' in [B]. Considering these two angles, I would like to analyze Sarvajñātman's explanation of the three kinds of definition.

ESSENTIAL DEFINITION

At first, Sarvajñātman explains the essential definition as follows:

> The definition, which directly differentiates the definiendum from other entities, is called the definition as the essential property of the definiendum, even if it is the essential property of the definiendum. [For example,] this in the ordinary world is 'The sky is hollow', 'Water is liquid', etc.,[15]

If [A] and [B] mentioned in the previous section are applied here, the factors of the essential definition will be as follows:

[A-1] Occurring in the definiendum as the essential property.
[B-1] Directly and entirely differentiating the definiendum from the non-definiendum.

Judging from the name called the essential definition, [A-1] is an expected factor. The questions, however, will remain: What does 'occurring in the definiendum as the essential property' mean? How can we know whether or not some properties are essential?[16] In Indian philosophy, since the definition is fundamentally a non-common property (*asādhāraṇadharma*) the definiendum is regarded as 'a possessor of property' (*dharmin*) in which a property is inherent. 'Occurring in the definiendum' also means that the definition occurs in the definiendum as being inherent in it. Originally the definition occurs in the definiendum as a property and the object meant by the word is distinct between the definition and the definiendum.[17] Sarvajñātman also understands it in the same manner. In saying 'occurring in the definiendum as the essential property', however, it seems to mean that this definition does not occur in the definiendum as a property but as a possessor of a property and that the object meant by it is not distinct from the defininendum.[18] When Sarvajñātman added the word '*api*' to '*lakṣyasvarūpam*' in the original Sanskrit text, he probably intended that some properties are originally the definition but that the essential property, which is not a property, is also regarded as the definition.[19]

Incidentally, the essential definition (*svarūpalakṣaṇa*) is interpreted in another manner.[20] For instance, in the sentence 'Earth is the possessor of smell (*gandhavatī pṛthivī*)',[21] 'the possessor of smell (*gandhavat*)' is called the essential definition of earth. Regarding earth, not only 'the possessor of smell' but also 'the state of possessing smell (*gandhavattva*)' is said to be its definition.[22] It is the fundamental distinction between these definitions that 'the state of possessing smell' is a property (*dharma*) of the definiendum, whereas 'the possessor of smell' is a property possessor (*dharmin*). The latter is not distinct from the definiendum and is logically equivalent to the definiendum. 'The state of possessing smell' is the definition in a strict sense, since the definition is a property according to Indian philosophy, while 'the possessor of smell' is the definition in a broad sense. Then 'the possessor of smell' is interpreted as the essential definition of earth.[23] The essential definition treated in the Advaita school also may mean the definition in a broad sense given in the form of a sentence. Sarvajñātman actually gives the examples of the essential definition in the form of a sentence like 'The sky is hollow' and 'Water is liquid'. In the Advaita school, however, the essential definition is never limited to this style,[24] because Sarvajñātman thinks that we can define earth as 'the state of a possessor of smell' but cannot define the sky as 'the state of hollow (*chidratva*)' nor water as 'the state of liquid (*dravatva*)'.[25] Moreover, in the case of 'the mane' to 'a horse' which is given as the example of the qualifying definition, even if it is stated in the form of the sentence like 'A horse is the possessor of the mane', it does not follow from this that 'the possessor of the mane' is the essential definition of a horse. The essential definition in Advaita school is regulated by the distinct standpoint from 'the definition in broad sense' mentioned earlier.

As for [B-1], it is important that the adverb 'directly' (*sākṣāt*) is added to the word 'differentiating'. If this adverb, on which the commentators do not give any explanations, is not added for a rhythm but for some other specific purpose, it may mean that Sarvajñātman divided the way of differentiating into 'directly' and 'indirectly'. The essential definition differentiates directly the definiendum from the non-definiendum while the other two definitions differentiate indirectly. The distinction between 'directly' and 'indirectly' may be as follows: When the definition differentiates the definiendum from the non-definiendum, it means that the definition differentiates its locus from the non-definiendum because the definiendum is the locus of the definition. As mentioned earlier, the essential definition is not a property of the definiendum but that which is not different from the locus. Therefore, in this case, the definition, which is not distinct from its locus, differentiates the definiendum from the non-definiendum. This can be the meaning of 'directly differentiating'. In other words, it is by means of itself, not of anything else, that the essential definition differentiates the definiendum. On the other hand, it can be the meaning of 'indirectly differentiating' that the definition differentiates the definiendum from the non-definiendum through the aid of the locus in which the definition is inherent.

Strictly speaking, the two factors of the essential definition are not distinct from each other. If some properties are provided with [A-1], they will be provided with [B-1], and vice versa. That is to say, if some properties occur in the definiendum as the essential property, they can differentiate directly the definiendum from non-definiendum.

Although, on the essential definition, Sarvajñātman does not discuss about 'being the reason of arising of the knowledge' which is one of the factors of the qualifying definition, this can be a factor of the essential definition. Therefore, it has one more factor:

[C-1] Being the cause of arising of the knowledge of the definiendum.

QUALIFYING DEFINITION

Next, the qualifying definition is explained as follows:

> And, what is the cause of arising of the knowledge, which is related to itself, of the definiendum is the definition as the qualifying property. For example, it is in such cases as the mane of

the horse.[26]

The factor of the qualifying definition stated here is only to be the cause of arising of the knowledge of the definiendum. If the factors stated in the previous section are added, the following three become the factors of the qualifying definition:

[A-2] Occurring in the definiendum as the qualifying property.
[B-2] Indirectly and entirely differentiating the definiendum from the non-definiendum.
[C-2] Being the cause of arising of the knowledge of the definiendum.

[A-2] is an expected factor. The most general example of the qualifying property is 'blue' in 'a blue lotus'. In this example, 'a lotus' is a locus and 'blue' is a property. Then, the object meant by the word 'blue' is distinct from that of 'a lotus'. In the Advaita school, a qualifying property is explained as 'the qualifying property corresponds to the result affirmatively and differentiates [the qualified entity from] others'.[27] An important point in this factor is that even if some properties are the qualifying property of the definiendum, they do not always become the qualifying definition. For example, though 'blue' is the qualifying property of 'a lotus', 'blue' does not become the qualifying definition of 'a lotus'. Even if the qualifying property is a differentiator, it cannot entirely differentiate the definiendum from the non-definiendum. When a non-definiendum was divided into the class of the same kind (*sajātīya*) and the class of a different kind (*vijātīya*), a qualifying property differentiates the definiendum only from the class of the same kind.[28] For example, although 'blue color' differentiates its locus from 'a white lotus' which belongs to the same class of 'a lotus', it does not differentiate 'a blue rose' which belongs to the different class of 'a rose'. Therefore, [B-2] is required as the second factor.

Well, [C-2] 'being the cause of arising of the knowledge of the definiendum' was not stated as the factor of the general definition mentioned earlier and was not contained in the factor of the essential definition. This factor probably means 'the cause to use a word (*pravṛttinimitta*)'. According to the example given by Sarvajñātman, 'a mane' becomes the cause to use the word 'the horse' because a 'mane' is the qualifying definition of the 'horse'. On the other hand, as it will be asserted in the next section that the accidental definition does not become the cause to use the word, 'a crow', which is the example of the accidental definition, does not become the cause to use the word 'Devadatta's house'. When we see a crow and judge from it 'This is Devadatta's house', does not the crow become the cause to use the word 'Devadatta's house'? For investigating this question we shall analyze two judgments on 'a horse' as follows:

[X-1] A horse is running.
[Y-1] This is a horse.

[X-1] is the judgment which gives us some information about 'a horse' and 'a horse' is the grammatical subject of this sentence. On the other hand, [Y-1] is not the judgment which gives us some information about 'the horse' but is the judgment which specifies some objects called 'this' to 'a horse' in the actual field and 'a horse' is the grammatical predicate of this sentence. In these two judgments, we can regard 'the mane', which is the qualifying definition, as the cause to use the word 'a horse'. Similarly we can show two judgments on 'Devadatta's house' given as the example of the accidental definition.

[X-2] Devadatta's house is small.
[Y-2] This is Devadatta's house.

As for [Y-2], 'a crow' can become the cause to use the word 'Devadatta's house',[29] while as for [X-2], 'a crow' is not regarded as the cause to use the word 'Devadatta's house'. This point is a distinction between the qualifying definition and the accidental definition. Originally [Y-1] is the judgment which differentiates 'this' from other than a horse, and [Y-2] is the judgment which differentiates 'this' from others than Devadatta's house, that is to say, they must be the judgment of differentiating 'this' from the whole non-definiendum. Since 'a crow' differentiates 'Devadatta's house' from other houses, it becomes the cause to use the word. When we make a judgment in the actual field, the 'differentiator' will be the cause to use the word certainly. The cause to use the word, which Sarvajñātman had in his mind, is not the case as such in [Y-1] and [Y-2], but only in the case such as [X-1] and [X-2]. And when we make a judgment of [X-1] or [X-2], we must know what 'a horse' or 'Devadatta's house' is and what they mean. Even if we do not know it precisely, we work on that assumption. If we interpret [C-2] as mentioned earlier, we are able to understand the meaning of the factor [C-2]. [Y-1] and [Y-2] are the judgments that do not concern the knowledge of 'a horse' and 'Devadatta's house'. The qualifying definition is first distinct from the accidental definition from the viewpoint of the way in which the properties occur in the definiendum. In addition to this, Sarvajñātman thought that the distinction between them depends upon whether they are the cause of arising the knowledge of the definiendum or not. [C-2] is one of the ways of determining the qualifying definition among the properties occurring in the definiendum.

ACCIDENTAL DEFINITION

The third kind of definition, the accidental definition, is explained as follows:

> What is not the cause of arising of the knowledge, which is related to itself, of the definiendum is held to the accidental definition, even if it is not the essential property of the definiendum. For example, a crow [is the accidental definition of Devadatta's house].[30]

Although the factors stated here are 'non-being the cause of arising of the knowledge the definiendum' and 'non-being the essential property of the definiendum', the following three will be the factors of the accidental definition:

[A-3] Occurring in the definiendum as the accidental property.[31]
[B-3] Indirectly and entirely differentiating the definiendum from the non-definiendum.
[C-3] Non-being the cause of arising of the knowledge of the definiendum.

Since I have already discussed [B-3] and [C-3], I would like to examine only [A-3]. The accidental definition is sometimes discussed in comparison with the qualifying definition.[32] According to Sarvajñātman, a distinction between them is the distinction between [C-2] and [C-3] stated in the former section. The most fundamental distinction, however, is a distinction in 'the way of being' between them. Some literature of the Advaita school explains the accidental definition as follows:

> The accidental definition is that which does not exist in the definiendum for all the time.[33]
> The accidental definition has no relations in the definiendum. Or, the accidental definition is that which is presumed as having

relations in it.[34]

For example, 'a crow' is said to be the accidental definition of 'Devadatta's house' because 'a crow' occasionally perches on Devadatta's house but does not perch always on it. In the case of 'the mane of a horse', it is not an accidental definition because 'the mane' is always related with 'a horse'. In other words, even if the accidental definition is explained as 'occurring in the definiendum', 'occurring' is temporary, and it is presumed that the accidental definition occurs in the definiendum. It does not really always occur in the definiendum. Therefore, it does not occur in all the definiendums, but it occurs only in a part of the definiendum. Sarvajñātman admitted that even the property that has fallen into the defect of narrow-application constitutes a definition. This is not based on the object on which the definition is given, but it is probably based on the self-will of the person who proposed the definition. A definiendum has many accidental properties. 'Devadatta's house' has not only 'a crow' but also other accidental properties. Then 'a crow' can be the accidental property of 'Yajña-datta's house'. Nevertheless, Sarvajñātman considered 'a crow' to be a definition which entirely differentiates Devadatta's house from all others. From this we cannot but infer that it is based on the self-will of the person who proposes the definition. In another school of Indian philosophy, the accidental property is not admitted as the definition. One of the reasons for this may lie in the point that the accidental definition is based on the self-will.

CONCLUSION

The characteristic of Sarvajñātman's theory of definition is to admit an accidental property as the definition. Therefore, the general definition of 'the definition' suffers from the defect of narrow-application. If some properties occur in the definiendum and they differentiate the definiendum from the non-definiendum, Sarvajñātman recognizes them as the definition. This is confirmed by the fact that he states the purpose of the definition as follows:

> Definition is [1] not to state the essential nature of the definiendum, [2] not to state that 'This word refers it,' either. It is [3] to state only that 'This is differentiated from all other entities'.[35]

Only the essential property will be recognized as the definition if [1] is the purpose of the definition. If [2] is the purpose of the definition, the qualifying property is also recognized as the definition. It is to recognize the accidental definition that [3] is the purpose of the definition. In Indian philosophy, other schools have probably considered [1] or [2] as the purpose of the definition. Sarvajñātman, however, rejects it.

All the topics for discussion of the Advaita school have some relation with the topic of *Brahman*. Although the theory of the definition also has relation with it, this theory has general importance. The topic of *Brahman* is fully explained with the general theory, not with the special theory. From this point, I have no doubt that Sarvajñātman's theory of the definition is important to all the Indian philosophical schools.

NOTES

1 '[*Brahman* is] that from which the origin, etc. (i.e., maintenance and dissolution) of this (=the universe) [proceed]' *janmādy asya yataḥ // Brahma-sūtra*, I,1,2.

2 Śaṅkara, the founder of the Advaita school, laid stress on Existence and Consciousness. It is the successor of Śaṅkara who refers to Existence, Consciousness and Bliss.

3 See *Pañcapādikāvivaraṇa*, p. 515, *ll*.7-8. Ed. by S. Subrahmanyaśāstrī, Varanasi, 1992; *Sarvadarśanasaṃgraha*, XVI, *ll*.903-904. Ed. by V.S. Abhyankar, Poona, 1978; *Vedāntaparibhāṣā*, VIII,4-9. Ed. by S. Sastri, Madras, 1984. Cf. M. Hiriyanna, *Indian Philosophical Studies I*, Mysore, 1957, pp. 98-103; T.R. V.Murti, *Studies in Indian Thought*, Delhi, 1958, pp. 72-87.

4 'Two Types of the Definition; *svarūpalakṣaṇa* and *taṭasthalakṣaṇa*', (in Japanese) *Journal of Indian and Buddhist Studies* (*Indo-gaku Bukkyo-gaku Kenkyū*), vol. 43, no. 2, 1995, pp. (86)-(89).

5 This paper is based on the following text, commentaries and translation: *The Saṃkṣepaśārīraka of Sarvajñātman critically edited with Introduction, English Translation Notes and Indexes* by N. Veezhinathan, Madras, 1972. *Anvayārthaprakāśikā* of Rāmatīrtha and *Subodhinī* of Puruṣottamamiśra (both of them are edited as Ānandāśrama saṃskṛtagranthāvaliḥ 83. 1918). T. Vetter, *Sarvajñātman's Saṃkṣepa-śārīrakam*, 1. Kapitel Einführung, Übersetzung und Anmerkungen, Wien, 1972.

6 Cf. *viśvodbhavasthitilayaprakṛtitvam asya cidvastuno yad asahāya-parigrahasya / tad varṇanīyam upalakṣaṇam eva kasmād brahmeti lakṣyapadaśaktyavirodhahetoḥ // Saṃkṣepaśārīraka*, I,519.

7 Here *svalakṣaṇa* and *upalakṣaṇa* refere to what *svarūpalakṣaṇa* and *taṭashtalakṣaṇa* mean respectively.

8 *lakṣyasya lakṣaṇam iha trividhaṃ prasiddhaṃ loke svalakṣaṇam amuṣya viśeṣaṇaṃ vā / yad vopalakṣaṇam imāni ca lakṣaṇena vyāvarṇayāmi pṛthag eva tu tat pratīhi // Saṃkṣepaśārīraka*, I,514.

9 Cf. Note 3.

10 Although Padmapāda refers to *svarūpalakṣaṇa*, he divides the definition into *upalakṣaṇa* and *viśeṣalakṣaṇa. dvividhaṃ hi lakṣaṇam upalakṣaṇaṃ viśeṣalakṣaṇaṃ ca // Pañcapādikā*, p.525, *ll*.2-3. (Ed. by S. Subrahmanyaśāstrī, Varanasi, 1992). Cf. *tac (=vyāvartakam) ca dvividham viśeṣaṇam upalakṣaṇaṃ ca // Nyāyakośa*, p. 697.

11 Cf. *tad brahmaṇo yadi viśeṣaṇarūpam iṣṭaṃ brahmeti lakṣyaviṣayasya padasya bhaṅgaḥ // Saṃkṣepaśārīraka*, I,520cd.

12 *lakṣyārthaniṣṭham upalabdham ato 'nyato 'rthān niḥśeṣato yad atiricya tad arthavastu / lakṣyaṃ nivedayati lakṣaṇam etad āhuḥ sāmānyalakṣaṇam idaṃ triṣu lakṣaṇeṣu // Saṃkṣepaśārīraka*, I,515.

13 Cf. *lakṣyārthaniṣṭham iti saṃbhavapradarśanārtham // Subodhinī* on *Saṃkṣepaśārīraka*, I,515. p. 406, *l*.20.

14 Cf. *sarvasmād atiricya vyāvartyety arthaḥ // Anvayārthaprakāśikā* on *Saṃkṣepaśārīraka*, I,515. p. 406, *l*.26.

15 *lakṣyasvarūpam api sad yad amuṣya sākṣād arthāntarād bhavati bhedakam etad āhuḥ / asya svalakṣaṇatayaiva tu lakṣaṇaṃ khaṃ chidraṃ dravaṃ jalam itīdṛśam atra loke // Saṃkṣepaśārīraka*, I,516.

16 Cf. *tatra svarūpāntargatatve sati vyāvartakaṃ svarūpalakṣaṇaṃ // Sarvadarśanasaṃgraha*, XVI, *ll*.904-5; *tatra svarūpam eva lakṣaṇaṃ svarūpalakṣaṇam // Vedāntaparibhāṣā*, VIII,5. We can understand nothing about the essential property from such explanations.

17 For example, the object meant by the word 'sky' is distinct from the object meant by the word 'hollow'.

18 Cf. *nanu svarūpasya svavṛttitvābhāvena kathaṃ lakṣaṇatvam ? iti cet, na; svasyaiva svāpekṣayā dharmadharmibhāvakalpanayā lakṣyalakṣaṇatvasaṃbhavāt // Vedāntaparibhāṣā*, VIII,6-7; *kathaṃ svarupasya lakṣaṇatvam, tasya dharmitvena dharmatvābhāvāt // Paribhāṣāsaṃgraha* on *Vedāntaparibhāṣā*, p. 230, *ll*.6-7. Ed. by P.B. Sāstri, Calcutta, 1883 śākābde.

19 'The essential property can distinguish [a possessor of property from others] as the bringing a difference in the same way as the property.' *dharmasyeva savarūpasyāpi vilakṣaṇatvena vyāvartakatvasaṃbhavād // Subodhinī* on *Saṃkṣepaśārīraka*, I,516. p. 407, *ll*.9-10.

20 In the following case, though it is doubtful that *svarūpalakṣaṇa* is translated 'the essential definition' the same translation is used to avoid the confusion. The translation of 'a descriptive definition' which Dr. Wada gave to it is probably right. Cf. T. Wada, *Invariable Concomitance in Navya-Nyāya*, Delhi, 1990, p. 100.

21 *gandhavatī pṛthivī // Tarkasaṃgraha*, X. (Ed. by Y.V. Athalye, Poona, 1974.), etc.

22 *pṛthivyā lakṣaṇam āha gandhavatīti // Tarkadīpikā*, p. 6, *ll*.18-19. (Ed. by Y.V. Athalye, Poona, 1974.), etc.; *gandhavattvaṃ pṛthivyā lakṣaṇam // Nyāyabodhinī*, p.7, *l*.17. (Ed. by Y.V. Athalye, Poona, 1974.), etc. I think that 'smell' can also be the definition of earth so that it may be stated by

the sentence of '*gandhaḥ pṛthivyā lakṣaṇam*'. Hiriyanna gives the example of 'the dew-lap (*sāsnā*)' to the cow as *dharmalakṣaṇa*. Cf. Hiriyanna, op. cit., p. 103.

23 Cf. Wada, op. cit., p. 100.

24 When Hiriyanna discusses on *svarūpalakṣaṇa* in the Advaita school he says that '*svarūpalakṣaṇa* in this sense is not considered in the article'. Cf. Hiriyanna, op. cit., p. 103. In the Advaita school, *svarūpalakṣaṇa* is not necessarily always shown by a sentence such as '*gandhavatī pṛthivī*'. For example, see '*satyādikaṃ brahmasvarūpalakṣaṇam*' (*Vedānta-paribhāṣā*, VIII,5). This expression is the same as the expression of '*gandhavattvaṃ pṛthivīlakṣaṇam*' (*Vedāntaparibhāṣā*, VIII,8) by which *taṭasthalakṣaṇa* is shown.

25 Cf. *na ca chidratvaṃ dharmaṃ ākāśātiriktachidratve mānābhāvād dravatvam pi dharmyabhedābhiprayeṇotkam* // *Subodhinī* on *Saṃkṣepaśārīraka*, I,516. p. 407, *ll*.12-13.

26 *svānuraktamatijanmakāraṇaṃ yat punar bhavati lakṣyavastuni / tad viśeṣaṇatayāsya lakṣaṇaṃ kesarādikam ivāśvavastuni // Saṃkṣepaśārīraka*, I,517.

27 *viśeṣaṇaṃ ca kāryānvayi vyāvartakam // Vedāntaparibhāṣā*, I,68.

28 *samānajātīyebhya eva nivartakāni viśeṣaṇāni viśeṣyasya, lakṣaṇaṃ tu sarvata eva // Śāṅkarabhāṣya* on *Taittirīyopaniṣat*, II,1, p. 283, *ll*.3-4. (*Ten Principal Upaniṣads with Śāṅkarabhāṣya*, Delhi, 1987). Cf. M. Biardeau, 'La définition dans la pansée indienne', *Journal Asiatique*, 245, p. 378.

29 Cf. *taṭasthalakṣaṇaṃ tu kākavat devadattagṛham iti / atrodāsīno 'pi kāka idaṃ devadattagṛham iti bodhayati // Nyāyakośa*, p. 697.

30 *svānuraktamatijanmahetutāṃ lakṣyavastuni nirasya lakṣaṇam / asvarūpam api tasya yad bhavet kākavad tad upalakṣaṇaṃ viduḥ // Saṃkṣepaśārīraka*, I,518.

31 Although '*upalakṣaṇa*' should be always translated 'the accidental definition' since it is considered as a property which originally differentiates something from others, the translation of 'the accidental property' was unavoidable in dealing it in comparison with *svarūpa* and *viśeṣaṇa*.

32 On *viśeṣaṇa* and *upalakṣaṇa*, Cf. Wada, op. cit., pp. 46-47.

33 *taṭasthalakṣaṇaṃ nāma yāvat lakṣyakālam anavasthitatve sati yad vyāvartakaṃ tad eva // Vedāntaparibhāṣā*, VIII,8. Cf. T.M.P. Mahadevan, *The Philosophy of Advaita*, Madras, 1957, p. 110. fn.3.

34 *yat yadasambandhi yatsambandhitayā kalpitam vā yal lakṣayati tat taṭasthalakṣaṇaṃ // Paribhāṣāprakāśikā* on *Vedāntaparibhāṣā*, p.5,*ll*.9-10. Ed. by A. Sastri, New Delhi, 1993.

35 *lakṣyasvarūpakathanāya na lakṣaṇāni nāpy asya vācakam idaṃ padam ity amuṣmai / vyāvṛttam etad akhilād itarārthajātād ity etad eva vadituṃ nanu lakṣaṇāni // Saṃkṣepaśārīraka*, I,523.

15

The Way to Liberation by Rāmānuja

SHOKEI MATSUMOTO

Rāmānuja explained that the means for reaching Liberation (*mokṣa*) is *bhakti*. *Bhakti* is usually explained as an easy practice different from the path of wisdom or the path of training. Nevertheless, *bhakti* as explained by Rāmānuja is not an easy path. According to the *Vedārthasaṃgraha*, *bhakti* refers to people longing for Liberation who worship without interruption the grace of God. Pleased by their practices, God rescues them from their sins. The spiritual devotion is solely to God.

This paper aims to examine the nature of the 'uninterrupted acts of worship' and the religious principles as implemented by later scholars. I will take a look at the religious principles as explained in the *Vedārthasaṃgraha*, examine the religious principles as written in the *Śrībhāṣya*, and then, examine the religious principles as found in the *Yatīndramatadīpikā*.

RELIGIOUS PRINCIPLES IN THE *VEDĀRTHASAṂGRAHA*

In the first work, *Vedārthasaṃgraha*, Rāmānuja says:

> When a person has caused the mass of evil *karman*, amassed during all his previous existences, to melt away by amassing unequalled good *karman*; when he has become wholly dedicated to God as a result of his taking refuge at His lotus-like feet; when he has acquired the moral qualities of *śama*, *dama*, *tapas*, *śauca*, *kṣamā*, *ārjava*, *bhayābhayasthānaviveka*, *dayā*, *ahiṃsā*, etc., and nourishe them by exercising them daily and applying to them his preceding knowledge of the true nature of the ontological orders gathered from the śāstras and corroborated by the teachings of the true *ācāryas*; when he devotes himself to the accomplishment of periodical and occasional acts corresponding to his station and stage of life, as the forms in which he is to worship the Supreme Person and avoids what is forbidden; when he throws himself altogether at the lotus like feet of the Supreme Person; when the

> darkness concealing his innermost self is dispelled by the grace of the Supreme Person who, supremely compassionate as He is, is pleased with the uninterrupted acts of worship that are dictated by the devotee's *bhakti* in glorification, remembrance, homage, salutation, mortification, exaltation, the listening to the description of His perfections and narrating them himself, meditation, adoration and prostration, etc.; then will he be able to attain the Supreme Person by virtue of his *bhakti*, which takes on the form of contemplation in the highest degree of lucid perception, directed to none but Him, uninterrupted, preeminent and held preciously dear.[1]

From this one can abstract the following religious principles:

(1) By accumlating good deeds one can destroy the effects of bad deeds of previous existences
(2) One has to devote oneself solely to God
(3) One has to acquire moral qualities
(4) One has to devote oneself to the accomplishment of periodical and occasional acts and avoid what is forbidden
(5) One has to dedicate oneself completely to God
(6) Make God feel pleased, and the darkness concealing one's innermost self will be dispelled by the grace of God.

With regard to the acquirement of moral qualities, Rāmānuja lists several forms of religious principles. The virtues are Tranquility (*śama*), Self-restraint (*dama*), Religious austerity (*tapas*), Purification (*śauca*), Endurance (*kṣamā*), Honesty (*ārjava*), Distinction between a situation of fear and non-fear (*bhayābhaya-sthānaviveka*), Mercy (*dayā*), and Harmlessness (*ahiṃsā*).

The concrete meaning of these terms is not explained in the *Vedārthasaṃgraha*, but Rāmānuja explains the terms used in the *Bhagavadgītā* in his *Gītābhāṣya*.

> Tranquility(śama): *śama* means control of the manas [by not having objects] (*GBh*. 10, 4).[2]
> Self-restraint(*dama*): *dama* is the suppression of the outer sense-organs by not having objects (*GBh*. 10, 4).[3]

According to this explanation, *śama* is the suppression of the *Manas*, and in *dama* the suppression of the other sense organs. In the *Bhagavadgītā* (18, 42), however, this relation is reversed and *śama* is the suppression of the outer sense-organs and Dama the suppression of the *Manas*.[4] Probably, this must have caused some confusion, in the way the moral qualities are summed up in the *Bhagavadgītā*; in 10, 4 it is in the order of *dama-śama*, and in 18, 42 it is in the order of *śama-dama*.

> Religious austerity (*tapas*): *tapas* occurs when suppressing enjoyment. It is physical pain as proven in the sacred books (*GBh.* 18, 42).[5]

'Suppression of enjoyment' indicates probably fasting. Not just simply causing pain to the body, it has to be in accordance with the sacred books.

> Purification (*śauca*): *śauca* means adapting to the rituals as laid down in the sacred books (*GBh.* 18, 42).[6]

In the *Tātparyadīpikā* it is written that *śauca* is divided into three kinds: mind, language and body. Namely, the purification of the mind, the purification of language, and the purification of the body. According to the explanation, *śukla* is purification of the mind through harmonized breathing (*prāṇāyāma*), etc.; the purification of language is correct language, based on the wisdom of *niyama*, etc.[7]; and purification of the body is cleansing.

> Endurance (*kṣamā*): *kṣamā* is the state in which, even when there are causes which could make the mind fluctuate, one does not let the mind fluctuate (*GBh.* 10, 4).[8]

In the *Bhagavadgītā* the word '*kṣānti*' is used instead of the word '*kṣamā*'. Rāmānuja explains this word as 'not letting the heart fluctuate, even when one is inflicted with pain by other people' (*GBh.* 18, 42).[9]

> Honesty (ārjava): *ārjava* is to adapt in the mind to other people and it is expressed as a bodily activity (*GBh.* 18, 42).[10]

In this moral quality 'thought' and 'action' can been explained as congruent.

> Distinction between a situation of fear or non-fear (*bhayābhaya-sthāna-viveka*): A situation of fear is when one has fear because of a mistake towards Bhagavat, a situation of non-fear is when one does not feel fear because one is full of enthusiasm to protect Him (*TD.* p. 143, l. 6).[11]

Mercy (*dayā*): [*dayā*] means not to inflict pain on other people (*TD.* p. 143, l. 6).[12]
Harmlessness (*ahiṃsā*): [*ahiṃsā*] means not to become the cause of pain for others (*GBh.* 10, 5).[13]

One can categorize and list the moral principles as follows:

Moral principles related to the self—tranquilization [of the Manas], the supppression of the sense organs, religious austerity, purification [of body, language and mind], endurance.

Moral principles related to other people — honesty, mercy, forbidding the destruction of life.

Moral principles related to God — the distinction between a situation of fear and non-fear.

One's own moral qualities should not be only of self-interest but also of altruism. Consider the moral quality of 'throwing oneself altogether for God': What makes me think of the words 'throwing oneself altogether' is the religious term *prapatti* as explained by the Pāñcarātra school. *Prapatti* means to give all of oneself to God. Nevertheless, I do not think we should consider 'throwing oneself altogether' and *prapatti* as meaning the same. If this meant Prapatti then it would be a principle on a higher level than others, which then have to be put on the highest position. Because 'throwing oneself altogether' is on the same level as other religious principles, it does not mean *prapatti*, but it refers to a physical ritual in which one 'throws one's whole body on the ground'.

Let us have a look at the moral quality of 'pleasing God'. There have been ten items listed in this regard: glorification (*stuti*), remembrance (*smṛti*), homage (*vandana*), salutation (*namaskṛti*), mortification (*yatana*), exaltation (*kīrtana*), listening to the description of His perfections and narrating them oneself (*guṇa-stava-vacana*), meditation (*dhyāna*), adoration (*arcana*), prostration (*praṇāma*).

In the *Tātparyadīpikā* some of the terms are explained.

Stuti means that one is talking about the virtues of God or what one glorifies God (*TD.* p. 143, l. 10).[14]
Yatana means what one does things like making a garden (a temple garden suitable for praising God) for Bhagavat (*TD.* p. 143, l. 10).[15]
Kīrtana means that one is reciting Bhagavat's name (*TD.* p. 143, l. 15).[16]
Vacana means what one is explaining to other people the virtues of

Bhagavat (*TD*. p. 143, l. 15).[17]

In order to satisfy God, the believers are asked to deliver uninterrupted acts of worship, such as praise, adoration, revere, worship, build temple gardens, recite, and prostrate oneself. One has to say that the *bhakti* method of Rāmānuja is quite a difficult one.

As we have seen before, self-interest and altruism are included in these principles. However all the religious principles are in general sacrifices to God. The religious principles as explained in the *Vedārtha-saṃgraha* were 'Principles of worship of God'.

RELIGIOUS PRINCIPLES IN THE *ŚRĪBHĀṢYA*

Rāmānuja explains in the *Śrībhāṣya* (I, 1, 1) that the means for *mokṣa* is one's remembrance-knowledge (*smṛti*) with the ability for continuity. This kind of remembrance-knowledge is explained in the word *bhakti*. He emphasizes that religious principles are the prerequisites for realizing *bhakti*.[18] He cites the explanation of the Vākyakāra (i.e. Taṅka) about the contents of the religious principles:

> The Vākyakāra also says in the following manner that firm remembrance-knowledge is the outcome of descrimination and others: —That (viz. firm remembrance-knowledge) results wholly from (1) *viveka* (discrimination), (2) *vimoka* (non-attachment), (3) *abhyāsa* (repetition), (4) *kriyā* (rite), (5) *kalyāṇa* (good conduct), (6) *anavasāda* (non-depression) and (7) *anuddharśa* (non-delight). This is known by reasoning (*sambhava*) and scriptural authority (*nirvacana*). — He also explains the true nature of *viveka* and others: — (1) *viveka* is the purification of the body by food that has not become impure, either on account of species or an abode or advantageous cause.[19] The scriptural authority for this is — 'When nourishment is pure, nature is pure. When nature is pure, memory becomes firm.' (*Ch. Up*. VII, 26, 2), (2) *Vimoka* is the absence of clinging to desires. The scriptural authority for this is — 'Tranquil, one should meditate on it.' (*Ch. Up*. III, 14, 1), (3) *Abhyāsa* means harping upon the thing begun, again and again. The scriptural authority quoted by the Bhāṣyakāra (viz. Dramiḍa) in support of this is here taken from the Smṛti — 'Always with the mind fixed on His form etc.' (*BhG*. VIII, 6), (4) *Kriyā* means the performance of the five great sacrifices etc., according to one's abilities. The scriptural authority is — 'He who performs works is the greatest of the knowers of Brahman.' (*Muṇḍ. Up*. III, 1, 4): also — 'Brāhmaṇas desire to know Him by reciting the Vedas, by sacrifices, by gifts, by penance, by fasting.' (*BĀ. Up*. IV, 4, 22), (5) *Kalyāṇas* consists of truth, honesty, mercy, gifts, harmlessness and

absence of greed. The scripture — 'He is to be reached through truth.' (*Muṇḍ. Up.* III, 1, 5), and 'To them alone comes this stainless Brahmaloka.' (*Praśna Up.* I, 16) etc., (6) *Avasāda* is non-brilliance and poverty of the mind arising from non-suitability of time and place, and from the recollection of objects of grief, etc. *Anavasāda* is the opposite of that. The scriptural authority for this is — 'This Self cannot be attained by one without strength.' (*Muṇḍ. Up.* III, 2, 4), (7) *Uddharśa* is the satisfaction derived from the opposites of that (i.e. depression); and the opposite of that is *anuddharśa*. That is to say, extreme satisfaction also is obstructive [to the production of the remembrance-knowledge]. The scriptural authority for this is — 'Having become calm, self-controlled ...' (*BĀ. Up.* IV, 4, 23).[20]

Here religious principles have been divided into seven categories:

(1) Purifying the body by avoiding impure food;
(2) Non-attachment to desire;
(3) Harping upon the thing begun, again and again;
(4) The performance of five great sacrifices;
(5) Gifts, harmlessness, etc.;
(6) Purifying of the mind;
(7) Establishing a tranquil mind.

When we compare these seven points from the *Śrībhāṣya* with the six points from the *Vedārthasaṃgraha*, we can see that they are very different, except for the part regarding the moral qualities of honesty, mercy and harmlessness. The religious principles of the *Śrībhāṣya* have no direct relation with God, except for the point about sacrifice. Self-cultivation and self-training, like purification of body and mind, are at the heart of it.

I would like to call the religious principles of the *Śrībhāṣya* the 'principles of self-cultivation', putting them against the 'principles of worship of God' of the *Vedārthasaṃgraha*. I will now explore how scholars of later generations responded to this two-sided Rāmānuja.

RELIGIOUS PRINCIPLES IN THE *YATĪNDRAMATADĪPIKĀ*

The *Yatīndramatadīpikā* is a handbook on Rāmānuja's thought, written in the seventeenth century by Śrīnivāsa. It consists of ten chapters, of which the seventh deals with religious principles. The context related to *bhakti* is as follows:

What is called *bhaktiyoga* is a continuous stream of remembrance-

> knowledge [of Brahman], uninterrupted like the flow of oil, and is characterized by the eightfold limb of *yama*, *niyama*, *āsana*, *prāṇāyāma*, *dhāraṇā*, Dhyāna and Samādhi. It is generated by the sevenfold discipline of *viveka*, *vimoka*, *abhyāsa*, *kriyā*, *kalyāṇa*, *anavasāda* and *anuddharśa*. Of these what is called *viveka* is the purification of the body by food that has not become impure either on account of species or abode or adventurous cause. *Vimoka* consists of non-attachment to desires. *Abhyāsa* is the continuous meditation of the perfect object. *Kriyā* means the performance of the five great sacrifices according to one's capacity. *Kalyāṇas* are such principles as truth, honesty, mercy, gifts, harmlessness and absence of greed. *Anavasāda* is freedom from dejection. *Anuddharśa* is the absence of exaltation. The meaning is that extreme satisfaction is obstructive [to the production of remembrance-knowledge]. Then *bhakti*, favoured by the sevenfold discipline, attains the likeness of direct intuition; it has 'final realization' as its limit. This 'final realization' may take place at the end of the present body or at the end of some other body.[21]

In the description above, we can see that there are eight religious principles beginning with *yama*. The terms of these principles correspond completely with the eight fundamental religious principles as explained by the Yoga school. What Śrīnivāsa did was to introduce the religious principles of the Yoga school instead of the religious principles *śama* and *dama* of the *Vedārthasaṃgraha*. He took the religious principles from the *Śrībhāṣya* over in their original form. Thus Śrīnivāsa chose the 'principles of self-cultivation' instead of the 'principles of worship of God'.

CONCLUSION

The following conclusions can be drawn:

(1) The religious principles explained in the *Vedārthasaṃgraha* are 'principles of worship of God'.
(2) The religious principles explained in the *Śrībhāṣya* are 'principles of self-cultivation'.
(3) In the *Yatīndramatadīpikā*, the 'principles of self-cultivation' are adopted.

The reason for the difference in the religious principles of the *Vedārthasaṃgraha* and the *Śrībhāṣya* is the coexistence of Ālvāl's tradition and that of the Ācārya in the thought of Rāmānuja.

In my earlier research on the vision of Rāmānuja on ritual, I indicated that there was a coexistence of different thoughts.[22] Rāmānuja speaks in the *Vedārthasaṃgraha* about rituals of worship as things 'to pleasure God', while in the *Śrībhāṣya* he refers to rituals as 'breeding wisdom'. The first view reflects the opinion from the standpoint of a believer of the Viṣṇu religion, while the second reflects the opinion of a religious leader of the Vedānta school.

That is also true in the case of the religious principles. The opinion of the religious leader of the Śrīvaiṣṇava school reflects the 'principles of worship of God', whereas Rāmānuja takes his standpoint of holding onto the traditional thought of the Vedānta school in 'principles of self-cultivation'. In the Commentary *Śrībhāṣya*, Rāmānuja does not express his own opinion, but records the theories of the old masters. What is the reason that the *Yatīndramatadīpikā* did not choose the 'principles of worship of God', but instead chose the 'principles of self-cultivation'? I think that this can be explained as follows. Once a religious school is established, one can introduce to a certain extent a new perspective on the theoretical level to answer the needs of the times, but even then there is a tendency on the practical level for traditional thought to remain strong. The *Yatīndramatadīpikā* introduced as principles of the first level the eight religious principles from the Yoga school. One can imagine a situation in which it is inevitable to rely on traditional principles as fundamental when introducing elements from other schools. When Śrīnivāsa entitled his work 'Light on Rāmānuja's Thought' (*Yatīndramatadīpikā*), he was actually not following the theories of Rāmānuja but the traditional theories of the old master Taṅka.

ABBREVIATIONS

BĀ. Up.: *Bṛhadāraṇyaka-Upaniṣad.*
BhG.: *Bhagavad-gītā.*
Ch. Up: *Chāndogya-Upaniṣad.*
GBh.: *Gītābhāṣyam*, ed. by P.B. Annagarācārya, Kāncīpuram, 1956.
Muṇḍ.Up.: *Muṇḍaka-Upaniṣad.*
Praśna Up.: *Praśna-Upaniṣad.*
ŚBh.: *Śrībhāṣya of Rāmānuja*, ed. by R.D. Karmarkar, Poona, 1959-1964.
TD.: *Tātparyadīpikā.* (*Vedārthasaṃgraha with the Gloss Called Tātparyadīpikā by Sudarśanasūri*, ed. by S.Ṣam.P.Ṣ. Ramamiśra-śraśāstrī, Benares, 1894.)
Vs.: *Vedārthasaṃgraha.* (*Rāmānuja*'s *Vedārthasaṃgraha*, by J.A.B. van Buitenen, Poona, 1956).

NOTES

1 *Vs.*, p. 126, l. 5f. so'yaṃ parabrahma-bhūtaḥ puruṣottamo niratiśaya-puṇya-saṃcaya-kṣīṇâśeṣa-janmôpacita-pāpa-rāśeḥ parama-puruṣa-cara=ṇâravinda-śaraṇāgati-janita-tad-ābhimukhyasya sad-ācāryôpadeśôpabṛṃhita-śāstrâdhigata-tattva-yāthātmyâvabodha-pūrvakâharahar-upacīyamā=na-śama-dama-tapaḥ-śauca-kṣamârjava-bhayâbhaya-sthāna-viveka-dayâhiṃsâdy-ātmaguṇôpetasya varṇâśramôcita-parama-puruṣârādhana-veṣa-nitya-naimittika-karmôpasaṃhṛti-niṣiddha-parihāra-niṣṭhasya parama-puruṣa-caraṇâravinda-yugala-nyastâtmâtmīyasya tad-bhakti-kāritânava=rata-stuti-smṛti-namaskṛti-vandana-yatana-kīrtana-guṇa-śravaṇa-vacana-dhyānârcana-praṇāmâdi-prīta-parama-kāruṇika-puruṣottama-prasāda-vi=dhvasta-svānta-dhvāntasyânanya-prayojanânavarata-niratiśaya-priya-vi=śadatama-pratyakṣatâpannânudhyāna-rūpa-bhakty-eka-labhyaḥ.

2 *GBh.* 10, 4, p. 88, l. 22, śamaḥ — antaḥkaraṇasya tathā niyamanam.

3 *GBh.* 10, 4, p. 88, l. 22, damaḥ — bāhya-karaṇānām anartha-viṣayebhyo niyamanam.

4 *GBh.* 18, 42, śamaḥ — bahyêndriya-niyamanam, damaḥ — antaḥkaraṇa-niyamanam. Cf. *TD.* p. 143, l. 3, śama-damau antaḥkaraṇa-bāhyêndriya-jayau.

5 *GBh.* 18, 42, p. 163, l. 7. tapaḥ bhoga-niyamana-rūpaś śāstra-siddhaḥ kāya-kleśaḥ.

6 *GBh.* 18, 42, p. 16., l. 8. śaucaṃ śāstrīya-karma-yogyatā.

7 *TD.* p. 143, l. 4. śaucaṃ-mānasa-vācika-kāyika-rūpenêti trividham. Rāmānanda Śukla (ed.), *Vedārtha-saṃgraha of Śrīmad Rāmānujayatīndra with the Commentary Candrikātilaka by R. Śukla*, Varanasi, 1991, p. 93, l. 17 f. śaucaṃ mānasaṃ prāṇāyāmâdiḥ vācikaṃ niyama-jñāna-pūrvaka-śabda-viṣayakatvaṃ, kāyikaṃ snānâdi.

8 *GBh.* 10, 4, p. 88, l. 20. kṣamā mano-vikāra-hetau saty apy avikṛta-manastvam.

9 *GBh.* 18, 42, p. 163, l. 8. paraiḥ pīḍyamānasyâpy avikṛta-cittatā.

10 *GBh.* 18, 42, p. 163, l. 8. ārjavaṃ pareṣu manônurūpaṃ bāhya-ceṣṭā-prakāśanam.

11 *TD.* p. 143, ll. 4-6. bhagavad-apacārâdinā bhīrutvaṃ bhaya-sthāna-vivekaḥ, tad-rakṣakatvâdhyavasāyâdinā nirbhayatvam abhaya-sthāna-vivekaḥ.

12 *TD.* p. 143, l. 6. dayā para-duḥkhâsahiṣṇutvam.

13 *GBh.* 10, 5, p. 88, l. 25. ahiṃsā para-duḥkhâhetutvam.

14 *TD.* p. 143, l. 10. stutir guṇa-kathanaṃ vandikṛtyam vā.

15 *TD.* p. 143, l. 10. yatanaṃ bhagavad-udyānâdi-karaṇam.

16 *TD.* p. 143, l. 15. kīrtanaṃ bhagavad-nāmôccāraṇam.

17 *TD.* p.143, l. 15. vacanaṃ parebhyo bhagavad-guṇānāṃ pratipādanam.

18 *ŚBh.* 1. 1. 1. p. 18, ll. 1-3.

19 Cf. *Śrībhāṣyam with Śrutaprakāśikā*, ed. by Śrī Uttamur T. Vīra-rāghavācārya, Madras, 1989, vol. I, p. 64, ll. 13-14, jāti-duṣṭāḥ kalañjagṛñjanâdayaḥ. āśrayaḥ — dravya-svāmī puruṣaḥ, abhiśasta-

pattita-caṇḍālâdi-dravyam āśraya-duṣṭam. ucchiṣṭakeśâdi-upahataṃ ni=mitta-duṣṭam.

20 *ŚBh.* 1. 1. 1. p. 19, l. 7-p. 21, l. 4. vākyakāraś ca dhruvânusmṛter vivekâdibhya eva niṣpattim āha — tal-labdhir viveka-vimokâbhyāsa-kriyā-kalyāṇânavasādânuddharṣebhyaḥ saṃbhavān nirvacanāc cêti. vivekâdīnāṃ svarūpaṃ câha. jāty-āśraya-nimittâduṣṭād annāt kāya-śuddhir vivekaḥ, iti. atra nirvacanam —'āhāra-śuddhau sattva-śuddhiḥ, sattva-śuddhau dhruvā smṛtiḥ.' (*Ch. Up.* 7, 16, 2) vimokaḥ kāmânabhiṣvaṅgaḥ, iti. 'śānta upāsīta' (*Ch. Up.* 3, 14, 1) iti nirvacanam. ārambhaṇa-saṃśīlanaṃ punaḥ punar abhyāsaḥ, iti. nirvacanaṃ ca smārtam udāhṛtaṃ bhāṣyakāreṇa, 'sadā tad-bhāva-bhāvitaḥ' (*BhG.* 8, 7) iti. pañca-mahāyajñâdy-anuṣṭhānaṃ śaktitaḥ kriyā' iti. nirvacanam — 'kriyāvān eṣa brahmavidāṃ variṣṭhaḥ' (*Muṇḍ. Up.* 3, 1, 4) 'tam etaṃ vedânuvacanena brāhmaṇā vividiṣanti yajñena dānena tapasânāśakena' (*BĀ.* '*Up.* 4, 4, 22) iti ca. satyârjava-dayā-dānâhiṃsânabhidhyāḥ kalyāṇāni, iti. nirvacanam — 'satyena labhyas' (*Muṇḍ. Up.* 3, 1, 5) 'teṣām evâiṣa virajo brahma-lokaḥ' (*Praśna Up.* 1, 16) ityādi. deśa-kāla-vaiṣamyāc chokavastv-ādy-anusmṛteś ca taj-janyaṃ dainyam abhā-svaratvaṃ manaso'vasādaḥ, iti. viparyayo'navasādaḥ. nirvacanam — 'nâyam ātmā bala-hīmena labhyaḥ' (*Muṇḍ.* Up. 3, 2, 4) iti. tad-viparyaya-jā tuṣṭir uddharṣaḥ. tad-viparyayo'nuddharṣaḥ, iti. atisaṃtoṣaś ca virodhîty arthaḥ. nirvacanam api — 'śānto dāntaḥ' (*BĀ. Up.* 4, 4, 23) iti.

21 Svāmī Ādidevānanda, *Yatīndramatadīpikā by Śrīnivāsadāsa*, Madras, 1949, p. 95, l. 6f.

[20] bhakti-yogo nāma yama-niyamâsana-prāṇāyāma-pratyāhāra-dhāraṇā-dhyāna-samādhi-rūpâṣṭāṅgavāṃs taila-dhārāvad-avicchinna-smṛti-santāna-rūpaḥ.

[21] sa ca viveka-vimokâbhyāsa-kriyā-kalyāṇâvasādânuddharṣa-rūpa-sā=dhana-saptaka-janyaḥ.

[22] tatra viveko nāma jāty-āśraya-nimittâduṣṭād annāt kāya-śuddhiḥ. vi=mokaḥ kāmânabhiṣvaṅgaḥ. abhyāsaḥ punaḥ punar ālambana-saṃśīlanam. śaktitaḥ pañca-mahāyajñâdy-anuṣṭhānaṃ kriyā. satyârjava-dayā-dā=nâhiṃsânabhidhyāḥ kalyāṇāni. anavasādo dainyâbhāvaḥ. anuddharṣas tuṣṭy-abhāvaḥ. atisantoṣaś ca virodhîty arthaḥ.

[23] evaṃ sādhana-saptakânugṛhītā bhaktiḥ darśana-samānâkārā antima-pratyayâvadhikā ca bhavati. sa cântima-pratyaya etac charīrâvasāne vā śarīrântarâvasāne vā bhavati.

22 Shokei Matsumoto, *A Study of Rāmānuja*, Tokyo, 1991, pp. 109-17.

16

Madhva's Salvation Theory*

HIROAKI IKEBE

INTRODUCTION

The *Bhagavadgītā* (*Gītā*) being a very important text of Hinduism, many philosophers have written commentaries on it according to their own point of view. Among them, Śaṅkara's *bhāṣya* is the oldest we have. This *Gītā* preaches three ways to liberation, i.e. *karmayoga*, *jñānayoga* and *bhaktiyoga*. However, because it does not strictly define the content and the mutual relationship of these ways, the commentators on the *Gītā* have interpreted it in their own way. Among them, Śaṅkara interpreted the *Gītā* as based on the intellectualism of the *Upaniṣads*, and he maintained that we can get emancipation only through knowledge, and do not need the performance of actions like sacrifice to get emancipation. Moreover, he defined *bhakti* as the means which assists knowledge or the shine of the knowledge, and he did not give an independent position to *bhakti*.[1]

After the commentary of Śaṅkara, Rāmanuja and Madhva wrote commentaries on the *Gītā*.[2] Rāmānuja maintained that by practice of actions, i.e. performing *karmayoga*, those who wish to get emancipation can get the higher *bhakti* to the God which is the direct means of getting the emancipation. He attached greater importance to the role of the *bhakti* in the ladder to emancipation. Moreover, he placed *bhakti* in the orthodox tradition of Brahmanism which attaches importance to the intelligence and meditation, by identifying the *bhakti* with them.[3] Madhva who flourished in the thirteenth century, also commented on the *Gītā*[4] from the position attaching importance to the role of the *bhakti*, like Rāmānuja. In this paper, we examine the position of the commentary of Madhva and elucidate the *karmayoga* and the *jñānayoga* in his system, i.e. their character, mutual relationships and functions in the ladder to emancipation.[5]

THE LADDER TO EMANCIPATION IN THE SYSTEM OF MADHVA

First, we examine the means of getting emancipation held by Madhva. He says in his GB. as follows:

> Emancipation is the highest goal of human beings.[6] And it (emancipation) will be got only through Viṣṇu's grace.[7] And it (Viṣṇu's grace) will be produced only through deep knowledge [of Viṣṇu].[8]

Thus the grace of Viṣṇu, the Supreme God, is the only means of gaining emancipation. We can get the grace of God only through the knowledge of his greatness. And Madhva maintains that *karmayoga*, *jñānayoga* and *bhaktiyoga* are necessary in order to obtain the grace and knowledge of God. We will examine how this can be done.

We can find the emancipation only through the grace of the God. In that case, how can we get the grace of the God? Madhva answers that we can get it through our *bhakti*.

> The supreme [God] who is pleased with *bhakti*, may give [*bhaktas*] an undistorted knowledge and better *bhakti*. [The supreme God] who is pleased with both of them, may give the revelation [Himself]. And also [He] may give a better *bhakti*. [He] may emancipate [*bhaktas* from *saṃsāra*] through both of them.[9]

Here is the figure of the ladder to emancipation according to this description of Madhva.

Step 1

God=pleased

Bhakti 1 ↑ ↓ *parokṣa-jñāna*

Bhakta

Step 2

God=pleased

Bhakti 2 ↑ ↓ *aparokṣa-jñāna*

Bhakta

Step 3

God=pleased

Bhakti 3 ↑ ↓ *mokṣa*

Bhakta

In this way, the supreme God is pleased with *bhakti*, and then He gives *bhaktas* two types of *jñāna*, i.e. knowledge, and *mokṣa*, i.e. emancipation by His grace. Moreover, we can understand that *bhakti* has three levels.[10]

How does Madhva define this *bhakti*? He says:

> *Bhakti* is called *sneha*, i.e. affection. [It is] the uppermost means [of getting the emancipation]. Through this [*bhakti*=*sneha*], we get the emancipation, while the other [means are] not [helpful]. The direct cognition [of God] is the means of getting this [*bhakti*].[11]
> *Bhakti* is called *sneha* which is based on the knowledge of the greatness [of God], and is very firm, and superior to all [other means].[12]

Thus, Madhva defines *bhakti* as *sneha* or affection. Moreover *bhakti* defined by him is not mere emotional affection, but intellectual affection which is based on the knowledge about the greatness of the God. We can clearly find this relationship between *bhakti* and knowledge in the ladder to emancipation.

KARMAYOGA AND JÑĀNAYOGA

What kind of roles do *karmayoga*[13] and *jñānayoga* play in the search for emancipation? First we confirm the meaning of the word '*yoga*'. Madhva defines the meaning of the word '*yoga*' as '*upāya*', i.e. means, or way.

> *Sāṅkhya* [means] rightly (*saṃyak*) to know (*khyāti*), understanding (*jñāna*). *Yoga* is the means (*upāya*), because this [*yoga*] unites [something to another]. The *Śabdanirṇaya* [says] that 'The *sāṅkhya* [means] rightly to see the truth. *Yoga* is the means of acquirement (*sādhana*).[14]

Therefore we can call *karmayoga* and *jñānayoga* 'the means with *karma*' and 'the means with *jñāna*'.

Although Madhva does not directly define *karmayoga* in his works, he classifies *karma* as a means of getting something into three types as BG. 4.17 does.

> The verse 'actions [should be known]' (4.17) does not mean that you will get the emancipation by merely knowing that [action], but means that you will get the emancipation only after fully knowing

> [actions]. And also it is said that 'God does not reveal [Himself] for those who do not know *karma, akarma* and *vikarma*. O sage! How can we get emancipation without it (God's direct cognition)?' The *akarma* [means] non-performing actions. The *vikarma* [means] bad actions, which are not the *karma* and the *akarma*, [it means] actions which are prohibited. Because [the *vikarma*] binds [us].[15]

Madhva classifies *karma* into actions (or *gahanā gatiḥ*, i.e. inexplicable, in the BG. 4.17d), non-performing actions and bad actions. It goes without saying that because of bad actions being prohibited, they are not the appropriate means of emancipation. Accordingly the question is the performance and non-performance of actions. Madhva mentions actions (*karma*), that bring emancipation, in his GB.

> Therefore you should not be a man whose motive is rewards of an action. The man whose motive is rewards of an action is one who performs for the sake of [acquisition of] rewards of an action. You are never such a man.[16]

Madhva maintains that when we perform actions, we should not expect any reward. Moreover he says that we should not be attached to non-performance of actions.

> [Objection] Then I will not perform actions.
> [Reply] 'You should not have [attachment to the non-performance of actions].'(BG.2.47d) [This passage] means that you should not be attached to non-performance of actions.[17]

On the other hand, he states the reason why we should not be attached to non-performance of actions.

> Because [by performing of actions which are not for the sake of any rewards] we will get only the reward called 'my grace', and not any other. And it is appropriate for us to wish for this [reward, i.e. God's grace].[18]

Madhva maintains that we can get God's grace and thereby emancipation, through our being engaged in unselfish actions, therefore we should perform actions. Moreover he maintains that although it is not appropriate to wish for the reward which gives us heaven, it is appropriate for us to wish for one which is the grace of the God. Consequently, the main point about the *karma* held by Madhva is that 1) we should perform actions without wishing for rewards, and 2) we should not be attached to non-performance of actions.[19]

He thinks about the distinctive feature of action in this way. Moreover, he places such an action in the ladder to the emancipation. In his commentary on the *Gītā* 3.4, he says that we cannot get emancipation without performing deeds.

> Knowledge is the only means of [getting the emancipation], but non-performance of actions is not.[20]
> If we could get the emancipation without performing actions, inanimate objects (i.e. stones, trees) also [would get the emancipation].[21]

It goes without saying that actions mentioned here are actions without wishing for rewards. In that case, why should we perform actions without wishing for rewards?

> That actions do not bind [us] will be through performing actions without wishing for [rewards].[22]
> If he does not perform actions, he does not get emancipation, which will be got through giving up actions with wishing for rewards and which is said beyond actions, i.e. *niṣkarmatā*.[23]

In short, why we should act without thought of rewards is that such conduct binds us in the *saṃsāra.* If we give up the *kāmyakarma*, actions do not bind us, consequently we will get emancipation. And Madhva calls giving up the *kāmyakarma* '*sannyāsa*'.

> *Sannyāsa* means giving up *kāmyakarma*.[24]

That is to say, *sannyāsa* means the performance of actions without wishing for rewards. However the BG. 3.4 preaches that we cannot get the accomplishment (*siddhi*) through the mere *sannyasana* (=*sannyāsa*). Therefore we cannot get the emancipation through the mere *sannyāsa*. Then how will we get the emancipation?

> For those who perform actions without wishing for rewards, through the purification of the internal organ, with knowledge, emancipation will be obtained.[25]

The performance of actions is not the direct means of getting the emancipation but it is the means of the knowledge. The relationship between the performance of actions and the knowledge will be dealt with later. On the other, the commentator Jayatīrtha defines the *karmayoga* as follows:

> *Karmayoga* is the performance of prescribed actions according to one's own *varṇa* and *āśrama* through giving up desire for rewards and with mind dedicated to God. . . . This *karmayoga* has two parts, the abandonment of desires and the performance of actions with mind dedicated to God. The former is called *sannyāsa* and the latter is metaphorically called *karmayoga*.[26]

That is to say, the *karmayoga* is the performance of prescribed actions according to one's own *varṇa* and *āśrama* through giving up the desire for rewards and with the mind dedicated to God, and has two parts, giving up desires (*sannyāsa*), and the performance of actions with the mind dedicated to God, which is metaphorically called the *karmayoga*.

We can say that this definition of the *karmayoga* by Jayatīrtha summarizes well the description by Madhva. In any case, 'the means with *karma*' can be summarized by saying that it is the performance of prescribed actions through giving up the desire for worldly rewards. Then where will the mind of those who have given up the desire for worldly rewards go? Madhva holds that the mind of those who have given up the desire for worldly rewards will go towards God. From the mind going towards God, *bhakti* will arise, and the desire to know God will arise too.

Next, we examine *jñānayoga*, which we can regard as 'the means with *jñāna*' in the same way as *karmayoga*. Although we cannot find the description of the definition of the *jñānayoga* in Madhva's commentaries on the BG, he says in his commentary to the *Brahmasūtra*

> The *Nāradīya*[*-purāṇa* says] that 'it is said that [we can get] the lower [grace] through [performing] actions [and] the middle grace through the *śravaṇa* etc., while it is supposed that [we can get] the uppermost [grace] through acquisition of knowledge. On the other hand, it is said that [we can get] heaven through the lower grace of *Viṣṇu* [and] the *janaloka* etc. through the middle [grace], while the uppermost [grace] gives [us] emancipation. The main means of getting knowledge is *śravaṇa*, *manana*, *dhyāna* and *bhakti*. Any other [means i.e. performing actions etc.] is not regarded as [the main means]. And no one has knowledge without them.'[27]

Here, 'getting knowledge' corresponds to getting *aparokṣajñāna* in the ladder to the emancipation. And we can regard '*śravaṇa, manana* and *dhyāna*' through which we can get the middle grace[28] as *jñānayoga*. This set of *śravaṇa*, *manana* and *dhyāna* corresponds to the three steps of training mentioned in the *Upaniṣads*, that is to say, the *śravaṇa* is the learning of scriptures, the *manana* is the consideration of the learned thing, and the *dhyāna*, *nididhyāsana*, is continuous meditation on *Brahman*. In the system of Madhva we can indirectly get the Supreme God through *śravaṇa* and *manana*.[29]

Next, in order to confirm the role of *dhyāna* in the path to emancipation, we examine the relationship between *jñāna* and *dhyāna*.[30]

> Mere knowledge is superior to the *abhyāsa*, i.e. repeated practice, which is not based on knowledge. *Dhyāna* accompanied by knowledge is superior to mere knowledge.
> And also in the *Ānabhimlātaśākhā* of *Sāmaveda* [it is said] that 'the knowledge is superior to mere *abhyāsa*, *dhyāna* [is superior to] this [knowledge]. And from this [*dhyāna*] the direct cognition of the God [arises], from this [*āparokṣya*] calmness arises.'[31]

From this description we can abstract the order as following:
Knowledge → *dhyāna* accompanied by knowledge → the direct cognition of God (*jñāna* → *sa-jñāna-dhyāna* → *āparokṣya*)

Moreover, Madhva mentions knowledge which we should get before *dhyāna*:

> '*Sāṅkhyena*' (BG.13.25) [means] through the knowledge about the nature of the God which is described in the *Vedas*. The performer of actions gets the direct cognition of the God after hearing, knowing, meditating. And one who has heard [gets the direct cognition of the God] after knowing, meditating. And the *sāṅkhya*, *parokṣajñānin*, [gets the direct cognition of the God] after meditating.
> And also the *Gaupavanaśruti* [says] that 'the performer of actions can see [the God] after hearing, knowing, meditating. And also one who has heard can see [the God] after knowing, meditating, and the who has the [indirect] knowledge [can see the God after meditating]. Because no one can see [the God] through any other method.'[32]

In short, before meditating we should have knowledge of the nature of God, i.e. *parokṣajñāna*, which is described in the Vedas, while we will find direct cognition of God (*aparokṣajñāna*) after meditation. Moreover, Madhva mentions the knowledge which a man who does meditation should have:

> In the *Nāradīya*, [it is said] that 'the mere knowledge [about the *yoga*][33] is superior to meditation done by those who do not know [*yoga*], while if man who does the meditation knows [it], his meditation is superior to the mere knowledge about [the *yoga*]. Direct cognition is superior to [this] meditation. And *bhakti* arises only through direct cognition, no other means [of getting the emancipation] is superior to [it].'[34]

That is to say, the knowledge which one who does meditation should have in addition to the *parokṣajñāna*, is knowledge of *yoga*. And this *yoga* is the *samādhiyoga*, *dhyānayoga*.

On *samādhiyoga,* Madhva says:

> The *samādhiyoga* which is the internal (mental) means of getting knowledge is argued in this chapter.[35]
> The meditation is said in this [chapter].[36]

Madhva maintains that in the sixth chapter of the BG, although *yoga* is the means of getting emancipation, the word *yoga* is specially used in the sense of the *samādhiyoga*, the *dhyānayoga*. Moreover he uses these two word, *samādhiyoga* and *dhyānayoga*, in the same meaning.[37] And this *samādhiyoga=dhyānayoga* is the internal (mental) means of getting knowledge, i.e. direct cognition of God. Therefore those who master this *samādhiyoga= dhyānayoga*, are called the *aparokṣajñānin*.

> 'One who wishes to mount the *yoga*' (BG.6.3a) is one who wishes to complete the means. 'One who has mounted' (6.3c) is one who has completed the means, it means one who knows directly.[38]

From above descriptions we can understand the order:
'*parokṣajñāna* → meditation(*samādhi*, *dhyāna*) → direct cognition of the God'.

This meditation in this order corresponds to *bhakti* 2 in the ladder to emancipation, and this meditation is the *dhyāna* in the three steps of the *jñānayoga*, *śravaṇa-manana-dhyāna*. And, although we can find knowledge of God through *śravaṇa* and *manana*, this knowledge is indirectly got through the scriptures, and is called *parokṣajñāna*, or the indirect knowledge of God. Accordingly *śravaṇa* and *manana* correspond to *bhakti* 1 in the ladder to emancipation, while through *dhyāna* corresponded to *bhakti* 2 we can get the direct knowledge about God, i.e. *aparokṣajñāna*.

However, we should pay attention to the fact that we can only gain knowledge through *śravana* etc. accompanied with the *bhakti*. Because, according to Madhva, ignorance is created by God,[39] therefore it is impossible for anyone except God to get rid of ignorance.

> And [the verse] 'I am not' (BG.7.25) means that the ignorance [depends] upon my wish.[40]

God is pleased with devotion of people, and in the form of giving grace, He will get rid of ignorance. Therefore we find emancipation only through the grace of the God.

The Relationship between Karmayoga and Jñānayoga

In the previous part we elucidated the content of *karmayoga* and *jñānayoga* according to the description in Madhva's commentaries on the BG. Finally, in order to place them in the ladder to emancipation, we examine the relationship between *karmayoga* and *jñānayoga*.[41]

In his commentary on the BG. 3.3 which preaches the two positions in this world i.e. the position of *sāṅkhya* with *jñānayoga* and the position of *yogin* with *karmayoga*, Madhva says:

> There are two types of human being. [One stands on] the position of knowledge with giving up the performance of actions in the stage of the householder etc., like [the position of] *Sanaka* etc., while [the other also stands on] the position of the knowledge, however at the same time he remains being the situations [of the householder, etc.], like [the position of] *Janaka* etc. [This verse] means that [both of them] stand on the position of my *dharma*.[42]

On this description, Jayatīrtha comments that the position of *Sanaka* etc. mentioned here corresponds to the position of those who perform the prescribed duties in the fourth stage of the life, while the position of *Janaka* etc. corresponds to the position of those who perform their *dharmas* prescribed in the first three stages, i.e. the stage of householder etc. Here, Madhva maintains that not only 'the position of the *sāṅkhya* with the *jñānayoga*', but also 'the position of the *yogin* with the *karmayoga*' is the position of the knowledge. He maintains that because we can only divide human being into two positions of knowledge, we cannot admit that there is a position of the only action. This Madhva's statement corresponds with his assertion that 'we cannot get emancipation through mere *sannyāsa* (he defined as the performance of actions without wishing for rewards)'. Moreover, he says that those who stand on the position of *sāṅkhya*, i.e. *Sanaka* etc., are also the *yogin*.

> Those who stand on the position of the knowledge are also those fit for performing actions [of the householder, etc.]. Therefore they (*Sanaka,* etc.) are *yogin*, too.[43]

That is to say, not only *Janaka* etc. are the *yogin*, but also *Sanaka* etc. After all, according to Madhva, we cannot distinguish between *karmayoga* and *jñānayoga*, because they are support each other, though they are not equal.[44]

Jñānakarmasamuccayavāda

However in the system of Madhva, the means of attaining emancipation is not the performance of actions but the *aparokṣajñāna*, and the performance of actions is the only means of getting knowledge.

> However those who perform actions without wishing for rewards also get emancipation through knowledge, much more those who get *aparokṣajñāna,* or direct cognition of the God, while the other means [except the knowledge] are not mentioned. Because in the *Nārāyaṇāṣṭākṣarakalpa*, it is said that '[the performance of] actions without wishing for rewards is for the sake of direct cognition of the God. However [if we get] direct cognition of the God, it is not necessary [for us to get] the other [means of getting] emancipation. All of this [performance of actions without wishing for rewards] will become the means of getting emancipation, if [the knowledge] will be put in [these performance of actions, while] the direct cognition [of the God] does not put anything in it for the *nirvāṇa*.' By the very reason, the necessity for the combination [of knowledge and action] is refuted.[45]

Therefore, Madhva rejects the *jñānakarmasamuccayavāda* which maintains that emancipation demands both *jñāna* and *karma.*[46] Moreover, it goes without saying that his claim is different from Śaṅkara's assertion — although he also rejects the *jñānakarma-samuccayavāda* — in his *Upadeśasāhasrī* 1.15, that 'because *jñāna* is incompatible with *karma*, therefore those who wish for emancipation should give up *karma*.'

Next, we examine the importance of *karma* for emancipation. First, *karma* is the means of getting the *jñāna*.

> *Karma* accompanied by *yoga* is the means of getting the *jñāna*. This [*jñāna*] is the means of getting emancipation.[47]
> Here (BG.) also, by the verse 'those who have the *buddhi*' (2.50) etc., it is said that *karmas* are the means of gaining *jñāna*.[48]

Because *karma* is the means of getting *jñāna*, it must be performed not only for *śravaṇa* and *manana* as the first and second steps, but also for *dhyāna* as the third step. Moreover, he says that we should perform actions after getting the *jñāna*.[49]

> And [although] the [mere] knowledge without performing actions is [the means for the cessation of the transmigration], it is not the means of getting the complete human goal.[50]
> Although those who have knowledge will gain emancipation for sure, the performance of purified actions increases bliss. However, the performance of the other actions decreases [their] knowledge.[51]

That is to say, even though we have got the emancipation through *Bhakti* 3 after the *aparokṣajñāna*, the bliss will increase through performing actions.[52] Madhva admits a gradation (*tāratamya*) of bliss in *jīvas* as well as in *muktas* who have attained emancipation.[53]

SUMMARY

We can sum up the points of Madhva's theory to emancipation as:

1) *karmayoga* and *jñānayoga* mean respectively 'the means with *karma*' and 'the means with *jñāna*'.
2) *karmayoga* is the performance of actions with the mind dedicated to God, without wishing for rewards, and is called *sannyāsa*.
3) *jñānayoga* is the three steps of learning, *śravaṇa*, *manana* and *dhyāna*.
4) We can get *parokṣajñāna* through *śravaṇa* and *manana*, and *aparokṣajñāna* through *dhyāna*.
5) Only God can get rid of ignorance, because ignorance is made by God. Therefore if we did *śravaṇa* etc. without *bhakti*, we would not get the knowledge.
6) We should do *śravaṇa* and *manana* with *Bhakti* 1 in the ladder to emancipation, while *dhyāna* with *Bhakti* 2.
7) Actions are a means of getting knowledge, while knowledge is a

means of getting emancipation. Therefore Madhva dose not admit the *jñānakarmasamuccayavāda*, because performing actions are indirect means of getting emancipation.

8) However we should perform actions after having gained knowledge, and the fruit of performing actions then (*jñānottamakarma*) is greater bliss.

TEXTS AND ABBREVIATIONS

GB. *Bhagavadgītābhāsya*, SMGa. vol. 1, Bhagavadgītāprasthāna, pp.1-164

GT. *Bhagavadgītātātparya*, SMGa. vol. 1, Bhagavadgītāprasthāna, pp.1-164

JT. Jayatīrtha.

JT. Ad GB. *Gītābhāshya of Sri Madhwacharya with Prameyadeepika of Sri Jayatirtha,* Bangalore: Poornaprajna Vidyapeetha, 1981.

JT. Ad GT. *Gitatatparyanirnaya of Sri Anandatirtha with the Commentary Nyayadipika of Sri Jayatirtha and the subcommentary Bhavadipa of Sri Raghavendratirtha,* Bangalore: Poornaprajna Vidyapeetha, 1987.

SMGa. *Sarvamūlagranthāḥ*, vol. 1, ed. by Bannaje Govindacharya, Uḍupi: Akhila Bhārata Mādhva Mahā Maṇḍala Publication, 1969.

SMGb. *Sarvamūlagranthāḥ*, vol. 1, ed. by K.T. Pandurangi, Bangalore: Dvaita Vedānta Studies and Research Foundation, 1993.

BIBLIOGRAPHY EXCEPT JAPANESE WORKS

Bhavani, S.K. 1995, *The Bhagavadgītā and its Classical Commentaries, A critical and Comparative Exposition,* Bangalore.

Mesquita, R. 1996, *Madhva und Seine Unbekannten Literarischen Quellen. Einige Beobachtungen,* Wien.

Narain, K. 1986, *An Outline of Mādhva Philosophy,* 2nd ed., Delhi.

Narain, K. 1986, *A Critique of Mādhva Refutation of the Śāṅkara School of Vedānta,* 2nd ed., Delhi.

Pandurangi, K.T. 1970, 'Central Teaching of the Bhagavadgītā According to Śrī Madhvācārya', in *GĪTĀ SAMĪKṢĀ*, Tirupati, pp. 41-50.

Pandurangi, K.T. 1993, 'Essentials of Bhagavadgītā', SMGb, pp. XIII-LII

Pandurangi, K.T. 1995, *Dvaita Vedānta Darśana of Śrī Madhvāchārya,* New Delhi.

Ramachandran, T.P. 1976, *Dvaita Vedānta,* New Delhi.

Sawai, Y. 1985, 'Śaṅkara's Theory of Saṃnyāsa', *Journal of Indian Philosophy* 14, pp. 371-7.

Shanbhag, D.N. 1990, *Śrī Madhvācārya and its Cardinal Doctrines,* Dharwad.

Sharma, B.N.K. 1981, *History of the Dvaita School of Vedānta & its Literature,*

2nd revised ed., Delhi.
Sharma, B.N.K. (tr.) 1989, *The Bhagavadgītā Bhāṣya of Śrī Madhvācārya*, Bangolore.
Sharma, B.N.K. 1991, *Philosophy of Śrī Madhvācārya*, revised ed., Delhi.
Shima, I. 1992, 'Historical Development of Salvation Theories Found in Commentaries on the Bhagavadgītā: From Śaṅkara to Rāmānuja', *Minami-asia Kenyū* (*Journal of the Japanese Association for South Asian Studies*) 4, pp. 1-14.
Sonde, N.D. (tr.) 1995, *The Bhagavad Gita Bhashya and Tatparyanirnaya of Sri Madhva*, Bombay.

NOTES

* I would like to express my thanks to Professor K.T. Pandurangi, Vice-Chairman of the Dvaita Vedānta Studies and Research Foundation, who kindly read this paper and gave me valuable suggestions.

1 I. Shima, 'Śaṅkara no Gītā Kaisyaku' ('Śaṅkara's Interpretation on the Bhagavadgītā: Jñāna, Karma and Bhakti'), *Naritasan Bukkyoo-kennkyūjo Kiyoo* (*Journal of Naritasan Institute for Buddhist Studies*) vol. 15, pt. 2, 1992, p. 200.

2 With regard to the commentary of Bhāskara which is older than that of Rāmanuja and Madhva, cf. K. Shyoshin, 'Bhāskara-saku Bhagavadgītābhāṣya niokeru Bhagavadgītā Inyooku ni tsuite' ('Citations from the Bhagavadgītā in Bhāskara's Bhagavadgītā-bhāṣya'), *Indo-Shisoshi-Kenkyu* (*Studies in the History of Indian Thought*), vol. 1, 1981, pp. 7-17. ; ditto, 'Dare no Tame no Gītā nanoka — Gītā-cyūkaishi niokeru Seitooha no Ichi-shiten — ' ('For whom is the Gītā intended? — A view point of the orthodox school inside the history of Gītā-interpretation — '), *Indo-Shisoshi-Kenkyu* (*Studies in the History of Indian Thought*) 6 (1989), pp. 53-66.

3 B. Kimura, 'Rāmānuja niokeru Jñāna-yoga 1' ('Jñāna-yoga of Ramānuja'), *Tokai-Bukkyo* (*Journal of Tokai Association of Indian and Buddhist Studies*), vol. 38, 1993, p.58.

4 Madhva wrote two commentaries on the *Gītā*, the *Bhagavadgītābhāṣya* and the *Bhagavadgītātātparya*. However, because his description is very brief it is often difficult to understand its meanings. Therefore we refer to the commentaries of Jayatīrtha, the *Prameyadīpikā* and the *Nyāyadīpikā*.

5 The main point of his salvation theory is briefly summed up in Pandurangi, 1970, pp. 41-50; 1993: pp. XIII-LII; 1995: pp. 68 71; Ramachandran, 1976: pp. 106-19. However they are not the treatise but the primer of the philosophy of Madhva. And salvation theory of Madhva is discussed in Sharma 1991: pp. 376-430, too. However, because this work 'aims at a fairly complete and comprehensive critical exposition of Madhva's philosophy, as presented in his own works__'(p. 11), he quotes phrases from all the works of Madhva, and does not intend to separately study GB. and GT. Therefore the aim of Sharma is different from ours. For that reason, we will not examine these works of earlier scholars in

detail, but only show the part concerned in following notes.
6 GB. ad BG. 2.24, p. 18, *ll.* 17-18.
7 GB. ad BG. 2.24, p. 18, *l.* 20.
8 GB. ad BG. 2.24, p. 18, *l.* 28.
9 GT. Introduction, p. 4, *ll.* 1-2.
10 These three levels of *bhakti* are designated by Jayatīrtha as *Pakvabhakti*, *Paripakvabhakti* and *Atiparipakvabhakti*. Cf. Pandurangi, 1970: pp. 46-47; 1995: p. 71; Sharma, 1991: pp. 398-9.
11 GT. Introduction, p. 4, *ll.* 5-6. Cf. Pandurangi, 1995: p. 71.
12 *Mahābhāratatātparyanirṇaya*, 1.85abc, SMGa, Itihāsaprasthāna, p. 8, *l.*3. Cf. Pandurangi, 1995: p. 70.
13 With regard to *karmayoga*, cf. Bhavani, 1995: pp. 95-139; Pandurangi, 1995: pp. 51-58; Ramachandran, 1976: pp. 109-10.
14 GT. ad BG. 2.39, p. 23, *ll.* 1-2.
15 GB. ad BG. 4.17, p. 53, *ll.* 12-14.
16 GB. ad BG. 2.47, p. 27, *ll.* 13-14. And cf. Pandurangi, 1970: p. 44.
17 GB. ad BG. 2.47, p. 27, *ll.* 14-15.
18 GB. ad BG. 2.47, p. 27, *l.* 15.
19 This kind of *karma* is called *niṣkāmakarma* in the Dvaita tradition. Cf. Pandurangi 1993: pp. XXV-XXXV; Ramachandran 1976: pp. 119-10; Sharma 1986: pp. 383-8. And Bhavani discusses the *niṣkāmakarma* of Madhva comparing with that of the Pañcarātra tradition and the Bhāgavata tradition (pp. 18-21).
20 GB. ad BG. 3.4, p. 39, *l.* 4.
21 GB. ad BG. 3.4, p. 39, *ll.* 5-6.
22 GB. ad BG. 3.4, p. 39, *l.* 13. And cf. Bhavani. 1995: p. 96.
23 GB. ad BG. 3.4, p. 39, *ll.* 3-4.
24 GB. ad BG. 3.4, p. 39, *l.* 17.
25 GB. ad BG. 3.4, p. 39, *l.* 18.
26 JT. ad GB. 5.1, p. 217, *ll.* 19-23.
27 *Brahmasūtrabhāṣya* ad *Brahmasūtra* 1.1.1, SMGa. vol. 1, Sūtraprasthāna, p. 6, *ll.* 2-5.
28 These lower and middle grace are different from the grace mentioned in the ladder to the emancipation.
29 With regard to *jñānayoga*, cf. Ramachandran 1976: pp. 110-12; Sharma 1986: pp. 407-9.
30 With regard to methods of meditation, i.e. *pratīka-upāsanā* and *bimba-upāsanā*, cf. Ramachandran 1976: pp. 111-12; Sharma 1996: pp. 410-16.
31 GB. ad BG. 12.12, p. 121, *ll.* 7-10.
32 GB. ad BG. 13.25-26, p. 130, *ll.* 1-4.
33 yogam iti śeṣaḥ / (JT. ad GB. 6.46-47, p. 271, *l.* 15).
34 GB. ad BG. 6.46-47, p. 72, *ll.* 14-16.
35 GB. 6, Introduction. p. 64, *l.* 15.
36 GT. 6, Introduction. p. 65, *l.* 1.
37 Cf. Sharma 1986: p. 408.
38 GB. ad BG. 6.3, p. 65, *ll.* 7-8.
39 With regard to God and ignorance, the *Viṣṇutattvanirṇaya*, one of Madhva's work, said that 'utpatti-sthiti-saṃhārā niyatir jñānam āvṛtiḥ /

bandha-mokṣau ca puruṣād yasmāt sa harir ekarāṭ' iti ca *skānde* (K.T. Pandurangi, ed. and tr. *Viṣṇutattvavinirṇaya*, Bangalore, 1991, §29). And cf. Pandurangi 1995: pp. 68-69; Ramachandran 1976: p. 106; Sharma 1986: pp. 416-24.

40 GB. ad BG. 7.25, p. 79, *l.* 1.

41 With regard to the relationship between *karmayoga* and *jñānayoga*, cf. Sharma 1986: pp. 383-8.

42 GB. ad BG. 3.3, p. 38, *ll.* 15-16.

43 GB. ad BG. 3.3, p. 38, *ll.* 17-18.

44 Cf. Bhavani 1995: pp. 104-8.

45 GB. ad BG. 3.31-32, p. 46, *ll.* 10-15.

46 Cf. Ramachandran 1976: p. 110; Sharma 1986: p. 384.

47 GB. ad BG. 2.51, p. 29, *l.* 32.

48 GB. ad BG. 3.20, p. 43, *l.* 22.

49 With regard to the performance of actions after getting the *jñāna* (*jñā-nottarakarma*), cf. Bhavani 1995: pp. 111-12; Sharma 1986: pp. 387-88.

50 GT. ad BG. 3.3-4, p. 38, *l.* 8. Cf. jñānamātraṃ karma vinā saṃsāra-nivṛttisādhanam api na sampūrṇapuruṣārthakaram iti bhāvaḥ / (JT. ad GT. 3.3-4, p. 101, *ll.* 1-2).

51 GT. ad BG. 3.3-4, p. 38, *ll.* 9-10.

52 With regard to *tāratamya*, cf. Ramachandran 1976: pp. 118-19; Sharma, 1986: pp. 397-406.

53 According to Madhva, the *mokṣa* has two aspects. One is disappearance of *duḥkha* and *ajñāna*, the other is acquirement of bliss. Cf. his commentary on the *Īśāvāsya-Upaniṣad* 11.

Abhyudaya and *Niḥśreyasa* in Bhartṛhari*

AKIHIKO AKAMATSU

INTRODUCTION

For a long time now while discussing the final goal of life, Indian authors have put forward the twofold distinction between *abhyudaya* and *niḥśreyasa*. In the *Manusmṛti*, *abhyudaya* is defined as the condition brought about by the activity of engagement (*pravṛtti*), while on the other hand, *niḥśreyasa* is explained as the state gained by the activity of disengagement (*nivṛtti*).[1] Broadly speaking, while the former means prosperity in this world and rebirth in heaven (*svarga*) within transmigration (*saṃsāra*), the latter means the supreme good that is complete and permanent freedom from transmigration (*mokṣa*).

This paper attempts to examine these two concepts which are met with in the *Vākyapadīya* of Bhartṛhari (*c.* fifth century). Bhartṛhari uses the word *abhyudaya* a total of eight times in the first Kāṇḍa of his *Vākyapadīya* and the *Vṛtti*.[2] Another word *niḥśreyasa* is never used;[3] nevertheless, special attention must be paid to the word *niḥśreyasa*. It is because K.A. Subramania Iyer asserted that Bhartṛhari mentioned *abhyudaya* and *niḥśreyasa* as two distinct aims of the study of grammar.[4] To begin with, I will summarize the discussion of Iyer.

As is well known, Patañjali (*c.* second century BC) enumerates the aims of the study of grammar in the *Paspaśāhnika* of his *Mahābhāṣya*. After having given a list of five practical aims according to the *Vārttika*,[5] Patañjali quotes 15 verses from the *Ṛgveda*, etc., and explains again the 13 new aims of the study of grammar, using these verses as a basis.[6] Iyer perceives two different concepts of *abhyudaya* and *niḥśreyasa* in the two verses quoted and explained therein. One verse goes as follows:

> But he who being knowledgeable as regards the difference (between correct and incorrect words) uses words correctly when

> he communicates (with others), he, knowing the propriety of words, obtains unending victory in the other world, but by (using) wrong words he incurs blemish.[7]
>
> One of the verses from the *Ṛgveda* (IV.58.3) runs as follows:
>
> Four horns, three feet he has, two heads, seven hands he has. Bound in three ways the bull loudly bellows. A mighty god has entered mortals.[8]

As regards the first verse, Patañjali explains: 'For just as *dharma* "merit (as shown in future existence)" lies in the knowledge of correct words, in the same way *adharma* "demerit (as shown in future existence)" lies in the knowledge of incorrect words also.'[9] This explanation agrees with the *Vārttika* 9 of the *Paspaśāhnika* which says: 'If one uses [the correct words] preceded by the study of grammar (*śāstrapūrvake prayoge*), *abhyudaya* results and that is equal to the Vedic statement [,i.e. just as *abhyudaya* results from the Vidhi of the Veda]. '[10] So one can easily concur with what Iyer says:

> The verse and the *Vārttika* tell us that the aim of the study of *vyākaraṇa* is the attainment of happiness here and beyond by acquiring merit (*dharma*) through the knowledge and the use of correct words.[11]

On the other hand, explaining the second verse, Patañjali says in conclusion that grammar must be studied so that we could be similar to the mighty god (*mahatā devena sāmyam*).[12] Iyer regarded this 'similarity with the great God' as referring to another aim of the study of grammar which is different from *abhyudaya*.

As is well known, Bhartṛhari built the grammatical and philosophical theory of language on Patañjali's tradition. Concerning his view on the aim of the study of grammar, he states that the Supreme Brahman is attained after having understood the science of grammar.[13] Iyer, after Vṛṣabhadeva's interpretation, considers this attainment of the Supreme Brahman as repeating the attainment of 'similarity with the great God' that Patañjali had already stated. And he concludes that Bhartṛhari keeps the two aims of the study of grammar, i.e. *abhyudaya* (happiness here and beyond) and *niḥśreyasa* (attainment of the supreme Good, i.e. *mokṣa*) quite distinct.[14]

As has been previously mentioned, Bhartṛhari never uses the word *niḥśreyasa* in his *Vākyapadīya*. Iyer insists nevertheless on the twofold distinction of *abhyudaya* and *niḥśreyasa* in Bhartṛhari's philosophy, for the following two reasons:

(1) In his *Mahābhāṣya-Dīpikā*, Bhartṛhari says: *dṛṣṭādṛṣṭa-phalābhyām abhyudayaniḥśreyasābhyām* (with the visible result and the invisible result, i.e. with *abhyudaya* and *niḥśreyasa*).[15] Iyer considered the visible result (*dṛṣṭaphala*) as being *abhyudaya*, i.e. happiness here and beyond, and the invisible result (*adṛṣṭaphala*) as being *niḥśreyasa*, i.e. liberation.[16]

(2) In his *Vākyapadīya*, Bhartṛhari distinguishes *śāstrapūrvaka-prayoga* and *śabdapūrvayoga*. As we have seen before in the *Vārttika* 9 of the *Paspaśāhnika*, the former leads to *abhyudaya*. According to Iyer, however, the latter is used in the context of 'the attainment of union with the ultimate Reality'. He says: 'The expression [*śabdapūrvayoga*] occurs in Vāk. I. 20 and four times in the *Vṛtti* on *Kāṇḍa* I. In all the occurrences, there is a reference to the attainment of union with the inner, eternal, undifferentiated, sequenceless Word.'[17] And only this *śabdapūrvayoga* ultimately leads to *niḥśreyasa*, i.e. liberation.

Hereafter, I shall examine these two points at some length in the following part.

DṚṢṬA / ADṚṢṬA

As mentioned above, Iyer, when making reference to a passage of the *MBhD* II as one of the bases for his affirmation, states that the visible result (*dṛṣṭa*) is *abhyudaya* and the invisible result (*adṛṣṭa*) *niḥśreyasa*. He interprets, on the other hand, *abhyudaya* as 'happiness here and beyond'. Are not these two statements contradictory? It is certain that *abhyudaya* as 'happiness here', e.g. one's prosperity in this world, is the visible result of a worldly activity. But *abhyudaya* as 'happiness beyond', e.g. one's rebirth in the world beyond, is not the visible but the invisible result of activities prescribed in the Vedas. It is impossible that this rebirth should be experienced in this world. If Iyer presupposed that *abhyudaya* should mean only the prosperity in this world, it would be possible to say that *abhyudaya* is visible. He emphasizes, on the contrary, the aspect of rebirth in heaven meant by *abhyudaya*. The rebirth in heaven is attained by virtue of *dharma* produced by the performance of Vedic activity. This *dharma* and, the *adharma* produced by the performance of bad deeds as well, are generally referred to as *adṛṣṭa* in Classical Sanskrit texts. Now we can investigate the examples of the usage of *dṛṣṭa/adṛṣṭa* in Bhartṛhari's works.

Passage 1: *yady apy eṣa pakṣaḥ syāt sādhuvad apaśabdā api vācakāḥ ity evam api dṛṣṭaṃ phalaṃ tulyam arthāvabodhaḥ / iha tu adṛṣṭaṃ phalam asty abhyudaya iti / ata āha -- evam ihāpi samānāyām arthāvagatau śabdena ca* (*MBh* I 8.20-21) *iti / abhyudayakāri ca bhavati* (*MBh* I 8.22) *iti ca bruvatā idam abhyupagataṃ bhavati avihitaparityāgād adharmo naśyata iti / anye manyante / tatparityāgāt adharmaḥ kevalaṃ na bhavati / ayam eva cābhyudayo yad atra enasā na yujyata iti/* (*MBhD* I 27.4-8)

Translation: 'Even though the position taken here is that also incorrect words (*apaśabda*), like correct ones (*sādhu*), convey meaning, and that therefore also the visible result (*dṛṣṭaṃ phalam*), understanding of meaning (*arthāvabodha*), is equal; there is here, as opposed to that (*tu*), an invisible result (*adṛṣṭaṃ phalam*), viz. that there is prosperity (*abhyudaya*). Therefore he (Patañjali) says: "So here too, though the conveying of meaning (*arthāvagati)* [by correct word (*śabda*) and by incorrect word (*apaśabda*)] is the same[, a certainty for *dharma* (*dharmaniyama*) is brought about only by correct word and meaning is not to be expressed directly (*abhidheya*) by incorrect word]." And when he (Patañjali) says "it (correct word) brings about prosperity (*abhyudaya*)", it is accepted by him that by abstaining from what is not enjoined (*avihitaparityāga*) *adharma* disappears. Others think that by abstaining from that *adharma* does merely not come about. The prosperity (*abhyudaya*) is merely this that here one is not connected with sin (*enas*).' (Bronkhorst 1987:87)[18]

This passage is a commentary on *MBh* I 8.20-22, which is a part of the *Paspaśāhnika*. One of the major problems discussed in the *Paspaśāhnika* concerns the aim of the study of grammar: What is the use of studying grammar, as the understanding of meaning is brought about even by incorrect words? Patañjali answers: Using correct words brings about *dharma* and *abhyudaya* with certainty. Following this discussion, Bhartṛhari says clearly in this passage that *abhyudaya*, which results from using correct words, is the invisible result (*adṛṣṭaṃ phalam*) and the understanding of meaning, which is caused by using not only correct words but also incorrect words, is the visible result (*dṛṣṭaṃ phalam*). It is Bhartṛhari who introduced the terms *dṛṣṭaphala/adṛṣṭaphala* into this discussion. The statement of Bhartṛhari that *abhyudaya* is the invisible result is in variance with Iyer's interpretation mentioned above: *abhyudaya* is the visible result. At this point, it need be asked: What does *abhyudaya* mean for Bhartṛhari? Does Iyer's rendering of *abhyudaya* as 'happiness here and beyond' do justice to what Bhartṛhari intended? Concerning this question, it is noteworthy that Bhartṛhari characterizes *abhyudaya* as absence of *adharma* or as being separated from sin, which is caused by abstaining from what is not enjoined, i.e. from using incorrect words. To this question, we will return afterwards (Passage 7).

> Passage 2: *tapasām uttamaṃ tapaḥ* (*VP* I 11b) / *yāni loke tapastvenābhikhyātāni brahmacaryādhaḥśayanodavāsacāndrāyaṇādīnī ye ca pavitratamāḥ svādhyāyās teṣām idaṃ dṛṣṭādṛṣṭaviśeṣaphalahetutvād abhikhyātatamaṃ tapaḥ* /(*Vṛtti* on *VP* I 11, 40.4-6)
>
> Translation: 'What is meant by "the best of all austerities" is this: Compared to what are considered to be austerities in the world like continence, sleeping on the ground, standing in water and progressive reduction and increase of nourishment according to the course of the moon and compared to what are considered to be the holiest forms of study, the study of the science of Grammar is the best form of austerity, because it leads to special results, visible and invisible.' (Iyer 1965:16-17)

This passage gives the view that the science of grammar brings about both the visible and the invisible results. Bhartṛhari does not say what they are respectively.[19] However, when we read the *Vṛtti* on the next verse, i.e. *VP* I 12, we will notice that each of them corresponds to the two results caused by using words. Bhartṛhari says: The collection of words, of which the grammatical correctness is established, is named 'supreme essence'; (1) because it is the conveyer of meaning (*vācaka*), and (2) because it is the cause of *abhyudaya* (*abhyudayahetu*).[20] As mentioned in Passage 1, the conveying of meaning is the visible result and *abhyudaya* is the invisible result.

> Passage 3: *jñāne śāstrapūrvake*[21] *vā prayoge 'bhyudayaḥ ity āgamāt pratipannānām upapattimātram āgamasyaivopodvalakam ity ucyate/ ihaiṣāṃ rūparasagandhasparśānāṃ pratyekaṃ samuditānāṃ ca dṛṣṭādṛṣṭaphalāḥ pratyarthaṃ yatāḥ śaktayaḥ parigṛhyante/ dṛṣṭaphalās tāvad viṣauṣadhyayaskāntavanaspatiprabhṛtīnām/ adṛṣṭaphalā nadyatīrthodakādīnām / śabdānām api keṣāñ cid uccāraṇe viṣāpaharaṇādi dṛṣṭaṃ phalam upalabhyate/ tathā sūktādīnām abhyāsād abhyupagamyate viśiṣṭam adṛṣṭaṃ phalam //* (*Vṛtti* 210.5-211.2) *yathaiṣāṃ tatra sāmarthyaṃ dharme 'py evaṃ pratīyatām / sādhūnāṃ sādhubhis tasmād vācyam abhyudayārthinām //* (*VP* I 156) *santi ceha dṛṣṭaphalāḥ kāścit pratiśabdaṃ śaktayaḥ ity āgamād evāvasīyate/ saty āgame sādhūnām api tathaivāvasīyatāṃ dharma-sādhanatvam ity ato 'bhyudayārthibhir anatiśankanīyāṃ smṛtim avicchinnaśiṣṭasamācārāṃ parigṛhya vyavahāre sādhava eva śabdāḥ prayoktavyāḥ*

// (*Vṛtti* 211.5-7) *sarvo 'dṛṣṭaphalān arthān āgamāt pratipadyate/* (*VP* I 157 ab)

> Translation: We say: For those who have understood through tradition (*āgama*) that *abhyudaya* lies in the knowledge [of correct words] (*jñāne*) and in the use [of correct words] preceded by the study of grammar (*śāstrapūrvake prayoge*),[22] every reasoning is only for confirming the very tradition. We accept in this world that *rūpa* (color), *rasa* (taste), *gandha* (smell) and *sparśa* (touch), whether individually or collectively, have the power to produce visible or invisible results, which are fixed in each object. While poison, medicinal herbs, magnet and trees, [23] etc., have the power to produce visible results (*dṛṣṭaphala*), wine and holy water, etc., have the power to produce invisible results (*adṛṣṭaphala*). In the case of words (*śabda*) also, when certain words are uttered, a visible result (*dṛṣṭaṃ phalam*) such as the counteracting of a poison is seen. Similarly, it is accepted that a particular invisible result (*adṛṣṭaṃ phalam*) is brought about by the repetition of a Vedic hymn, etc. It is to be understood that just as they have such powers, similarly the correct words (*sādhu*) have even the power to produce *dharma.* Therefore, those who desire *abhyudaya* should speak by means of correct words (*VP* I 156). We understand that every word has some power to produce visible results in this world only through tradition. Concerning the correct words also, in the same way [through tradition] we must understand that they are the means for the complete attainment of *dharma*, if there is such tradition. Therefore those who desire *abhyudaya* must use only correct words in worldly communication, while accepting the trustworthy tradition consisting of continuously transmitted practices of the śiṣṭas.[24] Everyone understands things having invisible results through tradition (*VP* I 157ab).

This passage makes it clear that *dharma* and *abhyudaya* are the invisible results of using correct words and that it is understood through tradition (*āgama*).

As has been mentioned, Bhartṛhari regards *abhyudaya*, attained by using correct words, as being the invisible result. We cannot accept, therefore, Iyer's statement that *abhyudaya* is the visible result.

ŚABDAPŪRVAYOGA

For Bhartṛhari, who considers the science of grammar as the first rung in the ladder of success and the correct road for those who desire liberation (*mokṣa*), [25] the *śabdapūrvayoga* must be an important term. This term seems to be used by Bhartṛhari in order to join his philosophy of language to a theory of practice. Before examining the conception of *śabdapūrvayoga* in Bhartṛhari's works, I will show the conclusions drawn by Iyer concerning this word:

> The position of Bhartṛhari, as I (=Iyer) understand it, is that the knowledge of the Science of Grammar and the use of the correct words as recognised in it leads to *dharma* which can do two things: (1) it can lead to *abhyudaya*, happiness here and beyond (2) it can enable the aspirant to practise *śabdapūrvayoga* that will, by stages, lead to his attainment of *mokṣa*. (Iyer 1969:146)

From this conclusion of Iyer's, we might think that the path forks into two directions leading to two different final goals, i.e. *abhyudaya* and *mokṣa* (= *niḥśreyasa*) beyond the point of attaining *dharma*, and that *śabdapūrvayoga* is the most important intermediate stage to the attainment of *mokṣa*. I will examine whether or not this is true.

> Passage 4: *śabdapūrvaṃ hi śabdasvarūpasyābhedatattvajñāne kramasaṃhāreṇa yogaṃ labhate / sādhuprayogāc cābhivyakta-dharmaviśeṣo mahāntaṃ śabdātmānam abhisaṃbhavan vaikar-aṇyaṃ prāpnoti / so 'vyatikīrṇāṃ vāgavasthām adhigamya vāg-vikārāṇāṃ prakṛtiṃ pratibhām anuparaiti / tasmāc ca sattānu-guṇyamātrāt pratibhākhyāc chabdapūrvayogabhāvanābhyāsākṣe-pāt pratyastamitasarvavikārollekhamātrāṃ parāṃ prakṛtiṃ pra-tipadyate* / (*Vṛtti* 47.6-48.3)
>
> Translation: (a) In fact, being guided by the correct words, when one knows the truth that the Word's own form itself is undivided, he gains *yoga* (union) by lumping all sequential items together (*kramasaṃhāra*). (b) Namely, when a particular *dharma* manifests itself in him through the use of correct words (*sādhuprayoga*), he, being united with the great Word itself, attains the stage free from the function of organs of sense (*vaikaraṇya*). (c) After having reached this pure state of the Word, he attains *pratibhā*, origin of the metamorphoses of the Word. (d) And from this state which is called *pratibhā* and is identical with the merest Being, he attains the Supreme Origin (*parāṃ prakṛtim*) in which all trace of the metamorphoses is completely lost, by making an attempt at prac-ticing that yoga guided by the correct words (*śabdapūrvayoga*).

This passage makes it clear that Bhartṛhari accepted five different stages from the first stage to the final goal, i.e. (1) the use of the correct words, (2) the attainment (manifestation) of *dharma* through it, (3) the attainment of *yoga* (union with the great Word), (4) the attainment of *pratibhā*, (5) the attainment to the Supreme One. As shown in my translation, I consider parts (a) and (b) of the passage as speaking of the same contents. Iyer regards passage 4 as 'describing the stages through which the grammarian goes in attaining *mokṣa*' (Iyer 1965:22).

> Passage 5: *tasmād yaḥ śabdasaṃskāraḥ sā siddhiḥ paramātmanaḥ / tasya pravṛttitattvajñas tadbrahmāmṛtam aśnute* //(*VP* I 144) *vyavasthitasādhubhāvena hi rūpeṇa saṃskriyamāṇe śabdatattve 'pabhraṃśopaghātāpagamād āvirbhūte dharmaviśeṣe niyato 'bhyudayaḥ / tadabhyāsāc ca śabdapūrvakaṃ yogam adhigamya pratibhāṃ tattvaprabhavāṃ bhāvavikāraprakṛtiṃ sattāṃ sādhyasādhanaśaktiyuktāṃ samyagavabudhya niyatā kṣemaprāptir iti* / (*Vṛtti* 201.8-202.3)
>
> Translation: Therefore the perfection of word is the attainment to the supreme ātman. One who knows the truth of its (= the word's) function attains the immortal Brahman (*VP* I 144). In fact, when the word itself is made perfect in the shape of being established as correct word (*sādhu*), the sin of incorrect words (*apabhraṃśa*) disappears. After that, when a particular *dharma* manifests itself [in him], *abhyudaya* becomes certain. And after having attained *yoga* guided by the correct words (*śabdapūrvakaṃ yogam*) through the practice of it (= the perfection of word by using correct words), one properly understands *pratibhā* that is having the truth as source, the origin of the metamorphoses of things, the Being, and being possessed of the powers of both object and subject. After that, the attainment of the supreme happiness (*kṣema*) becomes certain.

Although this passage also describes the five different stages as in the previous passage, it is noteworthy that the term *abhyudaya* occurs here. Iyer cited this passage as one of the sources of his proposition that Bhartṛhari states distinctly the two aims, i.e. *abhyudaya* and *niḥśreyasa* (= *kṣema*),[26] and he regarded the manifestation of *dharma* as the preliminary stage not only to *abhyudaya* but also to *mokṣa*. But it is impossible to read it from this passage. As this passage shows clearly, the manifestation of *dharma* and the attainment of *abhyudaya* happen simultaneously, and the two are synonyms. The next passage also makes this clear.

> Passage 6: *tatra sādhor yaḥ saṃbandho 'rthena sa jñāne śāstrapūrvake vā prayoge dharmābhivyaktāv aṅgatvaṃ prati-padyate*/ (*Vṛtti* 72.1-2)
>
> Translation: In that case, it is understood that the connection between a correct word and its meaning is the cause of the manifestation of *dharma* which lies in the knowledge [of correct

> words] (*jñāne*) and in the use [of correct words] preceded by the study of grammar (*śāstrapūrvake prayoge*).

In Passage 3, Bhartṛhari says: *jñāne śāstrapūrvake vā prayoge 'bhyudayaḥ*. Here he uses the word *dharmābhivyakti* (the manifestation of *dharma*) in place of *abhyudaya*. So it is clear that attainment of *dharma* is synonymous with attainment of *abhyudaya*. As mentioned in Passage 4, the attainment of *dharma* is the second stage, leading to the final goal, i.e. liberation. Therefore we reach the conclusion that the attainment of *abhyudaya* is one of the preliminary stages to the attainment of *mokṣa*. Now the question as to what *abhyudaya* means in Bhartṛhari's philosophy must be answered.

ABHYUDAYA IN THE BHARTṚHARIAN SENSE

> Passage 7: *tatra vyāvahārikīṣu sarvāsu vāgavasthāsu vyavasthitaḥ sādhvasādhupravibhāgaḥ puruṣasaṃskārahetur ekeṣām / paraṃ tu paśyantīrūpam anapabhraṃśam asaṃkīrṇaṃ lokavyavahārātītam / tasyā eva vāco vyākaraṇena sādhutvajñānalabhyena vā śabdapūrveṇa yogenādhigamyata ity ekeṣām āgamaḥ /* (*Vṛtti* 215.3-216.3)

> Translation: According to some, it is the cause of the perfection of a human being (*puruṣasaṃskāra*) to separate decisively correct words from incorrect words within all the states of words concerned with the worldly communication. The Supreme One (*para*), on the other hand, is *paśyantī*, and is free from incorrect word-form, and is pure and beyond worldly usage. Concerning this very Word, some have transmitted the tradition that it is attained by the study of grammar or through *yoga* guided by the correct words (*śabdapūrvayoga*), which is obtained by the knowledge of the correctness of words.

This passage belongs to the *Vṛtti* on *VP* I 159, which mentions the three kinds of stages of Word, i.e. *vaikharī*, *madhyamā* and *paśyantī*. The first part of this passage, referring to the states of words concerned with the worldly communication, may be regarded as concerning *vaikharī* and *madhyamā*. The latter part is about *paśyantī*, which is beyond the worldly communication. I cannot afford to go into details about these three kinds of Words. Here, it is noteworthy that the first part speaks of the use of correct words and the perfection of a human being as its result. As has been previously mentioned, the use of correct words brings about the manifestation of *dharma* or the attainment of *abhyudaya*. This 'manifestation of *dharma*' or 'attainment of *abhyudaya*' is replaced in this passage with 'the perfection of a human being'. Concerning this point, we should remember Bhartṛhari's conception shown in the last sentence of Passage 1: *abhyudaya* is merely this that one is not connected with sin in this world. Therefore we have come to understand the concept of *abhyudaya* in the Bhartṛharian sense: *abhyudaya*, which results from the use of corrects words, is the state of a human being free from sin, and is the state of his perfection in this world. Patañjali, as quoted at the beginning, stated that 'he, knowing the propriety of words, obtains unending victory in the other world, but by (using) wrong words he incurs blemish'.[27] Bhartṛhari, inheriting this idea in principle, excludes the notion concerning the 'world beyond' from *abhyudaya*, and puts it on a level of the dichotomy between merit and sin. The following passage shows this clearly:

> Passage 8: *tatra vāgyogavid śabdāpaśabdajñaḥ śabdān prayokṣyate nāpaśabdān/ prayogāc cābhyudayaḥ pratyavāyo vā na jñānād iti/* (*MBhD* I 10.21-22)
>
> Translation: 'He who knows the proper use of speech (*vāgyogavit*), though knowing [both] correct and incorrect words, will use correct words, not incorrect words. And prosperity (*abhyudaya*) or sin (*pratyavāya*) arises from the use [of words,] not from their knowledge.' (Bronkhorst 1987:56) [28]

In this passage, *abhyudaya* is in opposition to sin.

CONCLUSION

It is the notion generally accepted in the history of Indian thought that rebirth in heaven and liberation from transmigration are the two opposed final goals of human beings. Many texts discuss the opposition between the former gained by the Vedic ritual activities and the latter attained by *yoga* or asceticism. Subramania Iyer seems to have been so greatly influenced by this conventional view that he misinterpreted the Bhartṛharian idea concerning *abhyudaya*. As has been discussed earlier, in the philosophy of Bhartṛhari, the path starting with the use of correct words does not fork into two directions leading to two different final goals, i.e. *abhyudaya* and *mokṣa*. *Abhyudaya* is the last stage of perfection of a human being in this world and the preliminary stage of the attainment of liberation. The Science of Grammar is the door to bliss (*apavargasya dvāram*).[29] From the study of grammar, only one way leads straight to the final goal (*niḥśreyasa*),[30] i.e. liberation.

TEXT AND ABBREVIATIONS

MBh I:	*Mahābhāṣya* of Patañjali, volume 1, ed. Kielhorn
MBhD I:	*Mahābhāṣyadīpikā* of Bhartṛhari, Ahnika I, ed. Bronkhorst
MBhD II:	*Mahābhāṣyadīpikā* of Bhartṛhari, Ahnika II, ed. Palsule
VP I:	*Vākyapadīya* of Bhartṛhari, Kāṇḍa I, ed. Rau
Vrtti:	*Vṛtti* on *VP* I, ed. Iyer (1966)

NOTES

* The substance of this paper is based upon my article in Japanese 'Bhartṛhari ni okeru *abhyudaya* to *niḥśreyasa*' published in the *Tetsugaku-Nenpo* (*Annual of Philosophy*, Faculty of Letters of Kyushu University), no. 53, 1994, pp. 1-24. I would like to express my thanks to Mr. Anthony Black who was kind enough to revise and correct my English.

1 *Manusmṛti* 12.88-90.

2 *VP* I 156; *Vṛtti* 23.3, 27.7, 42.6, 202.1, 210.5, 211.6, 224.7. I treat the *Vṛtti* as a work of Bhartṛhari in this paper. Even if the *Vṛtti* was written by someone other than Bhartṛhari, I think there can be little doubt that Bhartṛhari and Vṛttikāra lived as contemporaries before Dignāga and Praśastapāda.

3 As to the words *apavarga* and *mokṣa*, which are regarded as synonyms of *niḥśreyasa* in the *Amarakośa*, Bhartṛhari uses the word *apavarga* in *VP* I 14 and *mokṣa* in *VP* I 16 in the context of discussing the final goal attained by the study of grammar.

4 K.A. Subramania Iyer, *Bhartṛhari, A Study of the Vākyapadīya in the Light of the Ancient Commentaries*, Poona, 1969, pp. 135-146.

5 *MBh* I 1.14.

6 *MBh* I 2.3-5.11.

7 *MBh* I 2.19-20: *yas tu prayuṅkte kuśalo viśeṣe śabdān yathāvad vyavahārakāle / so 'nantam āpnoti jayaṃ paratra vāgyogavid duṣyati cāpaśabdaiḥ*. Translation by D. Joshi and J.A.F. Roodbergen in *Patañjali Vyākaraṇa--Mahābhāṣya, Paspaśāhnika*, Poona, 1986, p. 43.

8 *MBh* I 3.15-16. Translation by S.D. Joshi, p. 52.

9 *MBh* I 2.22: *yathaiva hi śabdajñāne dharma evam apaśabdajñāne 'py adharmaḥ*. Translation by S.D. Joshi, p. 43.

10 *MBh* I 10.21 (*Vārttika* 9): *śāstrapūrvake prayoge 'bhyudayas tat tulyam vedaśabdena*. S.D. Joshi and J.A.F. Roodbergen treat this passage as the thirteenth *Vārttika*. For the interpretation of the word *vedaśabda*, cf. S.D.

Joshi, pp. 150-151.

11 K.A. Subramania Iyer, *Bhartṛhari*, p. 136. Kaiyaṭa too says that ɔy this verse [Patañjali] shows the fact that the study of grammar is the cause of *abhyudaya*. Subramania Iyer translates the word *abhyudaya* as 'happiness here and beyond' here, but he adds immediately: 'That by *abhyudaya* heaven is meant is made clear by Patañjali in his *Mahābhāṣya* on P. VI. 1.84, where he quotes an earlier text which declares that even a single word, properly understood together with the śāstra relating to it and correctly used yields him desired fruit in heaven.' The Sanskrit text suggested by Subramania Iyer runs as follows: *ekaḥ śabdaḥ samyag-jñātaḥ śāstrānvitaḥ suprayuktaḥ svarge loke kāmadhug bhavati* (*MBh* III 58.15). The same text is quoted by Bhartṛhari in his *Mahābhāṣya-Dīpikā* (*MBhD* I 11.1-2). And J. Bronkhorst translates '*svarge loke*' as 'in heaven and on earth'. I agree with J. Bronkhorst.

12 *MBh* I 3.22: *mahatā devena naḥ sāmyaṃ yathā syād ity adhyeyaṃ vyākaraṇam*. Cf. translation by S.D. Joshi, p. 53.

13 *VP* I 22cd: *tad vyākaraṇam āgamya paraṃ brahmādhigamyate.*

14 K.A. Subramania Iyer, *Bhartṛhari*, pp. 138-139.

15 *MBhD* II 39.25.

16 K.A. Subramania Iyer, *Bhartṛhari*, p. 137.

17 Ibid., p.141.

18 Translation of J. Bronkhorst, in *Mahābhāṣya of Bhartṛhari*, Fascicule IV: Ahnika I, critically edited by Johannes Bronkhorst, Poona, 1987, p.87. I added original Sanskrit words in parentheses, and with regard to the quotation from *MBh* I 8.20-22 (: *evam ihāpi samānāyām arthagatau śabdena cāpaśabdena ca dharmaniyamaḥ kriyate śabdenaivārtho abhidheyo nāpaśabdenety evaṃ kriyāmāṇam abhyudayakāri bhavatīti*), I inserted my translation with brackets according to this original text. As to the word *dharmaniyama*, cf. *MBh* I 8.1-6.

19 Vṛṣabhadeva translates 'the visible result' as 'wealth in this world' (*lābha*) and 'the invisible result' as 'liberation' (*mokṣa*).

20 *Vṛtti* on *VP* I 12, 42.6-7: *paramo rasaḥ iti / vācakatvād abhy-udayahetutvāc ca vyavasthitasādhubhāvaḥ śabdasamūho 'bhidhīyate /*

21 Iyer's edition has *śabdapūrvake*, but Śārudevaḥ Cāstrī's (Lahore 1934) has *śāstrapūrvake*. This reading is justified by the passage of Vṛtti 72.1: *jñāne śāstrapūrvake vā.*

22 See notes 9 and 10.

23 I cannot understand why *vanaspati* (Lord of the Forest, tree) is enumerated here. Is it possible to refer to the *Manusmṛti* 1.47: '(Trees) that have fruit but no flowers are traditionally known as Lords of the Forest; those that bear both flowers and fruit are called trees'(Translation of Wendy Doniger, *The Laws of Manu,* 1991, p. 8)?

24 The same idea is seen in the *Vṛtti* 82.1-4. For the conception of Śiṣṭas for Bhartṛhari, cf. M.M. Deshpande, The Changing Notion of Śiṣṭa From Patañjali to Bhartṛhari, *Asiatische Studien / Etudes Asiatiques* XLVII-1, 1993, pp.95-115.

25 *VP* I 16: *idam ādyaṃ padasthānaṃ siddhisopānaparvaṇām / iyaṃ sā mokṣasamāṇānām ajihmā rājapaddhatiḥ //*

26 K.A. Subramania Iyer, *Bhartṛhari*, pp. 138-139.
27 See note 6.
28 I added the original Sanskrit words in parentheses.
29 *VP* I 14a: *tad dvāram apavargasya vāṅmalānāṃ cikitsitaṃ / pavitraṃ sarvavidyānām adhividyaṃ prakāśate //*
30 The word *niḥśreyasa* means basically that, than which there is nothing better.

BIBLIOGRAPHY

Bronkhorst, Johannes, *Mahābhāṣyadīpikā of Bhartṛhari*, Ahnika I (Fascicule IV). Critically edited and translated with notes. Poona, 1987.

Iyer, K.A. Subramania, *The Vākyapadīya of Bhartṛhari with the Vṛtti*, Chapter I, English Translation. Poona, 1965.

Iyer, K.A. Subramania, *Vākyapadīya of Bhartṛhari with the Commentaries Vṛtti and Paddhati of Vṛṣabhadeva, Kāṇḍa I*. Critically edited. Poona, 1966.

Iyer, K.A. Subramania, *Bhartṛhari: A study of the Vākyapadīya in the light of the Ancient Commentaries*. Poona, 1969.

Joshi, S.D. and Roodbergen, J.F.F., Patañjali *Vyākaraṇa--Mahābhāṣya, Paspaśāhnika*, Introduction, Text, Translation and Notes. Poona, 1968.

Mahābhāṣya of Patañjali. Edited by Franz Kielhorn in 3 volumes, 1880-1885. 3rd revised edition by K.V. Abhyankar, 1962-1972. Poona.

Palsule, G.B, *Mahābhāṣyadīpikā of Bhartṛhari*, Ahnika II (Fascicule V). Critically edited and translated with notes. Poona, 1988.

Rau, Wilhelm, *Bhartṛharis Vākyapadīya*. Die *mūlakārikās* nach den Handschriften herausgegeben und mit einem *pāda*-Index versehen von Wilhelm Rau. Wiesbaden, 1977.

18

Indian Grammarians' Theory of Proper Names*

JUNZO TANIZAWA

In the history of the philosophy of language, the function of proper names is one of the most controversial topics. One of the main questions is whether or not proper names have senses, i.e. whether or not they *directly* refer to things without having senses. According to the descriptivist theory the sense of a proper name is given by the description(s) associated with it. At present many philosophers think that the descriptivist theory is mistaken and advocate the theory of direct reference of proper names. In India, Pāṇinian grammarians inquired into the meaning of words and in that context dealt with the topic of the meaning of proper names. In Sanskrit, the term supposed to be equivalent to 'proper name' is '*yadṛcchāśabda*' (arbitrary word), or in some cases '*saṃjñā*' (name), though the latter also means 'technical term'. My aim in this paper is to investigate the theory of meaning with respect to the *yadṛcchāśabda* and the *saṃjñā* advanced by Indian grammarians (*vaiyākaraṇas*) from the point of view of the contemporary controversy about proper names.

TWO ELEMENTS OF THE MEANING OF WORDS

It is well-known that Frege, with respect to the meaning of linguistic expressions, distinguished between sense (*Sinn*) and Meaning[1] (*Bedeutung*).[2] For example, the terms 'Phosphorus' and 'Hesperus' refer to the same object, Venus. Let us consider the two statements 'Hesperus is (identical with) Hesperus' and 'Hesperus is (identical with) Phosphorus'. The former is trivial, whereas the latter has a certain cognitive value. What, in spite of the fact that the two terms have the same referent, brings about this difference? According to Frege, in the case of a singular term, its Meaning is its referent and its sense is the manner of presentation of the referent. Therefore the statement 'a=b', even if the name 'a' and the name 'b' refer to the same object, has a certain cognitive value, unlike 'a=a', which is a tautology. A singular term refers to an object determined by its sense. Frege, moreover, asserts that an assertive sentence itself is a proper name of a truth-value; the Meaning of an assertive sentence is a truth-value and its sense is a thought (*Gedanke*) expressed by the sentence. The function of a sense of a singular term in a sentence is a contribution to thought and the thought is directly regarded as true or false.[3] Thus we should take his distinction of two elements of the meaning within the framework of his theory of truth and, furthermore, his idea of functional expressions.[4] Indian theories of meaning, on the other hand, have nothing to do with such a framework. It is, however, to be noted that, at least in the case of singular terms, such a distinction was also made by them.[5] According to early Pāṇinian grammarians, a word first *independently* means its own sense (*svārtha*) and then refers to a particular thing (*dravya*) determined by that sense.[6] A word's own sense (*svārtha*) has later become called its cause of application (*pravṛttinimitta*, PN), i.e. its cause on the basis of which the word is applied to its referent. The PNs *on the part of words' referents* are classified, in accordance with Indian traditional classifications of words, into four kinds: (a) an essential property as a whole (*jāti*), (b) a quality (*guṇa*), (c) an act (*kriyā*), (d) a relation (*sambandha*). For example, when we speak of a running black cow in front of us, 'the cow' is a term that has (a) as its PN, 'the black (cow)' is one that has (b) as its PN, 'the running (cow)' is one that has (c) as its PN, and 'the black cow' is one that has (d), i.e. the relation between the black and the cow, as its PN. And the complex expression 'the running black cow' has a complex PN composed of (a), (b), (c), and (d). Furthermore, Indian grammarians regard a word's own form (*svarūpa*) as the fifth PN, one *on the part of the word*, which will be discussed below in detail. With respect to a singular term, the PN *on the part of the term's referent* is, I think, equivalent to Fregean sense in that it determines the term's referent.[7] From this perspective, the question of whether or not proper names have senses leads, in the Indian context, to the question of whether or not *yadṛcchāśabdas* or *saṃjñās* have PNs *on the part of their referents*.

WHAT IS THE *YADṚCCHĀŚABDA*?

Let us examine the portion of the *Mahābhāṣya* (MBh) on the *Śivasūtra* '*ṛḷk*' in which the notion of *yadṛcchāśabda* is discussed in relation to the name '*ḷtaka*'. Bhartṛhari, commenting on that discussion in his *Mahābhāṣyadīpikā*, defines '*yadṛcchā (śabda)*' as follows:

> *Yadṛcchā* is, when there is no PN, what occurs or ceases to occur without any cause that lies in the word's referent which brings about its occurrence or ceasing. For example, the name '*Ḍittha*', whose cause (*nibandhana*) is only its own form (*svarūpa*), comes into use in the form of 'I give this name to this'. And in that case, it is always possible to cease to apply the name to this. Since, about the words whose causes are only their own forms, the forms cannot be represented by any forms other than their own, there are no other words which cause their application to cease. Thus the word '*ḷtaka*' is, if it is used as a name, a correct word whose cause is its own form because it is not due to any external cause and does not have any other word which prevents it from coming into use.........
>
> Some words have fixed meanings. They have fixed synonyms. They cannot be man-made because we cannot recollect who produced them. However, a certain set of words used as names, which are not applied to any fixed meanings, comes into use by means of human intention. We can thus say that a *jātiśabda* (word that express an essential property as a whole) is, when applied to the *jāti* (essential property as a whole), a *yadṛcchāśabda*, because it does not depend on any cause that lies in the referent, i.e. in the *jāti* itself.
>
> There are various applications of words by means of human intention, as for example 'By this there is such and such a *jāti*' or 'To that extent, there is such and such a *jāti*'. In that case it differs from a [genuine] *yadṛcchāśabda* in that it cannot be named by means of human effort. On the other hand, if it is, on the basis of a cause that lies in a *dravya* (particular thing), applied to the *dravya*, it is also a *jātiśabda*. However, since its referent is a *dravya*, it is a *dravyaśabda* (word that expresses a particular thing). We can think of a *guṇaśabda* (word that expresses a quality) in the same way. A *guṇaśabda* such as '*śukla*' (white), if applied to the universal (*sāmānya*) of the quality (*guṇa*), is a *yadṛcchāśabda*; and if it is applied to a quality that lies in a *dravya*, it is a *jātiśabda*, and also a *guṇaśabda* because it expresses a *guṇa*. In the same way a *kriyāśabda* (word that expresses an act) is ....
>
> In applications of three kinds of words, i.e. *jātiśabda*, *guṇaśabda* and *kriyāśabda*, words are fixed, and their meanings are also fixed. But in the application of the fourth word, *yadṛcchāśabda*, it is produced by a certain man.[8]

Thus a distinctive feature of *yadṛcchāśabda*s is their lack of PNs *on the part of their referents* and hence their referring is devoid of fixedness. According to the descriptivist theory of proper names,[9] the sense of, for example, the name 'Aristotle' is given by descriptions associated with it, such as 'the Greek philosopher who wrote *The Nicomachean Ethics*', 'the teacher of Alexander the Great', and so on. Indian grammarians would say that those descriptions express PNs *on the part of the referent* of the name 'Aristotle'. However, as shown above, they do not claim that proper names have PNs *on the part of their referents*. It follows that in Indian theories of meaning *yadṛcchāśabdas* do not have senses. However, is this view applicable to all uses of *yadṛcchāśabdas*?

In MBh on Pāṇini's *Aṣṭādhyāyī* (P.) 5.1.119 '*tasya bhāvas tvatalau*', Patañjali explicates how the suffix '*tva*' or '*tā*', which means the universal property (*bhāva*), can be attached to a *yadṛcchāśabda.*

> Then, since a person's name like '*Ḍittha*' [does not have as its meaning a *bhāva* that '*tva*' or '*tā*' stands for,] we cannot get a member (i.e. '*tva*' or '*tā*') that constitutes the compound. Therefore such compounds as '*Ḍitthatvam*', '*Ḍitthatā*' and '*Ḍāmbhiṭṭatvam*' cannot be formed. However there is a *primary Ḍittha* or *Ḍāmbhiṭṭa*. If a person does anything the *primary Ḍittha* or *Ḍāmbhiṭṭa* did, or if he has any quality the primary one has, people tell him 'This is your *Ḍitthatva*', or 'This is your *Ḍāmbhiṭṭatva*'.[10]

Kaiyaṭa comments on this part in his *Pradīpa* as follows:

> A *yadṛcchāśabda* like '*Ḍittha*' does not depend on any PN *on the part of its referent*, because it is applied according to one's intention. 'There is a *primary Ḍittha.* …………' means this: first we see a certain behaviour or a certain quality that belongs to *Ḍittha*, and then the word '*Ḍittha*' is figuratively applied to another person. In this case its PN is just his behaviour or quality............ The way we establish the relation between a name (*saṃjñā*) and the named (*saṃjñin*) is as follows: One superimposes a word's own form on its meaning and says that this is *Ḍittha.* It means that just as the word '*Ḍittha*' is applied to its meaning by means of its superimposition on the meaning, so a word's own form is superimposed on its meaning, and consequently a suffix like '*tva*' or '*tā*' is attached to it.
>
> Or others hold that there is an essential property (*jāti*) that inheres in one individual who undergoes changes according to different periods, i.e. his boyhood and so on, from his birth to death. Throughout the various periods we see the essential property in virtue of which we recognize that he is that same man, e.g., that *Ḍittha*. It is to the essential property that the suffix '*tva*' or '*tā*' is applied.[11]

As shown above, Kaiyaṭa bears three situations of utterance in mind: (1) the situation of naming, (2) the situation in which a certain proper name is figuratively applied to some person other than its original bearer because the former has the same behaviour or action as the latter has, for example, the situation in which we say of a great Japanese philosopher that he is a Japanese Wittgenstein,and (3) the situation in which we recognize one and the same essential property of an individual that persists throughout various periods and, seeing the property, we say that he (she) is Mr. (Ms.) so and so. Of these three, it is only in the case of (1) that proper names do not have their senses. We may naturally think that in (2) and (3) they have their senses. But it is to be noted that the seeming proper name in (2) is used not as a referring expression but as a predicate and hence we, in fact, cannot call it a proper name.

Let us turn our attention to *saṃjñā*s. According to Indian grammarians, we can divide them into (1) artificial (*kṛtrima*) or technical ones and (2) natural (*akṛtrima*), i.e. etymologically derivative ones. Some *saṃjñās* have both technical senses and etymological ones.[12] Thus *kṛtrima saṃjñās* belong to the class of *yadṛcchāśabdas* because they are arbitrarily named by human efforts.[13]

Bhartṛhari remarks in his *Vākyapadīya* (VP) as follows:

> In everyday language *saṃjñās* (names) depend on their own forms. Some of those are applied to their objects when there are any [etymological] causes, and others are applied even when there are not.
>
> In the grammatical literature *mahatī saṃjñās* (big names) are based on their own forms. When there are any [etymological] causes, they are inferred.[14]

Here *mahatī saṃjñās* are names such as '*kāraka*', '*upasarjana*', '*saṃkhyā*', '*sarvanāman*', and so on, which are composed of more than one syllable and have etymologically derived senses.

Of the above-mentioned two classes of *saṃjñās*, the *kṛtrimas* do not have etymologically derived senses while the *akṛtrimas* do, though referents of *akṛtrimas* may not be determined merely by those senses.[15] In Pāṇinian grammar '*ṭi*', '*ghu*', '*bha*' and so on are members of the former class and '*karmapravacanīya*',[16] '*sarvanāman*'[17]and so on are members of the latter. In ordinary language a name like '*Ḍāmbhiṭṭa*' belongs to the former and one like '*śatrughna*', which literally means 'destroyer of enemies' and refers to a brother of Rāma, or '*balabhadra*', which literally means 'strong' or 'powerful' and refers to Balarāma, belongs to the latter. The terms of the latter class are names based on descriptions both in grammar and in ordinary language.

As has been said, Indian grammarians lay emphasis on the fact that *saṃjñās*, even if they have etymologically derivative senses, have as their meanings their own forms. Bhartṛhari clearly states this point in the first chapter of VP. There the *saṃjñā* '*vṛddhi*', though it has an etymologically derivative sense in ordinary speech, has a technical sense in grammar according to P.1.1.1 '*vṛddhir ādaic*'.

> Just as words like '*vṛddhi*' and so on, based on their own forms, become connected with their named (*saṃjñin*) represented by the word '*ādaic*' (*ā,ai, au*) and so on, so the word '*agni*', based on the word '*agni*', becomes connected with the phonemes represented by the word '*agni*'.[18]

For example, according to the rule P.6.1.77 '*iko yaṇ aci*', '*y*', '*v*', '*r*', and '*l*' represented by '*yaṇ*', which is first based on its own form, are substituted for '*i*', '*u*', '*ṛ*', and '*ḷ*' represented by '*ik*', which is first based on its own form. In this case the form of the name (*saṃjñā*) is different from that of the named (*saṃjñin*). In the same way '*vṛddhi*', based on its own form, becomes connected with the named, '*ā*', '*ai*' and 'au' represented by '*ādaic*'. The word '*agni*', on the other hand, which has the same form as the *saṃjñin* in grammar,[19] based on its own form, becomes connected with the *saṃjñin*, i.e. the phonemes represented by '*agni*'.

From the fact that grammarians in general call into question forms of words and sentences, it follows that Indian grammarians, as in the example '*agni*', attach importance to forms of words. This point is also relevant to a solution of a problem that is characteristic of Pāṇini's grammar. Bhartṛhari remarks on the problem as follows:

> Before a name becomes connected with the named, it has its own form as its meaning. That is how it becomes suitable for the causes of the use of the sixth (genitive, *ṣaṣṭhī*) and the first (nominative, *prathamā*) case affixes.[20]

In the first place, according to P.1.2.45 '*arthavad adhātur apratyayaḥ prātipadikam*', the nominal stem (*prātipadika*) is defined as meaningful (*arthavat*). In the second place, according to P.4.1.1 '*ṅyāpprātipadikāt*', case affixes are appended after nominal stems, and then, according to P.2.3.46 '*prātipadikārthaliṅgaparimāṇavacanamātre prathamā*', one of the meanings of the first case (*prathamā*) is the meaning of the nominal stem. Thus in the sūtra P.1.1.1 '*vṛddhir ādaic*' one problem arises. This is a *saṃjñāsūtra* that defines the term '*vṛddhi*'. Therefore on reading this *sūtra* for the first time, or stipulating this definition, the first term '*vṛddhi*' has no meaning, and cannot be qualified as a nominal stem (*prātipadika*). The result is that, according to P.4.1.1 above, it cannot have the first case affix.

To avoid that problem, Indian grammarians assert that in this case the meaning of the term '*vṛddhi*' is its own form; with its own form as its meaning, the term becomes capable of suffixing a first case ending. On the other hand, for example, in the sUtra P.6.1.88 '*vṛddhir eci*', which is not a *saṃjñāsūtra*, the same problem does not arise, for '*vṛddhi*' in this case, in advance, has a fixed meaning by means of the definition shown above. Here it is to be noted that '*saṃjñā*' in grammar differs from '*saṃjñā*' in everyday speech in that it means a technical term on the basis of a definition. Thus Bhartṛhari says

> In the sūtra (P.1.1.1), since it (the *saṃjñā* '*vṛddhi*') has its own form as a meaning, a first (nominative) case affix comes after the *saṃjñā*. The situation that the mere meaning of the nominal stem [of the saṃjñin] is, as shown by the use of a sixth case affix [like '*ām*' of '*ādaicām*' in '*ādaicāṃ vṛddhiḥ saṃjñā*'], surpassed (vyatireka)[21] arises on the basis of the very meaning [of the *saṃjñā* '*vṛddhi*'].[22]

Next let us turn to the sixth case. Consider the phrase '*rājñaḥ puruṣaḥ*', in which we express a relation between qualifier (*viśeṣaṇa*) and qualificand (*viśeṣya*). The sixth case affix '*Ṅas*' is appended to the nominal stem '*rājan*' because here the meaning of the nominal stem '*rājan*' is surpassed (*vyatiricyate*); '*rājan*' here denotes the qualifier of the qualificand the nominal stem 'puruṣa' denotes.[23] In other words, the meaning of '*rājan*' here surpasses the mere meaning of the nominal stem (*prātipadikārthamātra*, see P.2.3.46 above).[24] In the same way in the sentence '*ādaicāṃ vṛddhiḥ saṃjñā*', the sixth case affix '*ām*' is appended to the nominal stem '*ādaic*' because here the mere meaning of the nominal stem '*ādaic*' is surpassed; '*ādaic*' here denotes the expressed (*vāçya*) of the expressor (*vācaka*) the nominal stem '*vṛddhi*' denotes. The meaning of '*ādaic*' here surpasses the mere meaning of the nominal stem. In this case, the stem '*vṛddhi*' must have a meaning other than *ādaic*, for otherwise the relation between the expressed and the expressor (*vācyavācakabhāva*) could not be established. Therefore it has its own form as its meaning. Thus the use of the sixth case affix '*ām*' of '*ādaicām*' is brought about by the meaning of the stem '*vṛddhi*', i.e. by its own form.

PRAVṚTTINIMITTAS OF PROPER NAMES: THEIR OWN FORMS

Saṃjñās have their own forms as their meanings in some contexts. This view can be connected with the view presented by Kaiyaṭa above, i.e. that we name something by superimposing a word's own form on it. We now return to the definition of '*yadṛcchāśabda*' made by Bhartṛhari, according to which a *yadṛcchāśabda* does not have any cause of application (PN) *on the part of its referent*. This does not mean that it does not have any PN at all. It has, as Bhartṛhari says, its own form (*svarūpa*) as the cause (*nibandhana*) of its use. Later Pāṇinian grammarians regard the form as the fifth PN, the PN *on the part of the term.*[25] Let us call the PN as a word's own form f-sense and put Bhartṛhari's definition of the *yadṛcchāśabda* as follows:

(1)*Yadṛcchāśabdas* do not have any Fregean senses.
(2) *Yadṛcchāśabdas* do have f-senses.

This view might suggest a solution of what is called Frege's puzzle,[26] i.e.the puzzle of identity statements. If proper names do not have any Fregean senses, how do identity statements such as 'a=b', 'Hesperus is (identical with) Phosphorus' and so on, have any cognitive values? The answer is, Indian grammarians would say, 'a' and 'b', or 'Hesperus' and 'Phosphorus' each have each their different forms, i.e. f-senses.[27]

I do not intend to say that Indian grammarians *did* solve Frege's puzzle. Such a view can, as Salmon pointed out,[28] be extended to other sorts of expressions, such as natural kind terms. According to this view, the cognitive value of 'Snow is white' would be different from that of '*Der Schnee ist weiss*', which is implausible.[29] And if the meaning of a name consists of its f-sense and its referent, the meaning of, for example, 'Phosphorus' may be given by the description 'the thing called 'Phosphorus''. If so, this argument may, as Kripke points out,[30] violate the noncircularity condition. Here, however, I cannot go into this matter in detail.

JĀTIŚABDAS AS *YADṚCCHĀŚABDAS*

Direct reference theorists deny that proper names have Fregean senses, and call proper names rigid designators, i.e. the terms that *rigidly* designate the same things in all possible worlds in which those things exist. The range of rigid designators, however, is not restricted to proper names. Kripke claims that natural kind terms have a greater kinship with proper names than is generally realized; they rigidly designate the same natural kinds in all possible worlds.[31] Indian grammarians, on the other hand, regard *jātiśabdas* that refer to the *jātis* themselves as *yadṛcchāśabdas* because those *jātiśabdas*, in such cases, do not have any PNs *on the part of their referents*. *Jātiśabdas* only have them when they refer to particular things determined by the *jātis*. Thus this view has a parallel with the direct reference theory of proper names in this respect: for Kripke and Putnam,[32] natural kind terms are equal to proper names in that both are rigid designators, and for Indian grammarians, *jātiśabdas* including as the main constituents natural kind terms, when they refer to the *jātis*, are equal to *yadṛcchāśabdas* in that both do not have any PNs *on the part of their referents*. We, however, should pay attention to a basic idea of Indian grammarians' theories of meaning: words except *yadṛcchāśabdas*, as shown above, have no beginnings, that is to say, are not man-made. Thus *jātiśabdas* that refer to the *jātis* are *yadṛcchāśabdas* from the point of view of their PNs, whereas they are not *yadṛcchāśabdas* in the literal sense, i.e. in the light of arbitrariness (*yadṛcchā*).

SAṂJÑĀS AND DESCRIPTIVE NAMES

The term '*yadṛcchāśabda*', in fact, does not altogether correspond to 'proper name', for it is possible for a *yadṛcchāśabda* to be applied to many objects if it conforms to the definition 'It does not have any PN *on the part of its referent*'. Consider the *saṃjñā* '*ṭi*', a *kṛtrima saṃjñā*. In this case we may say that '*ṭi*' is identified with the description '*aco'ntyādi*' in the definition of the *saṃjñāsūtra* P.1.1.64 '*aco'ntyādi ṭi*'. The term '*ṭi*', even if it is not a proper name, might be regarded as what G. Evans called a descriptive name,[33] whose reference is fixed by a certain description; it refers to whatever is a syllable beginning with the last vowel (*aco'ntyādi*) of a linguistic unit. Kripke, who makes a distinction between fixing a term's reference and giving its synonym, considers as an example of such names 'one meter'.[34] Suppose someone stipulates that one meter is to be the length of the stick *S* at the time *t*. He or she uses this definition, according to Kripke, not to give the meaning of 'one meter' but to fix the reference. It is not necessary but accidental or contingent that the stick *S* is one meter long at *t*. It may have a different length in another possible world. As a result, the meaning of 'one meter' is not given by the definition; the phrase 'one meter', which is a rigid designator, is not synonymous with 'the length of S at t'.[35] These arguments, however, are not applicable to the case of '*ṭi*'. To say that in some possible worlds *ṭi* might not be the *aco'ntyādi*, I think, does not make sense because the phrase 'the syllable beginning with the last vowel', unlike 'the length of the stick *S* at *t*', does not have the question of necessity. The term '*ṭi*' abbreviates the phrase '*aco'ntyādi*' and is synonymous with it. Therefore its PN is given by the description '*aco'ntyādi*', though Indian grammarians do not definitely say so. Thus it is just on the stage of the *saṃjñāsūtra*, i.e. at the time of naming, that it does not have its PN *on the part of its referent*. In the same way *jātiśabda*s do not have their PNs *on the part of their referents* when we give certain names to the *jāti*s, though, according to Indian grammarians, the name-giving in the case of *jātiśabda*s is impossible because they claim that words have no beginnings. That claim is inapplicable to the case of *yadṛcchāśabda*s as proper names.

CONCLUSION

From the fact that Indian grammarians define '*yadṛcchāśabda*' as 'the word that does not have any PN *on the part of its referent*', it does not follow that it has no sense or PN. What we may think of as a sense of a *yadṛcchāśabda* is as follows:

(1) The word's own form. We called it f-sense in order to distinguish it from Fregean sense. It might be claimed that this is a result of grammatical operations. Indeed Indian grammarians often attach great importance to a word's own form because it is necessary to do so in order to put various grammatical operations into practice, but f-senses might, as mentioned above, play a great role in our understanding of linguistic expressions, e.g. identity statements.

(2) A person's essential property that persists throughout his or her life. This is connected with the problem of personal identity, into which I cannot inquire in this paper. Here we can point out that in Sanskrit the suffix '*tva*' or '*tā*', which means a essential or universal property, can rather easily be appended to a nominal stem and that Pāṇinian grammarians make use of this notion of a person's essential property in order to explain the way the suffix is appended to a proper name. This condition is also applicable to the next.

(3) The sense of the description based on acts and qualities of the person. In this case the term that has the sense is not a genuine proper name in the sense that it is not a referring expression.

One of the reasons why a *yadṛcchāśabda*, or a *saṃjñā*, is not always a proper name or a singular term is that Indian grammarians traditionally regard word (*śabda*), meaning (*artha*), and the relation (*sambandha*) between the two as eternal (*nitya*). They paid attention to *yadṛcchāśabdas* because those words apparently violate the principle. What they were primarily concerned with is not the fact that those words refer to particular things or persons but the fact that they are *arbitrarily* applied to their referents.[36] Indeed some people did not regard the *yadṛcchāśabda* as a word because it violates the above principle.[37]

The fact that *yadṛcchāśabdas* are arbitrary words hardly seems to have led Indian grammarians to the view that proper names *rigidly* designate their referents.[38] They put emphasis on the arbitrariness of these words from the perspective of the time of naming. In their arguments, however, they tend to neglect, except in the context of the universal suffix '*tva*' or '*tā*', the way in which, in their community, people other than one who gave a name to something use that name.

NOTES

* This article is a revised and enlarged version of '*Yadṛcchāśabda* and *Saṃjñā*: From the Point of View of Proper Names', *Journal of Indian and Buddhist Studies (Indogaku Bukkyōgaku Kenkyū)* vol. 37-2, 1989, pp.17-22.

1. This term, a technical one, is capitalized to distinguish it from 'meaning' in ordinary usage.
2. Cf. Gottrob Frege, 'On Sense and Meaning', *Translations from the Philosophical Writings of Gottlob Frege*, ed. and tr. Peter Geach and Max Black, Oxford: Basil Blackwell, 1980, pp. 56-78.
3. Frege, 'Thoughts', *Logical Investigations*, ed. P.T.Geach and tr. P.T. Geach and R.H. Stoodhoff, New Haven: Yale University Press, 1977, pp. 4-5. Cf. Michael Dummett, *Frege: Philosophy of Language*, London: Duckworth, 1981, pp.152-9, 159-60, 180-6.
4. For more details on this matter, see Frege, 'Function and Concept', *Translations from the Philosophical Writings of Gottlob Frege*, ed. and tr. Peter Geach and Max Black, Oxford: Basil Blackwell, 1980, pp. 31-2.
5. Kaiyaṭa, a Pāṇinian grammarian, explicitly states the two elements of meaning as follows: It (i.e. meaning) is of two kinds: a word's referent (vācya) and its cause of application (*pravṛttinimitta*). (*Pradīpa* on P. 5.1.119). In addition to the two elements, Indian grammarians often take a word's etymological cause (*vyutpattinimitta*) as the third. However, what we should allow for in everyday speech is the former two.
6. *Mahābhāṣya*, ed. F. Kielhorn, Poona: Bhandarkar Oriental Research Institute, vol. 2, 1965, p. 424.

7. Here I do not intend to claim that both views are exactly the same. For the difference between the PN and Fregean sense, see my article (in Japanese) 'Imi no Niyōso: Bhartṛhari to Frege' (Two Elements of Meaning: Bhartṛhari and Frege), *Studies in Comparative Philosophy* (*Hikaku Shisō Kenkyū*) vol. 17, 1990, pp. 39-45.
8. *Mahābhāṣyadīpikā*, by V. Abhyankar and V.P. Limaye, Poona: Bhandarkar Oriental Research Institute, 1967, pp. 59-60.
9. See Frege 'On Sense and Meaning', p. 58; Bertrand Russell, 'The Philosophy of Logical Atomism', *Logic and Knowledge*, London: George Allen and Unwin, 1956, p. 243; John Searl, 'Proper Names', *Mind* 67, 1958, pp. 166-73. This theory is parallel in several respects to Indian grammarians' theory of *guṇasamudāya* (collection of properties). See J. Tanizawa, 'Pāṇinian Theory of *Guṇasamudāya*: Indian Cluster Theory', *Journal of Indian and Buddhist Studies (Indogaku Bukkyōgaku Kenkyū)*, vol. 39-2, 1991, pp. 6-10.
10. MBh, ed. F. Kielhorn, vol. 2, p. 366.
11. *Pradīpa* (in *Vaiyākaraṇamahābhāṣyam*, ed. Vedavrata, Rohtak: Haryaṇā Sāhitya Saṃsthānam, 5 vols, 1962-63), vol. 4, pp. 90-1.
12. The etymologically derived senses are, as mentioned in note 6 above, called *vyutpattinimittas*.
13. Cf. Yudhiṣṭhir Mimaṃsak, *Saṃskṛt Vyakaraṇ śastr ka itihas*, vol. 2, Sonipat: Rām Lāl Kapūr Trust, 1973, pp. 9-10.
14. VP 2.366-367. The reference to the second chapter of VP is to S. Iyer's edition: *The Vākyapadīya of Bhartṛhari* Kāṇḍa II , Delhi: Motilal Banarsidass, 1983.
15. Cf. H.P. Dvivedi, *Studies in Pāṇini*, Delhi: Inter-India Publications, 1977, pp. 12-15.
16. This term's etymological sense is as follows: *karma proktavantaḥ karmapravacanīyāḥ* (MBh, ed. Kielhorn, vol. 1, 1962, p. 346 (on P. 1.4.83)).
17. This term's etymological sense is as follows: *sarveṣām yan nāma tat sarvanāma* (MBh, vol.1, p. 88 (on P. 1.1.27)).
18. VP 1.59-60. The reference to the first chapter of VP is to S. Iyer's edition: *Vākyapadīya of Bhartṛhari* Kāṇḍa I, Poona: Deccan College Postgraduate and Research Institute, 1966.
19. Cf. P.1.1.68 '*svaṃ rūpaṃ śabdasyāśabdasaṃjñā*'.
20. VP 1.66.
21. For the meaning of '*vy-ati-ric*', see George Cardona, 'Anvaya and Vyatireka in Indian Grammar', *The Adyar Library Bulletin* 31-2, 1967-68, pp. 315-24. Cf. MBh, ed. Kielhorn, vol.1, pp. 461-2, p. 464. (on P.2.3.50); VP 3.14.6. (The reference to the third chapter of VP is to S. Iyer's edition: *Vākyapadīya of Bhartṛhari* Kāṇḍa III, part ii , Poona: Deccan College, 1973.)
22. VP 1.67.
23. See Cardona, 'Anvaya and Vyatireka in Indian Grammar', pp. 316-17. According to P.2.3.50 '*ṣaṣṭhī śeṣe*', sixth case affixes mean relations other than *kāraka*s and than the meanings of the nominal stems.
24. In this phrase, one may suspect that the mere meaning of '*puruṣa*' is surpassed and that, consequently, the first case affix cannot be appended

to the nominal stem '*puruṣa*'. For this problem, see Cardona 'Anvaya and Vyatireka in Indian Grammar', pp. 316-24; MBh ed. Kielhorn, vol.1, 1962, p. 464; VP 3.14.6.

25. See, for example, Puṇyarāja's commentary on VP 2.366; Helārāja's commentary on VP 3.1.2.
26. Nathan Salmon, *Frege's Puzzle*, Cambridge: The MIT Press, 1986, p. 7.
27. Salmon calls such a theory the verbal theory of information value. (*Frege's Puzzle*, pp. 71-2).
28. Salmon, *Frege's Puzzle*, p. 72.
29. Cf. Salmon, *Frege's Puzzle*, pp. 71-2.
30. Saul A. Kripke, *Naming and Necessity*, Cambridge: Harvard University Press, 1980, pp. 68-70.
31. Kripke, *Naming and Necessity*, pp. 127-8.
32. Hilary Putnam, 'The Meaning of 'Meaning'', *Mind, Language and Reality*, Cambridge: Cambridge University Press, 1975, pp. 229-35.
33. Gareth Evans, *The Varieties of Reference*, Oxford: Clarendon Press, 1982, p. 31.
34. Kripke, *Naming and Necessity*, pp. 54-6.
35. For more details on this matter, see Keith S. Donnellan, 'The Contingent A Priori and Rigid Designators', *Contemporary Perspectives in the Philosophy of Language*, ed. Perer A. French, Theodore E. Uehling, Jr., and Howard K. Wettstein, Minneapolis: University of Minnesota Press, 1981, pp. 45-60; Salmon, *Frege's Puzzle*, pp. 138-42.
36. Nāgeśabhaṭṭa, a Pāṇinian grammarian of the eighteenth century, attaches importance to the fact that *yadṛcchāśabdas* refer to particular things. See his Uddyota (in *Vaiyākaraṇamahābhāṣyam*, ed. Vedavrata) vol.1, p.70.
37. Cf. MBh ed. Kielhorn, vol.1, p. 20; Mīmaṃsak, *Saṃskṛt Vyakaraṇ śastr ka itihas*, vol. 2, p. 9. Some Indian grammarians assert that the relation between a *yadṛcchāśabda* or a *saṃjñā* and its meaning is eternal, to the effect that the term is capable of denoting any object. This view is not useful for understanding the use of proper names in ordinary language. See VP 2.363-365.
38. One could ask, Socrates might not be called 'Socrates' in some possible worlds. Kripke admits this possibility. So how can he assert that 'Socrates' *rigidly* designates Socrates in all possible worlds? This point, however, is not crucial for his idea of rigid designators. See *Naming and Necessity*, pp. 77-8.

19

The Ways of Mystical Realization in the Kashmir Śaivism

HIROHISA TODA

INTRODUCTION

Hinduism seems to be polytheism worshipping plenty of gods, who figure in Vedas, Epics and Purāṇas and factually have been adored by native folk through the ages. We know that major Hindu sects such as Śaivism and Vaiṣṇavism developed the mythological thoughts into theological theories in the medieval period. In the process they seemed to be influenced by the orthodox philosophical traditions such as Sāṃkhya, Vedānta, etc. Hinduism constructed monotheistic systems in which either Śiva or Viṣṇu is regarded as the only Supreme God. Even monotheistic sects are liable to tolerate the worship of many deities as appearances of the Supreme One. They do not exclude mythology and magical folklore respected by common people in order to invite many to their own sects. This tendency is not only a marked characteristic of Hindu religious sects but is seen in the universal religions having spread all over the world. If a sect firmly insists on its monotheistic dogma and is intolerant of popular beliefs, then perhaps it can hardly attract common people. Such a sect would be exclusively for the religious elite, for instance, the school of Trika or so-called Kashmir Śaivism that will be treated in this essay.

But first I wish to raise a question: Why is it that the tradition of the Trika school has not flourished today while the Śaivasiddhānta occupies the main position among Śaivite schools? Both schools belong to the Āgamic Śaiva school that held the Śaivite sacred scriptures (Śaiva Āgama, Tantra)[1] in high esteem, and constructed systematic theories based on them. We know well that the Trika advocates monistic (nondualistic) theology while the Śaivasiddhānta asserts dualistic one. Then, as a historical fact, the former disappeared but the latter prospers. What factors decided the destinies of these two schools?

In this essay we see examine the way to liberation (*mokṣa, mukti*) in the Trika system, the so-called Kashmir Śaivism. Let us contrast it with that of the dualistic Śaivism, namely, the Śaivasiddhānta.

OUTLINE OF THOUGHTS AND PRACTICES IN THE DUALISTIC ŚAIVISM

Śaivasiddhānta is traditionally called the dualist (*dvaita*) or rather the pluralist, for it asserts plural principles (*tattvāni*) and has a tendency to argue for the theory of dualism-cum-nondualism (*dvaitādvaita*) or difference-in-identity (*bhedābheda*). In the Śaivasiddhānta system there are two levels of principles or categories of real existence, namely, triadic primary principles (*tattva-traya*) and thirty-six secondary principles (*ṣaṭtriṃśat-tattvāni*).

The three primary principles are Lord (*pati*), Cattle (*paśu*) and Fetter (*pāśa*). These show respectively the Supreme God Śiva (*para Śiva, parama Śiva*), the individual soul (*aṇu, ātman*), and the causes of or conditions that places the soul in bondage to the material world. These principles are severally real existence. The individual soul is bound by bonds such as minute innate pollution (*āṇava mala*), impression of deeds (*karman*), material cause of the impure world (*māyā*), so that it takes on a material body, and its ability becomes limited.[2] The individual beings should be born in the material world several times and act according to religious practices and duties so as to mature or consume (*paripāka*) the pollution (*mala*) clinging to the embodied soul.[3] It is explained that God Śiva creates the material world overflowing with sufferings in order to give the individual beings an opportunity to consume their pollution.

Most sects of Śaivism enumerate the thirty-six principles (*ṣaṭ-triṃśat-tattvāni*)[4] that include the twenty-five principles of the Sāṃkhya system.[5] This fact, however, does not show that the Śaivites uncritically accept the thoughts of the Sāṃkhya. Śaivites are favourably inclined towards the Yoga system that adds the Creator Īśvara as the highest principle to the twenty-five. Śaivites attempt to subsume the framework of the principles of the Sāṃkhya system and to surmount its mechanistic or atheistic dualism by adding eleven higher principles to the twenty-five.[6] Śaivites install the eleven principles, namely, *śiva-tattva, śakti-tattva, sadāśiva, īśvara, śuddhavidyā, māyā,* and five *kañcuka*s (*kāla, niyati, kalā, vidyā, rāga*)[7] beyond *puruṣa*. This '*puruṣa*' does not mean the soul or spirit isolated from the material world as the term in the Sāṃkhya system.[8] It means that the individual self dwells in the phenomenal world.

According to the Śaivasiddhānta, the individual self (*puruṣa*) is limited by five factors (*kañcuka*s) which originate from the material cause (*upādāna*) called *māyā*, while he is in bondage to the phenomenal world made up by the developing transformation (*pariṇāma*) of the twenty-four principles from *prakṛti* to the five elements (*pañca-bhūtāni*).[9] So the thirty-one principles evolved from *māyā* are said to belong to the impure pathway or region (*aśuddhādhvan*). In contrast, the remainding five principles belong to the pure pathway or region (*śuddhādhvan*), in which there occurs the change of the divine situation of the primary cause named *bindu*, *mahāmāyā*, etc.[10] Towards the beginning of the change, *bindu* as nucleus holds all potential powers within and rests in stillness in the same way as the Supreme God Śiva. So the first principle is named *śiva-tattva*, which does not indicate God Śiva Himself.[11] The Supreme God Śiva is unchangeable and separated from all other principles. When the nucleus (*bindu*) is urged by Him, then *bindu* changes into *śakti-tattva*, *sadāśiva*, *īśvara* and *śuddhavidyā* in proportion to the balance of radiation of the divine powers. These are the powers of knowledge (*jñānaśakti*), of action (*kriyāśakti*) and of will (*icchāśakti*), which constitute omnipotence (*sarvārthakartṛtva*) and omniscience (*sarvajñatva*).[12] In this way, the thirty-six principles in the Śaivasiddhānta system are divided into two categories, namely, the impure (*aśuddha*) and the pure (*śuddha*). Further all of them belong to the category of bondage (*pāśa*) being separated from Supreme Śiva as the Lord (*pati*). Hence occur the double discontinuities or gaps inside and outside of the thirty-six principles.

The theory of the thirty-six principles is not only used for explaining the cosmogony but also one of the ladders of religious practices. These are, for example, yoga discipline, Tantric mysteries or esoteric rites, and daily rituals of worship. Attempting to approach the state of Śiva, yogins use the thirty-six categories as objects of meditation. As an initiatory ceremony at a Śaivite temple, a venerable master performs the ritual of symbolic assimilation (*nyāsa*). Touching parts of the body of his disciple, the master recites the corresponding incantations (*mantra*s) symbolically identifying each of these parts with the thirty-six principles.[13] Strictly it must be said that anybody performing such religious rites can hardly attain the supreme state, because there is discontinuity between the impure principles and the pure ones. Even if such a person attained the supreme state, i.e. *śiva-tattva*, still he/she could not become God Śiva Himself but only become similar to Him. Even though the person may think that he/she may be similar to God Śiva, there still is an absolute difference between the individual and God. Hence this system is called dualistic Śaivism.

It is difficult for a person to lead oneself to liberation (*mokṣa, mukti*). So it is necessary to devote him/herself to faith in God Śiva Who is merciful enough to relieve His creatures from miseries. In actual religious practices, a venerable master (*ācārya, guru*) substitutes for God Śiva and executes esoteric rituals promising future liberation to his disciples. Novices or ordinary believers should perform daily rituals of worship (*pūjā*) of God and preparatory rites of purification for initiation (*dīkṣā*) into the sect.[14] These religious practices are not contradictory to traditional ways or popular beliefs. It is important for the followers of the Śaivasiddhānta to perform religious actions such as daily rituals of worship, for the physical actions are effective in consuming the material pollution (*mala*) clinging to the individual soul.[15] Of course, the religious rites require high ability of the master and ardent devotion of disciples or believers to the master.

Common people living in the impure material world are quite distant from the pure region of God. However, if they ardently pray to God Śiva and solemnly perform rituals of worship in daily life, they may possibly approach the pure. And then God Śiva confers His grace (*anugraha*) upon them as a reward for their devotion (*bhakti*) and helps them climb up the higher steps towards Himself. Perhaps, it would be correct to interpret, in accordance with the doctrine of predestination, that since God does bestow His power (*śaktipāta*) of grace on them, people do begin to believe in God.[16] The gate to liberation is open to everybody regardless of wealth, social status, class discrimination, etc. The first requisite for bliss is faith, piousness. Probably this perspective is easily understood by many people. In addition, the manner of the religious practices in the Śaivasiddhānta system is not so extraordinary as to offend public order or common sense. The method is moderate enough to encourage ethics and morality, which a ruler or governing body favours.

As a historical fact, the Śaivasiddhānta order developed under the patronage of kings of several dynasties, i.e. Kalacuri, Cālukya, Coḷa, etc. The kings respected some of the Śaivasiddhānta teachers as royal preceptors at their courts, and offered patronage to build religious facilities such as temples and monasteries. The monasteries seemed to play the role of social and charitable institutions, which took care of the weak and the poor.[17] These religio-sociological circumstances brought the Śaivasiddhānta a long success while the theological efforts bore good results.

THOUGHTS AND PRACTICES OF THE MONISTIC ŚAIVISM

The Trika school, or the so-called Kashmir Śaivism,[18] was founded by the legendary master Vasugupta (*c.* AD 800-850) who wrote the *Śiva-sūtra.* His followers such as Bhaṭṭa Kallaṭa (*c.* AD 825-875), Somānanda (*c.* AD 875-925), etc., attempted to construct the nondualistic or monistic (*advaita, advaya*) theological system.[19] They compared, examined and synthesized different doctrines based on the Śaivite sacred scriptures (Śaiva Āgama). An outcome of such attempts is the *Tantrāloka* of Abhinavagupta (*c.* AD 950-1020). This is an encyclopedic work on Śaivite thoughts and practices referring to various traditions and doctrines and trying to integrate them. The Trika, literally meaning 'triple', seems to have consisted of three systems, namely, Āgama, Spanda and Pratyabhijñā.[20] The Āgama tradition is to be respected as the most authoritative basis of Śaivism. The Spanda system[21] aims at providing a new method for the mystic practice of yoga, which is different from the orthodox yoga of Patañjali. The Pratyabhijñā system appears to be seemingly comprehensive of every aspect of religion but is really oriented toward intellectualism (infra).

What is the first criterion of monistic Śaivism? Perhaps it is the dogma that the individual being is essentially the same as the Supreme God Śiva, or that the individual is identical with God Śiva. According to the monistic Śaivists, including the Trika, the individual has the same nature (*svarūpa*) and power (*śakti*) as God Śiva. Yet the individual is not aware of the truth on account of His power of concealment (*tirodhāna-śakti*). Perhaps the cause or the situation of bondage is an ignorance (*ajñāna*) of the essential nature of the individual self. Ignorance or imperfect knowledge (*apūrṇa jñāna*)[22] is sometimes symbolically called 'pollution'(*mala*) which is not the material thing at all.[23] Ignorance is of two types, namely, the individual or experiential (*pauruṣa ajñāna*) and the intellectual (*bauddha ajñāna*). The former can decrease by carrying on religious practices, i.e. the rite of initiation (*dīkṣā*), etc. The latter can diminish by studying proper (i.e. the monistic Śaivite) scriptures and treatises.[24] When ignorance turns into awareness, then bondage turns into liberation. Awareness of the essential nature of the individual is self-recognition of Godhood.[25]

While it is true that everyone has potential for divinity, it must be borne in mind that the aptitude for realizing divinity differs from individual to individual. Then the Trika has prepared several ways or ladders of mystical realization according to individual disposition, ability and intention. The following are the three or four means (*upāya*) and the six courses (*adhvan*).

Abhinavagupta enumerates four means (*upāya*s) as the four causes of realization through the discipline of yoga in his *Tantrāloka,* chapters 1 to 5, etc. He adds one, i.e. *anupāya* to the three means mentioned in the *Mālinīvijayottaratantra*[26] and the *Śivasūtra* of Vasugupta.
(1) *Anupāya* (literally meaning 'non-means') is a case wherein the truth is realized immediately without yoga discipline. That is, for example, enlightenment with some stimulus given by a reliable teacher.[27] *Anupāya* seems to correspond to *pratyabhijñā.*[28] (2) *Śāmbhavopāya* ('the means of Śaṃbhu, i.e. Śiva') is a case of mystical realization by the intuition (*parāmarśa*) beyond concept (*nirvikalpa*), in which will-power (*icchā*) is the important factor.[29] (3) *Śāktopāya* ('the means of Śakti') is a case of self-consciousness (*svātma-saṃvitti*) with the refining (*saṃskāra*) of concept (*vikalpa*) through repeated meditation (*bhāvanā*) with judgment (*niścaya*) by contemplative inquiry (*tarka*)[30] as the best among six components of yoga for Śaivite.[31] (4) *Āṇavopāya* ('the means of the minute, i.e. the individual') is another case of self-consciousness with the refining of concept through the yoga discipline. There are several ways of using various objects such as intellectual mind (*buddhi*), vital air (*prāṇa*), physical body (*deha*) and other external objects (*bāhya*).[32] The last one, the external objects, includes *maṇḍala,* alter, vessel, string of beads, book, *liṅga,* musical instrument, cloth, plastering (or fresco), idol, human body, etc.[33] These items, we presume, are not only to be used as objects of meditation but rather as equipments for rituals.

The six courses (*ṣaḍ-adhvan*)[34] are different ladders all leading to the religious goal. According to Abhinavagupta, these six are divided into two categories, namely, the expressing and the expressed. The former belong to the category of action (*kriyā*) relating to time (*kāla*), while the latter belong to the category of form (*mūrti*) relating to place (*deśa*).[35] The courses of the expressing category are: (1) the course of phoneme (*varṇa*), (2) of incantation (*mantra*),[36] and (3) of unit concerning word (*pada*). These are symbols representing hierarchy of divinity ruled by the Supreme God. The courses of the expressed category are: (4) of the causal function (*kalā*), (5) of principle or cosmic category (*tattva*), and (6) of realm of the universe (*bhuvana*). These represent the cosmogonic evolution emanating from the Supreme God. The six courses serve as intermediaries between the Supreme God and individuals so as to gradually progress with religious practice towards the mystical realization of God. In other words, the six courses are meaningful in the soteriological context rather than in the cosmogony one.

The course of the thirty-six principles (*ṣaṭtriṃśat-tattvāni*) is the most noteworthy of the six courses, for it is frequently used for religious practices such as yoga discipline and rites of initiation. Although the number of principles is the same and the names of ones are similar, the thirty-six principles of the monistic Śaivism are quite different from that of the dualistic. In the Śaivasiddhānta system, *śiva-tattva* is not the Supreme God Śiva Himself but one of the situations of the nucleus (*bindu*). In the Trika system, *śiva-tattva* is but God Śiva Himself, Who is the ultimate subject and primary agent causing every phenomenon in the world being immanent in Himself. *Śakti-tattva* is the active aspect of Śiva as a true agent, and inseparable from Him.[37] The Śaivasiddhānta defines *māyā* as the material cause (*upādāna*) of evolution in the impure region (*aśuddhādhvan*). On the other hand the Trika asserts that *māyā* is one of the powers (*śakti*s) of Śiva, which is the function of concealment (*tirodhāna*) causing obstruction in the realization of the truth.[38] As mentioned earlier, the principles of the Śaivasiddhānta system are divided into two categories—the pure and the impure pathways—because of the difference in mechanism or constitution. On the contrary, the Trika considers that there is no discontinuity among the principles. A series of them are manifestations (*ābhāsa*) of Śiva Himself by His active power (*śakti*). Accordingly, the thirty-six principles are very effective in religious practices such as yoga discipline, esoteric rites, etc., which require the regular order of ladder and the consistency of constitution. When a person aiming at liberation improves him/herself in the religious practice following the course set out in the Trika system, then the person may easily come closer to the goal. There are no flights missing in the series of steps leading to the top, which is, the realization of Śiva. It is different from the Śaivasiddhānta system.

The pattern of the six courses probably appeared in the early tradition of Śaivism before the systematization by Abhinavagupta. The six courses occur in the Śaiva Āgama such as the *Svacchandatantra,* the *Mālinīvijayottaratantra,* the *Netratantra,* etc., where these courses are used for the initiation rites (*dīkṣā*).[39] The Śaivasiddhānta also maintains that the six courses are useful for initiation, but at the same time its six courses have several differences with those of the Trika system in the details, for example, the constituent parts of each course, the meanings of these, the relation among courses, etc. Similarly the six courses are found even in earlier texts such as the *Sātvatasaṃhitā* (see Chaper 19 dealing with initiation) of the Pāñcarātra school of Vaiṣṇavism.[40]

Abhinavagupta respected the previous teachings on the six courses and attempted to adapt these to the Trika system in the latter half of his *Tantrāloka* dealing with initiation. According to him, the initiation or consecration (*dīkṣā*) consists of two processes, namely, the initiation of precept (*samaya-dīkṣā*) and the consecration for final liberation (*nirvāṇa-dīkṣā*).[41] The former is the rite of initiating precept so as to grant a believer the qualification of a Śaivite. The latter is the rite of purification, that is, consuming the pollution through the performance of symbolic assimilation (*nyāsa*) of the body parts of a disciple with the constituent parts of one of the six courses (*ṣaḍ-adhvan*), so as to guarantee the liberation at death. After the initiation executed by a venerable master (*ācārya, guru*), competent disciples may try to exercise the means (*śāmbhavopāya, śāktopāya* or *āṇavopāya*). Similarly, ordinary believers may perform daily rituals of worship by means of the six courses, following the method taught by the master. Moreover, Abhinavagupta explains the bestowing of God's power (*śaktipāta*) of grace (*anugraha*) in detail. He attempts to convince the believer of the effect of rituals, the importance of esoteric connection between a master and disciples. And he emphasizes the necessity of unconditional devotion to God Śiva and to the master as a substitute for Him.

Here, we must recall that in the monistic Śaivite system, the pollution (*mala*) is nothing but ignorance (*ajñāna*) of the essential nature of the individual self, and the liberation (*mokṣa*) is awareness (*jñāna*) of it. As regards the view that pollution was physical matter, the Śaivasiddhānta asserts that physical acts such as the rite of initiation and the daily rituals of worship could be effective in consuming the pollution. In the monistic Śaivism, daily rituals, etc., are not indispensable for liberation but subordinate to it, yet the immediate self-recognition, that is, *anupāya* is to be regarded as the best way to liberation. In spite of such intellectualism, why did Abhinavagupta explain about rituals in great detail? It could perhaps be that he was aware of the religio-sociological importance of the rites of passage, the duties of daily rituals and the leadership of a master in order to found, sustain and develop a newly rising religious association or movement, that is, the Trika. Abhinavagupta attempts to integrate various traditional teachings into the novel monistic system in his *Tantrāloka*. However, the fruit of his effort seems to be too complicated to be widely received by people.

METAPHYSICAL THOUGHTS OF THE PRATYABHIJÑĀ SYSTEM

The Pratyabhijñā system completes the monistic philosophy of the Trika school. Somānanda suggested the basic idea of the system in his *Śivadṛṣṭi*. Utpaladeva (AD 900-950) rearranged it and wrote a systematic textbook, the *Īśvarapratyabhijñā-kārikā* and its auto-commentaries advocating the doctrine more definitively. Abhinavagupta wrote two commentaries on it, namely, the *Īśvarapratyabhijñā-vivṛtivimarśinī* and the *Īśvarapratyabhijñā (laghu-)vimarśinī*. The descriptions in these commentaries are more consistent and successful in clarifying the idea of the monistic Śaivism than the *Tantrāloka*.

The word '*pratyabhijñā*' literally means 'recognition' and philosophically means 'self-recognition of the essential nature' in the soteriology context of the Pratyabhijñā system. Moreover, esoterically *pratyabhijñā* means that God Śiva recognizes Himself becoming the individual self, for He is considered to be the true agent of recognition.[42] Advocates of the Pratyabhijñā system deny the ordinary view of dualism making a distinction between the mind and the matter, or between the sentient (*ajaḍa*) and the insentient (*jaḍa*). They assert that the universe (*viśva*) is filled with the sentient, rather it is enshrouded in the divine consciousness (*saṃvid*), that is, God Śiva.[43] Similarly they deny another ordinary view of dualism setting up a discrimination between subjectivity (*pramātṛ, grāhaka*) and objectivity (*prameya, grāhya*). And they insist that the universe be filled with the subjective, for it is essentially identified with the ultimate subject (*paramārtha pramātṛ*), that is, God Śiva.[44] These may be the second and the third reasons why the Pratyabhijñā system is regarded as the monistic in Śaivism.

According to the Pratyabhijñā system, the Supreme God (*parameśvara*) Śiva is the ultimate subject, the true agent of all acts (*sarvakartṛ*), and the universal consciousness (*viśvamayī saṃvid*) containing every thing and causing every phenomenon in the world.[45] So that God Śiva is considered to be the transcendent beyond the universe (*viśvottīrṇa*) and the identical with the universe (*viśvarūpa, viśvātmaka*).[46] Even though individual matters in the phenomenal world seem to be physical and insentient, truly all of these are conscious substances (*cetana*) or sentient subjects (*ajaḍa pramātṛ*) being inside of Śiva as the universal consciousness. These are everlasting perfected existences that usually take rest (*viśrānta*) on Śiva in tranquility. When Śiva reflects on Himself and focuses upon an internal object resting on Himself, in other words, He controls the power of the intentional act of consciousness (*vimarśa*)[47] upon it, of His own voluntary will (*svātantrya*), then the internal object becomes the manifestation (*ābhāsa*) as an external thing with limiting factors such as time and place. And then the thing is as real as it manifests.[48] Similarly, individual subjects or agents are truly within Śiva and become manifestation with limiting factors owing to the power of Śiva.[49]

Philosophers of other schools conjecture on the cosmogony and assume material cause or prompting cause, and the process of creation or destruction of the world. So they attempt to discuss each other in vain. Advocates of the Pratyabhijñā system asserts that in reality there happen neither creation (*sṛṣṭi*) nor destruction (*saṃhāra*) of the universe. The truth revealed in the system is that there happen either manifestation (*ābhāsa, unmeṣa*) or concealment (*tirodhāna, nimeṣa*) of the everlasting perfected existence within Śiva.[50] This might be named the doctrine of 'realistic manifestation (*ābhāsa*)', which is quite different from the doctrine of illusion (*māyā*) asserted by the Advaita Vedāntin.

Let us look again at the dualistic theory of the thirty-six principles (*tattvas*), which is meaningful in explaining the cosmogony in accordance with the Śaivasiddhānta system. The theory, however, encounters difficulties in utility for religious practices on account of those double discontinuities inside and outside of the principles. Now the monistic theory of the thirty-six principles is meaningless to explain the cosmogony as long as the doctrine of realistic manifestation is maintained in the Pratyabhijñā system. According to the monistic system, there happens no creation but manifestation in the world, and all the principles are also manifestations of Śiva. Factually, the thirty-six principles are taken into consideration in the Pratyabhijñā treatises. We find two reasons for it. First, the teachers of the Pratyabhijñā have respect for the traditional doctrine on the principles occurring in the Śaivite sacred scriptures (Śaiva Āgama). Second, they admit the ladder of the principles to be useful for the religious practices aiming at liberation. We know, however, that physical acts such as the rite of initiation and the daily rituals are not necessary for liberation in the

Trika system which is inclined towards intellectualism.

The Pratyabhijñā system is optimistic about everything. According to this system, for example, the power of concealment (*tirodhāna*) of Śiva brings about the illusive factor (*māyā*) which conceals the truth and puts the unlimited conscious substance into limitation so as to make it manifest as an individual subject (called *māyā-pramātṛ* or *mita pramātṛ*) or an object.[51] Such an illusive function is also attributed to the grace of God Śiva, for He is so kind as to give us the opportunity for enjoyment in everyday life.[52] Empiric behaviour requires differentiation between subject and object. The differentiation might be caused by Śiva. So the fulfillment of empiric behaviour could be an evidence for proving the existence of Śiva.[53] In case this assumption is overestimated and applied excessively, it might lead to an uncritical acceptance of the existing situation, which is perhaps filled with evil. Abhinavagupta actually says that there is no bondage in truth.[54]

CONCLUSION

Śaivism built up the monotheistic theology according to the Śaivite sacred scriptures (Śaiva Āgama), yet it separated into two opposite sects or movements, namely, the dualistic system of Śaivasiddhānta school, and the monistic system of the Trika school (so-called Kashmir Śaivism). We have seen earlier the soteriological views of both systems, and the reasons why the Śaivasiddhānta prospers but the Trika disappeared. Needless to say, outward factors or the historical and sociological conditions invited the different destinations, yet we find inward factors or the theories and practices respecting liberation.

The Śaivasiddhānta maintains that the individual soul is separated far from God Śiva and too powerless and polluted to get closer to Him, and then a person aiming at liberation should be devoted to faith in Śiva, Who is so merciful as to relieve. According to this system, since the cause of bondage is material pollution clinging to the individual soul, the physical religious practices are effective in consuming the pollution. These views are probably acceptable to ordinary people. The former view is in accord with how this world is full of evil and suffering, and the latter view gives them good motivation for the rite of passage or the daily rituals, which seem to be easy for them to do. Thus, the thoughts and the practices of Śaivasiddhānta are attractive enough for people to develop the religious association.

The Trika asserts that the individual self is essentially the same as

God Śiva, but is not aware of the truth, and this ignorance is the cause or the situation of bondage, therefore a person aiming at liberation has only to recognize one's own nature by oneself. Thus, the teachings of the Trika basically incline towards intellectualism and respect for independent spirit; in other words, these are fit for the intelligent elite or the self-important one. Surely, the Trika treatises, i.e. the *Tantrāloka,* etc., refer to several ways to liberation including the ways of mystical realization such as the three or four means (*upāya*) and the six courses (*ṣaḍ-adhvan*). Nonetheless the way of self-recognition (*pratyabhijñā*) is considered to be primary, and the ways of rituals, etc., are regarded as secondary. Even though Abhinavagupta made efforts to adapt the various ways of rituals to the Trika system, yet his efforts were not so fruitful as to prolong the heyday of the system. The teachings might not attract people of common sense. We do find, however, the influence of the Trika mysticism upon the tradition of the Tantric school of Śākta. In addition to such a tendency of intellectualism, perhaps the above-mentioned view of the Pratyabhijñā system was so idealistic as to keep people away from the conversion, for ordinary people were actually confronted with irrational difficulties in this real world.

TEXT AND ABBREVIATIONS

GNP: *Gurunāthaparāmarśa* of Madhurāja, ed. by P.N. Pushp, Srinagar, 1960.
IPK: *Īśvarapratyabhijñākārikā* of Utpaladeva, ed. by R. Torella, Roma, 1994.
IPV: *Īśvarapratyabhijñāvimarśinī* of Abhinavagupta, ed. and tr. by K.A.S. Iyer and K.C. Pandey, 1938, 1950, 1954.
IPVV: *Īśvarapratyabhijñāvivṛtivimarśinī* of Abhinavagupta, ed. by M. Kaul Śāstrī, Srinagar, 1938, 1941, 1949.
MVT: *Mālinīvijayottaratantra,* ed. by M. Kaul Śāstrī, Srinagar, 1922.
PH: *Pratyabhijñāhṛdaya* of Kṣemarāja, ed. and tr. by Jaideva Singh, Delhi, 1963.
ŚD: *Śivadṛṣṭi* of Somānanda, ed. by M. Kaul Śāstrī, Srinagar, 1934.
ŚDV: *Śivadṛṣṭivṛtti* of Utpaladeva, see *ŚD.*
ŚP: *Śaivaparibhāṣā* of Śivāgrayogin, ed. by R. Balasubramanian and V.K.S.N. Raghavan, tr. by S.S. Suryanarayana, Madras, 1982.
ŚS: *Śivasūtra* of Vasugupta, ed. and tr. by Jaideva Singh, Delhi, 1979.
ŚSV: *Śivasūtravimarśinī* of Kṣemarāja, see *ŚS.*
TA: *Tanırāloka* of Abhinavagupta, ed. by Mukund Rām Śāstrī, Srinagar, 1918-1938; reprinted by R.C. Dwivedi and Navajivan Rastogi, Delhi, 1987.
TAV: *Tantrālokaviveka* of Rājānaka Jayaratha, see *TA.*
TP: *Tattvaprakāśa* of Bhojadeva.
TPV: *Tattvaprakāśavṛtti* of Aghoraśiva.

NOTES

1 Here I would like to use broadly the name 'Śaiva Āgama' as a general term for the scriptures concerning the worship of Śiva and Śakti, namely, 10 Śivāgamas, 18 Rudrāgamas, 64 Bhairavāgamas and Śaktitantras. It was thought that Śivāgamas are dualistic, Rudrāgamas are dualistic-cum-nondualistic and Bhairavāgamas are nondualistic, so that the former two groups belong to the Śaivasiddhānta and the third group belongs to the Trika. Although Śaktitantras are practised by the Śākta school that worships Goddess Śakti, these are respected by the Trika also. Cf. K.C. Pandey, *Abhinavagupta: A Historical and Philosophical Study*, 2nd ed., Varanasi, 1963, pp. 140-143; Alexis Sanderson, 'Śaivism and the Tantric Tradition', in S. Sutherland et al., eds., *The World's Religions*, London, 1988, pp. 668-670; Mark S.G. Dyczkowski, *The Canon of the Śaivāgama and the Kubjikā Tantras of the Western Kaula Tradition*, New York, 1988. However, such characterization is not strict but conventional. Even if a scripture is classified into Śivāgama or Rudrāgama, it is likely that a number of monistic descriptions are found in it. Even though an authority like Abhinavagupta interprets a scripture in the way of a nondualist, perhaps the purport of the scripture is literally dualistic. Cf. Alexis Sanderson, 'The Doctrines of the Mālinīvijayottaratantra', in T. Goudriaan, ed., *Ritual and Speculation in Early Tantrism*, New York, 1992.

2 According to *Tattvaprakāśa* and its *Vṛtti*, the individual soul is bound by five factors, namely, *āṇava-mala, karman, māyā, bindu* as a material cause of the pure world, and *rodha-śakti,* i.e. the obstructive power of concealment of Śiva.

3 *TPV* 6: *ata eva mayottīrṇatvān malarahitatvāc ca vidyāvidyeśvaraprāpter aparamuktitvam/ TPV* 11: *malaparipākasya śaktipātadvāreṇa mokṣa-hetutvāt/* Cf. Rohan A. Dunuwila, *Śaiva Siddhānta Theology: A Context for Hindu-Christian Dialogue*, Delhi, 1985, p. 132.

4 For details on several views on the thirty-six *tattva*s, see *ŚP*, p. 136; pp. 182-185. Cf. K. Sivaraman, *Śaivism in Philosophical Perspective: A Study of the Formative Concepts, Problems and Methods of Śaiva Siddhānta,* Varanasi, 1973, pp. 220-247. On the theory of principles by the authoritative interpreter Aghoraśiva in *TPV*, see the reliable study of Jorg Gengnagel, *Māyā, Puruṣa und Śiva: Die dualistische Tradition des Śivaismus nach Aghoraśivācāryas Tattvaprakāśavṛtti,* Wiesbaden, 1996.

5 The twenty-five *tattva*s are enumerated in the *Sāṃkhyakārikā* of Īśvarakṛṣṇa.

6 On the number of *tattva*s in various texts, see Hajime Nakamura, *Vedānta Tetsugaku no Hatten*, Tokyo, 1955, pp. 351-352.

7 *TP* 21-22.

8 *Sāṃkhyakārikā* 22-38.

9 On *pariṇāma* of *māyā* in the Śaivism, see Sivaraman, *Śaivism in Philosophical Perspective*, pp. 115-120.

10 According to Sivaraman, *Śaivism in Philosophical Perspective*, p. 552, n. 68, the synonyms of *bindu* are given in the *Ratnatraya* (of Śrīkaṇṭhācārya) 70, as following: *śabdatattvam aghoṣā vāg brahmā kuṇḍalinī dhruvam*

vidyā śaktiḥ parā nādo mahāmāyā.

11 *ŚP*, p. 183: *asya(=bindoś) ca śivādhiṣṭhitatvena śivatattvavyapadeśaḥ/* *ŚP*, p. 185: *anye tu pañcānām api śivadvārakaṃ lakṣaṇaṃ vadanti/ jñānamātrayuktena paramātmanādhiṣṭhitaṃ tattvaṃ śivatattvaṃ/*

12 *TP* and *TPV* 27-30.

13 Jun Takashima, 'Tantrism', in *Iwanami Kouza Touyou Shisou 6: Indo Shisou 2*, Tokyo, 1988, pp. 135-137.

14 For details on *dīkṣā,* see Hélène Brunner-Lachaux, *Somaśambhupaddhati,* vol. 3, Paris, 1977, introduction; Chaps. 1-5.

15 Hélène Brunner, 'Jñāna and Kriyā: Relation between Theory and Practice in the Śaivāgamas', in *Rituals and Speculation in Early Tantrism*, New York, 1992, pp. 11-13. P.S. Filliozat, 'The Concept of *Adhvan* in Śaivasiddhānta', *Wiener Zeitschrift für die Kunde Südasiens und Archiv für Indische Philosophie* 38 (1994).

16 Such view as the predestination seems to be influenced by the view of the Trika. Cf. Brunner, *Somaśambhupaddhati*, vol. 3, p. viii; Jun Takashima, 'Kashmir Śiva-ha ni okeru *upāya* to *śaktipāta* no Taikei', *Shūkyou Kenkyū* 60, 3 (1986), p. 70.

17 Dunuwila, *Śaiva Siddhānta Theology*, pp. 35-44.

18 This name was provisionally begun to use in the pioneering study: *Kashmir Shaivaism* by J.C. Chatterji, Srinagar, 1914.

19 Sanderson ('The Doctrines of the Mālinīvijayottaratantra', 1992, n. 28) reports the sources of the terms meaning the 'nondualism'. For example, *śivādvaitam* occurs in *GNP* 14b and *ŚDV*, p. 36; *śivādvaitapakṣaḥ* in *ŚDV*, p. 88; *śivādvayam* in *ŚDV*, p. 89; *śivādvayavādaḥ* in *IPVV*, vol. 3, p. 406; *īśvarādvaitam* occurs in *GNP* 40; *īśvarādvayavādaḥ* in *ŚDV*, p. 36, etc.

20 This is, however, one of etymologies of the name 'Trika'. Others are, for instance, the triad of *Śiva*, *Śakti* and *Nara*; the three levels of *śakti*, namely, *Parā* (supreme state), *Parāparā* (supreme-cum-nonsupreme state) and *Aparā* (nonsupreme state), etc.

21 For details on the Spanda system, see the magnificent works by Mark S.G. Dyczkowski, *The Doctrine of Vibration*, New York, 1987; *The Stanzas on Vibration*, Varanasi, 1994.

22 *MVT* 1.23cd: *malam ajñānam icchanti saṃsārāṅkurakāraṇam/* This passage is cited in *ŚSV* 1.2. See *TA* 1.25-26; *TAV* 1.26: *ajñānaśabdasya apūrṇajñānam artha iti/*

23 In the monistic system, *āṇava mala, māyīya mala* and *kārma mala* are nothing but incomplete awareness of Śivahood. *IPK* 3.15-16; *ŚDV*, p. 13. Cf. Sanderson, 'The Doctrine of Mālinīvijayottaratantra', pp. 287-289.

24 On *pauruṣa ajñāna*, see *TA* 1.41-43; 1.48-49. Also on *bauddha ajñāna*, see *TA* 1.36-37; 1.47; 1.50-51. Cf. Swami Laksman Jee, *Kashmir Śaivism: The Secret Supreme*, Srinagar, 1985, p. 102.

25 *TA* 1.155-157.

26 *MVT* 2.20-23. Cf. Takashima, '*upāya* to *śaktipāta* no Taikei', p. 59; n. 15.

27 *TA* 2.49ab: *guror vākyād yuktipracayaracanonmārjanavaśāt samāśvāsāc chāstraṃ prati samuditād vāpi kathitāt/*

28 It is suggested in *TA* 2.48cd: *idam uktaṃ tathā śrīmat-Somānandādi-deśikaiḥ.* In *TAV* 2.48, Jayaratha cites passages from *Śivadṛṣṭi*. Somānanda

does not apparently use the term '*pratyabhijñā*' in his *Śivadṛṣṭi*, but he surely has such an idea.

29 *TA* 3.274: *nirvikalpe parāmarśe śāmbhavopāyanāmani/* *TA* 1.144-146; 3.269.

30 *TA* 4.2-4; 4.9; *TAV* 5.5.

31 According to Patañjali's *Yogasūtra* 2.29, the yoga system consists of eight components (*aṣṭāṅga*), namely, *yama, niyama, āsana, pratyāhāra, prāṇāyāma, dhāraṇā, dhyāna, samādhi.* But Śaivites adopt another yoga system that is constituted of six components (*ṣaḍaṅga*), namely, *prāṇāyāma, pratyāhāra, dhyāna, dhāraṇā, tarka, samādhi.* *TA* 4.13-16; *TAV* 4.15-16, etc. Cf. Navjivan Rastogi, 'The Yogic Disciplines in the Monistic Śaiva Tantric Traditions of Kashmir: Threefold, Fourfold, and Six-Limbed', in *Ritual and Speculation in Early Tantrism*, New York, 1992. It is well known that these six components of yoga occur in the *Maitri Upaniṣad* 6.18 and the *Amṛtabindu Upaniṣad.*

32 *TA* and *TAV* 5.1-7; 5.157.

33 *TA* 6.3-4a: *maṇḍalaṃ sthaṇḍilam pātram akṣasūtraṃ sapustakam/ liṅgaṃ tūraṃ paṭaḥ pustaṃ pratimā mūrtir eva ca// ity ekādaśadhā bāhyam ...*

34 Cf. André Padoux, *Vāc: The Concept of the Word in Selected Hindu Tantras*, tr. into English by Jacques Gontier, New York, 1990, Chap. 6 'The Sixfold Course', p. 330f.; Brunner, *Somaśambhupaddhati*, vol. 3, pp. xiii-xxii.

35 *TA* 6.22ab; 6.34-35.

36 On *varṇa* in Tantric texts, see Padoux, *Vāc*, Chap. 5 'The Phonematic Emanation', p. 223f. On the magical power of *mantra*, see Jun Takashima, 'Tantrism ni okeru Kotoba no Jyuryoku', in *Iwanami Kouza Touyou Shisou 7: Indo Shisou 3*, Tokyo, 1989.

37 *IPVV* 3.1.1-2, vol. 3, pp. 256-265. Cf. Chatterji, *Kashmir Shaivaism*, pp. 62-65; Jaideva Singh, *Śiva Sūtras: The Yoga of Supreme Identity*, Delhi, 1979, p. xxii.

38 *IPK* 3.1.7cd-8: *tirodhānakarī māyābhidhā punaḥ// bhede tv ekarase bhāte 'hantayānātmanīkṣite/ śūnye buddhau śarīre vā māyāśaktir vijṛmbhate//* *IPV* 3.1.8, vol. 2, p. 234: *parameśvarasya māyāśaktiḥ.*

39 Cf. Padoux, *Vāc*, p. 331.

40 For details, see Brunner, *Somaśambhupaddhati*, vol. 3, pp. xvi-xix; Padoux, *Vāc,* p. 332; Hiromichi Hikita, *Hindu Tantrism no Kenkyū*, Tokyo, 1997, pp. 439-440.

41 On *dīkṣā* in the *Tantrāloka,* there are excellent studies by Jun Takashima: *La dīkṣā selon le Tantrāloka d' Abhinavagupta*, doctoral dissertation, Paris, 1990; '*Tantrāloka* ni okeru *dīkṣā:* Kashmir Śiva-ha ni okeru Initiation Girei', *Tokyo Daigaku Shūkyou Nenpou* 1 (1983), pp. 13-26, etc.

42 *IPV* 1.1.1, vol. 1, pp. 36-38.

43 *IPV* 1.1.2(1), vol. 1, p. 56: *yadi sa na prakāśate tathā ca jaḍaḥ na ca jaḍasya etat yuktam ity uktam nāpi ajaḍasya tasmāt saṃvitprakāśa eva ghaṭādiprakāśaḥ,... /*

44 *IPV* 1.5.12, vol. 1, p. 246: *tat sakalo'yaṃ tattvabhūtabhāvabhuvana-saṃbhāraḥ saṃvidi viśrāntaḥ tathā bhavati iti ... /*

45 *IPK* 1.4.8: *tan mayā dṛśyate dṛṣṭo'yaṃ sa ity āmṛśaty api/ grāhya-*

grāhakatābhinnāv arthau bhātaḥ pramātari// *IPV* 1.5.1, vol. 1, pp. 196-197: *avabhāsanam tat paramārthapramātari śuddhacinmaye antaḥsthitavatām tena saha aikātmyam,... /*

46 *IPV* 1.5.15-16, vol. 1, pp. 267-268: *sarvāḥ śaktīḥ kartṛtvaśaktiḥ aiśvarya-ātmā samākṣipati/ ... prakāśātmā parameśvaraḥ svātmānaṃ jñātrekarūpatvāt ajñeyam api jñeyīkaroti... yato hi ayaṃ ātmānaṃ parāmṛśati tato viśvanirbharatvāt tathā nīlāditvena cakāsti/* *IPV* 1.1.5(4), vol. 1, p. 76: *viśvaḥ pramātṛvargaḥ paramārthata ekaḥ pramātā sa eva ca asti/* *IPV* 1.3.7, vol. 1, p. 142: *yac ca navaṃ bhāsayati smarati vā tat vastutaḥ saṃvidā viśvamayyā tādātmyavṛttīti viśvamayaṃ pūrṇam eva iti navaṃ na kiṃcit ābhāsitaṃ smṛtaṃ vā syāt/*

47 *IPV* 4.1.4, vol. 2, p. 285: *viśvarūpasya bhagavataḥ ... /* *IPV* 3.1.1, vol. 2, pp. 212-213: *viśvaprameyīkaraṇapratilabdhatadviśvottīrṇapramātṛpadahṛdayaṅgamīkāra... /* *PH,* p. 54: *śrīmatparamaśivasya punaḥ viśvottīrṇaviśvātmakaparamānandamayaprakāśaikaghanasya ... /*

48 *Vimarśa* is the most important technical term for the Pratyabhijñā system. Various translations for *vimarśa* are listed in a precise work of Raffaele Torella: *The Īśvarapratyabhijñākārikā of Utpaladeva with the author's Vṛtti,* Roma, 1994, p. xxiv, fn. 32. Borrowing from the term of the Phenomenology, I would like to translate it into 'intentional acts of consciousness'.

49 *IPK* 1.5.7: *cidātmaiva hi devo'ntaḥsthitam icchāvaśād bahiḥ/ yogīva nirupādānam arthajātaṃ prakāśayet//* *IPV* 1.5.7, vol. 1, p. 228: *viśvarūpābhāsavaicitrye cidātmana eva svātantryaṃ kiṃ na abhyupagamyate svasaṃvedanasiddham/* *IPK* 1.5.21: *kevalaṃ bhinnasaṃvedyadeśakālaanurodhataḥ/ jñānasmṛtyavasāyādi sakramaṃ pratibhāsate//* *IPV* 1.5.21, vol. 1, p. 298: *ābhāsamānasya paramārthatvāt ... /* *IPV* 1.5.12, vol. 1, p.246.

50 *IPK* 1.4.8. *IPV* 1.4.8, vol. 1, pp. 190-191: *evaṃ samam eva svātmani nirmala-mukurasthānīye yat yugalakaṃ svasmāt prakāśarūpatvāt avyatiriktam avabhāsayati parameśvaraḥ ... /* *IPV* 1.6.8, vol. 1, p. 334: *prakāśātmā parameśvara eva yato dehādipramātṛtābhimānadaśāyām api vastutaḥ pramātā ... /* *IPV* 1.8.10, vol. 1, p. 422: *paramārthatas tu prakāśasya deśakālākārasaṅkocavaikalyāt ekatvam eva ity eka eva prakāśo'ntarviśrāntaḥ sa eva ca pramātā ucyate ... /*

51 *IPV* 2.4.6-7, vol. 2, p. 161: *antarābhāsamānasya tathārūpāparityāgenaiva bahirābhāsanaṃ nirmāṇam/* *IPV* 2.4.10, vol. 2, p. 173: *paramārthatas tu sa eva kramākramarūpaviśvasṛṣṭyādikṛtyapañcasvabhāvaḥ prakāśate/ cetano hi svātmadarpaṇe bhāvān pratibimbavad ābhāsayati iti siddhāntaḥ/*

52 *IPV* 3.1.7, vol. 2, p. 232: *māyāśaktiḥ punar acidrūpe śūnyādau pramātṛtābhimānaṃ prarūḍhaṃ dadhatī bhāvān api cinmayān bhedena abhimānayantī sarvathaiva svarūpaṃ tirodhatte āvṛṇute vimohinī sā/ tirodhānam atra na vilayanarūpaṃ mantavyaṃ ... /* *IPV* 2.3.2, vol. 2, pp. 71-72: *tena śūnyadhīprāṇadehādyupādhyāśrayasvīkārātmakasaṃkocaparigrahasaṃkucitāt māyāpramātuḥ ... /* *IPV* 3.1.9, vol. 2, p. 238: *evaṃ kalāvidyākālarāganiyatibhir otaproto māyayā apahṛtaiśvaryasarvasvaḥ san punar api prativitīrṇatatsarvasvarāśimadhyagatabhāgamātra evaṃbhūto'yaṃ mitaḥ pramātā bhāti,... /* *IPV* 3.1.7-8, vol. 2, pp. 232- 235.

53 As we know, there are two kinds of Tantrists, namely, *mumukṣu* who strives for liberation *(mokṣa, mukti)* and *bubhukṣu* who longs for enjoyment *(bhoga, bhukti)* or supernatural power *(siddhi)*.

54 *IPK* 1.3.7: *na ced antaḥkṛtānantaviśvarūpo maheśvaraḥ/ syād ekaś cidvapur jñānasmṛtyapohanaśaktimān//* *IPV* 1.3.7, vol. 1, p. 143: *anena śaktitrayeṇa viśve vyavahārāḥ/ tac ca bhagavata eva śaktitrayam yat tathābhūtānubhavitṛsmartṛvikalpayitṛsvabhāvacaitramaitrādyavabhāsan-am sa eva hi tena tena vapuṣā jānāti smarati vikalpayati ca/* *IPV*1.8.10, vol. 1, p. 422: *saṃvidāṃ jñānām aikyena vinā lokapaddhatiḥ lokamārgaḥ sarvo vyavahāro na saṃbhavet, saṃbhavati ca ayam, tasmāt aikyam āsām/* *IPV* 1.5.18, vol. 1, p. 283.

55 *IPK* 4.1.3: *svasvarūpāparijñānamayo'nekaḥ pumān mataḥ/ tatra sṛṣṭau kriyānandau bhogo duḥkhasukhātmakaḥ//* *IPV* 4.1.3, vol. 2, p. 284: *satyam, paramārthato na kaścid bandhaḥ, kevalaṃ svasmād anuttarāt svātantryāt yadā svātmānaṃ saṃkucitam avabhāsayati sa eva tadā svasya pūrṇasya rūpasya yad aparijñāṃ bhāsamānatve'py aparāmarśarūpaṃ tad eva kāraṇatvena prakṛtaṃ yasya sa pūrṇatvākhyātimātratattvaḥ puruṣa ity ucyate/*

From Soft Shoulders to Soft Skin, with the Progress of Religious Feeling in Tamil Society

TAKANOBU TAKAHASHI

Constanzo Gioseffo Beschi (1680—1747), an Italian, is one of the most popular missionaries among Tamil people and exceptionally well-versed in Tamil language and literature. However, he erroneously translated 'soft shoulders' as 'soft skin' in a couplet from the *Tirukkuṟaḷ* (fifth or sixth century AD), the most famous book in the history of Tamil literature. Expressions relating to 'shoulders' occur frequently in ancient Tamil literature (so-called Sangam literature), so a scholar versed in ancient literature should not have made such a mistake.

The aim of this paper is to explore why such a man as Beschi misunderstood the popular expression, by taking into consideration the social and cultural changes in Tamil history.

CONSTANZO GIOSEFFO BESCHI

Constanzo Gioseffo Beschi,[1] also known among Tamils as Vīramāmuṉivar,[2] was born on 8 November 1960 at Castiglione-delle-Stiviere, a town near Mantova in the Republic of Venice. At the age of eighteen (1698), he joined the Society of Jesus. It is said that he displayed a great talent for languages from his early years, and was well versed in Italian, Latin, Greek, Hebrew, Portuguese, Spanish, French, Persian, and Sanskrit (later, he learned Urdu, Telugu, and Tamil). In 1710, at the age of thirty,[3] he set sail from Lisbon for Goa. Soon after when he began missionary activities in Tirunelvelly and Madurai, he discarded his Western attire for the dress and signs of Indian *saṃnyāsis*, following the life-style shown by his predecessor, Roberto de Nobili (1577—1656), in order to assimilate with the vernacular way of life. Although, like other missionaries, he suffered greatly due to cultural differences as well as from water, heat, endemic diseases, snakes, animals, and persecution by native people,[4] he, along with missionary activities, mastered the vernacular languages, especially Tamil.

Beschi produced many writings in Tamil, which may fall into three categories: (1) Grammar books and dictionaries, (2) Jesuit theological, catechismal prose writings, and (3) poetic works. To show his remarkable mastery of Tamil and his deep knowledge of its literature, some of his works deserve mention. As for grammatical works, *Grammatica latino — tamulica ubi de elegantiori liguae tamulicae dialecto centamiḻ dicta cui adduntur tamulicae poeseos rudimenta* (1730: English version, *A grammar of the High Dialect of the Tamil Language termed Shen-Tamil*, tr. B.G. Babington, Madras, 1822) and *Grammatica latino — tamulica, ubi de vulgari tamulicae linguae idiomate koṭuntamiḻ dicto, ad usum missionarium Soc. Jesu.* (1738: English version, *A Grammar of the Common Dialect of the Tamil Language called koṭuntamiḻ composed for the Use of the Missionaries of the Society of Jesus*, tr. G.W. Mahon, Madras, 1848) were written for fellow missionaries. And Winslow,[5] Pope,[6] Caldwell,[7] and Vinson[8] used his works for their own grammar books and dictionaries.

Another grammatical work by Beschi is the *Toṉṉūlviḷakkam* (1728). This work follows the indigenous lineage of grammars, such as the *Tolkāppiyam* (first to fifth century) and the *Naṉṉūl* (thirteenth century), and contains all the five sections of grammar, i.e. *eḻuttu* (phonology), *col* (morphology), *poruḷ* (poetics), *yāppu* (prosody), and *aṇi* (rhetoric), in 370 verses. He also compiled the *Caturakarāti*, a Tamil dictionary, and is believed to have compiled Portuguese-Latin-Tamil, Tamil-Latin, and Tamil-French dictionaries.

Among Beschi's poetical products, the *Tēmpāvaṇi* 'The Insatiable Beauty' (1726) is the most famous. It is an epic poem on the life of St. Joseph, consisting of 3615 stanzas in 36 cantos in 3 books. In it, the author has used more varieties of *viruttam* metre (as many as 90) than in the *Kamparāmāyaṇam*.[9]

Along with these literary activities, he is well known for having introduced new symbols into Tamil scripts, for example, to distinguish the long vowels *ē* and *ō* from the short *e* and *o*.

'SHOULDER' IN TAMIL POETRY

The *Tirukkuṟaḷ*, also called the Tamil Veda,[10] is the most famous and popular work in the history of Tamil literature. The author, Tiruvaḷḷuvar, was probably a Jain of the fifth or sixth century. The work consists of

1330 couplets divided into 133 chapters of 10 couplets each: the first 38 chapters on 'virtues' (*aṟam*), the next 70 on 'wealth' (*poruḷ*), and the remaining 25 on 'love' (*kāmam*). From a terminological point of view, *aṟam, poruḷ* and *kāmam* more or less correspond to the Sanskrit terms *dharma, artha,* and *kāma* respectively. Due to the work's content structure, it appears to be a treatise on the 'three objects of life' (Sanskrit, *trivarga*). However, Tiruvaḷḷuvar's treatment is very different from those found in the Sanskrit treatises. This is especially true when he deals with 'love'; he faithfully follows the tradition of ancient love (*akam*) poetry.

Chapter 92 of the *Tirukkuṟaḷ* dealing with 'Prostitutes' is included in the second part on 'wealth', but its content reflects the tradition of ancient poetry. So, *Tirukkuṟaḷ* 919, one of the 10 couplets of the chapter, could be rendered as follows:

> The *soft shoulders* of maids with excellent jewels are a hell into which the mean and base are plunged.

Here, the expression 'maids with excellent jewels' is a stock phrase referring to 'prostitutes', and 'soft shoulders of maids' is also a cliche in ancient Tamil literature.

The original word for 'shoulder' is *tōḷ* which signifies both 'shoulder' and 'forearm'.[11] *Tōḷ* is one of the most frequently referred parts of women's body, along with 'eye', 'tooth', 'forehead', 'hair', 'breast', 'loin', and 'foot'. It is often used idiomatically for representing women's beauty, such as a woman of 'broad shoulders', or of 'soft shoulders/arms', or of 'bamboo-like forearms'. In the 271st poem of *Akanāṉūṟu* (one of the eight anthologies of the ancient period, consisting of 400 love poems), we find an example of a good combination of these phrases; '(a woman having) extended [shoulders] and soft forearms resembling a bamboo between joints'.[12] *Tōḷ* also implies a sexual meaning: among the expressions denoting a sexual union in ancient love poetry, 'to hold [a woman's] shoulders' occurs most frequently.[13]

The 268th poem of *Kuṟuntokai* (another anthology of the ancient period, containing 400 love poems) is a good example of this, in which the heroine's friend, who is one of the main *dramatis personae* in love poetry and always shows sympathy for the heroine's love affair, tells the heroine afraid of separation:

> That man who comes at midnight

when lightning severs
a snake's dark-hooded head,
and holds your soft shoulders
like bamboo:
I have not the strength to ask him
if he is going away;
I cannot ask him
if he will return.
What can we do,
my friend?[14]

Thus, the word 'shoulder' (*tōḷ*) is one of the key terms in ancient Tamil poetry. Nevertheless, Beschi translated 'shoulders' as 'skin' (*tōl*).[15]

SOCIAL, CULTURAL CHANGES IN TAMIL HISTORY

Why, then, did Beschi erroneously render such an important term as *tōḷ* ? If we were to jump to conclusion, we could say that Beschi must not have known the tradition of ancient Tamil literature.

The oldest Tamil literature extant, generally known as Sangam literature, the major portion of which can be assigned to the first to third centuries, contains some 2380 of short and long poems by about 470 poets.[16] The poems are classified by their contents or subjects into two main categories: love (*akam*) and war (*puṟam*) poems, the former being more than three fourths the total number of poems. They possess a highly conventionalized and sophisticated nature, and are quite indigenous, independent, and not imitative, even though people were, to some extent, familiar with Aryan culture and ideas, and there were some poets from north India including Brahmins, Buddhists, and Jains.[17] The characteristic features of Sangam literature in comparison with the Vedic and Sanskrit literatures are: (1) the subjects of the former are 'secular' while those of the latter are mainly 'religious', and (2) Sangam literature is a literature of 'common people' although some heroes are kings and elite people, while the latter is a literature of the cultural 'elite', such as kings, priests, and *nāgarika*-type of citizenry.

The 'secular' nature of ancient Tamil literature, especially that of love poetry, gradually became slighted, detested, and abhorred, as Tamil society and culture became Aryanized. Naturally, in the course of the sixth to ninth centuries, ancient literature became the 'thing of the past' and was 'studied' only by men of taste in Hindu monasteries from the tenth to fifteenth centuries. Banned by some Saivites in the seventeenth and eighteenth centuries, it finally fell into oblivion.

Aryanization of the Tamil country began in the fourth to sixth centuries AD[18]with the influx of northern culture, languages, religions and customs. Probably under the patronage of the Pallavas and the Kalabhras,[19] Brahmanism, Buddhism and Jainism began to flourish; especially the latter two became increasingly popular in their territories, which is known from the existence of the educational institutions belonging to these sects, for example, at Kanchipuram.

In the period between the sixth and the ninth century, often called the 'Bhakti period', Aryanization intensified under the Pandya-Pallava rulers, and Sanskrit began to hold an honoured place as the language of higher literature and culture. Turning to the religious field, Jainism, Buddhism, and Hinduism (Śaivism and Vaishnavism) were struggling to gain popularity, but gradually Hinduism became considerably popular through the *bhakti* movement, and Jainism and Buddhism began to wane. Hindu poet-saints went about from temple to temple chanting verses they had themselves composed. Some of them, adopting the techniques of ancient love poetry, sang devotional songs to God, like a heroine singing her love to her hero. However, in general, 'the interest in the old literary conventions and themes was vanishing and there were people who even hated and attacked the conception of *kaḷavu* ('pre-marital love', the present author)'.[20] As worship in the temples became common among laymen, new temples were built and older ones renovated, and life began to centre on the temples.

The period from the ninth to the thirteenth century reigned by the Cholas witnessed the greatest flowering. The Cholas sponsored the Hindu temples, endowing them with financial support. By this time, temples had fully become centres not only of life but also of arts and scholarship. An auther writes:

> The background of the times is also the background of the temples.... The importance of the temples also involves the importance of the priesthood. The priests were men with generations of culture and education behind them, and the Tamil kings were always generous patrons of talent. Since the Brahmin priests were nurtured on Aryan traditions which they jealously preserved through the ages, Sanskrit *purāṇic* lore, which had been gradually spreading from early days, now became the common man's property and fired the popular imagination.[21]

Tamil literature had so far preserved its independence, but in this period literary work became imitative or derived from Sanskrit literature.

The following period is, according to Jesudasan, 'the period of decadence for Tamil literature'.[22] The Tamil vocabulary was being deluged by Sanskrit words. Sanskrit dominated the literary world, and savants, mostly of Brahmin origin, developed the study of religious and philosophical literature using a hybrid language of Sanskrit and Tamil called *maṇipravāḷa*. There were some indigenous products like *antāti*, *kalampakam*, *kōvai*, *piḷḷaittamiḻ*, and *ulā*,[23] but their language was Tamil with a free mixture of Sanskrit. Ancient literature had fully become the product of the 'past' and the object of study for men of taste. Scholars studied its grammar, prosody, rhetoric, and poetics, and composed theoretical works and commentaries on them.

Since the Bhakti period, Saivism and Vaishnavism had joined hands in opposition to, firstly, Jainism and Buddhism, and then Muslims. Now that Hinduism was fully established, they parted. Under such circumstances, in the middle of the eighteenth century, there appeared some extremists. Two Saivites, Cāmināta Tēcikar and Civañāṉa Cuvāmikaḷ (or Civañāṉa Muṉivar), prohibited the study and reading of such works as the *Cilappatikāram*, the *Maṇimēkalai*, the *Cīvakacintāmaṇi*,[24] not to mention ancient literature, as 'immoral' and 'irreligious', and even the Vaishnavite works. They may very well be responsible for the change from indifference to ancient literature to open hostility against it. And ancient literature had completely fallen into oblivion until the third quarter of the nineteenth century when it was 'rediscovered' mainly by U.V. Swaminatha Aiyar (1855-1942), S.V. Damodaram Pillai (1832–1901).

Thus it is only natural that Beschi did not know the tradition of ancient Tamil literature, still less its key terms like 'shoulder'. So, it is quite probable that the expression 'soft shoulders' seemed odd to him so that he read it as 'soft skin' according to his personal or European aesthetic point of view.

CONCLUSION

The ignorance about ancient literature among Tamil pundits in the nineteenth century is vividly described in U.V. Swaminatha Aiyar's *Autobiography*.[25] Ancient literature was unknown to Europeans too, in those days. R. Caldwell (see note 7), for example, knew the *Tirukkuṟaḷ* and the *Cīvakacintāmaṇi* and regarded them as the earliest Tamil works of about the ninth or tenth century AD.[26] In his famous catalogue, John Murdoch (1819–1904, Scottish) does not refer to any ancient works except a fragmentary piece of the *Tolkāppiyam*.[27] Karl Graul (1814–

1864, German) was a great Indologist[28] and, according to Mohanavelu,[29] a 'bibliomania'. He collected and took with him to Germany as many as 150 rare Tamil books and manuscripts, but no ancient literature was included in his collection.[30]

It has so far remained uncertain, however, whether or not, or, to what extent the Europeans before the eighteenth century knew ancient Tamil literature. Beschi's misunderstanding of the term *tōḷ* affords us an important clue.

NOTES

1 Here are some studies on Beschi: P.S.J. Ceyrac, 'Father Beschi, Vira-Mamunivar', *Indica (The Indian Historical Research Institute, Silver Jubilee Commemoration Volume)*, St. Xavier's College, Bombay, 1953, pp. 54−60; Ignatius Hirudayam, *Christianity and Tamil Culture*, The Dr. S. Radhakrishnan Institute for Advanced Study in Philosophy, University of Madras, 1977; Meenakshisundaram, K., *The Contribution of European Scholars to Tamil*, University of Madras, Madras, 1974; Thomas Srinivasan, 'Beschi, the Tamil Scholar and Poet', *Tamil Culture*, Vol. III, Nos. 3 and 4, Tuticorin, 1954, pp. 297−313; K.V. Zvelebil, *Lexicon of Tamil Literature* (*Handbuch der Orientalistik*, 2 Abteilung, Indien, Band 9), Leiden: E.J.Brill, 1995.

2 This title was conferred on Beschi by Tamil pundits after the publication of his *Tēmpāvaṇi*. See Zvelebil, *Lexicon of Tamil Literature*, p. 92.

3 Another source tells us that it was in 1707.

4 In 1713, Beschi was even arrested and sentenced to death in Tirunelvelly, according to Meenakshisundaram, *The Contribution of European Scholars to Tamil*, p. 30.

5 Miron Winslow (1789−1864, American) is the author of a *Tamil-English Dictionary* (1862).

6 G.U. Pope (1820−1908, English); his main works are *A First Catechism of Tamil Grammar*, 1888; *The 'Sacred Kural'*, 1886; and *The Tiruvasagam*, 1900.

7 Robert A. Caldwell (1814−91, English) is regarded as the founder of Dravidian linguistics. His famous book is *A Comparative Grammar of the Dravidian or South Indian Family of Languages* (1st ed., 1856; reprint, Oriental Books Reprint Corporation, New Delhi, 1974; Asian Educational Services, New Delhi, 1987).

8 J. Vinson (1843−1926, French); one of his works is *Manuel de la langue tamoule* (1903).

9 The original title given by the author, Kampaṉ (ninth, tenth, or eleventh century?), is the *Irāmāvatāram* ('The Descent of Rāma'), but the one *Kamparāmāyaṇam* is by far well known. The number of stanzas ranging from 4 to 6 lines varies from 10569 to 12097 depending on editions.

10 The *Tirukkuṟaḷ* has eight other names: *Uttaravētam* 'The ultimate Veda',

Tiruvaḷḷuvar 'Saint Vaḷḷuvar' (the author's name), *Poyyāmoḻ* 'The never-failing word', *Vāyuṟai vāḻttu* 'Truthful praise', *Teyvanū* 'The divine book', *Potumaṟai* 'The common Veda', *Muppāl* 'The threefold path', and *Tamiḻmaṟai* 'The Tamil Veda'.

11 See *Dravidian Etymological Dictionary* (2nd ed.) 3564, 'Ta. *tōḷ* shoulder, arm. Ma. *tōḷ* shoulder. Ko. *tōḷ* upper arm, elbow to shoulder. Ka. *tōḷ(u)* the arm'.

12 *kāmpiṉ kaṇ iṭai puraiyum neṭumeṉ paṇaittōḷ.*

13 Other expressions alluding to sexual unions are: 'the lover embracing the lady-love','the lover consuming/enjoying the lady-love's "virgin beauty" (*nalam*)', and 'the lady-love embracing the lover's chest'. For more detailed information, see Takahashi, Takanobu, *Tamil Love Poetry and Poetics* (*Brill's Indological Library* No. 9), Leiden: E.J.Brill, 1995, pp. 70−71.

14 M. Shanmugam Pillai and David E. Ludden (tr.), *Kuṟuntokai − An Anthology of Classical Tamil Love Poetry*, Madurai: Koodal Publishers, 1976, p. 127.

15 This was pointed out for the first time by G.U. Pope in his *The 'Sacred' Kurraḷ of Tiruvaḷḷuva-Nāyanār*, London: W.H. Allen & Co., 1886, p. 305. Beschi's original text is: '*Delicata cutis meretricum, quae limites non habent, sed omnibus pecuniam dantibus se tradunt, internus est in quo merguntur viles atque infimae notae homines*'.

16 See S. Vaiyapuri Pillai (ed.), *Caṅka Ilakkiyam: Pāṭṭum Tokaiyum*, Madras: Puri Nilaiyam, 1967.

17 It is also known from the Tamil-Brahmi cave inscriptions (second century BC to second century AD) found in various parts of the Tamil area that Jains and Buddhists settled there at that time.

18 This period is sometimes called the post-Sangam period or the late classical period.

19 Of the Kalabhras (Kaḷappāḷar) we have no definite knowledge. Buddhadatta (*circa* last quarter of the fifth century), an elder contemporary of Buddhaghoṣa, refers to the reign of the blemishless Accuta Vikkantaṉ of the Kalabbhakula. The Vēḷvikkuḍi grant of probably the third quarter of the eighth century tells us that a cruel king called Kaḷabhra defeated many *ādhirājas* and established his sway over Madurai, among other Tamil districts (cf. P.T. Srinivas Iyengar, *History of the Tamils, from the Earliest Times to 600 A.D.,* New Delhi: Asian Educational Services, 1982 (reprint), pp. 528 ff., and also pp. 437−8 for the original text and his translation of the Vēḷvikkuḍi grant). The Kalabhras, denounced as cruel kings (*kali-aracar*), came and uprooted many *ādhirājas*, indigenous Tamil kings and upset the political order.

20 Zvelebil, K.V., *Tamil Literature* (*Handbuch der Orientalistik*, Zweite Abteilung, 2. Band, 1. Abschnitt), Leiden: E.J.Brill, 1975, pp. 119−20. This is suggested by a verse quoted as the 'Preamble' (*pāyiram*) of *Tiṇaimālainūṟṟaimpatu* ('One Hundred and Fifty Stanzas on the Garland of Settings').

21 Jesudasan, C. and H., *A History of Tamil Literature*, Calcutta: Y.M.C.A. Publishing House, 1961, pp. 129−30.

22 Jesudasan, *A History of Tamil Literature*, p. 202.

23 These are minor literary genres, generically called *prabandha* (Tamil, *pirapantam*), the total number of which traditionally comes to 96. *Antāti* is a poem in which the foot or feet, or the line of the last line of a stanza is identical with those in the first line of the following stanza. *Kalampakam*, literally 'mixture, combination', is a poem containing fourteen to eighteen sections. *Kōvai*, 'string, arrangement, scheme', is an anthology of 400 poems by a single poet, illustrating the love (*akam*) themes arranged as a continuous story. *Piḷḷaittamiḻ*, 'The Tamil of Childhood', is a poem describing the various stages of childhood. *Ulā*, 'Procession', is a poem describing how women of each of the seven stages of life are love-stricken at the sight of a hero as they see him coming along in procession. Regarding more detailed information about *prabandha*, see K.V. Zvelebil, *Tamil Literature* (*A History of Indian Literature* ed. by J. Gonda, Vol. 10, Fasc. 1), Wiesbaden: Otto Harrassowitz, 1974, pp. 193–219.

24 The *Cilappatikāram* is a Jain epic by Iḷaṅkō-v-atikaḷ of the fifth century, and the *Maṇimēkalai* is a Buddhist one by Cāttaṉar of the sixth or seventh century. These two are often called 'twin epics', as they contain some common stories and *personae*. The *Cīvakacintāmaṇi* is another Jain epic by Tiruttakkatēvar (ninth to twelfth century), basing on the story of Jīvandhara in Guṇabhadra's *Uttarapurāṇa*.

25 The original is in Tamil: *Eṉ Carittiram*, Makāmakōpāttiyāya Ṭākṭar U.Vē. Cāminātaiyar Nūl Nilaiyam, Ceṉṉai, 1950 (1st ed.: 4th ed., 1997). Translation: K.V. Zvelebil, *The Story of My Life, An Autobiography of Dr. U.V. Swaninatha Iyer*, 2 Parts, Madras: Institute of Asian Studies, Part I, 1990; Part II, 1993.

26 R. Caldwell, *A Comparative Grammar of the Dravidian*, p. 84.

27 John Murdoch, *Classified Catalogue of Tamil Printed Books, with Introductory Notices*, Madras: Christian Vernacular Education Society, 1865 (1st ed.: reprint, Madras, 1968).

28 Graul's works are compiled in his *Bibliotheca Tamulica*, 4 volumes, London-Leipzig, 1854–65 (1st ed.: reprint, Osnabrück: Otto Zeller, 1969).

29 C.S. Mohanavelu, *German Tamilology: German contributions to Tamil language, literature and culture during the period 1706–1945*, Madras: The South India Saiva Siddhanta Works Publishing Society, 1993, p. 102.

30 See, Mohanavelu, *German Tamilology*, pp. 199–207.